Reframing Japanese Cinema

Reframing Japanese Cinema

Authorship, Genre, History

Edited by
Arthur Nolletti, Jr.
and
David Desser

Indiana
University
Press

Bloomington
and
Indianapolis

The paper used in this publication meets the minimum requirements of American National Standard for Information Sciences—Permanence of Paper for Printed Library Materials, ANSI Z39.48-1984.

∞™

Manufactured in the United States of America

Library of Congress Cataloging-in-Publication Data

Reframing Japanese cinema : authorship, genre, history / edited by
   Arthur Nolletti, Jr. and David Desser.
      p.   cm.
   Includes bibliographical references (p.   ) and index.
      ISBN 0-253-34108-6. —
ISBN 0-253-20723-1 (pbk.)
      1. Motion pictures—Japan. I. Nolletti, Arthur, date.
II. Desser, David.
PN1993.5.J3R44   1992
791.43'0952—dc20   91-33659

1 2 3 4 5 96 95 94 93 92

Contents

ACKNOWLEDGMENTS

This anthology, like most critical studies, is first and foremost a communal enterprise. It would be impossible to name all those who have participated in it in some way or other, directly or indirectly. Yet the editors would be remiss not to acknowledge those people and institutions without whom this book could not have been realized. Our thanks to Allan Casebier for his astute reading of the manuscript and, in particular, for the invaluable suggestions he made to improve the introduction. Thanks, too, to the staff at Indiana University Press, especially to Joan Catapano, for being an enormously helpful, sympathetic, and expeditious editor. And special thanks to our fellow contributors, whose scholarship and critical expertise were equaled only by their unwavering commitment to the project.

David Desser would like to thank his colleagues and friends at the Unit for Cinema Studies, University of Illinois: Edwin Jahiel, Director; Richard Leskosky, Assistant Director; Lyn Petrie; and especially Debbie Drake. A special acknowledgment of the University of Illinois Center for Advanced Study must also be made. In Japan, David would like to thank Professor Hisakazu Kakeba and the Faculty of Sociology at Kansai University for an invitation to spend a pleasant summer in Osaka absorbing Japanese film and food. Also in Japan, he would like to thank Mi-chan, Domen-kun, Chiharu-chan, and Senji Taniuchi. A special thanks also to Victor Kobayashi, Dean of the Summer Session, University of Hawaii at Manoa, for organizing "A Conference on Cinema as a Window on Japanese Culture" in the summer of 1986, where this project found some of its authors.

Arthur Nolletti, Jr. would like to thank a number of people for rendering vital assistance. Ronnie Klein of the Framingham State College library staff tracked down much-needed information. Tacey Miller and Sachiko Fuji Beck most generously translated important research material from Japanese into English. Kyoko Hirano helped obtain photographic stills, and as always shared her vast knowledge of Japanese cinema. Arthur is also grateful to the following for the often animated and invariably stimulating discussions he had with them:

John Gillett, Kakehi Masanori, Victor Kobayashi, Sato Tadao, Shimizu Akira, Tochigi Akira, Uegusa Keinosuke, his students at Farmingham State, and the participants of the Gosho workshop at the University of Hawaii Summer Session in June 1990 (an extra thanks to Victor Kobayashi for organizing this workshop). Finally, Arthur is deeply indebted to Mitchell B. Fields, a superlative friend and teacher; Arthur and Vera Nolletti, Sr., his parents; and, above all, Diana, his wife, and Alexandra, his daughter. From beginning to end they provided manifold support and encouragement, and made this book a part of their lives.

The editors wish to express their thanks to the following sources for permission to reprint articles:

Joseph Anderson's "Spoken Silents in the Japanese Cinema; or, Talking to Pictures: Essaying the *Katsuben,* Contexturalizing the Texts" appeared in slightly different form in *Journal of Film and Video* 40, 1 (Winter 1988).

David Desser's "Toward a Structural Analysis of the Postwar Samurai Film" is a revised version of an article that originally appeared in *Quarterly Review of Film Studies* 8, 1 (Winter 1983).

Iwamoto Kenji's article originally appeared in Japanese as "Talkie shoki no hyogen" in *Koza Nihon eiga* (*The Iwanami Japanese Cinema Series*), Vol. 3 (Tokyo: Iwanami Shoten, 1986).

Max Tessier's article is a translation of "Nagisa Oshima, ou l'énergie meurtrie du désir," which originally appeared in *Le Cinéma japonais au présent* (Lherminier), Winter 1979–80. Permission for translation and reprint rights were granted by Editions des Quatre-Vents.

Stills for Gosho Heinosuke and *Woman of the Mist* reprinted by permission of Kawakita Memorial Film Institute and Japan Society.

A note on name order and English titles: Name order appears in the Japanese style, family name first and given name second. English titles used for Japanese films represent the most common English-language usage, typically the release title of the film, or the most frequently used translation title.

INTRODUCTION

Since the 1950s, Japan has been a major force in international cinema. The fact that Japan has also been the only non-Western nation to be, first, a leading military power in the modern era and, second, a leading economic force in our time, is not coincidental. For the motion picture has above all proven to be the art of the twentieth century, the art of modern man, of scientific, technologized, dynamic Western man, and it has been Japan's goal since the beginning of the Meiji era (1868) to compete on every level with the West.

As has been the case throughout much of the long, dynamic history of Japanese art and industry, the cinema entered Japan as a borrowing from elsewhere, in this case, the early French and American cinema. The Japanese were fascinated by film on two levels: as an example of Western technology, and as a priceless glimpse of these faraway but crucial cultures. Historians of the Japanese cinema report many instances of early film showings where the apparatus itself, the projector, attracted as much interest as the images projected. Cinema became very much a standard of value, associated as it was with the West, that is, with the very latest in modern, scientific achievements.

But if Japan has proven a significant adapter, it is equally adept at originality, so that cinema found its unique uses as well. As in France and the United States, early filmmakers were attracted to the world around them, so that the commonplace and the exotic in the hustle and bustle of Tokyo were quickly committed to film. Film's power as a documentary form also did not escape early Japanese filmmakers, who turned their cameras to events of the day (often re-creating these events, such as battles in the Russo-Japanese War in 1905). Most tellingly, however, film was often paired with theater, not simply with theatrical sources for film content (although that was common) but as part and parcel of a theatrical presentation. Thus, exterior locales of a Kabuki or a *shimpa* play (a revised, "modernized" version of Kabuki) would be filmed beforehand and integrated into the theatrical performance, with the actors frequently lip-synching the dialogue from behind or beside the curtain on which the film was projected.

The theatrical model of film would have even more far-reaching effects, however—effects which would also prove the uniqueness of the Japanese cine-matic adaptations and transformations. As in the traditional theaters (Noh, Ka-buki), women's roles were played by men (such actors were termed *oyama* or *onnagata*). In transferring plays into film, this practice was continued, and would be well into the 1920s. Another theatrical model was also transferred to film: the role of the *katsuben* (or *benshi*), the film explicator, narrator, commentator. A figure who sits apart from the action, as it were, but is very much implicated in the entirety of the aesthetic experience, can be found in many Japanese theatrical and narrative arts. Cinema was no exception. The institution of the *katsuben* continued in many cases even after intertitles were in common use, even, in rarer cases, when sound came to the cinema!

But while the cinema as art and institution was growing in Japan in the 1910s and 1920s along traditional artistic and industrial practices, the influence of the West, especially in the form of Hollywood, began to assert itself. The idea of a neo-monopolistic, vertically integrated industry appealed very much to Japanese producers, and something quite similar to the Hollywood studio model was quickly put into place, which would produce greater continuity of studio style and contract talent than even Hollywood's Golden Age could manage. At the same time that Western production practices were modeled, stylistic features of the West also came into play. While sometimes these borrowings bordered on the absurd (such as directors sporting jodhpurs and riding crops on the set, and issuing directorial commands in English to the Japanese-speaking cast and crew), the influence of Griffith-style editing patterns and scene construction and the displacement of *oyama* by women turned the Japanese cinema into an inter-national industry.

Like the classic Hollywood cinema, the Japanese cinema boasted the star system, with stars commanding incredible loyalty and popularity, which led to often astonishing prolificacy. As in Hollywood, stars became immediately associated with genre, which itself became the backbone and lifeblood of the industry.

At the same time that the star-genre system predominated, Japan gave rise to an astonishing variety of directorial talent which, within the restrictions of a genre-driven industry, demonstrated strikingly individualistic talents. Directors such as Ozu Yasujiro, Mizoguchi Kenji, Naruse Mikio, Gosho Heinosuke, and Shimazu Yasujiro, working in both silent and sound films in the prewar era, combined features of the Hollywood approach with traditional Japanese aes-thetic practices, sifted through their own unique talents and interests. These directors compare favorably, individually and as a group, with those of any other national cinema. Similarly, in the postwar era, Japan gave rise to world-class filmmakers, led of course by Kurosawa Akira, but also including Ichikawa

Kon, Kinoshita Keisuke, and Kobayashi Masaki. And when other national cinemas were invigorated by New Waves in the late '50s and early '60s, New Waves which arose out of particular cultural and cinematic forces, Japan, too, regained prominence with the likes of Oshima Nagisa, Imamura Shohei, Shinoda Masahiro, Yoshida Yoshishige and Suzuki Seijun.

Japan followed the West, however, in one important feature: the turn to television. This trend, which was apparent in the early '60s, by the '70s had virtually devastated the once-enormous industry. Even more than in the United States, the film industry in Japan is today a helter-skelter of independent productions and industrial malaise. It is, however, too early to write off the contemporary Japanese cinema as nothing more than either the major market for U.S. films outside North America, or a major player in the ownership and management of the new international film industry. Furthermore, while Japanese film style has become increasingly internationalized, Donald Richie has observed that

> new films continue to contain elements of earlier [Japanese] styles, either unconsciously or as pastiche, as nostalgia, as homage. . . . At the same time predilections, unexamined, often unnoticed, remain: a way of scripting, a way of composing a scene, a way of shooting, which is unmistakably Japanese. It is this Japanese way of ordering things, of choosing things, of creating things, and of revealing assumptions which no amount of internationalism can altogether suppress.[1]

We can only hope that Richie is right. In the meantime, much scholarly research needs to be done both on the rich historic past and on the small handful of major directors at work today. From these artists, and others like them, will come the occasional gems that will continue to command our attention and urge Japan to do what its greatest films have always done: look at itself honestly, boldly, without compromise.

The Scope of This Study

Writing in 1979, David Bordwell lamented that after two decades, Joseph Anderson and Donald Richie's *The Japanese Film: Art and Industry*

> remains . . . the most detailed history of the Japanese cinema in any Western language. Virtually all subsequent research finds its conceptual framework dictated by this magisterial work. Even Noel Burch, whose work is the most original to appear in recent years, continues to rely on data and arguments adduced in *The Japanese Film*. Valuable as it is, however, *The Japanese Film* has won the unfortu-

nate honor reserved for film books: to call a volume the "standard work" usually means that it is the *only* work.[2]

More than a decade later, the situation remains unchanged.

That this is so is surely a tribute not only to the pioneering effort on Anderson and Richie's part, but to the essential soundness of their observations and the thoroughness of their research. But it is also true that Western scholars have shied away from rewriting the history of Japanese cinema, content instead to deal with it piecemeal.[3] In the intervening years since the publication of their "standard work" on Japanese film history, the writing, the doing, of film history has become more complex. Since the publication of *The Japanese Film* in 1959, the very discipline of film studies has grown up, and with it has come the rise of academic film historians. A side effect, an unfortunate by-product, of this professionalization of the field has been perhaps a sense of intimidation—in a period when a major film scholar can write a more than six-hundred-page manuscript on the four-year period that D. W. Griffith spent at the Biograph Studios, conceiving of writing a history of the Japanese cinema in its ninety years of existence becomes too awesome a task to contemplate.[4] For that matter, when it came time to do a second edition of their own work, Anderson and Richie added new chapters, while leaving the earlier work intact.

Reframing Japanese Cinema continues this pattern, offering up critical and historical assessments that build upon, refine, or bring greater specificity to a variety of particular areas and issues. The areas and issues we have chosen reflect standard, contemporary cinematic concerns. David Bordwell noted in the same article quoted above that "Western accounts of the history of the Japanese film industry have stressed three variables: director, genre, and studio."[5] Our three areas differ only slightly: director (authorship), genre, and history.[6] We might note that these three areas reflect a recent historical trend within film studies; that contemporary academic cinema reached a level of intellectual and pedagogical significance in the late 1960s under the impetus of *auteurism*—the so-called auteur theory that grew out of the *Cahiers du Cinéma's La Politique des auteurs* in the 1950s, sifted through the journalistic theorizing of Andrew Sarris in the early 1960s, and invigorated by French structuralist theory as developed by British Cinestructuralists;[7] that auteurism was followed by the serious study of genre under the continuing impetus of structuralism and semiology within film studies; that film history, a sophisticated history which relies on a variety of primary sources (the films themselves, studio records, trade journals of the period, etc.), filtered through contemporary theoretical perspectives, has emerged as a profitable, even dominant movement within the discipline. Such headings as authorship, genre, and history are broad enough to encompass a variety of perspectives and approaches, but specific enough, we think, to be useful within the film studies context.

The organization into authorship, genre, and history also reflects the continuing validity of these categories within film studies. These paradigms have undergone constant reconsideration; they continue to do so today. A pattern of rethinking, refinement, rejection, and reinvigoration characterizes, for instance, the reception and continued relevance of auteurism. The essays gathered in the first section on directors illustrate many of the ways in which authorship has been scrutinized by a variety of theoretical approaches. In its initial phase, theories of authorship expressed a belief in a transcendental subject, one virtually outside historical circumstances who imposed, by sheer design and dominating creative intelligence, a personality upon a group of films. Refinements upon auteurism began to take into greater account not simply the collaborative nature of film, not simply the industrial circumstances in which films are made, and not simply even the social and political circumstances of the moment that bear upon their production and distribution. Rather, auteurism became part and parcel of a virtual *system,* one which reflected both the industrial and artistic practices of a period. A director became implicated in aesthetic possibilities and paradigms, very much a product of his or her period.[8] Arthur Nolletti, Jr.'s essay on Gosho in the 1930s attests to the importance of periodization in considering authorship.[9] Similarly, film directors were seen as implicated in another kind of system, an ideological one which constrained not only the technical and stylistic elements in which they worked but even more fundamentally the very system of representation which underlay the work.[10] Here Robert Cohen's essay on *The Life of Oharu (Saikaku ichidai onna,* 1952), Mizoguchi's exploration of a woman's fall into prostitution, stands as exemplary of the new auteurism.

Like auteurism, genre study has been highly influenced by new theoretical approaches and perspectives. Until the 1970s, genre study was primarily concerned with isolating the aesthetic and narrative patterns common across a group of films, the task at hand being to list icons (elements particular to the genre), identify conventions, analyze structure, and examine variations and transformations from one film to another within the group. Since the 1970s, under the impetus of feminist film criticism and other ideologically informed approaches, the focus on genre has led to a more generalized theorization of the link between genre and culture, as well as a rigorous investigation of the ways in which genre films are received and used by their audience. Indeed, because genre films most often are produced for mass consumption and because they reflect societal values and beliefs (as well as a need for those values and beliefs), they emerge as invaluable artifacts of their society, and even serve to redefine and mythologize the way that society sees itself.

As we have already said, genre films have been the backbone of the Japanese film industry. Thus, to understand Japanese cinema requires an appreciation of the genres that help shape it. Japanese cinema is traditionally divided into two all-inclusive categories: the *gendai-geki* (films set in contemporary times) and the *jidai-geki* (period films, most often set in the Tokugawa Era [1615–1868]). Within these categories, there are numerous divisions and subdivisions. Among the most important of these, historically and aesthetically, are the following: the Samurai Film, the *chambara* (swordplay films), the *shomin-geki* (films dealing with the everyday lives of the common people), the *nansensu* comedy (farce and slapstick), the *haha mono* (films about motherly sacrifice and suffering), the *Kokusaku eiga* ("National Policy Films" of World War II), and the *yakuza eiga* (gangster films).

While the Japanese and American cinemas share a reliance on genre, the particularities of genre differ significantly. The Samurai Film, for instance, while often compared with the American Western, dominated the prewar Japanese cinema, where it owed actually very little to the Western and a great deal to Japanese swordfight plays (*kengeki*), Japan's violent warrior past, and folktales and local heroes. A prewar cycle of films called *keiko eiga* ("tendency films") functioned as social-problem pictures drawn from contemporary issues in Japanese society. Postwar genres such as the *haha mono* or the *yakuza eiga* similarly owe nothing to the West and everything to the particularities of Japanese history, culture, and society.

Japanese cinema today continues to rely on genre, but with some new and noteworthy developments. One can see, for example, in such recent films as Itami Juzo's *Tampopo* (1987) and Hayashi Kaizo's *To Sleep So As to Dream* (*Yume miruyoni nemuritai,* 1986) genre mixing, overt intertextual play, and self-consciousness of form that is characteristic of postmodernism. Whether these developments will continue and how they might evolve into future genres and subgenres, no one, of course, can say. Nevertheless, in order to appreciate this playing with genre, we must first recognize and understand the generic patterns that preceded it. Hence the double importance of the essays on genre in this volume.

From informed accounts of auteurism and genre study has also come a reinvigorated notion of history. Currently one of the most active areas of film research is not simply film history but early cinema—the premodern condition. Now that film has stabilized as both an industry and an aesthetic system, it is perhaps understandable that researchers are eager to know the details of its origins. It might even be argued that as film has lost some of its mass appeal, its overwhelming influence on society, researchers desire to return to a time when the future of film was before it. And as film has stabilized to the point of becoming a classical field in its own right, with rules and regulations, paradigms and possibilities constraining it, with a language and textual system intact, there is a desire to know the moment when cinema was based on an entirely different set of premises, "a different logic of the relation between viewer and film . . . a different thinking about images and their presentation, [and] on a different conception of space and narrative."[11] Komatsu Hiroshi's essay on Japanese film before World War I represents a significant attempt to participate in this return to origins.[12]

Nor is it surprising that recent and continuing work in film history should similarly be concerned with the technical bases of the cinema. As we have mentioned, notions of cinematic style as reflective of authorial personality were subjected to rigorous ideological critique. But this in itself has come in for further refinement in terms of an understanding of technology's role in the filmmaking process.[13] Much interest and debate in the West has centered around the coming of sound to the cinema. The present volume now brings the case of Japan's adoption of sound to this debate with the essay by Iwamoto Kenji.

A return to origins of another sort characterizes the remaining essays in our section devoted to history. The focus on the late 1920s and the 1930s marks a return to a moment when the Japanese cinema was struggling to come to terms with, literally, an original cinema—a distinctly and distinctively Japanese cinema. The focus on the '30s originated with Noel Burch, as elaborated in his *To the Distant Observer* (1979). His conception of the 1930s as a golden age in Japanese cinema was a polemical stance meant to counter the prevailing view at the time that the 1950s constituted the high watermark of Japan's cinematic achievement. For Burch, the '50s marked merely the Japanese cinema's adoption of the dominant model established and promulgated by mainstream American moviemaking (the classical Hollywood cinema). It was in the '30s, according to Burch, that Japan was characterized by a unique mode of cinematic construction, one in many ways counter to the dominant Hollywood model. To prove his argument, Burch established what he considered unique principles of traditional Japanese aesthetics and attempted to demonstrate how these principles carried over into cinematic discourse. His main point was that Japanese filmmakers, while essentially aware of the Hollywood model, rejected it.

This anthology's focus on the '30s is meant both to carry on and critique Burch's notion of that decade as a period of uniquely Japanese filmmaking. The articles by J. L. Anderson and David Bordwell examine peculiarly Japanese narrative and stylistic modes, subjecting them to objective, detailed analysis in order to bring greater specificity to the issue of Japanese cinema's unique qualities. Clearly, the time has come for the Japanese 1930s to get the much-needed attention it deserves.

Our organizational model also reflects, we think, the history of the reception of the Japanese cinema within the United States. From a period of acclaiming directors (Kurosawa in the U.S., Mizoguchi in France), the West discovered Japanese genre, especially the Samurai Film; with the institutionalization of film studies, other directors (Ozu and Oshima especially) were uncovered, other genres were identified, and aspects of Japanese film history and aesthetics were revealed and debated.

The cliché has it (nonetheless true for its status as received wisdom) that Kurosawa Akira's *Rashomon* introduced the Western world to the Japanese cinema. Of course, it introduced only a part, a small part, of Japanese cinema to the West. It would be years before any pre–World War II films would come to be seen; but even in the case of postwar/post-Occupation films, only a small portion were seen here and in Europe. Japanese films were enabled to be seen here because, in no small measure, of the consent decree which forced the major U.S. studios to divest themselves of their theaters in the immediate postwar era. This opening up of theaters to films drawn from outside the Hollywood mainstream (U.S. independent feature filmmaking also arose significantly in this period) was aided as well by a near-precipitous decline in U.S. major film production. Further, the reception of Japanese films in the States was part of the larger "Art Film" phenomenon of the 1950s: films by Kurosawa and other Japanese directors were placed on a par with the emerging films of Federico Fellini and Ingmar Bergman. In fact, one can argue that films such as *Rashomon* (1951) and Mizoguchi's *Ugetsu monogatari* (1953), with their allegorical settings and symbolism, clearly anticipate Fellini's *La Strada* (1954) and Bergman's *The Seventh Seal* (1956).

From the Japanese perspective, the acclamation of *Rashomon* led to the creation of films specifically for export. Indeed, a major studio, Daiei, specialized in such films, having reckoned that the appeal of *Rashomon* rested on its exotic period setting. Hence the production of *Ugetsu monogatari* (much more decorous and languorous, much more overtly "exotic" than Mizoguchi's other films of the period); hence the distribution of Kinugasa Teinosuke's *Gate of Hell* (*Jigokumon*, 1953), whose use of color was exemplary within its exotic (to the West) Heian-era setting—a film infinitely less interesting than the director's films of the late '20s through the mid-'30s; hence even the distribution of an inordinate number of films by Inagaki Hiroshi. The apotheosis of the foreign film in the 1960s (the continuing careers of Bergman and Fellini, the fame of Antonioni, and, especially, the cresting of the French New Wave) saw the Japanese film further solidify a popular intellectual status. By 1970, then, the foreign film, or Art House, circuit of exhibition was as likely to see a Japanese film released as almost any other national cinema, and certainly more so than any other Asian cinema. And as the past was discovered within this commercial context (including, for example, the rise of nontheatrical distribution in 16mm for classroom and film society showings), the Japanese cinematic past became available, filling in the gaps in the cinema contemporary with *Rashomon* and the Daiei export cycle, and even, slowly but surely, the prewar films, insofar as they had survived the ravages of earthquake, bombings, and general neglect.

Reframing Japanese Cinema, then, belongs to an ongoing process of discovery and rediscovery. It fills in gaps, solidifies areas left sketchy by previous work, brings specificity to topics heretofore only surveyed—and introduces some new areas for further work. We have here brought to the fore many of the already well-known scholars of the Japanese cinema, who have contributed new essays to this volume. But in addition, we have included major work not previously available to the English-speaking world. There is in Japan a modern generation of film historians informed by contemporary critical theory and sophisticated historical methodologies. The articles herein written by Komatsu Hiroshi and Iwamoto Kenji were originally written in Japanese and are here translated into English for the first time. Similarly, the work of Max Tessier, translated from the French, continues the pioneering efforts in film criticism for which the French are justifiably acclaimed around the world. A lengthy tradition of French criticism of the Japanese cinema and French critical theory informs Tessier's challenging essay on Oshima Nagisa.

In conclusion, we hope to have produced a book which will define important historical, cultural, and aesthetic issues at work in the Japanese cinema while examining such subjects as individual directors, specific filmic texts, questions and concepts of genre within the Japanese cinema, and larger concepts, movements, and theoretical areas of concern within this complex, fascinating field.

ARTHUR NOLLETTI, JR. AND DAVID DESSER

NOTES

1. *Japanese Cinema: An Introduction* (New York: Oxford UP, 1990), pp. 84–85. For a detailed overview of the Japanese film industry, in particular the state of film production, distribution, and exhibition today, see Keiko McDonald, "Japan," in John A. Lent, *The Asian Film Industry* (Austin: U of Texas P, 1990), pp. 34–60.

2. David Bordwell, "Our Dream Cinema: Western Historiography and the Japanese Film," *Film Reader* 4 (1979): 48. At the time of this writing, Noel Burch's book *To the Distant Observer* (Berkeley: U of California P, 1979) was not yet available to Bordwell; he refers instead to an article of the same title in *October* 1 (Spring 1976): 32–46.

3. David Desser's own *Eros plus Massacre: An Introduction to the Japanese New*

Wave Cinema (Bloomington: Indiana UP, 1988) is certainly in this model, dealing primarily with the history of a certain segment of the Japanese film industry in the 1960s. Even Burch's *To the Distant Observer* is less a history of Japanese film than a history of a certain idea found within the history of the Japanese film.

4. Tom Gunning, *D. W. Griffith and the Origins of American Narrative Film* (Urbana: U of Illinois P, 1991).

5. Bordwell, p. 48.

6. Interestingly enough, in recent years the history of film has become quite regularly the history of film studios. See, for instance, Thomas Schatz, *The Genius of the System* (New York: Pantheon, 1988). And while Bordwell may be correct that the variables of director, genre, and studio are held by the West to account for the shape of Japanese film history, much work remains to be done on the history of individual studios in Japan. Thus far, they have certainly escaped the critical attention that American scholars have given to studios such as RKO, Warner Bros., M-G-M, Paramount, Fox, and United Artists.

7. It is certainly unnecessary to rehearse the history of the auteur theory. Those new to the field of film might profitably turn to Bill Nichols, ed., *Movies and Methods,* Vol. I (Berkeley: U of California P, 1977).

8. The work of David Bordwell is exemplary in this theorization of systematic possibilities and constraints. See, for instance, his *Narration in the Film* (Madison: U of Wisconsin P, 1988) and *The Classical Hollywood Cinema,* co-written with Janet Staiger and Kristen Thompson (New York: Columbia UP, 1985).

9. A forthcoming study from Donald Kirihara, *Patterns of Time: Kenji Mizoguchi in the 1930s* (Madison: U of Wisconsin P, 1992), also brilliantly demonstrates how authorship studies can be reinvigorated by a sensitivity toward conceptions of periodization, paradigms, and objective parameters.

10. We have in mind here the massive influence of feminist-influenced psychoanalytic theory. While this theory has abandoned auteurism in favor of genre and history, and abandoned production in favor of reception, it nevertheless has had considerable impact on notions of authorship. Among numerous theorizations and explications of feminist and psychoanalytic film theory, see, e.g., E. Ann Kaplan, ed., *Psychoanalysis and Cinema* (New York: Routledge, 1990). For a good example of reception theory, see Janice A. Radway, *Reading the Romance: Women, Patriarchy, and Popular Literature* (Chapel Hill: U of North Carolina P, 1984).

11. The quote is taken from Thomas Elsaesser, *Early Cinema: Space, Frame, Narrative* (London: BFI, 1990). Along with the work by Gunning cited above, and recent publications by Charles Musser, this book is itself indicative of the dynamic attention being paid to cinema's originating moments.

12. While the Elsaesser book cited above pays some attention to British, French, German, Italian, Russian, and Scandinavian cinema to complement its dominant focus on American moviemaking, no mention is made of the Japanese cinema.

13. A controversial study that takes technology as predeterminate of most features of film production and film theory is Barry Salt, *Film Style and Technology: History and Analysis* (London: Starwood, 1983).

Part One

Authorship

Woman of the Mist and Gosho in the 1930s

Arthur Nolletti, Jr.

Today very few Japanese films enjoy theatrical release in the United States and Europe—far fewer than in the halcyon days of the 1950s and 1960s when Kurosawa and Mizoguchi made such a tremendous impact. Since the 1970s, however, touring retrospectives have provided a unique opportunity to discover some of the treasures of Japanese cinema past and present, and to sample firsthand the richness and vitality of its art. Some of these retrospectives have been devoted to the "Golden Age" of the 1930s, war films, Japanese comedy, and individual actors and actresses. But doubtless the most important have been the major retrospectives on master directors. In the 1970s the West finally got a real look at the work of Ozu; in the early 1980s, Naruse Mikio received this honor; and in the late 1980s, it was Gosho Heinosuke's turn.

Long recognized by the Japanese as one of their most preeminent directors, Gosho (1902–81) excelled in the *shomin-geki,* the drama of the everyday life of the lower and middle classes. His films express a fundamental belief in humanistic values, almost always depicting common people and their problems with a mix of humor and pathos. The most characteristic mood of a Gosho film, in fact, is one of laughter-through-tears, what the Japanese call *nakiwarai.*

Nolletti's essay, which deals with Gosho's work in the 1930s—the first of his two most productive periods—examines how he built on the *shomin-geki* and departed from it. Nolletti discusses a number of films, but focuses primarily on *Woman of the Mist (Oboroyo no onna,* 1936), one of Gosho's most personal works of the period, and one that merits re-evaluation, for "it contains many of the elements of a film classic" ("Special Issue on Director Gosho Heinosuke," Film Center of Tokyo National Museum [1974]: 24). Here Nolletti not only analyzes Gosho's themes, narrative strategies, and visual style but shows how he blends elements from two genres—the *shomin-geki* and the romantic melodrama—and why.

For further reading, see John Gillett, "Heinosuke Gosho: A Pattern of Living," The National Film Theatre Booklet (March 1986): 3–7; William Johnson, "The Splitting Image: The Contrary Canon of Heinosuke Gosho," *Film Comment* 27, 1 (January-February 1991): 74–78; Arthur Nolletti, Jr., "*Where Chimneys Are Seen*," in *Magill's Survey of Cinema: Foreign Language Films,* ed. Frank N. Magill (Englewood Cliffs: Salem Press, 1985), Vol. 7, pp. 3360–65; Sato Tadao, *Obake entotsu no sekai. Eiga kantoku Gosho Heinosuke no hito to shigoto (The World of Phantom Chimneys: The Movie Director Gosho Heinosuke, the Man and His Work)* (Tokyo: Noberu Shobo, 1977); David Shipman, *The Story of Cinema* (New York: St. Martin's Press, 1982), pp. 967–968; and Max Tessier, *Images du cinéma japonais* (Paris: Henri Veyrier, 1981), pp. 56–57, 63–65.

Relatively unknown in the West, Gosho Heinosuke (1902–1981) is recognized as one of Japan's greatest directors.[1] Like Shimazu Yasujiro, his mentor at Shochiku's Kamata Studio in the early 1920s, he specialized in the *shomin-geki,* the drama of the everyday lives of the lower-middle classes. His career spanned forty-three years, beginning in 1925 with *Spring in Southern Islands (Nanto no haru),* his directorial debut, and ending in 1968 with *Seasons of the Meiji Period (Meiji haru aki),* a feature-length puppet film. During that time he made a total of ninety-nine films, working in a wide range of genres that included nonsense (*nansensu*) comedy, light comedy, romantic melodrama, family drama, social drama, and the *jidai-geki* (period film). All of these films are imbued with his basic belief in humanistic values, as well as a wholehearted commitment to express the true and most authentic feelings of human beings. Further, these films illustrate his particular style of lyricism, the mixture of pathos and humor that makes one want to laugh and cry at the same time—a style that has come to be known simply as "Goshoism."

Gosho established himself as an up-and-coming director in 1927 with *The Lonely Roughneck (Sabishiki ranbomono),* his fourteenth film. However, he achieved his greatest critical and popular success in the '20s with *The Village Bride (Mura no hanayome,* 1928), a tale of a beautiful, physically handicapped

Gosho Heinosuke. Photo courtesy of
Kawakita Memorial Film Institute and
Japan Society.

young woman that many consider his first masterpiece. Dealing with common
people, it not only demonstrated his compassion for the oppressed and physically handicapped, but it also criticized feudal values.

Although Gosho's career was long and distinguished, it was by no means
untroubled. Projects unsuited to him and two protracted bouts of tuberculosis
took their toll. So, too, did the establishment of "national policy" films during
the war (which morally and temperamentally he could not make). Finally, there
were various conflicts with the studios; of these, the most serious and bitter was
over his support of the union in the Toho labor strikes of the late '40s. These
troubles notwithstanding, his work not only thrived but flowered, especially in
the '30s and in the immediate postwar period.

During this latter period, he made a series of films that many regard as his
best: *Once More* (*Ima hitotabino*, 1947), a sumptuously produced love story that
takes place before, during, and after the war; *Dispersing Clouds* (*Wakare-gumo*,
1951), about a young female student's self-discovery while staying at a convales-
cent home; *Where Chimneys Are Seen* (*Entotsu no mieru basho*, 1953), a warm

examination of two couples living in a poor industrial section of Tokyo, and Gosho's most acclaimed work; *An Inn at Osaka* (*Osaka no yado,* 1954), a meticulous study of a young insurance company employee's relationships at a small hotel; and *Growing Up* (*Takekurabe,* 1955), a superb adaptation of Higuchi Ichiyo's classic story of a young girl fated for a life of prostitution.

During the '30s, his first sustained creative period, he produced a rich variety of films, beginning with Japan's first successful talkie, *The Neighbor's Wife and Mine* (*Madamu to nyobo,* 1931), and ending with *The Song of the Flower Basket* (*Hanakago no uta,* 1937), a light-hearted look at human relationships in a small *tonkatsu* (pork cutlet) restaurant in the Ginza. It was a decade in which he experimented—with sound, with adapting literature to film, and perhaps, as one of his assistant directors suggests, with the limits of expression offered by film itself.[2] But most of all it was a decade in which he made significant developments in his art.[3]

This essay will examine those developments. Section I will provide a short overview of the period, emphasizing the nature of his themes, the make-up of his *shomin-geki,* and the all-important relationship of his dramas and light comedies. Section II will offer a close textual analysis of one of his least discussed but most accomplished and representative films, *Woman of the Mist* (*Oboroyo no onna,* 1936). Here we will examine his narrational and visual strategies and his mix of genres and moods in order to arrive at an understanding of what "Goshoism" is, how it functions, and what it signifies in this specific '30s text.

I

Gosho's work in the '20s clearly paved the way for his even finer achievements of the '30s. He had found what was to be his characteristic theme: the life of common people in all its beauty and sorrow. Moreover, his visual style—which would remain consistent throughout his career—had already begun to take shape by the time he made his second film, *The Sky Is Clear* (*Sora wa haretari,* 1925). Known as the director who "uses three shots where others use one," he later attributed his style to two sources. From haiku, he—like other Japanese directors, as well—learned abbreviation, association, and a sensitivity to nature and the seasons. From Ernst Lubitsch, whose *Marriage Circle* (1924) he had seen over twenty times, he learned analytical editing—the use of hundreds of individual shots to capture even the most minuscule nuances of character and emotion. In addition, he had a special fondness for the moving camera, which he deployed to underscore social and psychological connections between people and to give added depth to his images.

From 1925 to 1941 Gosho worked exclusively at Shochiku, where studio head Kido Shiro made the *shomin-geki* one of the company's specialties. To a certain degree, then, Gosho's subjects, themes, and dramaturgical choices can be seen as variations and transformations on a genre defined and developed by studio policy.[4] Yet we must not forget that the *shomin-geki* was in actuality a broad, all-inclusive genre. As such, it was able to accommodate an often wide and disparate range of material and moods, among them farce, light comedy, lyricism, social criticism, and melodrama. In short, the mixture of ingredients is all, and in the hands of Gosho and other outstanding directors, the genre exhibited remarkable variety in structure, thematic emphasis, and, most of all, style.

All of Gosho's '30s films are essentially *shomin-geki,* but more specifically they belong to a variety of subgenres, including light comedies, *nansensu* (nonsense) comedies, "salaryman" films, family dramas, social dramas, adaptations of literature, and *shitamachi* films (dealing with life in old downtown Tokyo). Although these categories are helpful in studying Gosho, they must be used with caution, because there is a great deal of overlapping between them. Thus, to take one example, *Burden of Life (Jinsei no onimotsu,* 1935) is at once a "salaryman" film, a family drama, a social drama, and of course an example of *shomin-geki.*

No discussion of Gosho's work in the '30s can possibly be complete without taking into account his light comedies, *The Neighbor's Wife and Mine, The Bride Talks in Her Sleep (Hanayome no negoto,* 1933), and *The Groom Talks in His Sleep (Hanamuko no negoto,* 1935).[5] Regarded in their day simply as "entertainments," today they are considered classics. Yet critics still tend to ignore these films, which is a mistake, for as Sato Tadao has aptly pointed out, they played an integral role in Gosho's development.[6]

Virtually plotless, these comedies take a wholly trivial matter and use it as a springboard for a succession of silly—some would even say "stupid"—gags. These gags almost always build to a climax in which the major characters come together to resolve any and all problems. Rarely is there an explicit statement of theme, or even a suggestion that any theme is intended. As for the tone, it is predominantly gentle, warm, and affectionate; Gosho invites us to laugh as much with his characters as at them, saving his occasional ridicule for those most deserving it—the envious or incorrigible, or both—those most ripe for comic comeuppance.

Partly inspired by American silent comedies, these farces were enormously popular with Japanese audiences, who doubtless found them not only entertaining but liberating. Indeed, these films obviously satisfied two diametrically opposed needs. First, they caught the spirit of the neighborhood and community, emphasizing an underlying solidarity between people and showing the simple joy in living.[7] And second, they invariably spoofed and dramatized the societal and familial pressures brought to bear on individuals.

Consider, for instance, the two nonsense comedies, *The Bride Talks in Her Sleep* and *The Groom Talks in His Sleep*. Typical of such comedies, they have to do with a bizarre, embarrassing, and thoroughly exaggerated social situation. The titles of the two films announce their central conceit. In *The Bride* the question is: does the eponymous heroine talk in her sleep? In *The Groom* this question is asked about the husband. Wholly insignificant, this issue is treated by all the characters as if it is of earth-shattering importance. Hence family, friends, and neighbors alike gather round to give advice, satisfy their own curiosity, and, in short, meddle. In both films, the young newlyweds must ultimately stand up for their right to handle what is an entirely personal matter, regardless of how silly or insignificant it may be. Thus, in hierarchical-minded Japan, these nonsense comedies provide a wonderfully delightful way of celebrating *ninjō* (personal desire) without undermining the claims of *giri* (social obligation).

Generally speaking, discussions of *The Neighbor's Wife and Mine*—which was made before the two nonsense comedies—tend to concentrate exclusively on the formidable technical problems Gosho faced—and solved—in turning out Japan's first successful talkie. As a result, the film's importance as a *shomin-geki* comedy is often overlooked. Even Anderson and Richie conclude that it is "perhaps unimportant to Gosho's status as a director,"[8] apparently forgetting that the film is the first of his surviving works—his fortieth!

A playful tribute to Western (American) influences and a gentle satire of bourgeois manners, it has to do with a playwright suffering from writer's block. In addition, he has to contend with a never-ending succession of distractions: a cat screeching outside his window, his baby squalling, his daughter needing to be taken to the bathroom, and, finally, the last straw: a lively jazz band rehearsing next door. Of course, the writer is more than eager to find an excuse not to work. First, he refuses to get out of bed; then—determined to put a stop to the neighbor's music—he goes next door, only to end up partying. He even gets drunk. All of this is naturally played for laughs by Gosho and gagman Fushimi Akira as they poke fun at the foibles of human nature and the follies of middle-class life.

Yet, while the film overall maintains its light tone as a *shomin-geki* comedy, it also brings some psychological nuances to the characters. Hence the husband, though good-natured and genial, repeatedly indulges in infantile behavior. At one point, in order to block out the noise from next door, he even goes through a series of antics: covering himself with a blanket, plugging his ears, tying a cloth around his head, and finally hiding inside a large wooden trunk. When all this fails, he tries to convince his wife to talk to the offending neighbor. Unsympathetic, she refuses.

The comedy is perhaps at its richest and most suggestive in its delineation of the wife. Although she is by no means perfect, she is hard-working, nurturing (especially to her children), and unfailingly practical (when she finds a coin, she immediately scoops it up, since money is at a premium). Forever urging her husband to get to his work (much to his dismay and irritation), she is understandably distraught when he plays mah-jong, continually procrastinates, and stays on next door to party. Of course, the party poses an additional threat to her. Feeling that she cannot compete with the Westernized charms of Madame, who dresses, smokes, and postures like a Hollywood vamp, she fears for her marriage. She also is jealous. (No doubt this is why she later asks her husband to buy her some Western clothes; kimonos simply aren't "modern.") To be sure, Gosho makes it clear that she overreacts to her husband's visit next door; after all, he has simply gone next door, not run off with another woman.

Even so, Gosho treats her feelings with understanding and sympathy. In one particularly striking shot—the kind of inserted close-up that shows his Lubitsch-like attention to psychological detail—he conveys the anxiety and insecurity she feels by having her take the large ornamental pin from her hair (*kanzashi*) and bend it in the palm of her hand. In yet another shot, we see her alone at work in the kitchen, feeling abandoned and singing a plaintive song.

In keeping with the mood of light comedy, however, Gosho develops her character only so much and no more. Mostly he hints at her strengths, weaknesses, and vulnerability through the kinds of probing images described above. But that is enough to give the comedy a degree of gravity and realism that otherwise it would lack. And, interestingly, it makes the happy ending, in which husband and wife are once more reunited, all the more happy.

Lightweight but hardly insignificant, Gosho's three *shomin-geki* comedies share with his '30s dramas many of the same themes and concerns: a special feeling for the plight of women, a preoccupation with social and domestic pressures exerted upon the individual, and an identification with the joys and sorrows of ordinary people's lives. This sharing is not surprising, of course, since throughout the decade Gosho worked in both genres at the same time; thus, a give-and-take is to be expected.

Yet not only have critics frequently minimized this give-and-take, they have failed to examine the contributions of these comedies to the dramas. Basically, Gosho's light comedies served him in two different ways. First he doubtless learned that by their very nature, they were unable to accommodate subtle humor or in-depth examinations of character. (There is really not much more characterization in *The Groom Talks in His Sleep,* made in 1935, than there is in *The Neighbor's Wife and Mine,* made four years earlier.)

Second, and far more important, he came to recognize how comedy could enrich his dramas. Hence his unique mix of humor and sentiment that is invariably gentle and warm even when it includes farce, satire, and irony. Time and again—not only in the '30s but throughout his career—he used this mix to bring balance to his material, to temper what might have been tragic or, as we have seen in the light comedies, merely trivial.

This tempering quality, this combining of moods, works hand in hand with Gosho's mixing of genres, and produces what one critic calls "a kind of warm and sincere relationship born in pathos."[9] It is this quality, above all else, that pervades his dramas of the '30s: *L'Amour (Ramura,* aka *Aibu,* 1933), a silent melodrama about a humble country doctor's relationship with his loyal daughter and profligate son; *Dancing Girl of Izu (Izu no odoriko,* 1933), a lyrical adaptation of Kawabata Yasunari's classic tale of the doomed love between a young itinerant dancer and a Tokyo college student—and an early landmark in the *junbungaku* (pure literature) movement;[10] and *Burden of Life,* which we need to consider briefly.

Focusing on child-parent relationships, *Burden* has to do with the indifference and animosity that a middle-aged white-collar worker (a "salaryman") feels for his last remaining child at home, a nine-year-old son. Filled with acute insights about family relationships, this "slice of life" drama makes especially fine use of humor in the climax. Earlier the father's harsh treatment had caused the boy and his mother to move out of the house. But one day the boy, forgetting that he no longer lives at home, ends up walking there after school by force of habit. Soon he and his father, who by now has come to see the error of his ways, are reconciled. When the mother hears this, she is not only greatly relieved but overjoyed and cannot wait to get home. In the final shot we see her riding home in a taxi, all the while urging on the driver with "go faster, faster." The scene is quintessential Gosho: something funny, sad, ironic, and moving all at the same time.

Burden has also been praised for its emphasis on character rather than plot. Frequently moving beyond the central narrative, Gosho creates a series of small, deliberately casual episodes that convey what Noel Burch calls "the family's life-stream."[11] In these episodes he takes time to look at various family members. Some of these characters serve to advance the plot more than others, but all of them exist chiefly to bring the flavor of life as it is lived to the film and to show their basic warmth and humanity. In short, *Burden of Life* illustrates that by the mid-'30s Gosho's *shomin-geki* was increasingly devoting itself to character studies.

So far we have discussed the nature of Gosho's light comedies, their relationship to his dramas, and the essential quality of "Goshoism" itself. Before turning
to an examination of *Woman of the Mist,* however, we need to consider the way in
which Gosho's art was almost certainly shaped by his childhood and upbringing.

Born in 1902 in the Shitamachi region of Tokyo, Gosho was an illegitimate
child. His father, a prosperous tobacco merchant, never married his mother, a
geisha of great beauty; but when Gosho was five years old, his father's legitimate
son died, and Gosho's life changed forever. Taken by his father, he was named
heir and groomed for a position in the family business. He was also told at the
time that he could no longer call his natural mother "mother." After that he did
so only once, when she was on her deathbed.[12] Yet as he himself later said, he
was genuinely loved by his father and grandfather, and had a happy and full
childhood. While this is doubtless true, it is probably no less true that he always
remained very sensitive to the complex nature of his circumstances, and even
felt guilty. There was, on the one hand, the situation of his mother, and his
brothers and sisters—a life that was far from easy. (A beloved younger brother
suffered from infantile paralysis and lost the use of one leg.) By contrast, his life
was filled with every conceivable advantage. In fact, as part of his informal
education, his grandfather introduced him to the arts, and his father took him
along to the tearoom/restaurants and geisha houses that he loved to frequent—
a milieu that Gosho would later depict in his films with great affection.

What Gosho could not help but appreciate, in short, were the contradictions
in life—and the fact that nothing was black or white. He saw the plight of his
mother, the serious illness of his brother. But he also saw the goodness and
generosity of his father and grandfather, and so he could not cast them in the
roles of his mother's oppressors; indeed, he couldn't even identify them as the
principal cause of her suffering. What Gosho came to realize was that no one
was to blame.[13]

It is this knowledge, this unerring sense of life's injustices, contradictions,
and complexities, that lies at the heart of Gosho's films, giving them an ex-
pansiveness and generosity of spirit. Only through humor and sentiment, and
laughter and pathos, could he surmount these contradictions and make sense of
them. Indeed, only through mixtures of genre and mood could he capture the
flavor and fullness of life itself.

II

Perhaps none of Gosho's extant films of the '30s is more representative of his
style, themes, and concerns than *Woman of the Mist.*[14] Arguably his most mature

work of the period, it is, first of all, an outstanding example of the *shitamachi* film, yet another subgenre of the *shomin-geki* that Shochiku specialized in.

The Shitamachi was the eastern part of pre–World War II Tokyo, the old downtown neighborhoods consisting of merchants, craftsmen, and other members of the bourgeois class. It was an area that Gosho knew intimately, one that he and other Shochiku directors depicted as a place where "warm people help each other along while wittily bantering among themselves."[15] These directors, none more so than Gosho,

> excelled at expressing the delicately refined humanity of the families and relatives of the cities and the local societies. They hated grandiosely moralistic themes. They preferred casual humor and pathos. Excluding wildly theatrical conflicts as boorish, they were charmed by the kind of story in which a slight misunderstanding between well-intentioned people gives rise to a conflict which is then skillfully resolved by a wise person.[16]

This description fits *Woman of the Mist* except for one important detail: its central conflict is the result of something far more serious than "a slight misunderstanding." Indeed, as we shall see, the casual and often affectionate observations of daily life that characterize the *shomin-geki*—and *shitamachi* film—are gradually tempered by the pathos and tragedy of romantic melodrama, thereby resulting in an especially rich and moving drama. In fact, it is Gosho's combining of these two distinct genres that makes *Woman of the Mist* one of his most formally accomplished works of the '30s.

Based on an original story idea by Gosho himself,[17] the film focuses on two families: Bunkichi (Sakamoto Takeshi) and his wife, Okiyo (Yoshikawa Mitsuko), a childless, middle-aged couple who run a dry-cleaning shop in downtown Tokyo; and Otoku, Bunkichi's widowed sister (Iida Choko), and her only child, Seiichi (Tokudaiji Shin), a law student. Otoku works as a maidservant in order to send her son to school, his success being her greatest goal in life. She becomes distraught, however, when she learns that he is reading novels instead of concentrating on his studies. Thus she asks her brother to speak to him. Sympathetic to mother and son alike, Bunkichi tells his nephew that there is nothing wrong with reading novels so long as he does his studies, too. Seiichi takes this advice to heart, but shortly afterward, he falls in love with Teruko, a delicate bar hostess (Iizuka Toshiko), and she becomes pregnant. Not knowing what to do, Seiichi turns to his uncle for help.

Like Gosho's best *shomin-geki, Woman of the Mist* is essentially a character study. At first the central protagonists seem like stock types in domestic comedy: the henpecked husband, the shrewish wife, and the profligate son, among others. But this is exactly the initial impression Gosho wants to create, for he means to reveal his characters, in all their contradictions and complexities, little by little. Thus, we cannot safely assume that we know them until the very end.

Of the five major characters, the most developed—and the most different from what he first appears to be—is Bunkichi. Initially, he strikes us as something of a bumpkin—a naive, henpecked little man susceptible to flattery. In fact, in the opening scene, we see him pretty much through his wife's eyes as he allows the local synod to talk him into canvassing the neighborhood to raise funds. "Isn't this a bit beyond you?" Okiyo asks at one point, making her feelings unmistakably clear. Yet, while Bunkichi frequently looks her way for approval—an act that Gosho's connecting pan shots between husband and wife underscore—he simply cannot resist being flattered. "I'm the only one who can do it," he boasts. But far from convinced, she asks, "Are you sure?" After the synod has gone, he meekly tries to defend himself by explaining, "I'm being counted on." But Okiyo will have none of this. She reminds him about the last time he volunteered for the group, and how it ended in disaster. Then she scoffs, "Aren't you easy!"

Gosho not only gradually qualifies our first impression of Bunkichi, but in time totally reverses it. This process gets underway in the next scene when Otoku asks him to speak to Seiichi about neglecting his studies. "He's in your hands," she later tells Bunkichi, a directive that acquires even greater meaning in the course of the narrative as Bunkichi becomes surrogate father and good angel to his nephew. As such, we see another side to him: his warmth, sensitivity, common sense, and, above all, wisdom. Consequently, when he first speaks with his nephew, he doesn't reproach him or insist on anything. Rather, he acknowledges two equal obligations: the one Seiichi owes his hard-working mother (*giri*) and the one he owes himself, namely, the right to seek more out of life than what is offered in his studies (*ninjō*).

Recognizing the need to find a balance between the demands of *giri* and *ninjō*, Bunkichi is the advocate of the middle path, the proverbial golden mean (*chūyō*). This is the path he takes when he intervenes to save Seiichi and Teruko from ruining their lives when she becomes pregnant. He thus devises a bold plan in which he not only claims to be the father of Teruko's child but also insists that Okiyo and he adopt it, an act that puts his marriage at considerable risk. In resolving this delicate problem, he clearly reveals his true nature to be courageous, selfless, and caring. Yet, in order to keep the entire matter and his pivotal role in it a secret, he masks most of his true nature and plays the unapt fellow that the world takes him to be.

Even so, Bunkichi is not all goodness and nobility. On the contrary, away from his wife's vigilant eye, he quickly finds his way to restaurants and tearooms, where he is not averse to getting drunk. There is also a bit of the con man in him. Thus, while he genuinely loves his nephew, he is not above using him to get money from his wife and his sister. (On one occasion, he even interrupts Otoku while she's giving a singing lesson—a source of extra income—and bluntly demands, "Give me all the money you've got!" on the pretext that Seiichi's teacher is eating and drinking with them.) Far from damning Bunkichi in our eyes, these flaws—actually, peccadilloes—endear him to us all the more, for they prove that he is thoroughly human. Moreover, they flesh out the portrait of a man that only Seiichi, Teruko, and we the viewers are privileged to see.

Although less individualized than Bunkichi, the other main characters still manage to surprise us, thanks to the subtle shading and depth that Gosho gives them. On the face of it, Seiichi seems a rather conventional young man. Yet he is also an idealist and something of a quester who is trying to fulfill that part of himself that his law studies deny. It is this desire that leads him to literature, and to make the claim that "only in novels are there really humane things," a claim that his uncle tells him simply is wrong. It is in part this same desire that leads to his romance with Teruko, for after all, what better affirmation of one's humanity is there than love? "A good boy," as he is described in the film, Seiichi is basically decent and honorable. But when Teruko becomes pregnant, he discovers that he is wholly unprepared to deal with the situation. Until now he has gone through life untested. Thus, in an important sense, the film is about Seiichi's rite of passage from youth to manhood—a rite that proves both painful and inescapable.

Throughout the film, however, the qualities that make Seiichi particularly interesting as a character are his shyness, indecision, and lack of social graces. These qualities illustrate not only his youthful innocence but also his vulnerability and confusion. Even at the synod meeting, where—at his uncle's request—he gives the group much-needed legal advice, he becomes ill at ease, self-consciously rubbing the back of his neck and stammering when the members thank him and compliment him. He is even more uncomfortable when he first meets Teruko, and finds himself seated alone with her at the restaurant in which she works. In fact, though he is attracted to her, he can barely make conversation. Far from being put off by his behavior, however, she does everything in her power to make him more comfortable. Indeed, she understands him almost immediately.

Ultimately a conventional figure of womanly self-sacrifice. Teruko is like a devoted heroine on the *shimpa* (popular melodrama) stage who gives up her life to benefit the career of the man she loves and of whom she feels, to some degree, unworthy. Typical of such heroines, she even takes upon herself any and all blame when she becomes pregnant and sees herself as a burden. "I'm a bad woman," she tells Seiichi. And though it is true that she has seduced him, it is no less true that he loves her and has acted, albeit reluctantly at times, of his own free will.

Interestingly enough, before her sacrifice is required by the drama, Teruko is carefully individualized and even somewhat unconventional. Once a geisha, but now determined to make it on her own, she is independent-minded and worldly wise (though not hardened or cynical in the least). That she is drawn to Seiichi in the first place suggests her own purity of heart and innocence; that she takes the initiative in their relationship by telling him outright that she likes him and by arranging to meet him again indicates the extent to which she is her own person.

Yet, despite her specific qualities as an individual, she remains throughout the film the "woman of the mist," a woman forever destined to be an outsider. Her lack of a real place in the world is underscored by the fact that her very identity is tentative and uncertain. Hence she is known by two different names. To Bunkichi, she is Kotaro, the name she had as a geisha when he first knew her (and when, it is suggested, they may have been lovers). To Seiichi, however, she is Teruko, the name she now goes by in her work as a bar hostess—the name that she has chosen in order to begin a new life. A creature of considerable pathos, Teruko is admirable not just because she possesses delicate and inexpressible feelings but because she comes to accept transitory happiness as her fate. Nevertheless, as we shall see, there is a certain ambiguity in the sacrifice she makes for Seiichi and the very pathos it generates, just as there is ambiguity in Seiichi's career being saved.

Okiyo and Otoku, the last of the main characters, are in certain respects alike. Okiyo at first seems shrewish, even downright stingy, for besides trying to monitor Bunkichi's behavior (especially his drinking), she holds the family purse strings, and is frugal when it comes to giving him spending money. Yet, she gives him money, even though she knows that he soon will be broke and will ask for more. She also knows that she will not refuse him. In fact, despite appearances, Okiyo and Bunkichi are happily married, their playful banter and acceptance of certain roles—wife/mother, husband/child—evidence of a warm, comfortable relationship. Okiyo's good-hearted and generous nature, however, is perhaps best seen in her relationship with Teruko, who she thinks is the mother of Bunkichi's child. Indeed, it is a tribute to her character that when Teruko dies, she faults herself for not having been even kinder to the young woman! This is the Shitamachi spirit at its best. True, Okiyo has to be flattered and cajoled by Otoku into forgiving her husband and adopting the baby. But her anger and hurt are perfectly understandable, especially when we stop to consider that she has been unable to give Bunkichi children and that she forgave him for infidelity in the past on the condition that it never happen again.

Like Okiyo, Otoku is basically good-natured and warm-hearted. But in her determination to see Seiichi become a success, she is often stubborn and forever trying to control him. In his words, she's "nosey and noisy." When he understandably "rebels" by reading novels, she overreacts and is even comical in her moaning and complaining. Her best qualities emerge in her dealings with other people. When a student patron at the restaurant where she works asks her to ignore his large unpaid bill and bring him more food, she gently scolds him but serves him anyway. When Okiyo threatens to divorce Bunkichi, Otoku does a remarkable job soothing her sister-in-law's feelings; indeed, she proves herself a veritable expert on human nature. Finally, when she befriends Teruko, she tends to her every need. She even chastises Bunkichi for failing to give the young woman a waist-warmer, apparently a necessity for expectant mothers. No matter that she believes Teruko is bearing her brother's child. If she knew the truth, chances are she would be just as kind, just as pragmatic—eventually.

No less important than characterization in *Woman of the Mist* is the way in which Gosho blends the *shomin-geki* and the romantic melodrama. Like *Burden of Life,* the early scenes of *Woman* in particular treat the customs, interactions, and unhurried lives of its characters with a casualness and documentary-like feel—what Noel Burch calls, in discussing another of Gosho's films, an "unaffected approach."[18] Here gentle comedy and irony predominate, and certain actions seem just details in the ups and downs of family life. The most significant example of this is Otoku's request that Bunkichi talk to her son. Only later do we realize that this detail functions as a vital plot thread in the skillfully woven fabric of the finished film. Indeed, the film seems to be virtually plotless until midway through, when (in the twenty-second of the film's forty-one scenes) Gosho introduces the catalyst to the dramatic action, Teruko's pregnancy. From this point on, *Woman*'s narrative becomes far more conventional, and the predominant tone shifts to one of seriousness and pathos. Still, Gosho retains enough of the earlier comedy to temper the increasingly tragic mood, and to underscore the fact that despite the hardships they suffer, his characters manage—as always—to prevail.

Besides being characterized by a blending of different genres and moods, Gosho's narrative is organized as a series of interrelated personal sacrifices, beginning with Otoku's years of hard work to put Seiichi through school and ending with a sacrifice that preserves and protects all those that have gone before it: Seiichi's decision to abide by Teruko's will and not reveal that he is the father of her child. In between these opening and closing sacrifices, there are four others: Bunkichi's naming of himself as Teruko's lover; Teruko and Seiichi's promise to Bunkichi never to see each other again; Okiyo's forgiveness of

Bunkichi's "infidelity" and acceptance of Teruko's child; and Teruko's final rejection of Seiichi.

Within this overall structure, Gosho—like all filmmakers—uses various forms of parallelism and repetition to unify his film and develop and intensify the dramatic conflicts. Among the most important of these forms are parallel motifs, such as compositions, repetition of paradigmatic shots, recycling of principal locales and setting, and a form that often incorporates many of these: the double scene. Situated at different points in the narrative, each of these two scenes treats the same characters in the same setting in much the same situation. As the word *much* suggests, the duplication is not exact, but that is precisely what Gosho wants, for ultimately the progression and development of his narrative depend upon the principle of contrast and differentiation, and our recognition of this principle. Gosho's double scenes, then, are in effect mirror images of one another in which he relies on not only narrative form but also visual strategies by echoing specific camera angles, movements, and compositions.

Take, for instance, the double scene in which Otoku and Seiichi confront each other in their home. The first of these scenes—scene 5—occurs early in the film; the second—scene 24—comes in the middle, and serves as a catalyst for the rest of the dramatic action. Both scenes deal with the nature of Otoku and Seiichi's relationship, and the struggle for power in that relationship. In the first scene, there is never any question that Otoku remains in control. It is Sunday morning. She is in the kitchen, preparing breakfast; he is upstairs in his room, surrounded by books and reading (probably surreptitiously). On this particular morning, Otoku has arranged for Bunkichi to drop by to talk with Seiichi. Expecting him any minute, she thus hurries Seiichi along so that he will be dressed and finished eating. In the process we are given a clear and accurate view of their relationship as a contest of wills in which each is locked into a fixed role. Wanting the best for her son, but troubled by his behavior, she ends up constantly ordering him around in an effort to retain control. Thus, no sooner does she see him than she greets him with a rapid succession of comments: "Not washing?" "That's terrible," "You look filthy," and "Make it quick." In turn he mostly tries to ignore her, but before long he obediently goes off to wash, gargle, and do what he is told.

As might be expected, Gosho visually reinforces Otoku's domination of Seiichi. Thus, in the final shot of the scene, as they are seated for breakfast, Gosho privileges her in the frame by locating her in the center and by giving us a full view of her face. By contrast, Seiichi is seated in the lower left-hand corner, his back turned to us. Gosho also relies on other visual strategies to bring depth and nuance to the relationship. When Otoku first calls Seiichi for breakfast, the camera—representing her point of view—pans to the bottom of the stairs. That it stops there instead of moving any higher suggests her realization that Seiichi's room is his domain, a place where she has no power. As he descends the stairs, however, he knowingly enters his mother's domain. What he sees and how he feels is conveyed by Gosho's subjective camera, which now assumes the young man's point of view. Thus, we not only observe Otoku toiling and rushing around (perhaps more than is necessary) to get the breakfast just right for her son—we also get a sense of how harassed and smothered he sometimes feels living under her roof.

Nothing is exactly resolved in this scene. In fact, Gosho trusts his viewers to have the sensitivity and intelligence—and experience—to know that the young man loves his mother, appearances notwithstanding, and that no matter how painful the conflict between them may be, it is an inevitable part of life. The son must find his own way and grow up to be independent; the mother must gradually let go.

By the time of the second scene, much has happened. Two scenes earlier, Seiichi has learned from Teruko that she is pregnant, and loving her, he means to do right by her. In the scene that follows, however, his situation becomes even more complicated when a well-meaning co-worker tells Otoku that she has seen Seiichi with a woman, a remark that sends Otoku rushing home immediately in order to confront him. During the course of this confrontation, which occupies the last scene of this double scene, we see Otoku's domination of Seiichi come to an end. We also see Seiichi deliberately throw away the chance to assert himself, for not only is he shackled by feelings of fear and guilt over his involvement with Teruko, but he cannot bring himself to add to his mother's grief by telling her the truth.

At first Otoku seems in control as usual. Repeatedly asking if he is seeing a woman, she does most of the talking, while he says little, looks visibly uncomfortable, and seems more or less trapped at the small table where he is seated. At one point he adjusts his collar; at another, he even picks up a book, as if he intends to read. But, determined to have answers, she quickly pulls it out of his hand and tosses it aside. "Who is she? I'd like to meet her," she says, half-pleading, half-demanding.

Seiichi, however, is far from indifferent to his mother's pleas and demands. This becomes evident when she bursts into tears, upbraiding him with, "And I trusted you! Have I worked so hard for this?" Here Gosho cuts to a close-up of his face. On it we see shame and guilt, feelings that are exacerbated by his knowledge that she also worked hard and sacrificed to help his father become a lawyer—an effort that went for naught. Thus, Seiichi lies, telling her what she wants to hear: that there is no woman in his life. Given his body language here and throughout the scene—the pained expressions, the constant fidgeting with his clothing, the frequent avoidance of eye contact, and, perhaps most telling of all, the fact that he covers his face—it is difficult to believe that Otoku would be taken in for a second. Yet, taken in she is, no doubt because she so desperately needs to be. Grateful and relieved, she weeps, calls him "a good boy," and apologizes for being foolish. Moments later, she is once again immersed in the comforting rituals and routines of daily life.

This scene is particularly enriched by the way that Gosho reworks visual strategies and elements of *mise-en-scène* from the first scene. Hence his use of the stairs setting. About halfway through this second scene, Seiichi finds himself standing face to face with Otoku and being forced to repeat his lie. So repugnant is his own behavior to him, and so great are his feelings of shame, that he moves away from her at the first opportunity. He cannot look her in the eye. Yet rather than escape to his room, though no escape is possible, he sits at the bottom of the stairs. From this safe distance, it is somewhat easier to lie.

In the first scene Gosho used a subjective moving camera to communicate Seiichi's point of view as he came down the stairs. In this scene, however, Gosho does not follow Seiichi's movement with even so much as a functional pan. Rather, he gives us a single shot in which Seiichi simply walks into the frame and sits down: as blunt and objective a recording of the action as one can imagine. Quite clearly, then, Gosho does not wish us to empathize with the young man, as we did before. Instead he seems to be asking us to watch, to consider, and to understand the gravity of the situation.

Doubtless the most striking instance of Gosho's repetition of visual strategies is to be found in the closing shot. Like the closing shot of the first scene, it is a two-shot of Seiichi and Otoku. But, as we might suspect, this time it is not Otoku who visually dominates the frame. Praying at the family altar, she is located in the left background, while Seiichi—seated once more at the table—is in the right foreground, and is therefore the larger figure. Even so, his visual dominance is subtly qualified by the empty space at the center of the frame and by his own behavior. Thus, after watching his mother briefly, he turns away and lowers his head, wiping away a tear. She has touched him deeply, and he has spared her. But in doing so, he has betrayed Teruko and his love for her. Caught in a clash of conflicting loyalties, he is not strong enough to solve the dilemma he is in, and he knows it. Consequently, in the very next scene, he pays his uncle a visit. "I'm in a bind," he says, asking for help.

In discussing Gosho's narrative structure and use of double scenes, we have examined many of the most salient characteristics of his style, including some of his visual strategies. Now we need to concentrate on the two principal influences on his style—the haiku and Lubitschian *découpage*—and how they function in the film. Nowhere are these forms more strikingly used than in the montage sequence that traces the development of Seiichi and Teruko's love affair. Exacting forms, they both make use of omission, condensation, and suggestion; but, as we shall see, Gosho calls upon each form for a somewhat different task.

Because of its very brevity, the haiku—most often a poem of seventeen syllables—can render only the outline of its subject, the essence of what the poet sees and feels: in short, the high moments. Left to the reader is the task (and pleasure) of filling in the details, making the connections and associations necessary to complete the poem.[19] Consider, for example, one of Gosho's own haiku, in fact the very last that he wrote:

> *Hana oboro*   Along the misty, flower-strewn road,
> *Hotoke izanau*   Buddha beckons—
> *Sanpomichi*   Come stroll along.[20]

These lines, which very nearly say outright that the poet expects to die soon, offer a series of concrete, serene images: "misty, flower-strewn road," "Buddha beckons," and finally, an invitation that is all the more inviting because of its casual and informal tone, "Come stroll along." Like all haiku, this poem is simple, and elegant in its simplicity. It requires the reader to see and feel in these particular images the sense of calm and peace, the promise of tranquility that emerges only after one passes through the austerity of life itself. As such, it is at one and the same time highly concrete in its images and thoroughly allusive and suggestive in its meaning.

In *Woman of the Mist* the montage sequence functions as visual haiku in two distinct ways. Structurally, it relies on the principles of omission, condensation, and suggestion, providing viewers with "high moments" only and expecting them to fill in the rest. Tonally, it creates a specific mood and atmosphere in its depiction of the physical settings and environment. Situated halfway through the narrative, this sequence is made up of the following seven scenes (scenes 16–22):

16. Seiichi receives a letter, which he tells Otoku is from a friend at a rival school. She remarks that lately this friend has been writing often.
17. In the privacy of his room, Seiichi reads the letter. From Teruko, it asks him to meet her the next day at the same place.
18. One evening as Seiichi and Teruko walk together, they discuss what will happen if his mother and uncle find out that they are seeing each other. Teruko also asks Seiichi to walk her home.
19. Outside her apartment building, she invites him in. Not yet ready to accept her invitation, he hesitates.

20. Seiichi, his face filled with uncertainty, follows Teruko down the hall-way to her apartment, only to leave after a few minutes.
21. Sitting alone on a bench overlooking the city, Seiichi is deep in thought, presumably about his relationship with Teruko.
22. Teruko tells Seiichi that she is pregnant; he promises to stand by her and accept his responsibility.

As this outline suggests, Gosho's structure of the couple's evolving relationship is marked by ellipsis. Certain information is withheld; specific actions are omitted. Even the period of time covered is hard to determine. Is it a matter of weeks, a few months, or possibly longer? To be sure, scenes 18–20 seem mostly straightforward. The events they cover are confined to a single evening, their chronology is relatively clear, and their basic point is unambiguous—i.e., Seiichi and Teruko have not yet become lovers. Nevertheless, even these scenes are characterized by ellipsis. Between scenes 19 and 20, for example, Seiichi obviously changes his mind. No less important is the way in which Gosho manages to keep one step ahead of us when it comes to the exact stage of Seiichi and Teruko's relationship. Thus, in scene 17 we are surprised to learn from Teruko's letter that the relationship is already underway—having begun, as it were, be-

Ill-fated lovers Teruko (Iizuka Toshiko) and Seiichi (Tokudaiji Shin). Photo courtesy of Kawakita Memorial Film Institute and Japan Society.

tween scenes, off-camera. And in the next scene we are once again surprised when we discover that Teruko and Seiichi's relationship has already turned serious.

This montage sequence, however, is at its most elliptical in the last two scenes. In scene 21 we see Seiichi alone but have no way of knowing whether or not this scene immediately follows scene 20. If it does, then perhaps he is trying to decide whether to return to Teruko's apartment, which he has left rather abruptly. At any rate, Gosho deliberately keeps us in the dark until scene 22, the closing scene. Then we see Seiichi reading a book inside Teruko's apartment, and suddenly learn that she is pregnant. In short, the haiku-like gaps and omissions in this sequence have the effect of moving forward the relationship from one major stage to another, imparting a strong determinism into the story and making it seem as if events are beyond anyone's control. Thus, Seiichi and Teruko's love seems doomed from the start.

Gosho's treatment of the physical environment to evoke atmosphere and mood and to comment upon the dramatic action also shows the influence of haiku. This is particularly true of scenes 18–20, in which Seiichi and Teruko meet. It is evening. We see them walk along a crowded, brightly lit street, then turn off onto a quiet side street where they sit on a park bench for a few minutes. Although they are alone and although he gives her a gift—cosmetics, which she accepts with more politeness than enthusiasm—the mood is neither romantic nor carefree. On the contrary, it is one of uncertainty and anxiety, in which he tries to assure her (and perhaps himself, as well) that he can handle the situation if his family finds out about them. As they continue walking, now to Teruko's apartment, the streets are dark and empty, and suddenly it seems very late. A heaviness and gloom hangs over the couple, and in the background the muted sound of a train adds a note of melancholy. This mood intensifies as they reach Teruko's apartment. "It's a humble building," she says, apologetically. "Sort of," he answers, sensing, and fearing, that she is about to invite him in. Gosho never actually shows Seiichi accept her invitation, but he does show him follow her very tentatively down the long, gray hallway that leads to her apartment—a passageway completely devoid of design or decoration. And that is enough, for the very blandness of this setting, along with the small, cramped quarters of the apartment, serves to underscore the pervasive feeling that what Seiichi and Teruko are doing is, at one level, wrong.

Indeed, from the very beginning, the lovers never seem to experience any real joy or happiness. Seiichi is forever vacillating, claiming in one scene that he does not care what others think of his relationship with Teruko, only to contradict himself in the next scene. Teruko, on the other hand, sees in Seiichi her last chance for happiness; and though she knows that to take advantage of his naivete, his uncertainty, and his genuine love for her is neither wise nor wholly right, she does so anyway. It is, in a real sense, her last chance to bring beauty into her life.

So far we have spoken of the influence of haiku on this montage sequence in terms of structure and tone. But perhaps there is a third type of influence, as well—what might be termed *metaphoric*. Hence in scene 20, the moment Seiichi arrives at Teruko's apartment, he sets down a bonsai plant that he has been carrying for her since scene 18. This plant plays no further role in the scene; indeed, it is never subsequently seen or mentioned. Why, then, has Gosho bothered introducing it in the first place? One reason may be that its presence in scenes 18–20 helps make it clear that the time covered is a single evening. Yet, the real reason for its presence, I think, lies in the special meaning and resonances that this plant has for Japanese audiences. A tree of enduring interest and beauty, the bonsai is said to teach the meaning of patience and humility to the owner in the five, ten, fifteen, or twenty years that it takes to grow. Similarly, in contemplating a single leaf, one can find peace and harmony in the quiet rhythms of nature itself. As one writer has said, "It is not what we do to these plants that is important, but what they do to us. The need for patience, humility, and peace is universal. So too is the power of the bonsai."[21] Quite clearly, we should not attempt to "explain" what was intended to be oblique, evocative, and suggestive. Suffice it to say that in the image of the bonsai Gosho conveys all our hopes and fears, and all our deepest feelings for these young lovers. Such is haiku.

Lubitschian *découpage,* the other major influence on Gosho's style, is best exemplified by the last scene of this montage, particularly in its use of close-ups of props and other details to reveal the psychology and often complex feelings of the characters. Like Lubitsch, Gosho employs a piecemeal editing style that often locates these props and details ("plastic material") in cutaway shots; but unlike the Lubitsch of *The Marriage Circle*—the Lubitsch that influenced him most—Gosho also relies on a mobile camera (most often in the form of a pan) to underscore the relationship between any given character and the prop or detail being isolated.

In this scene, in which Teruko tells Seiichi that she is pregnant, there are four especially significant close shots of plastic material. The first of these shots, an insert of a miniature Buddha, takes place soon after she returns to her apartment, where Seiichi is waiting. Understandably trying to delay giving him the news, she warms her hands and asks if he has waited long. But there is only one thing on his mind. "How was the hospital?" he asks obliquely. She does not answer, but walks over to a chest of drawers, on top of which sits the miniature, glass-encased Buddha. In close-up we see her hand lightly rub it, a gesture that suggests not only her continued reluctance to answer but her silent plea for strength and support. "Relax," she says quietly, perhaps as much to herself as to Seiichi. Then, after bowing before the Buddha, she declares, "I don't want to be your burden." When he replies that she is not, she says—almost apologetically—"Don't worry. I'll raise your child."[22]

What weighs on Teruko's mind is not just the pregnancy but her complicated feelings regarding Seiichi. Put simply, she wants to relieve him of any responsibility at the same time that she needs him to take responsibility—and, in fact, desperately wants him to do so. But she will ask or hope for nothing. Rather, she will put herself in the hands of Buddha.

Throughout the scene, Gosho emphasizes the sense of confusion, the palpable fear, and the undeniable pain that both Seiichi and Teruko experience and often try to keep to themselves. Having revealed Teruko's feelings in the first close-up, in the second Gosho focuses on those of Seiichi. Hence, immediately following Teruko's announcement that she is prepared to rear the child on her own, Gosho gives us an insert shot of Seiichi's school cap, which is casually tossed on the floor and almost completely covers the book it rests on. The meaning is unmistakable: now Seiichi suddenly realizes that what he has formerly treated with indifference—his career in law, for which the cap and the book are metonyms—is probably lost to him forever. Acutely aware of what he is thinking, Teruko insists that she can work a little and that she can even emigrate to China.[23] She then glances at a photograph on the wall, a picture of herself as a geisha.

The third significant example of a Lubitschian close-up, this shot of the photograph parallels that of Seiichi's looking at his cap and book. Here too there is a sudden and undiluted confrontation with harsh reality; here too there is the sense of seeing oneself as if for the first time. Thus, Teruko realizes, with painful clarity, what trying to take up the life of a geisha again will mean for her: not just hardship and struggle, but almost certainly prostitution. Perhaps Seiichi understands all of this as well, for he addresses her tenderly as "Teru" for the first time in the film. He also seems more genuinely selfless than he has ever been before. "Let me think about this a bit more," he says. Then he adds, "I'll be a full grown man shortly. I'm ready to be a father." Teruko thanks him for his kindness, but still cannot bring herself to ask for anything.

Even so, at the close of the scene Seiichi takes his most decisive action yet. Placing his hand affectionately on her shoulder, he rubs it gently, thereby not only comforting her but implicitly making a vow to stand by her. He then reinforces this vow with a simple and eloquent action that is captured in the fourth and last insert shot. Thus, he picks up a hinged picture frame containing a photograph of her in geisha dress, and slowly closes it. With this act, he in effect promises that she will never have to return to her past life because her life is now with him. Overwhelmed with gratitude and deeply relieved, Teruko no longer resists Seiichi's offer to assume responsibility, but now rushes to his side and embraces him. Weeping, she says, "I really worry." And once again she apologizes: "I'm a bad woman."

The scene, however, is not quite over. In fact, although the lovers seem united, it ends on a disturbing note, for instead of returning Teruko's embrace, Seiichi stands stiffly, allowing himself to be embraced. It is as if, in spite of his best intentions, he still remains indecisive. Indeed, as the next scene proves, such is the case.

Although Gosho is indebted to Lubitsch for his cutting style and use of plastic material, in the last analysis his visual style is very much his own: an artful orchestration of hundreds of static shots and numerous moving camera shots. In fact, in the scene just discussed, Gosho's combination of close shots and the mobile camera has a richness and range that we have barely touched on. Take, for example, the close shot of Seiichi's discarded cap and book. It is preceded by the following two shots: (1) a pan shot that assumes Seiichi's actual point of view as he quickly looks away from one of Teruko's dolls (clearly a symbol of their child) to Teruko herself; and (2) a close (objective) shot of Seiichi himself. Together these three shots function as a succinctly expressive unit that conveys Seiichi's feeling of panic, of being simultaneously trapped, overwhelmed, and powerless. Indeed, in this example and throughout the film as a whole, Gosho uses a panning camera to connect characters, to show the emotional and psychological ties that bind them—as here, where Seiichi recognizes the inexorable ties between Teruko and himself. But in addition, in this present scene the orchestration of cuts, close-ups, and moving camera shots has the effect of visually bringing Teruko and Seiichi together in the frame only to separate them time and again—an expression of their imperiled, tentative relationship. Hence another reason why we find little comfort in their closing embrace.

Earlier in this essay I said that what ultimately emerges as the dominant mood in the last half of *Woman of the Mist* is pathos: the privileging of passion, sentiment, and emotionalism that is characteristic of melodrama. This pathos mainly results from the increasing emphasis on Teruko's plight. However, interwoven with this pathos and counterbalancing it—if only for a short time—is the comic, casual, and documentary-like flavor of the *shomin-geki*. How does Gosho shape and use these two moods, alone and in conjunction with each other? And to what purpose? In answering these questions, we will arrive at a fuller understanding not only of the film's specific themes and concerns but of "Goshoism" itself.

Gosho relies on the *shomin-geki* to help dramatize Teruko's plight and make it as poignant as possible. He does this by contrasting it with Bunkichi and Okiyo's marital problem, which serves as the central interest for three scenes. Although the first of these scenes is as tense and dramatic as any in the film—it is here that Bunkichi tells Okiyo about his supposed affair and illegitimate child—the two scenes that follow are characterized by gentle, ironic comedy.

This is especially true of the scene in which Otoku convinces her understandably hurt and angry sister-in-law not to divorce Bunkichi. In this scene—the wittiest and perhaps most psychologically incisive in the film—Otoku assumes the role of mediator to patch up the breach as quickly as possible. By turns she cajoles, soothes, flatters, scolds, and counsels Okiyo, finally getting her to agree that it is in her best interest to take Bunkichi back *and* to adopt the child. (It helps, of course, that to some extent Okiyo wants to be talked into doing both.) At one point, Otoku even produces a handy photograph of Seiichi—as a baby, no less!—to help persuade Okiyo of the joys of motherhood. Thus, when Bunkichi shows up unexpectedly, Otoku has little to do but put the finishing touches on a job well done. Scolding him in private, she ushers him in to the room where Okiyo is sitting. He tells Okiyo that he has been worried about her; she asks, "Really?" clearly wanting to hear more; and Otoku—recognizing that the moment is propitious—invites her to join Bunkichi and her for a drink of sake. In short, the couple is "remarried," harmony is restored, and in the next scene—just as Otoku predicted—Okiyo ends up the talk of the town for being an extraordinarily open-minded and forgiving wife.

As we have said, these scenes serve to moderate and offset the pathos inherent in Teruko's situation. They do this in part because of their good-natured and warm-hearted humor, which is characteristic of the *shomin-geki* and the *shitamachi* modes. But they also do this because of their cunning location in the narrative. Following the scene in which Teruko informs Seiichi about her pregnancy, and preceding the one in which she banishes him from her life, these scenes temporarily draw us away from her, in effect demonstrating that life is not only tragedy and suffering.

And yet, in the long run, these same scenes, far from muting or minimizing Teruko's plight, serve only to deepen it, for the more we see the bonds and community that the other characters share, the more we come to realize what she has been permanently denied. Indeed, there is no small irony in the fact that only by rejecting Seiichi can she become a member of his family and enjoy a sense of community, if only until the baby is born. This irony is never more striking than when Otoku, completely ignorant of the baby's paternity, visits her, and treats her as if she is in fact a beloved daughter-in-law.

Having established this particular irony, for the remainder of the film Gosho reinforces and intensifies the pathetic element, and with it the mood of melodrama. Stylistically, he achieves this in a number of ways. Thus, in the scene in which she banishes Seiichi from her life, Gosho expresses her feelings of longing, isolation, and despair through a combination of *mise-en-scène,* editing, shot distance, and performance gestures. Seiichi, in spite of his promise to his uncle never to see Teruko again, appears at her apartment to plead with her to marry him. "I must have lost my mind," he declares, referring to his failure to come forward as the father of her child. But she implores him to accept what must be and sends him away. As Seiichi leaves, Gosho keeps his camera close on her: "Seiichan, I am sorry," she says, urging him to "study hard." In the next shot, Gosho subtly dollies back to capture the look of anguish on her face and the tension in her body as she hears Seiichi close the sliding door behind him. A cutaway shot reveals what she sees in her mind's eye: Seiichi walking away dejectedly. A medium shot follows in which she watches him from a window. Gosho holds this shot briefly, then cuts to the closing shot—a long one in which she is swallowed up in the space of the nearly empty room. Finally yielding completely to her feelings, she bends over, prostrate with grief. She has done what she felt had to be done.

Gosho also reinforces and intensifies pathos by concentrating almost entirely on the drama of separation, self-denial, and repression that is central to the mode of melodrama. In particular in two of the film's last scenes—Teruko's deathbed scene and the confrontation between Seiichi and Bunkichi at her wake—Gosho's narrative posits one obstacle after another in order to show the impossible gap that exists between his characters' personal desires and the chances of realizing those desires. Thus, even on her deathbed, when Bunkichi offers to bring Seiichi to her, Teruko refuses. "Tell him to study hard and be a great man," she says, in effect displacing her desires onto Seiichi, and leading Bunkichi to weep. But although Teruko is unquestionably the figure of greatest pathos in the film, she is by no means the only one. There is also Seiichi. Obviously having been advised not to attend the wake, he nonetheless shows up, filled with guilt and remorse about Teruko, and insisting on telling the truth about their relationship. Yet once more he is prevented from doing so by Bunkichi, who urges him to respect the "purity" of Teruko's love and sacrifice—and do what will be of benefit to others. Seiichi reluctantly obeys, but seems a broken young man. In both of these scenes, the pathos deepens not just because Teruko and Seiichi are denied their own desires, but because they too deny those desires, an act that is admirably selfless and undeniably sad.

The final scene of the film once more weds the worlds of the *shomin-geki* and melodrama. Decidedly bittersweet, it is set in the student bar/restaurant where Otoku works. But now there are no customers singing and drinking, no litany of orders being shouted out by the waitresses, for the restaurant is closed.

In long shot we see Otoku go to one of the tables to clear away the dirty dishes and stack them on a tray. Joined by two co-workers, she refers to Teruko, saying, "We're in mourning." They offer condolences. "It's a pity," one says, ruefully. "The good die young," adds the other. They then leave her to finish her work. In the closing shot, as she heads to the kitchen, Gosho's camera dollies out, a movement that serves to put everything in perspective: life goes on.

Even though there are only a few occasions in the last third of *Woman of the Mist* when we are led to laugh and cry at the same time, Goshoism is pervasive. However, it is a Goshoism that compels us not only to empathize with the sorrows, joys, and deeply human qualities of the characters but to reflect on the disquieting ambiguity surrounding Seiichi and Teruko's fate.

At first glance, Gosho seems wholeheartedly to approve of, even laud, Teruko's and Seiichi's personal sacrifices for the common good. In this respect he seems basically conservative, upholding the traditional values of loyalty and duty to family, emperor, and "the spirit of Old Japan" (*yamato-damashii*) that were being espoused by the military in order to check liberalism and Western ideas. Yet, as we shall see shortly, Gosho was fairly progressive for his day. In 1936, the year in which *Woman of the Mist* was made, the military movement was at its height,[24] and, like other artists, Gosho was forced to find ways to disguise any criticism he might have of the social system or political climate.

In *Woman of the Mist* Gosho outwardly conforms to the times by having Seiichi and Teruko submit to the will of their elders. Yet so sustained and intense are the emotion and sympathy he elicits for these two characters, denying themselves as they do, that the result is a deep and abiding ambiguity, in which their sacrifices come across as something less than ideal and good. How does Gosho achieve this ambiguity? Not surprisingly, by recourse to melodrama, which often disguises its social criticism by treating social crises in highly personal and emotional terms. Such is the case here. Indeed, we soon find ourselves asking a series of perhaps unanswerable questions: Although Seiichi's career and future have been saved, hasn't he in fact lost something even more valuable by not marrying Teruko, by not claiming his child? As for Teruko, hasn't she been punished far in excess of her "sin"? Indeed, what is her sin, apart from her sexual past (as a geisha) and her love for Seiichi, and why does its absolution require an act of "purity"—i.e., her death?[25]

These questions, though they may be unanswerable, have one thing in common: they lead us to discover for ourselves one of Gosho's most important themes—the belief that "human individuality [is] the most precious thing in the world."[26] Seen in this light, Seiichi and Teruko become far more than doomed lovers; they represent the desires of those individuals who want something more than society is willing or able to give. Indeed, in their desire to marry for love, they anticipate a democratic (Western) value that even today remains in opposition to the long-standing practice of arranged marriages.

In defending the need for individuality, Gosho does not mean to suggest that traditional values of duty and loyalty are to be rejected. Rather, he means to imply, once more, that the claims of family and individuals, *giri* and *ninjō* need to be constantly weighed and balanced. Bunkichi, Otoku, and Okiyo do the best they can, and while in the end they fall short, in their basic human decency, they represent society at its best. Like Bunkichi, Gosho advocates *chūyō*, the golden mean; but unlike him, Gosho acknowledges, with a single-mindedness of purpose and dedication, the need of the individual. Indeed, Gosho, ever sympathetic to the downtrodden, understands what it means to be a "woman of the mist," an individual on the periphery of society whose dreams and desires are unlikely to be realized.

In conclusion, in its themes and concerns, its emphasis on character, its visual and narrational strategies, and its mixing of moods, *Woman of the Mist* is clearly representative of Gosho in the '30s. As almost always, the *shomin-geki*, the drama of the everyday life of common people, serves as the foundation for his work. Yet, as we have also seen, he draws on melodrama, and with it pathos, creating the mood of laughter-in-tears that is popularly known as "Goshoism." In *Woman of the Mist*, however, his blending of melodrama and the *shomin-geki* goes beyond the usual notion of "Goshoism," prompting us to deeper feeling and thought about the many contradictions—and injustices—that are part of life. Thus, *Woman of the Mist* is more than a character study or a melodrama or a *shomin-geki* drama. It not only sums up Gosho's work in the '30s but also effectively points the way for his work to come.

NOTES

1. In the '50s a few of his films played in the West, most notably *Yellow Crow* (aka *Behold Thy Son* [*Kiiroi karasu*, 1956]); *Growing Up; Where Chimneys Are Seen* (aka *Four Chimneys*); and *An Inn at Osaka*. These last two films also showed at European festivals. Apparently, Gosho's first film to play theatrically in the U.S. was *A Daughter of Two Fathers* (aka *The Situation of the Human World* [*Hito no yo no sugata*, 1928]) with Tanaka Kinuyo. It shared a double bill in New York City with Harry Langdon's *Soldier Man*, and was reviewed by the *New York Times* on March 12, 1929, p. 26.

In the '80s, renewed interest in the Japanese film past gained Gosho international attention. A few of his '30s films were included in the touring package "Before *Rashomon*: Japanese Film Treasures of the '30s and '40s." There were also retrospectives exclusively devoted to him: at the Cinémathèque Française (1984–85), the National Film Theatre in London (March 1986), the Tenth Hong Kong International Film Festival (1986), and the Museum of Modern Art and Japan Film Center (1989–90), among others.

In addition, a retrospective of his films was the main event at the twentieth edition of Verona's International Film Week, April 6–12, 1989.

For an excellent introduction to Gosho, see Joseph Anderson and Donald Richie, "The Films of Heinosuke Gosho"; Mark Le Fanu, "To Love Is to Suffer"; and "Heinosuke Gosho," in *World Film Directors*.

2. Kakehi Masanori, "Gosho Heinosuke no sekai" ("The World of Gosho Heinosuke"), p. 125.

3. Unfortunately, only slightly more than a half-dozen of the 36 films he made in the '30s are extant. (Among those lost is *Everything That Lives* [*Ikitoshi ikerumono*, 1934]), an examination of social injustice that Anderson and Richie consider one of his four best films [*The Japanese Film*, p. 355]). The only consolation—and it is not a small one—is that the surviving films are among his most popular and critically praised of the day. Thus, we can feel reasonably confident that they provide an accurate picture of his themes and style, even if that picture is ultimately incomplete.

4. David Bordwell in *Ozu and the Poetics of Cinema*, p. 164, discusses this matter in relation to Ozu's work, but it also holds true for Gosho.

5. Although all three of these films may rightly be classified as *shomin-geki* comedies, *Bride* and *Groom* are frequently referred to as "nonsense comedies." *Neighbor*, on the other hand, is almost always referred to simply as a *shomin-geki* comedy. This distinction, when made, is made for a historical reason: *shomin-geki* comedy evolved out of nonsense comedy and *shomin-geki* drama.

6. "Le Point de vue sur les cheminées fantomes" ("The Point of View on the Phantom Chimneys"), p. 72.

7. This idealization of the old neighborhood and communal solidarity continues today in Japanese film in Yamada Yoji's Tora-san series, *It's Tough to Be a Man* (*Otoko wa tsurai yo*), and is one of the chief reasons for the enormous popularity of this long-running series.

8. *The Japanese Film*, p. 73.

9. Kyoko Hirano, "Heinosuke Gosho," p. 226.

10. In twentieth-century Japanese literature, a distinction is made between *junbungaku* (pure literature) and *taishūbungaku* (popular literature). In Japanese film, the *junbungaku* movement first took shape in the '30s when filmmakers began adapting "the better kinds of Japanese literature" (Anderson and Richie, *The Japanese Film*, p. 123).

11. *To the Distant Observer*, p. 259.

12. Kakehi, p. 124.

13. Sato, "Le Point de vue sur les cheminées fantomes," p. 72.

14. The title *Oboroyo no onna* is difficult to translate into English because there is no equivalent word for *Oboroyo*, which in Japanese means something like "the night of a hazy moon." Thus, the film has various English titles: *Woman of Pale Night*, *A Woman of the Misty Moonlight*, *Woman of the Mist*, and even *Moonlit Night Lady*. Of these, *Woman of the Mist* is the most frequently used.

15. Sato Tadao, "Tokyo on Film," p. 2.

16. Ibid.

17. In crediting himself for the original story idea, Gosho uses the name "Goshotei," his signature as a haiku writer. Also worth noting is that Gosho based Iida Choko's character on one of his relatives and that the actual screenplay was written by Ikeda Tadao, one of Shochiku's leading writers and an expert at describing the Shitamachi scene. See Firumu Sentā, ed., *Gosho Heinosuke kantoku tokushū*, p. 18.

18. *To the Distant Observer*, p. 287.

19. Harold G. Henderson, *An Introduction to Haiku*, pp. 1–8.

20. Quoted in Kakehi, p. 125. See also Kakehi, "Reminiscences of Gosho," p. 8.

21. Claude Chidamian, *Bonsai*, p. 12.

22. During the Gosho workshop that I conducted at the University of Hawaii Summer Session on June 4, 1990, Shimizu Akira of the Japan Film Library Council pointed out that today Teruko would probably have an abortion. But no such possibility existed in the 1930s, because abortion was illegal. For the past several decades, however, abortions have been legal in Japan, and can be obtained for medical or economic reasons under Article 14 of Japan's Eugenic Protection Law. This change is reflected in Gosho's 1956 film *Twice on a Certain Night* (*Aru no futatabi*), in which the heroine (Otowa Nobuko) has an abortion chiefly because her husband (Sano Shuji) is out of work.

23. This reference to China is the only specific allusion to the war Japan was waging there. This war and the establishment of the puppet regime of Manchuko earned Japan worldwide condemnation in the '30s, but as Donald Keene notes, "for the Japanese who participated in the colonization of Manchuria, life was immeasurably better than it had been at home" (*Dawn to the West,* p. 858). References to China as a place to find work appear in films as late as Ozu's *Brothers and Sisters of the Toda Family* (*Todake no kyodai,* 1941). See Bordwell, *Ozu and the Poetics of Cinema,* p. 282.

24. Anderson and Richie, *The Japanese Film,* p. 102.

25. In the last part of the film, questions also arise as to the exact nature of Bunkichi's feelings for Teruko. In the scene in which he visits her on her deathbed, and again in the scenes of her wake, he is genuinely grief-stricken, and even weeps. At first we imagine that this is because he has come to admire her, and thus cannot help being moved when she suddenly takes ill and dies so young, a victim of unkind fate. Yet, Gosho continually foregrounds Bunkichi in these scenes, showing us his deep and abiding sorrow, and often in close-up. Thus, these feelings begin to seem ambiguous, all the more so when we recall that he has known Teruko in the past—in a relationship that is itself ambiguous. Nothing is made of these ambiguities; indeed, they are not even acknowledged in the film. Still, we cannot help but wonder: Was Bunkichi once in love with Teruko? Is he still? Only he, Gosho, and writer Ikeda Tadao know for sure.

26. Anderson and Richie, *The Japanese Film,* p. 356.

WORKS CITED

Anderson, Joseph L., and Donald Richie. "The Films of Heinosuke Gosho." *Sight and Sound* 26 (Autumn 1956): 77–81.

―――― . *The Japanese Film: Art and Industry.* Expanded edition. Princeton: Princeton UP, 1982.

Bordwell, David. *Ozu and the Poetics of Cinema.* London: British Film Institute; Princeton: Princeton UP, 1988.

Burch, Noel. *To the Distant Observer: Form and Meaning in the Japanese Cinema.* Berkeley: U of California P, 1979.

Chidamian, Claude. *Bonsai: Miniature Trees.* New York and Princeton, N.J.: D. Van Nostrand, 1955.

Firumu Sentā [Film Center], ed. *Gosho Heinosuke kantoku tokushū* [*Special Issue on Director Gosho Heinosuke*]. Vol. 21. Tokyo: Film Center of the Tokyo National Museum of Modern Art, 1974.

Hall, Mordaunt. "The Screen: A Japanese Production." *New York Times,* 12 March 1929, p. 26.

"Heinosuke Gosho." *World Film Directors. Vol. I: 1890–1945.* Ed. John Wakeman. New York: H. W. Wilson, 1987, pp. 401–406.

Henderson, Harold G. *An Introduction to Haiku.* New York: Doubleday, 1958.

Hirano, Kyoko. "Heinosuke Gosho." In *Directors/Filmmakers: The International Dic-*

tionary of Films and Filmmakers. Vol. II. Ed. Christopher Lyon. Chicago: St. James Press, 1984, pp. 225–226.

Kakehi Masanori. "Gosho Heinosuke no sekai: Gosho Heinosuke no entotsu no mieru basho o megutte" ("The World of Gosho Heinosuke: About His Work *Where Chimneys Are Seen*"). In *Nihon eiga o yomu: paionia tachi no isan (Reading Japanese Film: Heritage of the Pioneers).* Tokyo: Dagereo Shuppan, 1984, pp. 115–138.

———. "Reminiscences of Gosho." In *Heinosuke Gosho,* The Tenth Hong Kong International Film Festival, Presented by the Urban Council (1986), pp. 1–44.

Keene, Donald. *Dawn to the West: Japanese Literature of the Modern Era—Fiction.* New York: Holt, Rinehart and Winston, 1984.

Le Fanu, Mark. "To Love Is to Suffer: Reflections on the Later Films of Heinosuke Gosho." *Sight and Sound* 55 (Summer 1986): 198–202.

Sato Tadao. "Le Point de vue sur les cheminées fantomes." Trans. from Japanese into French by Patrick de Vos and Cecile Sakai. In *Le Cinéma japonais de ses origines à nos jours,* Deuxième Partie. Paris: La Cinémathèque Française, 1984, pp. 71–77.

———. "Tokyo on Film." Trans. Larry Greenberg. *East-West Film Journal* 2 (June 1988): 1–12.

Why Does Oharu Faint? Mizoguchi's *The Life of Oharu* and Patriarchal Discourse

Robert N. Cohen

Unquestionably the most fascinating and frustrating critical problem regarding Mizoguchi Kenji has to with his attitude toward women. For many critics he is an impassioned defender of women's rights who feels that women have little choice under the Japanese patriarchy but to sacrifice themselves. Their only way out is to develop spiritual strength to transcend their oppression. In *The Life of Oharu* (*Saikaku ichidai onna,* 1952), the eponymous heroine falls from high position and eventually becomes the lowest type of street prostitute. Critics frequently have contended that by the end of the film she has attained transcendence. Cohen corrects this view. In fact, his reading of the film shows that Mizoguchi's attitude toward women was ambiguous at best and often disparaging. As Cohen explains, most of the action of the film is told in flashback from Oharu's point of view. After telling her story, she faints, and it is this act which is the starting point for Cohen's essay. Drawing on Freudian and modern psychology, as well as feminist theory, he asks whether Oharu is not herself subject to some kind of neurosis, and whether her point of view as represented in her flashback might not also be subject to some kind of neurotic distortion. At the same time he examines how the patriarchy of Mizoguchi's film uses various strategies, such as shot/reverse shots and the system of the look (or gaze), to control the heroine.

For further reading, see Dudley Andrew, "Saikaku ichidai onna," in *The International Dictionary of Films and Filmmakers: Volume 1—Films,* ed. Christopher Lyon (Chicago: St.

James Press, 1984), pp. 403–405; Robert Cohen, "Mizoguchi and Modernism: Structure, Culture, Point of View," *Sight and Sound* 47 (Spring 1978): 110–118; Kawabe Kazuo et al., "What *Life of Oharu* Has to Offer" ("Zadankai: *Saikaku ichidai onna* ga teiki suru mono"), *Shinario* 23 (June 1967): 14–26; Alain Masson, "Revers de la quietude (sur quatre films de Mizoguchi)" ("The Other Side of Quietude: On Four Films by Mizoguchi"), *Positif* 212 (November 1978): 26–28; Joan Mellen, *The Waves at Genji's Door* (New York: Pantheon, 1976); Donald Richie, "Kenji Mizoguchi," in *Cinema: A Critical Dictionary*, Vol. 2, ed. Richard Roud (London: Martin Secker and Warburg, 1980), pp. 696–703; and David Williams, "Kenji Mizoguchi," in *World Film Directors: Volume One—1890–1945*, ed. John Wakeman (New York: H. W. Wilson, 1987), pp. 787–803.

There is little doubt today in the West that Mizoguchi's most important subject has been the plight of the Japanese woman. At the same time, we realize that Mizoguchi was a director of commercial films, and consequently, that his work represents an institutional discourse, the structure and ideology of which inform this subject matter. Thus in view of the general feeling that the women in his films are essentially powerless to affect their lives in the narratives,[1] the concept of patriarchy offers a way to discuss the limitations placed on them at the level of discourse. It is here that we can approach the apparent ambiguities of his films and ask questions concerning the sources of pleasure in his texts, the function of women as object and icon, and the subjective positioning of both male and female characters.

It is, therefore, the purpose of this essay to apply the Western theory of patriarchy to one of Mizoguchi's most prominent films about women, *The Life of Oharu* (*Saikaku ichidai onna*, Shin Toho, 1952).[2] This late film seems especially suited for such an analysis, not only because the common interpretation of the film becomes increasingly doubtful under such scrutiny, but also because *Oharu* is an example of Mizoguchi's film style at its most enigmatic. It is largely a work in the director's characteristic style (long takes, great camera-to-subject distances, editing strategies based on a ninety-degree rule), but more important, it also includes several instances of the shot/reverse shot, which establishes a specific character point of view, and which is almost nonexistent in Mizoguchi's other films.[3] What is most significant, of course, is that the reverse shot is the linchpin of classical Western film and the most fundamental structure of patriarchal discourse as it has been defined in Western film theory. Therefore, an evaluation of the ways the reverse shot functions in *Oharu* will tell us how well the film either confirms or contradicts the patriarchal implications underlying the Western film, whose conventions the Japanese understood so well.

The fate of Mizoguchi's heroine, for example, at the end of *Oharu* exemplifies the precarious interpretation that critics have offered for Oharu's becoming the itinerant priest. It is the consensus of opinion that Oharu triumphs in her unwitting battle to overcome an oppressive society. She is said to "transcend" her life on earth, and in Audie Bock's phrase, as the priest Oharu "prays for all humanity."[4] Clearly this spiritual victory is one that is exclusively reserved for women in Mizoguchi, and in a revealing passage Dudley and Paul Andrew associate it with the woman's special vision.

> Most frequently, the women in Mizoguchi's films scream with their glance. . . .
> They see through the system, through the audience, into the structure of an
> impersonal cosmos. Revolt thus leads the way to a kind of stoic contemplation,
> which in his late films Mizoguchi seemed to prize beyond all other goals.[5]

The woman's access to vision notwithstanding, it is one of the functions of patriarchy to position women as objects of contemplation, as symbols for what they lack in the signifying structures of the narratives. Men, Dudley Andrew and Paul Andrew tell us, "initiate the actions . . . carry on the way of the world . . . are suited for action, progress."[6] According to the theory of patriarchy, however, it is as active subjects of the discourse that men become the controllers of the look and vision that functions to objectify women as passive objects. It is, therefore, hard to maintain the view that Oharu triumphs at the end of the film when to achieve this position she is kept passive in the discourse, denied a sexual identity at the end of the film, and made to assume the guilt of others.

In the West, patriarchy has been a major subject of feminist theory for at least fifteen years.[7] For this study, however, the works of two authors are especially important: Laura Mulvey and her pioneering essay "Visual Pleasure and Narrative Cinema," and Mary Ann Doane, particularly *The Desire to Desire*. The former essay and its subsequent elaborations have established the "system of the look" as the basic cinematic figure by which patriarchy structures male desire in the Western film and positions women as both "masculine spectators"[8] and feminine objects of the screen spectacle. It is the essential instability of such structures of subject positioning and desire which has led feminist critics particularly to the issues that Doane addresses—namely, the characteristics of melodrama conceived as a specific kind of patriarchal discourse where women are defined primarily in relation to forms of narcissism and neurosis. Doane's work in this area is exemplary for what it allows us to observe about Oharu's psycho-pathology and in relation to the unique tension between the forms of audience identification and distance that characterize many of the director's films.

Since psychoanalysis forms the basis of these concepts and their application, it is important to point out initially that there are at least two related aspects of Mizoguchi's film that have profound psychoanalytic consequences: Oharu's failed search for a stable identity, and the fact that she faints three times over the course of the narrative. *Oharu* traces the fall of the title character from her exalted life as a court lady through the separate strata of seventeenth-century Japanese society until she lands as a common street prostitute. Told largely in flashback from Oharu's point of view, the story portrays her life as a series of crises in which she is unable to establish herself in any socially defined role, whether it be as mother, daughter, wife, geisha, concubine, or nun. The flash-back of these events culminates in Oharu's fainting for the last time. The con-vergence of these two occurrences thus authorizes an interpretation based on their cause-effect relationship, whereby Oharu's fainting must be seen as a reaction to the form and the content of her memory. Such a radical response on the woman's part suggests a desire to avoid deep-seated anxieties caused by the knowledge that her sense of self is not stable or secure. In Freudian terms, Oharu's predicament is succinctly described by Philip Rosen in the following passage:

> Primary experiences of identity are constructed against a radical anxiety, sum-marized as castration anxiety. Processes of desire, sexuality, and fantasy are intertwined with consciousness of self, which is produced to counter against the founding anxiety and is always in dialectic with it. As a result, the normal experi-ence of identity occurs only on condition that its basic processes are hidden from the "I" thus constructed. This is an essential Freudian point: There is always a fundamental *mis*recognition involved in the individual's desire to find—or recog-nize—his or her self as stable and secure.[9]

Accordingly, Oharu's fainting at the end of the flashback represents the failure of this process of "misrecognition." Since fainting itself is often taken as a corollary for blindness where the individual displaces a perceived psychic threat onto the site of the body,[10] Oharu's fainting can be taken as a neurotic response to her memory where castration anxiety threatens to enter the text at the end of the flashback. The woman's narration of her past therefore can be analyzed as Oharu's Oedipal journey, and her fainting suggests its irresolution. Patriarchy, however, has a stake in the outcome of the discourse, and it is through this influence that the Hollywood film regularly represses the full ex-pression of woman's sexual identity. Similarly, in Mizoguchi's film we will try to apprehend an analogous system of patriarchal influences that can explain the repression of the Japanese woman and the conversion of her body into the symptoms of her cinematic illness.

In the Hollywood film, patriarchy asserts itself most conspicuously through the subordination of the female characters by the controlling gaze of the male. According to Laura Mulvey, because men are the central characters of most Hollywood films, it is through an identification with the male protagonist that the spectator enters the action of a film. Point of view, and particularly the shot/reverse shot, place men in a position to control the narrative by possessing the gaze that marks them as subjects who look and women as objects to be looked at. Pleasure is established for the character, and by identification for the spectator, in looking at women as objects of a male desire. Men thus actively control women and the narrative by controlling the look.

In *Oharu,* there are two series of reverse shots that position Oharu as the subject of the look, and both bracket the woman's flashback. In the opening sequence in the famous hall of Buddhas, there are four shots of Oharu looking at the statues intercut with three point-of-view shots of what she sees. In the last, her gaze rests on one statue, and over this figure the face of Katsunosuke, her first lover, is superimposed twice. At the end of the flashback, we have a similar series of POV shots that establish Oharu in relation to the statues. From a medium long shot of Oharu inside the hall, there are two shots of her looking at the statues and two POV shots of what she sees. In the second, the statues go out of focus,[11] and in the following shot of recognition, Oharu projects a great sense of fear and then she faints.

In these examples Oharu assumes the position of the subject, whose look objectifies the man, Katsunosuke. According to these series of shots, we have two potentially subversive moments within the discourse if it is actually being governed by the laws of patriarchy. According to Mulvey's characterization of the woman in patriarchy as possessing a "to-be-looked-at-ness,"[12] Oharu's active look constitutes a reversal. There are several issues, however, in *Oharu* which govern the woman's access to the look and foreground her essential "to-be-looked-at" position. Most of these center around the polarities set up in the text between the possibilities of seeing and being seen.

First off, the interior of the temple acts as a certain haven for Oharu, given the fact that throughout the film she is forever being banished from place to place, turned out, as it were, from areas associated with stability and belonging to those scarcely offering safe repose. It is in this inner chamber that Oharu has her fullest access to vision. It is here, too, that she has access to her memory, which recalls her past and her relationship with Katsunosuke, the retainer of lesser rank, who is beheaded for his affair with her. Therefore, there is little doubt that Oharu's gaze inside the temple is an erotic look that sets up her pleasure as a major signifying element of the text. Simultaneously, it is Oharu's very access to vision and the accessibility of her past, of Katsunosuke, and her self, which are rendered problematic throughout the film. This is clearly speci-fied in Oharu's gesture of ceremoniously removing her scarf during the first temple scene, at the precise moment she realizes that one of the Buddhist statues reminds her of Katsunosuke. Here she reveals herself openly and freely for the first time in contrast to the opening shots of the film where, as a common street prostitute, Oharu conspicuously keeps her face hidden.[13]

The contrast further reveals not only that the film will be about Oharu's inner journey, but also that her desire for knowledge will take precedence over her relations with the world around her. This is clearly specified through the inner/outer dichotomy where outside the temple Oharu recoils from her femi-nine position as someone who is seen—the prostitute who shuns revealing her face—but inside, she actively positions herself as the subject who sees. Since the text establishes that this latter desire is indistinguishable from Oharu's desire for Katsunosuke, her self-image is inexplicably bound up with him. Oharu's position in the text at the threshold of memory thus places her as the voyeur, as someone who wishes to see without being seen. This position, which is denied to women in terms of psychoanalytic theory, points to the possible explanation that Oharu suffers in the film because she possesses a desire forbidden by its overriding patriarchy. It is almost as if her gesture of removing the scarf is the key which unlocks a Pandora's Box of memories that inauspiciously culminate in her fainting at the end of the flashback.[14]

Additionally, the shot/reverse shot preceding the flashback is characterized by Katsunosuke's fundamental absence from the film's historical present. He is objectified only within Oharu's imagination. Oharu, therefore, retains an essen-tially feminine position by becoming the subject of a daydream. Doane raises this issue in her discussion of what she calls the "medical discourse films" of the Hollywood cinema during the 1940s, in which she refers to Freud and Breuer and their study of female hysteria: "For it is daydreaming which instigates the illness in the first place—an uncontrolled and addressee-less daydreaming."[15]

Oharu thus seems to have access to a subject position only in relation to Katsunosuke as an object of fantasy. It is consequently only in this position that Oharu as the woman may become active within the discourse. Throughout the rest of the film, in both the flashback and the action after she faints, Oharu is represented passively, as the object of the desire of others.

Oharu's subjectivity in this early scene also suggests another of Doane's observations. Like the illnesses which play a part in medical discourse films,

Oharu's fainting, "implicat[es] woman's entire being."[16] She is not merely an object of spectacle possessing a body that functions only to be looked at by men. When her entire being is at stake, the woman's body, in Doane's phrase, becomes "fully a signifier" of that which is invisible, by which she means that the woman's body signifies an illness. Her status in the discourse thus shifts from the "spectacular" to the "symptomatic." Likewise, Oharu can assume a subject position normally reserved in the classic cinema for the male subject without provoking a crisis in the film's overall patriarchy. This implies that patriarchy can be operating in *Oharu* even though Oharu's body escapes being "entirely" signified as "an object of male vision." Equally, it is possible that Oharu has access to the look in this early sequence only on condition that she remain castrated and other throughout the remainder of the film.

In the system of the look, as Mulvey first proposed, the woman is constituted as an icon for the pleasure of the male, but it is ultimately an ambiguous pleasure, for the woman in the classic text represents the threat of castration for the male spectator. To determine whether or not Oharu as an image represents such a threat requires an examination of two aspects of Mizoguchi's film. One is that Oharu is totally objectified during the course of the flashback, turned into an object of pleasure for a succession of male characters. The second stems from the fact that Oharu is treated differently under the law than her first lover. For the crime of sleeping with someone of a differing rank, Katsunosuke is condemned to die by beheading, while Oharu is banished.[17] Both sentences are established in the narrative as legal consequences of the patriarchal law in Japan that seeks to maintain the rigid vertical hierarchy of social relationships. Within the parameters set up in the discourse, the woman's "fall" is thus represented as a series of lesser banishments, where each time a relationship "fails," she is sent away, put, as it were, out of sight. In this way, Oharu receives special but unequal treatment and is punished by a law that is characterized by treating the woman's whole body as the offending object. Oharu is thus identified as a woman who, like her counterpart in the classic Western text, is represented as being "overpresent."[18]

Being constituted as the female and singled out for special treatment and punishment, Oharu therefore symbolically represents that which must be repressed. As she moves through and is moved by the narrative during the flashback, she is "read" by each of the male characters after Katsunosuke's death as a feared object. Her banishment then becomes a series of textual positions that identify Oharu as the object of a desire whose goal is "not to see" the woman as a threatening presence. This goal is clearly the sole possession of the patriarchal forces that structure the text. What is demanded of Oharu by the male characters is in effect a complete silencing of her femininity and her complete exclusion from collective life.[19] Oharu is thus compelled to give up her access to the look, thereby taking on the guilt of others and repressing her sexuality. All of this is played out against a series of conflicting positions centered around Oharu as both the desired and the feared object.

Each of these general tendencies of the Mizoguchi text suggests that Oharu's image in fact does represent sexual difference, and consequently the castration threat for the male spectator. Its clearest expression occurs in the next-to-last episode of her flashback. Earlier, on the same night that Oharu enters the temple as the aging prostitute, she is stopped by a man, who she thinks is a customer. She carefully covers her face to keep him from seeing her true age. They enter a cheap inn, and the man then leads her near a back room where several young pilgrims sit around a table. They all crane their necks to get a glimpse of Oharu's face, which she still keeps conspicuously hidden. With all male eyes toward her, the man removes Oharu's scarf and raises his lantern to give the others a clearer view of her. He says, "You want a girl. Take a look at this witch." The men stare and then look away self-consciously while the man tells them that if they wish, Oharu will lead them in a life of sin. He then thanks her and pays her off. She looks at the coins and then stops. Returning to the men, Oharu suddenly hisses at them with a demented air, hunches her back, and assumes the pose of a cat, clawing at them as if to pluck out their eyes.[20] The men recoil from her, when again she stops, looks back at the money, laughs, and thanks them. She then leaves with the men's voices nervously laughing off-screen.

The first thing to notice is that this scene is consciously ironical. For this man, who so unabashedly uses Oharu as an object, is one of the few throughout the entire film to acknowledge Oharu for what she is now: a ridiculous aging courtesan. He restates her own self-knowledge about what she has become in order to survive. He therefore acknowledges her true feminine identity, but not only does he do it for the wrong reason, he does it too late. This fact is of primary significance because as Doane makes clear, "mistiming" is one of the fundamental requirements of pathos, part of what Franco Moretti calls the "rhetoric of the too late."[21] The depth of Oharu's humiliation in this scene is a result of this mechanism which is "related to a certain construction of temporality in which communication or recognitions take place but are mistimed."[22]

It is not only the man's "too late" recognition of Oharu that distinguishes this scene, but also the heroine's self-recognition of what she has become. This explains Oharu's sense of irony, while at the same time it provides her motivation for assuming the pose of the cat. This position refers back to the sequence where Oharu turns a cat loose on the merchant's wife, who has humiliated her by forcing her to cut off her long, beautiful hair. The moment in both scenes thus represents Oharu's castrating desire for revenge. The nervous laughter of the pilgrims in the inn signifies their half-realization of this threat. However, Oharu quickly realizes the futility of her gesture in the later scene, which suggests a further reference to Doane's comments on female narcissism:

> In his article, "On Narcissism: An Introduction," Freud compares the self-sufficiency and inaccessibility of the narcissistic woman to that of "cats and the large beasts of prey" (as well as that of the child, the criminal, and the humorist). The cat is the signifier of a female sexuality which is self-sufficient, and, above all, objectless.[23]

Oharu's primary position throughout her narration as the object of repression thus undercuts her aggressive stance as the cat. Her sexuality, which the man singles out for special consideration, offering it as a lure and a trap for the young men under his care, becomes blunted and "inaccessible." The viewer is made aware of these conflicts and their effects on Oharu's character precisely because of the pathos of the scene, and the distance separating Oharu from her original desires.

The scene's importance in the discourse, however, as the culminating episode of Oharu's reminiscence comes from the power of the woman to take over the control of vision. She is taken into the inn and used by the man as a visual sign of the forbidden object. In this way, she is offered to the pilgrims as an aberration of their sexual desires. Once Oharu sees the bitter irony of the situation, however, she seizes control and flaunts her "to-be-seen-ness," turning the men's aggressiveness back on them and mocking her position as the object of the look. To some extent, she thus holds out the threat of castration as a desirable position both for the pilgrims and for the male spectator.[24] This ambivalence, however, is immediately dissipated again through Oharu's control of vision as she looks down at the money in her hand and laughs. The men's eyes follow her gesture, moving from the woman's body to the money. Through this move their discomfort is assuaged.

This gesture in effect relates Oharu to the money as a commodity which increases the pathetic nature of her degradation. It also represents an additional feature of pathos characterized by Doane as "a sense of disproportion—between desires and their fulfillment or between the transgression . . . and the punishment associated with it."[25] Any sympathy the viewer may feel at this point in the text is derived from this sense of the disproportion between Oharu's original "sin" and these obvious consequences. These associations link Oharu through her aggressive behavior not only to the merchant's wife, but also to her liaison with Katsunosuke. Thus her whole life as portrayed in the flashback comes to bear on these few gestures, and it is Oharu's control of the trajectory of vision that makes this possible even without a shot/reverse shot structure.

Even though it remains an oversimplification to see Oharu's figure in itself throughout the film as an icon for the castration threat, the text acknowledges her sexual difference in this scene through the laughter of the men, which is kept off-screen. As Oharu walks away in silence, she comes to embody that difference and lack which the discourse sets up through the *mise-en-scène* and its sound track. Through a unique form of suture, the men's voices create the perception of absence, which, like the suturing effect of the shot/reverse shot, stimulates, as Kaja Silverman says, a desire "to see more."[26]

According to orthodox suture theory, the breaking up of scenographic space into character point-of-view shots forces the spectator to become aware of the frame, and thus the limitations on his ability to control what he sees. "He discovers that he is only authorized to see what happens to be in the axis of the gaze of another spectator, who is ghostly or absent."[27] This "absent one" is conceptualized as the "speaking subject," which is a position in the classic narrative that is never acknowledged within the film.

In the Mizoguchi text, which generally eschews the point-of-view shot, there are invariably elements of the *mise-en-scène* that force an awareness of the frame onto the spectator and the limits it poses on what he can see. Without articulating an absent gaze, the Mizoguchi text continually marks absence as a function of the controlling third-person view. Characters stand just off-screen during dialogue scenes which continue across the frame line or, as in the scene at the inn above, character voices emanate from an off-screen space before, during, and after the central action. In none of these constructions is there an explicit subject who is articulated as different from the speaking subject of the film.

We can theorize a difference, however, that is set up through the absence which is signified through off-screen space. The voices of the pilgrims at the inn signify this absent field, and it is the text's refusal to return to them that implies the existence of an absent, speaking subject. As Silverman shows in her reading of Hitchcock's *Psycho,* "The whole operation of suture can be made more rather than less irresistible when the field of the speaking subject is continually implied."[28] This implication, I would argue, constitutes an essential structural tension that underlies a great many of Mizoguchi's most idiosyncratic scenes in terms of their difference from Western classical film. Held within the third-person, nondifferentiated shot, the movement and framing of characters continually articulates a system of discourse predicated on presence and absence, "unmediated, 'unsoftened' by the intervention of a human gaze."[29]

An extreme example of this process occurs in Katsunosuke's beheading scene, in which the sword itself functions to center vision and structure absence without a human subject. In this one-shot scene, Katsunosuke dictates his final message to Oharu, and then the camera leaves the man and centers the sword in the frame as the executioner prepares to carry out the sentence. Through a series of camera and object movements, the blade enters and exits the frame as the central identifying presence until the camera pans up with it, and the blade slashes out of frame, leaving an almost blank sky to mark its absence. The executioner then steps back into frame, the sword with him, at which point the camera reframes the blade and then pans down its length until the scene fades to black.

Here there is no mistaking the symbolic power invested in the sword merely by its central presence in the discourse. Its movements establish its link to the castrating power of the law. Not only is the actual beheading accomplished off-screen, with the movements of the sword standing for Katsunosuke's death, but the articulation of excessive absences in such a scene of heightened spectacle no doubt intensifies the spectator's anxiety concerning what is kept off-screen. Without a shot/reverse shot, the scene powerfully manipulates the viewer's frustrated desire to see in such a manner that only the fade to black can reassert the viewer's right to control.

Not all of *Oharu*'s reverse shots are as radical as this example. In fact, the initial scene inside the hall of Buddhas essentially duplicates the orthodox suturing process which introduces the field of the Absent One. Whenever we have a one-shot of Oharu looking at the statues, Katsunosuke, whose face has been superimposed there, becomes the signifier of absence. His absence from the frame alternated with hers creates this conventional suturing effect. What is further evident, however, is that at the end of the scene, Mizoguchi organizes the images so that they disavow this absence and lack as in the Western cinema, by producing again this desire to see more. In this case, the "more" is not another shot of Katsunosuke but the entire content of the flashback, which Mizoguchi places immediately after a final shot of Oharu looking. Her fantasy/daydream is thus tied to the hermeneutic code associated with Katsunosuke's presence in this early scene, and the spectator's desire to learn Oharu's story is substituted for Katsunosuke's absence in the last shot of the reverse-field figure.

The motivating forces behind the film's long flashback can thus be ascribed to those elements of patriarchy that function to disavow absence and lack, which, Mulvey proposed, imply the castration threat for the male spectator. Her two proposals for disavowal have to do with the ways narratives progress and the ways they are interrupted through fetishizing the female as an icon. Both strategies have their place in *Oharu*.

In the first instance, what Mulvey calls voyeurism, the patriarchal text attributes to the heroine characteristics that establish her guilt. In Oharu's memory of the events of her life, this is indeed the case. Katsunosuke offers her personal devotion and the promise of a true loving relationship through marriage. He first says to her, "I want to make you happy," and in his final message, he urges, "Please find a good man and have a good life with him. But, be sure to marry only when there is true mutual love." Then to the executioners, he says, "I hope the time will come when there is no social rank." This is the message Oharu takes away, when she questions her father, "If we love each other, what if our ranks are different?" Oharu, therefore, explicitly believes in the philosophy which Katsunosuke voices, and her response to it is to faint in the man's arms the first time she hears it, thereby giving herself to him. In this way, with a show of feminine overemotionalism, she expresses her femininity, which makes her more susceptible to the ideal he represents. Throughout the flashback, Oharu is continually reminded of this ideal, if only in an abstract way. Only once does she again refer to Katsunosuke, even though the ideal he represents to her colors the spectator's response to her fall by its pathos. As indicated before, a sense of disproportion informs the pathetic discourse, a distinction "between desires and their fulfillment." Oharu's suffering and her "tragedy" throughout the subsequent episodes thus evolve in her memory as a consequence of her uncompromising moral stance and the restrictive social laws which make her liaison with Katsunosuke a "just" crime.

In contrast to this reading of the flashback, Oharu is not punished simply for being gullible, or for actually marrying a man of inferior rank, but for sleeping with him, for committing an error in conduct. Therefore, even though the disparity in their social ranks signifies the violation of the law, it is her sexual nature specifically for which she is punished. The patriarchal law exerts its control over her by banishing her from Kyoto and, consequently, by contributing to her loss of parental esteem, which has the effect of converting Oharu into an object of exchange. She is returned to her family in exchange for giving up her feminine "to-be-looked-at" nature. She is reconstituted as a daughter, and her return to her family, characterized by her father as the destruction of family honor, is the text's mark of the denial of her sexual nature. The text pushes her into a regressive position, and her words to her father, which combine the concepts of love and social rank, further deflect the spectator's attention away from Oharu's sexual guilt. Her "moral" crime and its extension in the betrayal of her father are thus the marks of disavowal characteristic of the voyeuristic strategy.

Oharu's return to the family's provincial home closes the opening sequence of the film and constitutes an essential paradigm for the subsequent action of the flashback. In each of the following episodes, Oharu enters into a new relationship as the object of an exchange, the purpose of which can be ascribed to the desire of patriarchy to control Oharu and her sexuality. In the sequence preceding Oharu's sojourn with Lord Matsudaira, for example, the "search for the ideal beauty" episode, Oharu is discovered dancing with a group of provincial daughters. In the only male point-of-view shot of the flashback, Oharu is singled out and taken away from the other dancing women. To cover over the immediate threat of castration this suturing instance signifies in classical narrative, Matsudaira's messenger falls to his knees and proclaims, "I'll buy her." Immediately, the merchant agrees to act as intermediary, and the narrative resumes with Oharu's father selling his daughter to the lord. In this way, the lack enunciated through the "Absent One" in the reverse shot of Oharu dancing is disavowed by the resumption of narrative which converts the woman into an object of exchange. She is selected for this position, as in each of the following episodes, because her femininity meets the needs of the men who purchase her. Likewise, she is eventually banished from each relationship when this femininity seeks expression and recognition through a sexuality that is invariably problematic.

This view of Oharu as a commodity is structured by the discourse itself, whose logic determines the actions and thoughts of the woman throughout the flashback. Thus in each episode of her fall, Oharu's problematic sexuality is expressed primarily through the woman's body. Most often it is her inherent "to-be-looked-at" nature which puts Oharu's social position into jeopardy, when the mere sight of her elicits a male desire that ultimately forces her away and down to the next level of degradation. Often, however, individual parts of her body are singled out for special treatment. Her hair is cut by the jealous wife of the merchant as a way to erase the visual attraction Oharu holds for her husband. In the Matsudaira sequence, it is the uterus, the center of female reproduction, which is the focus of her appeal—she is brought there to have a child—and when she is no longer needed, she is pathetically separated from the lord and her child. As a commodity, therefore, Oharu is represented exactly like the typical woman in the Western maternal melodrama, where

> the texts bring into play the contradictory position of the mother within a patriarchal society—a position formulated by the injunction that she focus desire on the child and subsequent demand to give up the child to the social order. Motherhood is conceived as the always uneasy conjunction of an absolute closeness and a forced distance.[30]

This distance between Oharu and her child dominates the last part of the narrative and creates the great pathos of the film. We can see that the text, therefore, contains two major narrative threads: one which involves the social law and Oharu's relation to it, and another, the patriarchal law that controls her sexuality and her reproductive identity. Significantly, it is the commodification of the heroine through the discourse that transforms the first into the second. After Katsunosuke is beheaded, there is almost no mention of the social law and rank that he represents in Oharu's explicit memory. She becomes no social crusader for societal reform, no activist trying to make a martyr out of Katsunosuke and his courageous stance for the rights of the individual. Instead she devotes herself to the simple pursuits of happiness and personal satisfaction as a woman, and the fact that she acknowledges herself as a commodity in these pursuits represents the deflection of her desire from an identification with others to an identification with herself. To extend the former into the action of the flashback would mean a critique of the patriarchal basis of Japanese society. Since we can argue that the purpose of the flashback is to uphold the patriarchy of the discourse, it is the woman who is put at fault and not society.[31]

This explains why Oharu's memory is overwhelmingly preoccupied with feelings and experiences associated with being victimized. This too explains why Oharu is kept from her son at the end of the film. She is guilty, not, as Matsudaira's vassals contend, because Oharu has humiliated the clan by her life of degradation, but simply because she has lived her life as a Japanese woman.

At the same time the patriarchy of Mizoguchi's text invokes the mechanism of voyeurism to control the heroine during the extended flashback, investigating her guilt and meting out punishment, it simultaneously establishes the beauty of Oharu's position, overvaluing her through the mechanism Mulvey describes as fetishistic scopophilia. This form of disavowal converts the woman into a fetish object for the male spectator whereby her beauty is substituted for the threat she invariably poses as the signifier of sexual difference.

In many ways, the description of this mechanism in *Oharu* takes us to the heart of one of the most idiosyncratic aspects of Mizoguchi's style: the tension so often displayed in all his films between identification and distance. These are the moments when Mizoguchi's camera will hold the characters in long shots during moments of great emotional significance.[32] In *Oharu,* these examples occur in an extreme form, sometimes functioning like a coda for the preceding action, and often followed by a fade to black. There are four instances of the technique: the scene of Oharu's attempted suicide after Katsunosuke's parting note, the last shot of the geisha house sequence, the last shot of Oharu playing the samisen after catching a glimpse of her son, and the last shot in the film of Oharu as the traveling priest. The examples are similar to but somewhat different from Mizoguchi's overall tendency to maintain a generally large camera-to-subject distance and do not indicate the full range of meanings that the technique entails. Their usage in *Oharu,* therefore, is a unique instance of

Mizoguchi's style which functions to fetishize the figure of the woman within the specific patriarchal context of this film.[33]

Most commentators on this aspect of Mizoguchi's work hold the concepts of identification and distance as binary oppositions.[34] The typical features of Mizoguchi's distanciation are thought to weaken the spectator's identification with the characters on the screen, thereby increasing the viewer's autonomy and powers of discrimination. The Mizoguchi distance is thus assumed to be Brechtian in being a critical strategy which deconstructs the transparency of the traditional classical codes. These codes, in turn, are believed to support the fact that Mizoguchi's films are most often intense melodramas of extreme pathos. Distance is considered an antidote to the overemotionalism that his films constantly approach, but which often fails to materialize because of the lack of audience involvement with the characters. Conversely, however, as the examples from *Oharu* show, it is the very foundations of melodrama, its great emotionalism and its pathos, that the Mizoguchi distance intensifies in this film. Based on the concepts of disproportion and mistiming, these scenes make the woman into a fetish object, not by emphasizing distance over identification but by combining the two processes.

In each of the four scenes we take to correspond to Mulvey's second category of patriarchal disavowal, a sense of disproportion characterizes Oharu's relationship with something she lacks. It is this distance between Oharu and the object of her desire that provides the pathos of each scene. In the suicide attempt, it is Katsunosuke that Oharu mourns, and whom she attempts to join in death by trying to kill herself. The camera keeps her and her mother in long shot as they run through the bamboo grove, and their dialogue informs the viewer directly about these issues. The subject of the scene is thus Katsunosuke's death and Oharu's distant response to it. Likewise, in the geisha house, the subject of the entire preceding segment is money, its power to corrupt, and Oharu's refusal to succumb to its lure. In the last shot of this scene, Oharu stands in the extreme background as the counterfeiter is led away by the police. The restaurant owner and the others who are left in the frame throw down the bogus coins in disgust while Oharu stands above in all her geisha finery, representing her distance from money and power. Outside the temple after Oharu has been thrown out of the nunnery, it is her child from whom she has been separated. She watches him from afar, and then she sits in front of her samisen and cries. And in the final shot of the film, the long shot frames Oharu as the priest, her distance from any identifiable sexuality marked through her ambiguous dress.

In each of these cases, the spectator's ability to understand the emotions in the scene without the use of close-ups comes from the relationship established in the text between the character and the explicit intent of the scene expressed through either dialogue or action. At times this relationship is easier to read than at others. In the suicide attempt, it is Oharu's loss of Katsunosuke that determines her emotions. In the scene following Oharu's viewing of her son, it is her separation from him that motivates her depression. At the geisha house, it is Oharu's lack of money in relation to the rest of her life; in the final shot, it is her lack of a feminine identity and more. It is less important, however, in Mizoguchi's discourse to know exactly what the character feels, because knowing less does not make the shot less emotional. In fact, the scenes often become unbearably emotional because of the distance that is represented between Oharu and what she desires. This emotion is, therefore, intensified through the mistiming that the sense of disproportion signifies. As Doane again observes, "Moving narratives manifest an unrelenting linearity which allows the slippage between what is and what should have been to become visible. What the narratives demonstrate above all is the irreversibility of time."[35] It is this aspect of *Oharu* that results from its general picaresque form with its precise cause/effect structure punctuated by these "interruptions" which heighten and foreground Oharu's position as the one who suffers. It is at these moments that the temporal aspect of Mizoguchi's film as melodrama functions to create the most intense feelings of pathos.

The lack of closeness between the spectator and Oharu in these scenes represents the lack that Oharu represents as a woman, and thus her position as the fetish object. This is established through the distance and temporality that are specific marks of the Mizoguchi text as melodrama. Simultaneously, the beauty of the compositions and the position bestowed on Oharu as an aesthetic object mark her as a fetish for the male viewer. Oharu becomes appealing both as a signifier of suffering and as an aesthetic object, "satisfying in itself," as Mulvey says. In this position, the woman comes closest to representing a sign of disavowal for the male spectator.

Significantly, Mizoguchi's brand of fetishism does not break up Oharu's body into parts through separate shots, dwelling on her face or figure. Instead, it frames her whole body, which emphasizes its completeness, but places it against a background which seems more complete, more narratively significant than the immediate action implies. Noel Burch has commented on the "surplus of iconographic signs" in Mizoguchi's distancing shots where the environment included in the frame signifies elements seemingly extraneous to the narrative.[36] Far from diluting the narrative at these points, however, Mizoguchi's distance intensifies it, especially in scenes such as the above, where what the heroine lacks in the fiction implies its completion through the overdetermined environment which contains her. Her whole body then takes on this symbolic aspect of absence and lack, and it is only through the long shots, through the various distancing devices, that Mizoguchi is able to accomplish this unique form of disavowal. More significant still is the fact, as Doane admirably demonstrates, that an identification between the woman and her body signifies a narcissism that is a specific pathological condition of women caught up in the male desire of most mainstream narratives.

By the logic that patriarchy imposes on Oharu's character, her memory gains the force of a psychic trauma which triggers her fainting as a hysterical attack. In Freudian terms, "the nucleus of an hysterical attack . . . is a memory, the hallucinatory reliving of the scene which was significant for the illness."[37] This return of the repressed, again according to Freudian theory, takes the form of the projection onto others of the guilt an individual feels over the events in memory. This kind of distortion in the memories of victims of hysteria conforms to the pattern of guilt that places Oharu as the one who is wronged by others in her own personal narrative. The crucial point is, nevertheless, that "the returning portions of the memory are distorted by being replaced by analogous images from contemporary life; thus they are distorted only in one way—by chronological shifting but not by the formation of a substitute."[38]

This explanation underscores Katsunosuke's prominence in Oharu's memory. Her relations with him, placed in her memory as the initial cause of her suffering, become the founding relationship of her psychic life and function as the paradigm for all Oharu's future relations with others. Katsunosuke becomes her ego ideal, which is a position in the actual chronology of her life that should be taken over by her father. In the logic of her "distorted" memory, however, Katsunosuke is substituted for her father, and his loss comes to represent her failed search for happiness, pleasure, and identity. Oharu's flashback, therefore, must represent her Oedipal journey, and its chronological distortions signify the fact that it remains unresolved. Her memory takes on the forces of a defense in which Oharu projects all her neurotic fears onto Katsunosuke. The social wrongs which plague her throughout memory become projections of her own internal fear that she has been wronged. It is this anxiety concerning Oharu's unresolved Oedipal conflicts, as well as her fear of having been castrated, which threatens her at the conclusion of the flashback and which motivates her fainting.[39] Her defense is unsuccessful, however, for as Freud commented, "with the return of the repressed in a distorted form, the defense has failed."[40]

This failure of Oharu's defenses suggests that Oharu's narration of her life as a memory is directly responsible for her fainting, and thus for the woman's illness. Doane's analysis of the medical discourse films, however, tells us that when a heroine becomes the narrator of her memories, the process can have one of two functions: it can be therapeutic or "disease-producing."[41] In the American films, which so often include psychoanalysis within the narratives, the former is characterized by the presence of a doctor who listens to the woman's narration and interprets her illness, while the latter, as we have seen before, is associated with daydreaming. According to Doane, the daydream

> feeds that narcissistic self-sufficiency to which women are always prey. The woman's narrative acumen is thus transformed into the symptom of illness. Her narrative cannot stand on its own—it must be interpreted. Narration by the woman is therefore therapeutic only when constrained and regulated by the purposeful ear of the listening doctor.[42]

Oharu's narration thus seems disease-producing, while at the same time it is contained within a controlling discourse which "constrains and regulates" it. It therefore combines both functions. Her fainting after the flashback confirms her illness, while the signs of patriarchy within the discourse suggest how it is being controlled.

The containing discourse that regulates the woman's memory need not be the courtroom setting, the psychoanalytic session, or the hospital bed, which are the typical institutional arenas in the medical discourse films which guarantee that the male doctor will discover the "truth" of the woman's illness. As Doane makes clear, the controlling discourse is much more an issue of who controls the image. In *Oharu*, we remember that just preceding the flashback Oharu is positioned as the subject of the discourse, whose specific point-of-view shots project Katsunosuke's image onto the Buddhist statue. It is from this enunciating position that the woman's narration follows. It would seem, therefore, that Oharu's flashback controls the image, thus authorizing her point of view as the controlling presence of the memory; nevertheless, this is not altogether the case.

First there is the fact that Oharu's point-of-view shots, as well as the flashback, are framed by the film as a whole. In the classic text, the seemingly narratorless aspect of the discourse provides the "reality effect" of the film when the diegesis is introduced in the third person. This is the case in *Oharu*, which begins with the shot of Oharu walking alone on the grounds outside the temple. The flashback in such a context must be marked in some way differently from this surrounding enunciation. In Mizoguchi's film, as in the medical discourse examples, however, the woman's subjective point of view never returns as an explicit mark of enunciation once the flashback has begun. Thus the events of Oharu's memory are accorded the same value in the discourse as the surrounding action and are granted the same truth as the overall discourse itself; in effect the surrounding discourse validates the truth which it contains. This validation is strengthened by the fact that the last action Oharu remembers is a repetition of the opening shot of her on the temple grounds. It is marked in her memory, however, with an absence of sound—the words of the couple Oharu observes no longer appear on the sound track—and the implication arises that the woman's memory is somehow incomplete, lacking in relation to its more powerful, authoritative surrounding context.

The second mark of the discourse which devalues the authority of Oharu's subjectivity occurs in the last one-shot of her just preceding the flashback. After Oharu is positioned as the subject of the look, and Katsunosuke is established as the object of her glance, there follows the shot of Oharu removing the scarf. This tight medium shot, the closest to an American shot in Mizoguchi, is characterized by an extremely self-conscious attitude on the part of the heroine. Her eyes focus inward after she slides off the scarf, and then she leans against a pillar in a repose of passive contemplation, her eyes falling downward. Simultaneously, the shot contains an overaccumulation of filmic codes, which, while signifying the transition to the past that takes place in Oharu's mind, also establishes the power of the discourse itself to place Oharu in this position. At the beginning of the shot, *gagaku* music is inserted to represent not only the transition into the flashback, but equally the courtly role that Oharu assumes in the following sequence. Second, the camera slightly reframes the character as the scarf slides off her head with an almost gratuitous movement, the beauty and elegance of which serve again to prefigure Oharu's courtly role and sensitivity. Third, there is a dissolve that punctuates the shift back in time.

The accumulation of these filmic effects marks the author's presence within the discourse and signifies the presence of the "speaking subject" of the text. Oharu's ability to control her flashback is thus undercut by this sign of her lack of power which keeps her as a symbol of difference and lack for the male spectator. Her memory is, therefore, a daydream by Doane's definition, but one which is itself subject to the control of the text's inherent patriarchy, the purpose of which, we can assert, is to confirm Oharu's basic narcissism. Her fainting at the end of the flashback thus authenticates her basic illness as a mark of disavowal. Like the woman's film in America during the 1940s, Oharu's illness is inscribed onto her body, and similar to her portrayal in the Western film, "the trauma of the woman is total."[43]

The patriarchy that controls Oharu during the flashback also determines the course of the action after she faints by reactivating what Silverman has called patriarchy's "compulsory narrative of loss and recovery."[44] After Oharu faints in the hall of Buddhas, the narrative resumes with her reunion with her mother, the news that her father is dead,[45] the final recovery of her son, their separation, and her transformation into the traveling priest. All of the events are portrayed not only using the familiar motifs of visibility and invisibility, but also by invoking the logic of Oharu's guilt at it has been portrayed during her recollection.

The penultimate sequence of the film is Oharu's reunion with the Matsudaira clan. She returns to them in hopes of being reunited with her son, who has now become their leader. Instead, she is chastised by the Matsudaira vassals for behavior inappropriate for the mother of their new lord and is pronounced guilty of shirking her social obligations. She is again sentenced to banishment after being allowed one last look at her son. Her attempt to get near him is played out in a grand spectacle as Oharu rushes toward the boy, only to be restrained by the men, who are both horrified of her power and afraid of their own vulnerability. With koto rhythmically punctuating their chase, the men lose Oharu somewhere on the castle grounds. The sequence ends in a stunning deep-focus shot of the vassals charging back and forth in the background, while in the center of the frame sits Oharu's palanquin, the "mysterious basket," to borrow from Proust, which will presumably carry her off into a life in exile.[46] Oharu has thus finally escaped her ultimate "to be looked at" position. Therefore, the film should end with this last shot of the sequence: Oharu, unseen, her whole body hidden from the gaze of the spectator, away from the eyes of the Matsudaira vassals, submerged in herself, in the basket, symbol of prison and the womb.

Oharu's complete banishment from the text, however, despite the fact that it is based on the logic of the feminine within the discourse, must be disavowed by its underlying patriarchy. This explains the necessity of the final scene, which places Oharu as the begging priest, to fulfill the desire of the narrative that she repent for her guilt. Her lack of sexual identity is thus made beautiful and "satisfying in itself" as Oharu is transformed and overvalued as the priest. Religion in this case becomes the mark of denial for the woman's narcissistic wound. She becomes a religious object only as a substitute for what she lacks as a woman in the discourse. Her so-called transcendence is thus an imaginary concept forced on the spectator, who must assume the position of the male subject.

There is still an ambivalence here that comes from the pathos of the scene. While Oharu's religious conversion signifies the male desire to disavow her ultimate castrated condition and by association his own, the use of *gagaku* music tends to undercut this position.[47] When Oharu sees the pagoda in the distance after she leaves the houses where she begs, she stops to pray, and the music recalls her past life specifically with Katsunosuke. This aural signifier brings back Oharu's original transgression as an element of the discourse and serves as a reminder to the male spectator of the inescapability of Oharu's past. This juxtaposition of past and present, a result of the text's pathos, reaffirms, as we have previously seen, the "slippage between what is and what should have been" and solidifies the spectator's own position as lacking.

The composition of the scene substantiates Oharu as the beautiful object, the self-sacrificing woman, who is captured within an environment whose symmetry is meant to represent her completeness. The melodramatic requirements of the narrative, however, keep reminding the spectator of what has come before and what might have been in a manner that contests Oharu's completeness as a traveling priest. What comes back to the spectator is the sense of what Oharu now lacks, of what has become absent through her fetishized conversion into a religious object.

The beauty of such a position and the artistic consequences of Oharu's conversion finally tend to fetishize the distance Mizoguchi establishes between the spectator and the screen. This seems an inevitable mark of a Japanese desire that patriarchy control its own ambivalence. As Doane again observes, "In a patriarchal society, to desexualize the female body is ultimately to deny its very existence."[48] Since women do exist in Mizoguchi and in Japan, but remain, at least in *The Life of Oharu*, representations of lack and desire, they are subject to procedures of disavowal which elevate them into symbols of suffering and beauty. Beautiful but lacking, whole yet fractured, women in Mizoguchi signify the fundamental misrecognition at the heart of the director's patriarchal discourse.

NOTES

1. Compare the following: "What his two types of heroine have in common is a singular pathos—the fate of the long-suffering ideal woman is as grim as that of the spiteful rebel" (Audie Bock, *Japanese Film Directors* [Tokyo: Kodansha International, 1978], p. 41); "If women revolt against the system of prohibitions, exchanges, and hierarchy that men have established, it is because they see right through to the end of this system and sense its futility" (Dudley Andrew and Paul Andrew, *Kenji Mizoguchi: A Guide to References and Resources* [Boston: G. K. Hall, 1981], p. 28).

2. The film is based on the novel *Koshoku ichidai onna* of 1686 by Ihara Saikaku. See *The Life of an Amorous Woman and Other Writings,* ed. and trans. Ivan Morris (New York: New Directions Books, 1963), pp. 121–208.

3. See Robert Cohen, "Mizoguchi and Modernism: Structure, Culture, Point of View," *Sight and Sound* 47, 2 (Spring 1978): 110–118.

4. Bock, p. 42. See also the interpretations of the film's ending in Keiko McDonald, *Mizoguchi* (Boston: Twayne, 1984), pp. 114–116; and in Dudley Andrew, "The Passion of Identification in the Late Films of Kenji Mizoguchi," in *Film in the Aura of Art* (Princeton: Princeton UP, 1984), pp. 176–177.

5. Andrew and Andrew, p. 29.

6. Ibid., p. 28.

7. The concept was introduced into film theory by feminist critics at the same time

Lacan's psychoanalysis began its ascendancy. For the purposes of this study, the following selective readings are noteworthy: Claire Johnston, "Towards a Feminist Film Practice: Some Theses," in *Movies and Methods,* ed. Bill Nichols, Vol. 2 (Berkeley and Los Angeles: U of California P, 1985), pp. 315–327; Paul Willemen, "Voyeurism, the Look, and Dwoskin," *Afterimage* 6 (1976): 40–50; B. Ruby Rich, "In the Name of Feminist Film Criticism," in *Movies and Methods,* Vol. 2, pp. 340–358; Stephen Heath, "Difference," *Screen* 19, 3 (Autumn 1978): 51–112; Janet Bergstrom, "Enunciation and Sexual Difference," *Camera Obscura,* Nos. 3–4 (1979): 33–70; Laura Mulvey, "Visual Pleasure and Narrative Cinema" and "Afterthoughts on 'Visual Pleasure and Narrative Cinema' Inspired by *Duel in the Sun* (1946)," in Mulvey, *Visual and Other Pleasures* (Bloomington and Indianapolis: Indiana UP, 1989), pp. 29–38; and Mary Ann Doane, "Film and the Masquerade—Theorizing the Female Spectator," *Screen* 23, 3–4 (September–October 1982): 74–88; Doane, *The Desire to Desire: The Woman's Film of the 1940s* (Bloomington and Indianapolis: Indiana UP, 1987); E. Ann Kaplan, *Women and Film: Both Sides of the Camera* (New York: Methuen, 1983); Mary Ann Doane, Patricia Mellencamp, and Linda Williams, eds., *Re-vision: Essays in Feminist Film Criticism* (Frederick, Md.: University Publications of America, 1984); Teresa de Lauretis, *Alice Doesn't: Feminism, Semiotics, Cinema* (Bloomington: Indiana UP, 1984); Gaylyn Studlar, "Masochism and the Perverse Pleasures of the Cinema," in Nichols, ed., *Movies and Methods,* Vol. 2, pp. 602–621; Kaja Silverman, "Suture [Excerpts]," in *Narrative, Apparatus, Ideology: A Film Theory Reader,* ed. Philip Rosen (New York: Columbia UP, 1986), pp. 219–235.

8. See Mulvey, "Afterthoughts on 'Visual Pleasure,' " p. 30.

9. Philip Rosen, "Introduction: Text and Subject," in *Narrative, Apparatus, Ideology,* p. 160.

10. See J. Laplanche and J. B. Pontalis, *The Language of Psychoanalysis,* trans. Donald Nicholson-Smith (New York: Norton, 1973), p. 56.

11. In McDonald's commentary on this scene, she describes a different set of circumstances that I am unaware of: "The statues once more metamorphose into the faces of those who wronged her: Lord Matsudaira and the merchant Kabei" (*Mizoguchi,* p. 114).

12. "Visual Pleasure and Narrative Cinema," p. 11.

13. For a contrary interpretation of this gesture, see Dudley Andrew, p. 177.

14. For a comprehensive discussion of the Pandora's Box metaphor as it relates to this interior/exterior motif and the portrayal of women in melodrama, see Mulvey, "Introduction," in *Visual and Other Pleasures,* pp. x–xii. Cf. Mizoguchi's use of the palanquin near the end of the film.

15. *The Desire to Desire,* p. 53.

16. Ibid., p. 39.

17. On the relationship between castration and decapitation in terms of gender distinctions, see Tania Modleski, *The Women Who Knew Too Much: Hitchcock and Feminist Theory* (New York and London: Methuen, 1988), pp. 19–20.

18. Doane, *The Desire to Desire,* p. 39.

19. For a discussion of how Japanese ideology might function in this context in relation to Lacan's formulations concerning mirror identification, see Scott Nygren, "The Pacific War: Reading, Contradiction, and Denial," *Wide Angle* 9, 2 (1987): 69–70.

20. McDonald calls Oharu's mime "playing the witch," in reference to the old man's words to describe her to the pilgrims. See *Mizoguchi,* pp. 113–114.

21. Doane, *The Desire to Desire,* p. 91.

22. Ibid.

23. Ibid., p. 51.

24. On the possibility that castration might hold an attraction for the Japanese spectator, see Peter Lehman, "The Art of Making Films: An Interview with Oshima Nagisa," *Wide Angle* 4, 2 (1980): 58, and Lehman, "The Mysterious Orient, The Crystal Clear

Orient, The Non-existent Orient: Dilemmas of Western Scholars of Japanese Film," *Journal of Film and Video* 39, 2 (Winter 1987): 12–15. In contrast to Oharu's position as the manipulator of vision, see Kaja Silverman's comments on *Lola Montez* and *Gilda* in "Suture," pp. 230–235.

25. *The Desire to Desire*, p. 86.

26. "Suture," p. 221.

27. Daniel Dayan, "The Tutor-Code of Classical Cinema," in *Movies and Methods*, ed. Bill Nichols, Vol. 1 (Berkeley and Los Angeles: U of California P, 1976), p. 448.

28. "Suture," p. 224.

29. Ibid.

30. Doane, *The Desire to Desire*, p. 50.

31. On the logic of commodity fetishism, see ibid., p. 32.

32. Noel Burch argues for a "kind of reverse codification" in Mizoguchi's distance, where the more intense the drama, the farther away the camera is positioned (*To the Distant Observer: Form and Meaning in the Japanese Cinema* [Berkeley and Los Angeles: U of California P, 1979], pp. 236–244).

33. For a variety of relevant comments on distanciation from a feminist perspective in relation to Hitchcock's films and their apparent affinity to Mizoguchi, see Modleski, pp. 8–9, 41–42.

34. For a counter argument, see Dudley Andrew. For the more accepted view, see David Bordwell, "Our Dream Cinema: Western Historiography and the Japanese Film," *Film Reader* 4 (1979): 52–57; Bordwell, "Mizoguchi and the Evolution of Film Language," in *Cinema and Language*, ed. Stephen Heath and Patricia Mellencamp, pp. 101–117; and Burch, especially pp. 225–237.

35. *The Desire to Desire*, p. 91.

36. Burch, p. 236.

37. For Freud's comments on the nature of these traumatic scenes, see Sigmund Freud, *The Origins of Psycho-Analysis: Letters to Wilhelm Fliess, Drafts and Notes, 1887–1902*, ed. Marie Bonaparte, Anna Freud, and Ernst Kris, trans. Eric Mosbacher and James Strachey (New York: Basic Books, 1977), p. 21, n. 3; p. 22.

38. Ibid., p. 152.

39. As a symbol of the castration fear, Katsunosuke's image in the hall of Buddhas has a number of implications in relation to the concept of doubling. See Juliet Mitchell, *Psychoanalysis and Feminism* (New York: Vintage Books, 1975), p. 84. Also, Saikaku's original book on which Mizoguchi based his film contains a variety of interesting castration symbols. See, e.g., Morris, pp. 121, 194.

40. Freud, p. 153. This passage also suggests additional psychological interpretations of Oharu's becoming the priest at the end of the film.

41. *The Desire to Desire*, p. 53.

42. Ibid., pp. 53–54.

43. Ibid., p. 68.

44. Quoted in Modleski, p. 12.

45. In Andrew and Andrew, the plot summary of *Oharu* states that Oharu is informed about the death of Lord Matsudaira, not her father (p. 136).

46. See note 14 above.

47. Burch was the first to point out the special attention Mizoguchi gave his sound tracks and the almost experimental quality that results from the interplay between sound and image. See Noel Burch, *Theory of Film Practice*, trans. Helen R. Lane (New York and Washington: Praeger, 1973), pp. 94–97.

48. *The Desire to Desire*, p. 19.

Ikiru: Narration as a Moral Act

David Desser

In this essay, Desser focuses on three pairs of Kurosawa films to show that the latter in each pair is in some sense a "remake" of the former. In each instance of a "make and remake," he highlights some aesthetic, structural, or thematic issue at the heart of the pair, an issue insufficiently addressed in the first instance that thereby necessitated and justified the remake. These issues include the use of spatial and narrative structures, theatricalization, and an objective analysis of style (camera movement, placement, *mise-en-scène,* shot length, etc.). After briefly commenting on the first two pairs—*The Men Who Tread on the Tiger's Tail (Tora no o fumo otokotachi,* 1945) and *The Hidden Fortress (Kakushi toride no san akunin.* 1958); and *The Lower Depths (Donzoko,* 1957) and *Dodeskaden* (1970)—Desser examines at length the third and most complex "pair": *Drunken Angel (Yoidore tenshi,* 1948)/*Rashomon* (1950) and *Ikiru* (1952). As Desser says, *Ikiru* may well be the richer for borrowing not from one but from two films. From *Drunken Angel* it borrows thematic concerns, but from *Rashomon* it takes "both significant stylistic and thematic concerns." Thus, in its posing of questions regarding life and death and heroism and action, *Ikiru* undergoes bold shifts in point of view and narrative style that serve to show the *Rashomon* principles at work, but always to a different end.

For further reading, see David Bordwell, *Narration in the Fiction Film* (Madison: U of Wisconsin P, 1985); Seymour Chatman, *Story and Discourse: Narrative Structure in Fiction and Film* (Ithaca: Cornell UP, 1978); Dennis DeNitto and William Herman, *"Rashomon,"* in *Film and the Critical Eye* (New York: Macmillan, 1975), pp. 243–271; Patricia Erens, *Akira Kurosawa: A Guide to References and Resources* (Boston: G. K. Hall, 1979); Stanley Kauffmann, *"Rashomon,"* in *Living Images: Film Comment and Criticism* (New York: Harper and Row, 1974), pp. 316–324; Stephen Prince, *The*

Warrior's Camera: The Cinema of Akira Kurosawa (Princeton: Princeton UP, 1991); and George M. Wilson, "On Narrators and Narration in Film," in *Narration in Light: Studies in Cinematic Point of View* (Baltimore and London: The Johns Hopkins UP, 1986), pp. 126–144.

Jean Renoir, in a famous saying, pointed out that a director essentially makes only one film, has only one story to tell. A number of unarguable auteurs give clear credence to this notion in an obvious way. Alfred Hitchcock made two versions of *The Man Who Knew Too Much* (1934 and 1956); Howard Hawks remade his *Ball of Fire* (1942) into *A Song Is Born* (1948); John Ford remade *Judge Priest* (1934) as *The Sun Shines Bright* (1953), and reworked *Three Bad Men* (1926) into an adaptation of *Three Godfathers* (1949).

Such practice is perhaps even more common in Japan, where one can quickly point to Ozu Yasujiro's remake of *A Story of Floating Weeds* (*Ukigusa monogatari,* 1934) as *Floating Weeds* (*Ukigusa,*1959), or *I was Born but . . .* (*Umarete wa mita keredo . . . ,* 1932) into *Ohayo* (1959); Ichikawa Kon's two versions of *Harp of Burma* (*Biruma no tategoto,* 1956 and 1983); and the career of Inagaki Hiroshi, where we find two versions of the *Samurai Trilogy* (*Musashi Miyamoto,* 1940 and 1954–56) and two retellings of *The Life of Matsu the Untamed* (*Muho Matsu no issho,* the first in 1943, the second as *Rickshaw Man* in 1958). That these men were in essence (and often in fact) their own producers when they remade their own films convinces us of their own overt desires to redo an earlier film, even beyond the manner in which all of these directors continually rework, repeat, and refer to motifs found in earlier films. That they were in a sense *allowed* to remake an earlier film within the commercial context in which they all worked is also not surprising. Anywhere from six to thirty years passed between versions, and, especially in the days before revival theaters, television, and videocassettes, few members of the audience could be expected to recall the original version in any significant detail. We also note something else: that in most of these instances (and others throughout film history to which one could point), the remakes add another dimension to the film, typically color cinematography.[1] (The only exception on the above list is Ford's *The Sun Shines Bright.*)

We might assume that the motives on the parts of directors such as Hitchcock, Hawks, Ford, and Ozu in remaking one of their own films went beyond the commercial use of color cinematography, that they had in mind something more important to them, even if, as seems to be the case with Ford, it was a strictly personal desire. We might say that they were concerned with aesthetic problems, which could indeed include the problem of color filmmaking. (Additional factors could be the use of a greater budget, the addition of diegetic music, freedom from censorship, etc.) Yet in many of these instances the motive does not seem especially notable, in that the remake is by no means demonstrably superior to or even more interesting than the original; commercial considerations might indeed have been the primary factor in directing the remake (again with the exception of Ford's *The Sun Shines Bright*).[2]

Kurosawa Akira has never remade a film from earlier in his own career. Yet we can find significant reworkings on a more profound level than the mere repetition of motifs common in the films of the many directors who qualify as auteurs. And we can clearly see in such significant reworkings of earlier films the aesthetic problems with which Kurosawa was concerned. This is to say that perhaps Kurosawa was dissatisfied with an important aspect of an earlier film and wanted to try it again under new, improved circumstances; perhaps he felt at a later date that he was better prepared to deal with an issue he had raised at an earlier time—a rethinking, a reconceptualization of a certain problem. Such major reworkings on Kurosawa's part can be found in both thematic and stylistic domains; Kurosawa conceives of each film as raising certain issues and the film itself as a working through of these concerns.

For instance, we can see a variety of concerns in Kurosawa's early film *The Men Who Tread on the Tiger's Tail* (*Tora no o fumu otokotachi*, 1945). Thematically we can point to a struggle between feudal ideology and a more modern perception worked out in the relationship between the samurai retainers and the character portrayed by Enoken, the famous comic actor, with whom they come into contact. Stylistically, in this tale of border-crossing, we can see a concern with cinematic space. Both concerns, the ideological and the cinematic, reappear in *The Hidden Fortress* (*Kakushi toride no san akunin*, 1958).[3] Here the aesthetic problem of Cinemascope was of clear concern to Kurosawa, as it was to many Japanese directors at this time. Or we can look to *The Lower Depths* (*Donzoko*, 1957), where the aesthetic issue Kurosawa raised for himself was the question of theatricalization. The film is less an adaptation of Gorky's *The Lower Depths* than it is of the famous and influential Shingeki version of Gorky's play. The issue, the aesthetic problem, of theatricalization was dealt with again, later, in *Dodeskaden* (1970). This film is by no means merely a color version of the earlier film, for not only is the story completely different (sharing only the theme of denizens of the lower depths), but color is problematized in the same way theatrical space was in the earlier film. However, of all the films in Kurosawa's career which may be said to be reworkings of problems raised in earlier films,

Ikiru (1952) is no doubt the richest. And it might be the richest because it borrows, problematizes, issues raised in not one but two earlier films, *Drunken Angel* (*Yoidore tenshi,* 1948) and, most of all, *Rashomon* (1950).

From the point of view of "remakes and reworkings," *Ikiru* seems initially most clearly indebted to *Drunken Angel.* The problem Kurosawa wanted to deal with in the earlier film was thematic: What does it mean to be a hero in modern times, under ordinary circumstances? He cast Shimura Takashi in the lead role, the drunken angel of the title, as a doctor in postwar (contemporary) Japan struggling against a polluted environment (a fetid pool in a slum neighborhood) to cure his patients of T.B. His problems are complicated by neighborhood gangsters (*yakuza*), one of whom (played by Mifune Toshiro) contracts T.B. himself. The question of ordinary heroism partially escaped Kurosawa—as portrayed by the dynamic Mifune, the character of the *yakuza* was so extraordinary, and his struggles against tuberculosis and a returning gang boss (*oyabun*) so interesting, that the film shifted focus despite Kurosawa's intentions.[4] Thus when he again confronted the problem of heroism in a contemporary context, he re-starred Shimura Takashi but did not cast Mifune Toshiro at all—revealingly, the only Kurosawa film made between 1947 and 1965 not to star Mifune.

However, closer examination reveals that *Rashomon* was very much on Kurosawa's mind when he made *Ikiru.* Here we see both significant stylistic and thematic concerns being readdressed. Thematically, *Ikiru* may be said to continue addressing the problem raised by *Rashomon:* how to live in an existential world, a world rendered meaningless by the death of certainty, by the death, that is, of God. We note that the woodcutter of *Rashomon* who decides to take the baby into his own family (by which action the priest has his faith restored in mankind after the horror, the horror, he has previously witnessed) is portrayed by Shimura Takashi—the same actor who stars in *Ikiru.* Kurosawa uses *Rashomon* to explain the meaninglessness of the world, and presents a solution only at the end, in a scene not found in any of the source stories for the film.[5] *Ikiru,* on the other hand, begins in a world rendered meaningless, and the bulk of the film addresses the question of action in such a universe. Stylistically, Kurosawa explores two interconnected notions raised first in *Rashomon:* point of view and narrativity. *Rashomon,* of course, is infamous on this point, though perhaps the ways in which Kurosawa modulates point of view, finds ways to implicate a *cinematic* narrator in this tale of subjectivity, are less well understood. *Ikiru* situates a narrator, a narrating agent, from the start, and then demonstrates a variety of other narrational strategies, including, as it were, a demonstration of the *Rashomon* principle late in the film. *Ikiru,* then, must be seen as a significant film in the director's career not simply because it reworks aspects of earlier films, but because it readdresses the important thematic and technical problems with which the earlier works were concerned. In so doing, Kurosawa addresses vital thematic issues and foregrounds complex cinematic problems.

It might be best to address the problem of narration first, for that is quite naturally the first thing that confronts us when watching any film. Who, what, when, where, how—these not only are principles of journalistic writing, but they underlie the methods and procedures of the fiction film. Whose story is this; and why this person and not some other? What will happen to this who; when will it, or when did it, occur; where and how did it come to pass? In a sense, so much of the work of the narration of the classical film is devoted to repressing these questions. The mechanisms of narration are repressed under the weight of the drive of the plot; the cause-and-effect chain begins *in medias res* so that we do not ask the question of origin. That is to say, we must not ask not only the question, Why this character and not some other? but also the question, Who has chosen this character and not some other? We may see this issue problematized quite deliberately at the start of Hitchcock's *Psycho* (1960). We are informed of location (place and time) via subtitles. Then the camera, unmotivated by an individual agent (unassigned point-of-view shot), seeks out a particular space, the hotel room in which we find Marion Crane and her lover. Thus we are permitted to ask retrospectively, What would have happened if the camera had chosen to look at, to spy upon, the goings-on in the *next* room? In this film so much concerned with looking (as is Hitchcock's *oeuvre*), not only is the audience implicated in the character of Norman, but the narrating agent implicates himself (Hitchcock the auteur). *Psycho* thus makes explicit, it foregrounds, the implicit, the hidden, elements of the classical narrative.

Rashomon, too, may be looked at from this point of view. The film seemingly confronts us with explicit narrators, the characters who tell their stories, whose stories we see. The characters tell stories to each other, huddled around the fire beneath the ruined gate or in the bright glare of sunshine at the outdoor court. It is these stories, these conflicting tales of seduction and death, that have most interested audiences and critics. For here we seem to find the thematic glory of *Rashomon*, the question of the relativity of truth; how to live one's life in an absurd world, a world rendered absurd by the theory of relativity. After being confronted by four conflicting tales, the audience has, it seems, to choose: it must select one story over the others as being true, or, correctly, must assume that all stories are equally true and false, that truth itself is uncertain. Thus we might be tempted to say that one of the messages of *Rashomon* is that point of view is everything.

Rashomon modulates point of view by playing with cinematic structures. Our first inclination is to understand the film as possessing different narrative times. There seems to be a present tense—that of the three men at the ruined gate (typically called "the framing story"); and *two* levels of past tense—the first, more immediate past, of the trial, and then the past of *that* tense, the tales told at the trial. We initially construe these past tenses as "flashbacks"—the wood-cutter at the gate: "I was walking through the forest and I came across the following things. . . . " We construe them as flashbacks given our experience of earlier films which seem to utilize such a structure. It is only when we realize that these "flashbacks" tell competing, differing accounts that we must call them something else. Bruce Kawin uses the term "mindscreen."[6] They thus move from some identifiable past tense into a more vague "conditional" tense. We note that these stories are all first-person narratives in that the narrator is explicitly identified, but their time sequence, rather than being in the past, is better expressed as being elsewhere, at some (non)time. The stories themselves are not related by a subjective, first-person camera. Such a technique, one would immediately assert, would be most obnoxious (as, for instance, in the American *film noir*, *Lady in the Lake*, 1946). Yet Kurosawa is careful to demonstrate that the point of view in question is questionable. That is, within these narrated tales, Kurosawa modulates point-of-view structures to imply both the first-person elements of the tales and the presence of *another* narrator.

This other narrator is implicated in a number of sequences. For instance, the woodcutter's first walk through the forest is built by a number of shots, and a number of different kinds of shots, including subjective angles from his point of view. But there seems to be another point of view present, a kind of watchful camera—camera distance and angle not only clearly *not* from the woodcutter's point of view but clearly somehow to be taken as another.[7] Of especial impor-tance here is the manner in which Kurosawa handles what initially seem to be straightforward point-of-view shots. For instance, at one point the woodcutter stops and looks—we see him look, and the next shot initially seems to be what he is looking at. Distance from the object and angle on it give every indication that this is so. However, in this second shot, we suddenly see the woodcutter emerge from the forest in the background. That is, he walks into the shot we take to be his point of view. The exact same structure is utilized in a second sequence: the woodcutter stops and looks; we see him look; and we take the next shot to be what he is looking at. But again, he appears in the shot. It is as if Kurosawa had taken the point-of-view shots from within a mirror, the camera placed at the point of view of the *mirror* image. The camera is equidistant from the object as the woodcutter and looking at the same angle. Finally, the wood-cutter's "mindscreen" comes to an end with a point-of-view shot—except this time the point of view is clearly identified: It belongs to the corpse of the dead husband.[8]

Point of view is also interestingly handled in the tale told by the bandit. He blames a gust of wind for the events which take place. He was, he tells us, relaxing on the ground by a tree when he saw a woman and her husband. A gust of wind came up and blew the woman's veil off her face. At that moment, the bandit claims he knew he had to have that woman. And Kurosawa indeed shows us such an occurrence, with the bandit opening his eyes, seeing the woman riding by, and the veil lifting off her face, from the bandit's point of view. The camera even pans upward along the woman's body in this point-of-view shot. But the sequence begins with a kind of God's-eye view, a long shot in a magnificent forest, the bandit revealed to be a small figure in this configuration. Again, this other point of view is alluded to, but in view of the film's theme, that God is dead, this "God's-eye view" is ironic. Or perhaps not so ironic, for this point of view belongs to the narrating agent, a human storyteller, seeking values in a world rendered absurd precisely by the death of God.

Playing with point-of-view structures within allegedly first-person narrations serves to throw the entire film into highlight. That is to say, if we are naive enough to believe what each individual character says, we are equally naive to accept the framing story at face value—naive, that is, to accept the framing story as anything other than a story. The final scene of *Rashomon* is not simply happening, as if by magic, or as if we were voyeurs into the lives of others. This scene is being presented to us for a purpose by someone, a narrating agent, who might reflect the values of the director, Kurosawa the auteur. Given that this scene was an addition by Kurosawa to the Akutagawa sources, we may claim that it somehow addresses the problem the majority of the film invokes—the problem of the relativity of truth. We are being told something, by someone, for some reason.

This implicit narrator behind the scenes of *Rashomon* is made explicit by *Ikiru* which, in fact, plays with a variety of narrative structures and points of view, which equally foreground the idea of our being told something. The opening shot, for instance, foregrounds an omniscient narrator, via a voice-over overtly asserting, "This is an X-ray of the stomach of the story's main character." The use of a voice-over explicitly identified not with a character (as is usual in Hollywood films which utilize the voice-over technique) but with a narrator who, as it were, *stands apart from the action,* recalls the narrator of the classical Japanese theater, and even, perhaps, the *katsuben* of the early cinema.[9] Like the narrator who functions so importantly in the plays of Chikamatsu, for instance, Kurosawa's narrator makes moral judgments and guides our feelings and perceptions with the aim of teaching a lesson.

Kurosawa not only literalizes a narrating agent but, with this shot of an X-ray, plays with the idea of omniscience, of being able to get into the character's mind—here we get into the character's body! From a shot of the X-ray, the film dissolves to a shot of Watanabe (not a direct cut as Richie claims).[10] X-ray and character are visually linked through this dissolve, a shot which significantly recurs in reverse, as it were, when near the end of the film Kurosawa dissolves from Watanabe's face to his mourning picture at the wake. We make the assumption that X-ray and figure, linked by dissolve, are of the same person, the person who we are told is the hero of our story. One minute later into the film, Kurosawa again has a close-up of Watanabe, the voice-over returning to tell us that yes, indeed, this is the hero of our story—although at the moment it would be boring to talk about him. The voice-over is interrupted for a short while as Miss Odagiri is embarrassingly forced to relate a joke which only she finds funny (but which the audience takes as symbolic of Watanabe and of bureaucratic life). The voice-over returns again to continue to berate the hero, only to be dropped as a primary narrative device (the voice-over recurs only once more, much later in the film). But at the film's start it serves the function of foregrounding narrativity, of bringing to the fore the fact that this is a film about a particular person being *told* to us, told to us, therefore, for some particular reason.

Having foregrounded an omniscient narrator, Kurosawa moves to an extended subjective camera sequence, whose length and formal patterning are quite daring. The sequence begins when a group of women come to City Hall to complain about a fetid pool in their neighborhood. Their first stop in the bureaucratic maze which will eventually confound them is the Citizen's Section, headed by Watanabe. They first ask for help from one of Watanabe's assistants, Sakei, who then discusses it with Watanabe. We see, first, an objective shot of the women talking to Sakei. The camera then pans left to follow him to Watanabe's desk (two shots). Watanabe tells Sakei to send them elsewhere. Sakei then exits the frame, and the camera remains on Watanabe for slightly more than half a minute. Then we get the scene of Miss Odagiri's joke and the narrator's berating of Watanabe. The film then cuts to the women's group, this time at the station where they were presumably told to go. Kurosawa begins the subjective camera sequence by opening the shot with the women screen right, the man they are talking to screen left. The camera dollies in and pans left to look directly at the bureaucrat, assuming the women's point of view. Then in a series of still shots linked by wipes (fifteen shots for two and one-half minutes), the camera/women confront a variety of bureaucrats, each of whom sends them to another station. Finally, they return not to the first station of this sequence but to *Watanabe's* station, where the camera now dollies back and pans right to reveal the women and Sakei. This exact reversal of the camera movement which began the sequence provides a formal closure—although this precise sequence did not begin at Watanabe's station, the women's journey through the bureaucracy did. Moreover, as this scene ends, we learn that Watanabe is not at his desk, that he is "out today," which is to say that the extended first-person camera sequence in a sense initiated by Watanabe, ends at a later narrative time.

The omniscient narrator who can peer into the characters' bodies also allows us views of characters' thoughts via flashbacks from Watanabe's point of view (he remembers alone in his house). Again, as with the extended first-person camera sequence, Kurosawa does not rely on this technique very heavily. It functions, on one level, to demonstrate the variety of narrative strategies available to Kurosawa and to film in general. Watanabe, having just learned he has cancer (which we already knew from the voice-over narrator showing us the X-ray), goes home. Alone in the house, he plaintively calls for his son, Mitsuo. Kurosawa shows us five memories Watanabe has, memories of death (his wife's funeral), discussion of remarriage, error (his son gets caught in a run-down in a baseball game), illness (his son at the hospital with appendicitis), and separation (his son going off to war in a troop train). The flashbacks are handled, in one respect, quite conventionally. They are initiated by a close-up of Watanabe's face, a direct cut to his wife's picture, followed by a dissolve to a shot of Watanabe, Mitsuo, and Watanabe's brother and sister-in-law riding in a car following a hearse. Watanabe's voice-over calling "Mitsuo" links present and past tense. Further, a brilliant formal transition on Kurosawa's part also links past and present in the sequence in which Watanabe sits down in the past tense at the baseball game, sits down in the present tense, followed by a cut to Watanabe moving down in the frame in the hospital elevator.

Although Watanabe is identified as the hero of the film, Kurosawa does not feel obligated to focus on him in every scene. That is to say the omniscient narrator chooses on a number of occasions to reveal things to us that are unknown to Watanabe. For instance, we know he has cancer before he does; we see the doctor and his staff discuss their feelings about cancer after Watanabe leaves the hospital. We are privy to a heartless conversation between Mitsuo and his wife about how to spend Watanabe's money. We see Watanabe's co-workers discussing his absence; we witness a conversation between Mitsuo and his uncle and aunt about his father's seemingly strange behavior—the uncle thinks Watanabe has a mistress. Most radically, however, we see events after Watanabe dies.

Two-thirds of the way through (84 minutes into this 134-minute film), Watanabe succumbs to the cancer. Here, Kurosawa again shifts narrative styles in a daring manner. He intercuts objective shots of the wake with a number of first-person narrations—true flashbacks, in this instance, for in contrast to the first-person narratives of *Rashomon,* we are not asked to doubt the veracity of the events. Rather, the *present* tense created in this sequence shows the *Rashomon* principle at work. At his wake, Watanabe's co-workers and superiors convince themselves that Watanabe alone was not, could not have been, responsible for draining the fetid swamp and building a playground. Their flashbacks continually contradict this assertion as we see over and over that it was indeed Watanabe's lone tenacity which pushed the project through. Thus if we were wondering, in *Rashomon,* why people delude themselves, how memories could simply be so wrong, so different, we see in this extended sequence in *Ikiru* the process by which people construct a world-view out of their own inner needs.

I have claimed that *Ikiru* deals thematically with two issues raised in earlier films: the question of ordinary heroism raised in *Drunken Angel* and the problem of life's meaning in an existential, absurd world posed in *Rashomon.* The question of heroism is unarguably one of Kurosawa's authorial characteristics. He raises it along two axes: extraordinary and ordinary, the axes corresponding to works in *jidai-geki* (period films) and *gendai-mono* (modern stories). Kurosawa puts forth visions of extraordinary heroism in *The Men Who Tread on the Tiger's Tail, Seven Samurai (Shichinin no samurai,* 1954), *The Hidden Fortress, Yojimbo* (1961), and *Sanjuro (Tsubaki Sanjuro,* 1962), among others, extraordinary because of the nature of the actions (combat) and the degree of competence the heroes possess.[11] However, heroism is possible, Kurosawa claims, under real-life contemporary conditions, seen in not only *Drunken Angel* and *Ikiru* but also *The Quiet Duel (Shizukanaru ketto,* 1949), *The Bad Sleep Well (Warui yatsu hodo yoku nemuru,* 1960), *High and Low (Tengoku to jigoku,* 1963), and *Red Beard (Akahige,* 1965).

At some level, however, heroism is always extraordinary; it may not be a matter of possessing some kind of superior skill, but if it were easy to be a hero, everyone would be one! Rather, heroes in period and modern films find themselves living in precarious times, precarious in that external forces are no longer strong enough to command action, no longer able to compel certain types of (acceptable) behavior. Thus both types of heroes must *choose* the kind of action they will take. They must, that is, *act* heroically. This is where the concept of heroism meets the notion of existentialism in Kurosawa's work, seen most clearly in *Rashomon* but implicit in most of his works (implicit precisely because the characters, living in chaotic times, must choose a course of action). It is crucial for a proper and full understanding of *Ikiru* to recognize the kind of choice Watanabe makes, i.e., what it is that he chooses to do. And in so doing we note the similarity of his choice to the course of action chosen by the heroes of all Kurosawa's other films: the choice between right and wrong, seen not metaphysically (religiously) but ethically. For in every instance, even the blackly comic *Yojimbo,* the heroes choose to help others.

We may partially account for the popularity of *Rashomon* in the West by its explicitly existential tone. *Rashomon* is an existential allegory: God is dead, there are no eternal verities. It can be argued that *Rashomon,* like a number of important films of the 1950s, finds its existential tone from the Atomic Bomb experience, from the existence of the Bomb (obviously more clearly, immediately, and personally felt in Japan than elsewhere, as Kurosawa's *Record of a Living Being* [*Ikimono no kiroku*, 1955] superbly demonstrates). The ruined gate at which the action takes place seems to have been bombed; the priest's recollection near the start of "weird" births and bizarre climatic conditions clearly points to radiation mutations and the like; and the historical setting at a crucial juncture in Japanese history—the change from the Heian world of noble courtiers to the samurai of the Kamakura shogunate—represents a rift in culture comparable to the defeat of Japan in the Pacific War, the American Occupation, and the renunciation of the emperor's divinity. But the existential tone does not predominate, for we must recall the added scene of the woodcutter taking the baby. The woodcutter makes a sacrifice, does something for someone's good. He asserts not only that to act is to live, but that to act for the benefit of others is still possible in such an absurd world.

The question of how "to live" is certainly at the forefront of *Ikiru* since, as Richie points out, the Japanese title "is the intransitive verb meaning 'to live.' "[12] The question of what it means to live is posed by the existential dilemma of death—since human beings are doomed to die, what is the meaning of life? Watanabe is sentenced to die, as is all humankind, the only difference being that Watanabe knows exactly how and when it will occur. Thus Kurosawa dramatizes, makes immediate, the question which inevitably befalls us all. The fact of death, the death sentence as it were, imposed upon Watanabe combines with the meaningless world in which Watanabe "lives." The narrator asserts that it was the drudgery and bureaucracy of City Hall which rendered Watanabe a living corpse, a mummy, as Miss Odagiri calls him. Thus not the Atomic Bomb but modern life is to blame here. The question of how to live in such a world might, then, come down to a matter of attitude. Watanabe's attraction to Miss Odagiri stems from her energy, her "aliveness." Yet she claims, when asked her secret of life, that "I only eat and work." This seems to lend support to Richie's assertion that Watanabe has found meaning, "has discovered himself through *doing*." (He compares the existentialist tone of the film to the works of Sartre, Camus, Kafka, and Dostoevsky, finding support for this latter comparison by recognizing that Dostoevsky is Kurosawa's favorite writer.)[13] Richie insists that it is not what one does that matters, but merely that one acts. He claims, for instance, that "in *Seven Samurai* only action matters—whether one was a good samurai or a bad robber is meaningless."[14] This is an astonishing claim, which must simply be reckoned as wrong. For by extension, it would mean that the action taken by the woodcutter in *Rashomon* is no more or less admirable than the commoner stealing the baby's blanket; that the doctor in *Drunken Angel* was not especially admirable in trying to help the gangster; that the doctor in *Red Beard* should have taken a more prestigious, higher-paying position; that the businessman in *High and Low* should not necessarily have paid the ransom which saved the life of his chauffeur's son! It is also contradicted by what, in fact, Miss Odagiri *does*—she makes toys which she says makes her feel connected to all the children in Japan. Thus we need to ask ourselves how we would feel about Watanabe if, rather than having a park built for a working-class community, he had continued to explore the bizarre nightlife of Tokyo as he does early in the film with the drunken writer. Or if indeed Miss Odagiri were his mistress, as Watanabe's brother tries to claim for much of the film. Surely the kind of action taken is crucial to our appreciation of Watanabe, and to Kurosawa's view of man as an ethical being, as one who must choose to act rightly in the face of absurdity. That is what heroism means; that is what it means to live.

It is also what it means to make films, to explore at different times and in different ways the various issues which are of concern. Certainly, as a film artist Kurosawa is entitled, even obligated, to explore aesthetic and formal issues of his chosen medium. But formalism has never been enough for Kurosawa, and, in fact, despite the attention paid to issues of form by Western critics of the Japanese cinema, it was never enough for any major Japanese film artist. Films are, above all, *about* something, and the question of remakes and reworkings in the careers of major directors primarily revolves around reconsiderations and restatements of major thematic, ethical, and moral concerns. Once Kurosawa had found the true meaning of heroism in *Ikiru,* he could restate its major characteristics in films such as *Seven Samurai* and *Red Beard.* And he could also find this hero at odds with a changing world, as in such films as *Record of a Living Being* and *The Bad Sleep Well.* Or, having defined heroism, he could safely turn to realms in which there were, could be, no heroes, presaged by the formal configurations of *Throne of Blood* (*Kumonosu-jo,* 1957), and made more sadly explicit in *Dodeskaden, Kagemusha* (1980), and *Ran* (1985). The fact of authorship, then, the mere tracing of recurring motifs and formal repetitions, is less important than the question of authorship, the questions and issues with which an author struggles over the course of a career.

NOTES

1. "Colorization" perpetrators attempt to claim a certain originality for these colorized efforts. Indeed, the U.S. copyright office seems to agree, allowing black and white films in the public domain to be copyrighted by the company which colorizes them. On the other hand, the Film Preservation Act will work toward at least noting that

substantial changes have been made to films which have been colorized (while attempting to prevent this atrocity from occurring with other films).

2. See Tag Gallagher, *John Ford: The Man and His Films* (Berkeley: U of California P, 1984), pp. 284–301.

3. See David Desser, *The Samurai Films of Akira Kurosawa* (Ann Arbor: UMI Research P, 1983), pp. 92–97.

4. See Donald Richie, *The Films of Akira Kurosawa*, rev. ed. (Berkeley: U of California P, 1984), pp. 49, 53.

5. See Richie, p. 71.

6. Bruce Kawin, *Mindscreen: Bergman, Godard, and First-Person Film* (Princeton: Princeton UP, 1978). See especially pp. 84–87. For a discussion which basically rejects Kawin's notion of "mindscreen," see Edward Branigan, *Point of View in the Cinema: A Theory of Narration and Subjectivity in Classical Film* (New York: Mouton, 1984), pp. 216–221.

7. The kind of point of view I have in mind here is most interestingly utilized by John Carpenter in *Halloween* (1978), where the camera becomes associated with "the monster" (Michael) even without the typical sequence of point-of-view shots (point/ glance-point/object). See for instance, Vera Dika, "The Stalker Film, 1978–1981," and J. P. Telotte, "Through a Pumpkin's Eye: The Reflexive Nature of Horror," in *American Horrors: Essays on the Modern American Horror Film*, ed. Gregory A. Waller (Urbana: U of Illinois P, 1987), pp. 86–101, 114–128. For an excellent discussion of how such point-of-view shots may be handled, see Branigan, pp. 103–121.

8. This is to say, the shot of the woodcutter reacting in horror is, in screenplay language, "POV corpse." POV corpse shots exist in only a few other films—Dreyer's *Vampyr* (1932) and Welles's *The Magnificent Ambersons* (1942) come to mind, as does Itami Juzo's *The Funeral* (*Ososhiki*, 1984). In fact, these shots are so frequent in Itami's film as to become both a running gag and a significant part of the overall theme.

9. See Joseph Anderson's essay in this volume for a discussion of the variety of narrative art forms in Japan and the *katsuben*'s role in the cinema.

In the West, we often make sweeping statements relating a particular strategy in a Japanese film to an aspect of Japan's traditional culture, as if the strategy were deliberate or the culture so ingrained as to be a "natural" part of a filmmaker's repertoire. While it is true that the Japanese people are extraordinarily culturally literate, in the case of Kurosawa we need not speculate on his knowledge of such institutions as the *katsuben*, and how they functioned. His own brother, Heigo, was a *katsuben*. See Akira Kurosawa, *Something like an Autobiography*, trans. Audie Bock (New York: Alfred A. Knopf, 1982), pp. 74–75.

10. Richie, p. 89.

11. I have called this element of "competence" the concept of "professionalism" which separates the hero from ordinary citizens, protector from protectee. See *The Samurai Films of Akira Kurosawa*, pp. 141–144.

12. Richie, p. 86.

13. Richie, p. 94 (emphasis in original). See also *Ikiru: A Film by Akira Kurosawa*, edited with an introduction by Donald Richie (New York: Simon and Schuster, 1968), p. 10.

14. Richie, *Ikiru*, p. 10.

Oshima Nagisa, or The Battered Energy of Desire

Max Tessier

Translated by Marise C.
Thompson and
Arthur Nolletti, Jr.

The most widely known of the Japanese New Wave directors of the 1960s, Oshima Nagisa is also the most controversial. Breaking with the traditional humanism of such classicist directors as Ozu, Kurosawa, and Kinoshita, he developed his own themes and created a variety of styles appropriate for each theme. Refusing to align himself with any given political party or ideology, he has remained an outspoken critic of his country. One of his predominant themes is the linkage of sex and revolution to represent the "positive energy" of human beings and their most overt defiance of societal conventions. In "Oshima Nagisa, or The Battered Energy of Desire" (which originally appeared in *Le Cinéma japonais au présent 1959–1979,* and which here appears for the first time in English translation), Tessier investigates the career of Oshima through 1978, beginning with the director's highly publicized battle with Shochiku over the company's withdrawal of *Night and Fog in Japan* (*Nihon no yoru to kiri*) from theaters in November 1960. Tessier focuses on the most central and recurrent of Oshima's concerns: his criticism of the 1960s revolutionary movement; his attempt to develop his own "authentic subjective consciousness"; his rejection of the so-called victim syndrome; his determination to do away with sexual taboos; his interest in "criminal behavior"; and his feeling for the plight of the Korean minority in Japan. Tessier also discusses Oshima's continuing experimentation in film language, such as his use of sequence shots in *Night and Fog in Japan,* multiple techniques in *Diary of Yunbogi* (*Yunbogi no nikki*, 1965), and elaborate flashback structures in *Violence at Noon* (*Hakuchu no torima*, 1966) and *The Ceremony* (*Gishiki*, 1971). As Tessier makes clear, some of Oshima's stylistic experiments, like some of his films, are more successful than others. Throughout the essay Tessier shows how and why Oshima's work is engaged in a complex and everchanging dialectic with Japan of the 1960s and 1970s. Also included in this essay is "Oshima on Oshima," the director's own statement of his political and aesthetic credo, prompted by the *Night and Fog* incident.

For further reading, see Audie Bock, *Japanese Film Directors* (Tokyo: Kodansha, 1978), pp. 309–337; Noel Burch, "Nagisa Oshima and Japanese Cinema in the 60s," in *Cinema: A Critical Dictionary*, Vol. 2: *Kinugasa to Zanussi*, ed. Richard Roud (London: Martin Secker and Warburg, 1980), pp. 735–743; Ian Cameron, *Second Wave* (New York: Praeger, 1970), pp. 63–98; David Desser, *Eros plus Massacre: An Introduction to the Japanese New Wave Cinema* (Bloomington and Indianapolis: Indiana UP, 1988); Stephen Heath, "The Question Oshima," in *Questions of Cinema* (Bloomington: Indiana UP, 1981), pp. 146–164; Dana Polan, "Politics as Process in Three Films by Nagisa Oshima," *Film Criticism* 8, 1 (1983): 35–41; Sato Tadao, *Oshima Nagisa no sekai* [*The World of Oshima Nagisa*] (Tokyo: Tsukuma Shobo, 1973); Max Tessier, "Entretien avec Nagisa Oshima" ("Interview with Nagisa Oshima"), *Positif* 267 (May 1983): 8–11; Maureen Turim and John Mowitt, "Thirty Seconds over . . . Oshima's *The War of Tokyo* or *The Young Man Who Left His Will on Film*," *Wide Angle* 1, 4 (1977): 34–43; and Special Oshima Issue, *Wide Angle* 9, 2 (1987).

For the majority of Western viewers, *In the Realm of the Senses* (*Ai no koriida*, 1976) revealed a filmmaker whose whole being is held in the extreme tension of a sexual drive perceived as a deadly force. In fact, the film was but the explicit and sum total of fifteen years of work permeated by this drive—a drive closely linked to the feeling of failure and death and taken as the ultimate physical, almost physiological, resistance to the power of the state over the individual. The obsessive search for sexual ecstasy by Kichizo and Abe Sada is the culmination of a work practically dedicated to the assertion of desire in all its shapes and forms, and opposed to inference by the "reprehensible activities" of humankind, politics included. Because of films such as *Night and Fog in Japan* (*Nihon no yoru to kiri*, 1960), *Death by Hanging* (*Koshikei*, 1968), *The Ceremony* (*Gishiki*, 1971), and *Dear Summer Sister* (*Natsu no imoto*, 1973), Oshima was often thought to be first and foremost a political director from the radical left. Perhaps at one time this was true, but it is also true that Oshima always mistrusted party politics, and that the political element in his work is only a means—as good as any other—to spark the positive energy of human beings and to channel their desire. In a text written after the *Night and Fog in Japan* incident,[1] Oshima was already pointing out this concern: "The greatest obstacle to the influence of art in present-day Japan, and within it, is the politicization which enslaves art." This was a rather bold statement at a time when the entire current of progressive cinema was strongly politicized and subject to a number of dogmas held by parties still hardly de-Stalinized. Besides, we know that Oshima always refused to belong to any influential party and was criticized just as much by the JCP (Japanese Communist Party) as by liberals for his attitude and his criticism of the humanism held in esteem from Kurosawa to Imai.

Ideological Revolution and Transformation of the Language

One of Oshima's favorite targets while he was going through an extremely difficult period after being fired by the Shochiku Company was the notion of "the victim syndrome" in the majority of Japanese films. This view held that many Japanese had been victims of the war without really searching for its profound causes or attempting to go beyond that stage fifteen years after the defeat. Oshima, like many of his radical colleagues, violently criticized this idea. He also criticized the reaction of postwar intellectuals who, while condemning the "call to the victim syndrome of the people" issued by progressive humanists, were trying to appeal to the presumed desires of the people—or what Oshima calls its "subjective will." This "subjective will" took symbolic form in "the movements of group singing" found in most progressive films and which Oshima mocks in his own films. Oshima, therefore, criticized this "subjectivistic" tendency and sought to go beyond the pseudo-subjectivity of a movement which spoke to the "subjective will of the people," and which was embodied in a visceral way in the struggle against the *Ampo-toso*, or the U.S.-Japan Security Treaty, a struggle led in 1960 by extreme leftist movements. In a major text written by Oshima in 1963, one can read:

In the history of the Japanese people's movement, this struggle will always remain extraordinary because, for the first time, a subjective consciousness appeared. Even if it was only a pseudo-subjectivity, it provided the basis for the meeting of movement and organization. What was needed at the time and the lesson that had to be drawn from the struggle itself was to regroup these pseudo-subjectivities, denounce their pseudo-nature and also to eradicate them so that the movement might become a truly subjective movement. None of this came about.[2]

In other words, ideological radicalization was not carried far enough, in spite of the fact that there was a force of similar leaning inside the movement. But this force was too weak to reach the level of an "authentic and determined subjective consciousness."

As for Oshima, he—and co-scriptwriter Ishido Toshiro—attempted to express this position in his key work of that time, *Night and Fog in Japan,* the almost clandestine making of which brought about not only his first break with Shochiku but also his career as an independent filmmaker. This film, shot in 1960 after the success of *Cruel Story of Youth* (*Seishun zankoku monogatari,* 1960), and the title of which is a conscious homage to Alain Resnais's *Night and Fog,* which Oshima greatly admired, was and remains a landmark in the history of Japanese cinema. This is, first of all, because it boldly tackled a political topic that was still hotly debated (and because Oshima was vehement in his criticism of the traditional, "pseudo-subjective" left). But, second, the film was revolutionary in style, for Oshima had understood that there could not be an ideological revolution without a political transformation in the language of film.

Filmed entirely in sequence-shots—forty-five of them in all, forty-three according to some—*Night and Fog in Japan* rejected the objective, chronological narrative so loved by the movie company, replacing it with a flashback structure that was intentionally and outrageously theatrical, and highly subjective in attitude. *Night and Fog* was already using the multidimensional structure that Oshima would pick up again and refine in *The Ceremony* ten years later. During the wedding ceremony of Nozawa Kazuaki, former activist in both the JCP and that branch of the Zengakuren (student militant group) still linked with it, and Harada Reiko, a member of the new Zengakuren, now split from the Party, light is shed on the internal and external contradictions born of the events of May–June 1960, when violent demonstrations occurred against the *Ampo-toso,* which the Japanese Diet nevertheless ratified—in opposition to the majority of public opinion. The intrusion of Ota, hunted by police because he took part in the demonstrations by helping the wounded Reiko reach a hospital in a journalist's car, astonishes everyone and brings discord to the wedding ceremony that was to be the symbol of reconciliation among the diverse tendencies of the movement. Starting from this disruptive intrusion, Oshima interweaves all the elements which serve to point out the failure of the JCP in confronting the *Ampo-toso* and in preventing neo-Stalinist tendencies from gaining the upper hand in its own internal organization. This failure is seen when Nakayama invites all the participants at the wedding banquet to return to the Party—at the very moment when Ota has finally been arrested by the police.

The film has an extremely complex structure (so much so that one needs several careful viewings to digest all its elements). It moves from flashback to flashback, during which the characters present their position and their own experience of the events. Out of this strategy a critical political discourse emerges that finally holds the JCP members responsible for the failure of the action taken against the bid for power of the pro-American government. After this, Oshima calls on intellectuals (his audience) not to repeat this error. Declaring that the real subject of his film was politics, he stated: "I attempted to develop a revolutionary critique of the revolutionary movement, comparing the movement of the 1950s to that of the 1960s." It is probably from this film and the repercussions which followed that Oshima developed a great distrust of the influence of politics over filmmaking or art; therefore, he did his utmost to break away in order to nurture his own authentic subjective consciousness, taking sex and crime as his essential themes, and resorting to subjective imagination as an empirical method instead of realistic and political analysis.

He had already explained his systematic use of sequence-shots (or "one-scene, one-shot") in an article as being a "method to avoid interrupting the director's flow of consciousness and [a method] to attach greater importance to real time."[3] This technique was intensified by the use of sudden bursts of light, quite theatrical, which would illuminate one or another part of the scenery or action without Oshima otherwise indicating that it was a flashback. The characters watch and comment upon their past actions just as they would watch those of other protagonists actually there.

Needless to say, Shochiku would never have authorized the shooting of the revolutionary, incendiary bomb that *Night and Fog* was if they had known for one instant what it was about. On the one hand, after the great commercial impact of *Cruel Story of Youth* (usually christened *Naked Youth* for export), in which Oshima had—in his own words—"attempted to capture the substance of modern times in acts of cruelty," the company was quite ready to put its trust in him to repeat this daring success. On the other hand, Oshima, knowing the risks he would be taking if he revealed the content of his project, was clever enough to keep the scenario secret until the day before shooting began. (The shooting itself was completed in a few days in order to avoid eventual changes by the management, or even their stoppage of the film.) Thus, the film was not shot against the will of Shochiku, but rather without their knowing it. Disconcerted by this "product," they pulled the film from distribution four days after its release (on November 9, 1960), using as a pretext its commercial failure, which was made worse by the failure of Yoshida's film *The Blood Is Dry* (*Chi wa kawaite iru*), on the same bill. In reality, the day before the film was withdrawn, a violent political event had taken place: the assassination of Asanuma Inejiro, leader of the Japan Socialist Party, by a nationalist student. Thus, Shochiku's action was certainly not unrelated to this political event. Of course, Oshima was not fooled as to the meaning of their decision, and he accused Shochiku of withdrawing the film for political reasons. This brought about an increasingly stubborn posture on the part of the company, which practically impounded the film, refusing any request for a showing, even in private. Logically, Oshima and several of his fellow filmmakers walked out on Shochiku and created their own independent company, Sozosha (Creation Company), in 1961.[4]

Eclecticism and Experimentation

In spite of the extreme financial difficulties that Oshima was experiencing at that time of his life, it took him less than a year to shoot his next film, *The Catch* (*Shiiku*, 1961).[5] A personal adaptation of a novel by Oe Kenzaburo, it recounts the guarding of a black American POW by some Japanese farmers on the eve of the armistice in July 1945; his lynching following conflicts that tear apart the village community; and the transfer of responsibility for the murder onto a young refugee, who is then killed. We thus recognize a little of the structure of *Night and Fog in Japan* in the introduction of a character who serves to explode the tensions in a seemingly close-knit community. Again, Oshima rejected the social realism of his predecessors and filmed in long sequence-shots, often with a telephoto lens, to maximize and extend the "flow of consciousness of the director" which he had talked about earlier. Rejecting their responsibilities, first by doing away with their undesirable hostage, whom the authorities had asked them to guard until the end of hostilities, then later by naming a "phony culprit," the villagers again present themselves as victims of the conflict thrust upon them. This situation gives Oshima a new opportunity to attack the myth of the "victim syndrome" created in the turmoil of the defeat. One may think, incidentally, that the black airman, fallen from the sky, appears to be the embodiment of evil in the eyes of the superstitious villagers, but Oshima never endorses this interpretation or any explicit symbolic interpretation in his works.

After this film, which was a commercial failure, Oshima went through a lean period, and despite a few television activities, he had to accept some commissioned work so as not to be doomed to silence. At the request of Okawa

Hashizo, an actor at Toei, Oshima then shot *Amakusa Shiro, the Christian Rebel* (*Amakusa Shiro tokisada,* 1962), which recalled the insurrection of Japanese Christian farmers against the seventeenth-century shogun, and the failure of the movement led by Amakusa, who was beheaded at the end, and whose head was put on display for the inhabitants of Nagasaki as an example. From the very first, the subject suited Oshima, who of course made it a point not to concoct a *jidai-geki* (historical film) in the traditional style but rather to employ his sequence-shot technique. However, his use of this method, which was too repetitive and already overutilized, was not convincing, and the film—according to Oshima himself—was a failure, with the added burden of a budget inadequate for this kind of production. It was also a commercial flop, which forced Oshima to return to television and writing criticism for almost three years. During this time he could reflect on the dangers of excessive theorizing.

It was only in 1965 that he was able to resume "normal" film activities by signing a distribution agreement (a compromise?) with Shochiku, his former company, which would be taking only a limited amount of risk by distributing films produced by Sozosha. The first outcome of this agreement was a film considered "commercial," *Pleasures of the Flesh* (*Etsuraku,* 1965), a brilliant stylistic exercise on a sensual subject quite fashionable in those days when "eroductions" (erotic films) were flourishing, and which Oshima's inventive talent saved from being trite. The use of very long takes and numerous tracking shots in color and Cinemascope for erotic scenes was aesthetically justified in this film, the mannered style being a means to explore the eroticism of bodies. Doubtless a "minor" film in Oshima's canon, it nevertheless forshadowed his concern with ripping to shreds sexual taboos, a concern which was to characterize his next films. It also proved to Oshima that "his commercial value was not diminished."

In the same year Oshima, already eclectic on principle, made a medium-length feature composed of still photographs, *Diary of Yunbogi* (*Yunbogi no nikki*), inspired by the diary of a ten-year-old Korean boy, which Oshima saw as "the Korean version of *Boy* [*Shonen,* 1969]." *Yonbogi* started Oshima's special interest in the Korean minority problem in Japan, another taboo which he tackled in two important films: *Death by Hanging* (1968) and *Three Resurrected Drunkards* (*Kaette kita yopparai,* 1968). In the montage technique of still photographs and sounds that he used for *Yunbogi,* Oshima had discovered the possibility of a multiple technique, and the appropriateness of one form for each subject, a form born of the context of the film. He therefore refused to impose a single style on all of his films as most great Japanese masters did. He used this multiple technique again for *Band of Ninja* (*Ninja bugeicho,* 1967), a curious experiment in animation adapted from a popular comic strip by Shirato Sanpei.

In this film the illusion of movement was created by extremely dynamic editing, and the sound track was filled with percussive onomatopoeia dear to the Japanese.

A "Criminal" Cinema

Violence at Noon (*Hakuchu no torima*, 1967) marks a turning point both thematically and aesthetically in a greatly diversified life's work that reached its zenith in *The Ceremony* (1971) and *In the Realm of the Senses* (1976). Based on a short story by Takeda Taijun, *Violence at Noon* has for its main character Eisuke, a sexual psychopath who commits a series of rapes and crimes in the vicinity of a village in central Japan. The complicity linking Eisuke and Shino, a village woman who excites his desire, in some ways recalls the themes of Imamura, particularly *Intentions of Murder* (*Akai satsui*, 1964). But whereas Imamura describes a passionate love relationship between the rapist and his victim, Oshima presents the notion of "crime out of conviction," i.e., a crime that might not be justified, as is usually the case, by recourse to social context (poverty), moral context (justice), or political context (strategy), but which is made logical only by the very desire of the criminal who totally accepts his "madness." Oshima says that he got this idea while working on the script, and tells how the idea took shape later. "I decided to make my character an obsessed, demonic criminal, someone who feels inside himself a powerful urge to do evil without necessarily knowing *why*. When I passed this stage, I arrived at the idea of 'crime of conviction' or 'uncontrollable necessity.' This is the way I analyze the ground I covered."

Of course, even though the obsessed Eisuke is arrested by the police at the end, in keeping with the news item which inspired the film, there is no moral conclusion drawn by Oshima. Rather, he is interested in the actions of the character only as an incarnation of the "Ma" (Evil or Devil, in this sense), and finds the roots of this evil in the primitive, non-Westernized Japanese beliefs that Oshima has alluded to many times. This theme of the "demonic sexual crime" is taken up again in some later films: *Japanese Summer: Double Suicide* (*Muri shinju nihon no natsu*, 1967), *Death by Hanging* (1968), and the more recent *Empire of Passion* (*Ai no borei*, 1978), also inspired by a news item from the past. Totally abandoning the predominant characteristics of his previous films, including the theatrically stylized *mise en scène* and the sequence-shot technique, Oshima fulfills his desire in the latter film to experiment with a new technique, fragmenting space radically and excessively in order to express the multivocal vision of several characters in the drama: "What is most important to me is each time to create a film in which the subject matter and my 'capricious will' ('Wagamamasa') may be in essential agreement." "Now," he adds, "my intention while making a film is to reach reality by means that go beyond reality, or to arrive at surrealism by means of realistic elements"[6]—a double-edged declaration in which Oshima justifies his approach by a very Godard-like turn of phrase. Thus, in *Violence at Noon* the use of telescopic flashback montage, in which no particular point of view prevails except that of one character followed by that of the filmmaker shooting him, ensures an intriguing dialectic of consciousness. The film, magnificently photographed by Takada Akira, consists of more than two thousand separate shots, almost all of them stationary. Noel Burch sees in this film and in the one following it (*Band of Ninja*) "significant attempts to come to terms with certain aspects of the radical montage of Eisenstein's silent films." He also detects the decisive influence of writer-reformist Yoshida Shoin, who, in pre-Meiji Japan, praised madness (as a way to break free of social stagnation).[7] Sato Kei, one of the key actors in Oshima's group, brings Eisuke's lucid madness to life with considerable power, especially in his projection of "demonic evil" as defined by Oshima. In fact, Oshima told journalists that he himself was that "demonic rapist in broad daylight" and concluded that "to make a film in the world in which we live is primarily a criminal act." This resolute, conscious criminal act was already making Oshima an outlaw in tightly controlled Japanese society long before the court action regarding *In the Realm of the Senses*.

Sexual and criminal obsession also fuels *A Treatise on Japanese Bawdy Song* (*Nihon shunka-ko*, 1967), as well as *Japanese Summer: Double Suicide* (1967), *Diary of a Shinjuku Thief* (*Shinjuku dorobo nikki*, 1968), *Death by Hanging* (1968), and *Three Resurrected Drunkards* (1968).

In these five essential titles from his works, Oshima, even more resolutely than before, thrusts us into the heart of the "imagined" world. The "imagined" encompasses not only what is dreamed or unreal but also the affirmation of one's desire and the reconstruction and realization of a subjective time and space that objective reality denies. Indeed, Oshima is not the only filmmaker who explores the fields of imagination. One can find such a preoccupation in Imamura, Yoshida, and Teshigahara, among others; but as always with Oshima, the exploration is radical, essential, and unlike any other. In this period when he pushed his experiments in structure and form as far as possible, even to the point of being esoteric as in *Japanese Summer*, he attacked everything which, conceretely or symbolically, might represent the Japanese state and the notion of power. Against these he fought tenaciously.

In this respect the case of "R," Lee Jun U, charged with murdering and raping a high school girl in 1958, is significant. Starting from a news item,[8]

Oshima employs what we might call a "strategy of the fantastic," his aim being to deny the legality of the death penalty, as well as the very notion of guilt, which the young Korean refuses to acknowledge. After a parodic reenactment of the crime, "R" willingly agrees to be executed a second time, but only after he has convinced himself of his moral innocence—even though he killed. A fictitious psychodrama, *Death by Hanging* is one of Oshima's most complete assaults on the Japanese state, which he considers the very foundation of every crime and every injustice. As he had already done in *A Treatise on Japanese Bawdy Song,* Oshima holds up to ridicule the symbols of the imperial state, particularly the most central and revered symbol of all, the *Hinomaru,* the flag of the rising sun, the sacred emblem of Japan—and a leitmotif in the majority of his films. In front of the *Hinomaru* (literally, "the circle of the sun"), the "negative" characters perform whatever might be considered sacrilegious, such as a crime or a sexual act. "R," a Kafkaesque character, but also a protagonist in a new theater of the absurd, is spiritually the elder brother of the youngster in *Boy* whose parents force him to fake accidents in order to obtain compensation from motorists caught in the trap. A "criminal" being in spite of himself, he remains an Innocent, even though he never tries to escape or refuses to cooperate.

These two films stand in opposition to a whole tradition of Japanese cinema (of which Shochiku was the self-appointed champion, thanks to Kinoshita). In particular they illustrate one of Oshima's chief characteristics: his denial of sentimentality, or any appeal to the audience's emotions or feelings of pity which might elicit the "victim syndrome." The case of *Boy* is typical: wherever the material lends itself to the possibility of sentimental melodrama or compassion for the fate of the unfortunate child or parents, Oshima sharply turns away from this emotion by resorting to ellipsis or by introducing imaginary scenes, which force the spectator to reach the level of "surreality" sought by the filmmaker. Not only does Oshima exonerate the boy's parents for their "criminal" act, he also admits that he considers this family to be the equivalent of the "Holy Family" of Christianity. Here again is an assault on a fundamental taboo of Japan, the family. On the surface, *Boy* looks like a "classical" film in its form, with a clear concern for a purer style than in Oshima's previous films. But if this is so, it is probably a subjective reaction against that series of films in which Oshima continually explodes the elements of the language, forcing upon the audience mental gymnastics that he is not always sure they can do.

Therefore, *Japanese Summer: Double Suicide* and *Three Resurrected Drunkards,* together with *Diary of a Shinjuku Thief,* are landmarks in an investigation of language that constitutes a radical break from the syntax of Japanese cinema. In the first film, Oshima carries to extremes his taste for theatrics, as well as his symbolism, which is hard to decipher for anyone unfamiliar with the contemporary references made to the period when the film was shot. The people who gravitate around the central figure of the killer, labeled "gun-toting devil"—a criminal dear to Oshima—are excessively absurd, halfway between avant-garde theater and a comic strip leaning toward the fantastic. Meijiko is an androgynous-looking creature. Wearing his hair short on the right, long on the left, white in front and black in back, he impassively observes the symbolic images of Japan in uniform: the military, the police, students, Shinto priests. In an urban decor used because of Tokyo's fascinating, anarchic shapes, silhouettes are painted or cut out on the walls or on the ground, and everywhere, of course, we find the obsessive *Hinomaru*. Meijiko meets a man (played by Sato Kei) who lives with the obsession that he will be assassinated by a killer, perhaps a white man, and accompanies him in his search. The film, impossible to summarize, is a long game of hide-and-seek. At the end, almost all of the characters are killed: the two protagonists, a few *yakuza* and the police, and the two lovers in a "double suicide," a Japanese tradition of lovers' suicide that here is transposed by Oshima into an act of (futile) rebellion against the state. Filled with anarchy and nihilism, and obsessed by destruction and nothingness, *Japanese Summer: Double Suicide* gets lost in Oshima's fascination with his own structural elements. Nevertheless, it succeeds in communicating this fascination to the viewer.

While this film is profoundly tragic and examines most of Oshima's obsessions, *Three Resurrected Drunkards*—one of his most clearly Godardian works—returns to the serious topic of the Korean problem, but treats it in the mode of parody and comedy, with allusions to Japanese comedies unknown in Europe. For Oshima, above all, the film provides the opportunity to demonstrate his virtuosity in the handling, even the manipulation, of film language. The film chooses as its "heroes" three young Japanese students whose uniforms are stolen by one of three Koreans trying to avoid being drafted for Vietnam by their country. For fun, the Japanese assume the identity of the three Koreans. When both groups finally meet, the Koreans try to kill the Japanese to take over their identities. Oshima denies that he wanted to make a "political comedy" because he likes paradox, yet the film is preoccupied with paradox, to say nothing of the fact that Oshima has great fun misleading the audience with his formal play. The use of the repetition of language is obvious: halfway through the film, Oshima virtually returns to the opening scene (except for a few telling details) in which the Korean army deserter steals the uniforms from one of the Japanese students—hence the knowingly provoked reaction of the audience, who generally blame the projectionist for having put on the wrong reel. Behind its apparent "hoax," the film was a personal way of expressing opposition to the Japanese government's attitude toward the Vietnam war. A sort of manifesto in the style of "We are all Koreans . . . ," it ends with the three Japanese students' being mistaken for the Korean deserters and sent off to Korea.

Naturally, Oshima's daring language did not please Shochiku, which distributed the film. Withdrawing it from the market, the company canceled its agreement with the director, thus repeating the *Night and Fog in Japan* episode. Therefore, Oshima's next films—which were still being produced by his Sozosha (Creation) Company—found distribution through the independent circuit of the Art Theater Guild (ATG), which had already distributed *Band of Ninja* and *Death by Hanging*. In fact, this small-scale circuit of a few theaters in the large cities of Japan was especially well suited to the style and ambitions of Oshima and other independents, almost all of whom used it.

Continuing with his personal method to undertake a frontal attack on the taboos of Japanese society, Oshima resumed his investigation of sexuality in *Diary of a Shinjuku Thief*. The title pays homage to the works of Jean Genet, whose book is displayed in the bookstore, the main locale of the film. The action takes place in Shinjuku, a Tokyo district which, much more than today, was the symbol of student political activism (it was the site of many demonstrations and violent acts in the years of the student uprising, between 1968 and 1971). "The film is about a young man and a girl seeking the right moment to reach sexual climax. At the same time, it is the story of Shinjuku and its riots. I attempted to express Shinjuku as an area of disruption through these two young people and the various characters with whom they have contact" (Oshima). Among these characters is one of the leading figures of Japanese avant-garde theater, Kara Juro, whose company is giving a performance in a traveling "red tent" called *Akai Tento*. Interestingly, Oshima resorts to color in the middle of a black-and-white film for the outdoor performance of one of the company's plays. In this play Birdey, the young man, has the opportunity to reveal himself by becoming an actor, while Umeko, the girl linked to him since her attempted theft in a bookstore, finds herself influenced by Kara's wife, Ri Reisen, a Korean. During a night of student riots in Shinjuku, Birdey and Umeko finally achieve sexual satisfaction together. In this semidocumentary film, which is shot in a very free style (hand-held camera, 16mm, black-and-white and color) and which gives the impression of lack of control on the director's part, Oshima insists on the assertion of the self and the importance of sexual awakening as a catalyst for liberated, revolutionary attitudes in the struggle against the repression of the state. He also asserts the supremacy of desire over any transmitted culture, however liberal—a culture symbolized here by the Kinokuniya bookstore of Shinjuku, whose manager plays himself. The multiple commentaries (from teachers, actors, friends of Oshima, his close collaborators) on sexuality,

Diary of a Shinjuku Thief.
Birdey (Yokoo Tadanori) and
avant-garde theater figure Kara
Juro. Photo courtesy of Max
Tessier.

theft, crime, and repression link the sequences of the film, which otherwise seem to have been edited in an intuitive and totally haphazard manner.

Oshima uses some of this new methodology again in *The Man Who Left His Will on Film* (*Tokyo senso sengo hiwa,* literally *Secret Story of Postwar Tokyo,* aka *He Died after the War,* 1970), in which Motoki, a student, and the members of his "Posi-Posi" group act their own parts. Motoki discovers that he is incapable of filming the street uprising that radicals named the "Tokyo War" at the time of the post-1968 demonstrations. He finally commits suicide, leaving his fantasies behind on film. As always with Oshima, the film also reflects his own uncertainties at a time when he might have begun to have doubts about the future of his strictly political attitude; nevertheless, he continues his struggle against the ascendancy of the state.

The Man Who Left His Will on Film is undoubtedly a rough draft of a film, unsatisfying, but necessary to the development of the next film, which today more than ever appears to be the summation of Oshima's work to date, *The Ceremony,* or better still, *The Ceremonies* (1971). In this film, Oshima reveals his innermost feelings in nearly perfect form. Through the history of the wealthy Sakurada family, ruled by the patriarch Kazuomi (Sato Kei) and symbolized by the cycle of various official ceremonies (weddings, births, deaths) that mark the family's life, Oshima examines contemporary Japan, its postwar history (1945–1970), the authority of the father/state, what it means to be Japanese today, his own role as an artist, and many other concerns. Subverting the structure of the family chronicle so dear to classical filmmakers such as Ozu, Naruse, and Kinoshita, he creates a succession of extremely complex flashbacks that can be compared to those in *Night and Fog in Japan*. The director's "flow of consciousness" is still active. Here too banquets are interrupted, family contradictions come to light, and characters express themselves in songs, whether military, romantic, bawdy, or political. (This is one of Oshima's leitmotifs in a nation that perennially expresses itself through song.) Oshima, however, adds a few episodes of his own invention that send the film over into fantasy and surrealism once again: the wedding without a bride, one of the most startling scenes in a film which contains many startling scenes; the intrusion of the fascinating character Tadashi, who evokes Mishima Yukio the writer by arranging his suicide like a piece of theater—and in the same year, too; the expedition to the island where Terumichi, the Sakurada heir, rejects his inheritance by committing suicide, thus breaking the continuation of the family; and the final sequence of the imaginary baseball game, when Masao listens to the sound of the Japanese land, the same sound that he used to listen to as a child—a sequence that ends in a long, black shot, ominous and threatening.

A film of surreal beauty, *The Ceremony* owes an enormous debt to Narushima Toichiro, the cameraman;[9] Toda Jusho, the set designer;[10] Takemitsu Toru, the composer;[11] and Oshima's family of actors.[12] The film is an admirable example of teamwork serving a director who sees it as a kind of spiritual and political legacy, and who senses the end of a period of liberty, as well as the end of the myth of absolute "independence" in a system that is suffocating.

Oshima then made *Dear Summer Sister* (1973), a parable on the return of Okinawa to Japan, and something of a disappointment after such an impressive work as *The Ceremony*. Despite evidence of Oshima's further exploration in film language, the improvisation method, which had proved itself in *Diary of a Shinjuku Thief* and *The Man Who Left His Will on Film*, now falls flat and only underlines the repetition of previous elements without breathing new life into them or probing them more deeply. Oshima fails to render acceptable a symbolic system too vague and ambiguous to be really meaningful. In any event, the film was the swan song for Oshima and his most eminent colleagues as independent producers.[13] Thus, in 1974, thirteen years after its formation, Oshima announced the dissolution of the Sozosha Company. He declared that "the task of Sozosha has been fulfilled," and that "the system of independent production no longer fits our times"—a declaration which was filled with bitterness and which

scarcely managed to hide an acknowledgment of failure and an intensified nega-
tivism. Actually, Oshima was implicitly admitting that any struggle is sporadic
and that each fight must find a new form if the previous one has failed.

In the Realm of the Senses: International Breakthrough

Salvation came from abroad. The success of several of Oshima's films at festivals
bore fruit: a French producer (Anatole Dauman) made Oshima the tempting
offer of a co-production, and Oshima accepted, making what became the first
"hardcore" masterpiece of international erotic cinema, and a genuine legend: *In
the Realm of the Senses* (1976).

So much has been written about the film that it is unnecessary to go into
detail, except to emphasize the fact that Oshima's direction—a far cry from his
previous stylistic audacity—is essentially focused on the painstaking observation
of the lovemaking of the couple Abe Sada (Matsuda Eiko) and Kichizo (Fuji
Tatsuya), and on the idea of time-space as a no-exit situation, an enclosed world.
In other words, Oshima does not allow his characters to leave their room except, literally, to justify their attitude in the days of militarism (hence the parade
of soldiers in front of Kichizo) and, figuratively, through the expedient device of
infrequent "imaginary" sequences. Here Oshima returns to one of his favorite
themes: not only the "sexual crime" but the ability of human beings to expend
their energy in the most complete and positive way. The "immoral" behavior of
the couple is a defiant challenge to a time when a man had a duty to expend his
energy in the army, while a woman was to remain in the home, devoting herself
to the bearing of children.

Paradoxically seen in Japan in a mutilated and censored version (with masking, blurred images, and truncated screen), *In the Realm of the Senses* became
the subject for a test of strength between Oshima and the "Japanese state"
that had been postponed for a long time. This test took the form of a long-term
court action against the filmmaker and his publisher, the main charge being
hypocritically directed at the book published upon the release of the film, and
not at the film itself. The lawsuit is still going on, and its outcome will probably
decide the fate of censorship in Japan. [Editor's note: Oshima won the case in
1982.]

Oshima's last film to date is *Empire of Passion* (literally, *Ghost of Love*,
but clumsily titled *The Realm of Desire* by its French producer—an example
of commercial calculation that proved fruitless). Once again, Oshima examines
crime and sex, this time in the rural Japan of the Meiji era (1895). But paradoxi-

In the Realm of the Senses. The enclosed world of Kichizo (Fuji Tatsuya) and Abe Sada (Matsuda Eiko). Photo courtesy of Max Tessier.

cally, the film suffers from a meticulous, almost academic, treatment, its aesthetic beauty being much too studied and its form serving only to emphasize its thematic indebtedness to *In the Realm of the Senses* and other Oshima films. A surprising, unexpected film from Oshima, it is the work of an already mature artist. But it makes one wonder if he has not fallen into the trap of success, for it also betrays a certain dearth of inspiration, while reminding us of the Japanese film scene which does not allow him to make films according to his wishes, except on a very low budget. In spite of Oshima's habitual mockery of the established order, the final intrusion of the police in the lovers' house—a beautiful image that once again refers to the *Hinomaru*—followed by the lovers' being tortured, sufficiently points to the fears of a filmmaker worried about Japan's future and the danger of a rebirth of nationalism—a danger that he feels is stronger in Japan than anywhere else.

An open, eclectic filmmaker, never imprisoned by one ideology or one party, relentlessly questioning his country and the power which rules over it, Oshima remains a unique figure in the history of Japanese cinema, even in its contemporary phase. More than any other filmmaker, he has helped to shake off the weight of the past through his innovative works—works that are often elusive and outrageously individual, fascinating in their very excesses, and, above all, Japanese to the core in their thematic and formal language. We can only fear that Oshima, who has always insisted on the need to make his films in Japan, may accept an international arrangement, thereby cutting off his creative roots. However, his film career already is the expression of an inner echo which resonates within him, like the echo of the Japanese land in Masao's head in *The Ceremony*.

NOTES

1. See "On the Subject of Uncalled-for Political Criticism," in "Oshima on Oshima," the appendix to this essay.

2. "The Condition and Subject of Japanese Cinema after the War" ("Sengo, Nihon no eiga no joyu to shutai"), *Positif* 143 (October 1972). Several extracts are reprinted here (between quotation marks).

3. Quoted by Jean-Paul le Pape in his French translation of "Oshima par lui-même" ("Oshima on Oshima").

4. For more on this matter, see Oshima, "Filmmakers Should Not Rely on the Conscience of the Masses" (translated into English as "Oshima on Oshima").

5. "The Palace Production" was created especially for this occasion, since Sozosha (Creation) was not yet in operation.

6. From an unpublished interview with Oshima, 1967.

7. Cf. Noel Burch, *To the Distant Observer: Form and Meaning in the Japanese Cinema* (Berkeley: U of California P, 1979), p. 330.

8. *Death by Hanging* is only one example of an Oshima film inspired by a current or past "news item." Other such films are *Violence at Noon; Diary of a Shinjuku Thief; Boy; In the Realm of the Senses;* and *Empire of Passion.*

9. Narushima Toichiro collaborated with Oshima on *The Man Who Left His Will on Film* and *The Ceremony* and directed a full-length feature in 1972, *Time and Memory (Seigenki).*

10. Toda Jusho, one of the most accomplished Japanese production designers, worked with Oshima from *Violence at Noon* to *Empire of Passion.*

11. Takemitsu Toru, undoubtedly the most prominent of contemporary Japanese composers, wrote the music for *The Man Who Left His Will on Film; The Ceremony; Dear Summer Sister;* and *Empire of Passion.*

12. In addition to his team of scenarists (Ishido Toshiro, Tamura Tsutomu, Sasaki Mamoru, Adachi Masao) and technicians, Oshima has gathered around him an easily recognizable "family of actors" in his films. Among the most familiar are Koyama Akiko (Mrs. Oshima), Sato Kei, Watanabe Fumio, Toura Mutsuhiro, Komatsu Hose, Matsuda Masao, Tonoyama Taiji, and also co-scenarists Ishido Tohiro and Adachi Masao (during the period of *Death by Hanging*).

13. In effect, Oshima stopped making films for three years before the co-production of *In the Realm of the Senses,* as did Yoshida after *Martial Law* (1973) and Teshigahara after *Summer Soldier* (1972), and Imamura's *History of Postwar Japan as Told by a Bar Hostess* (1970) initiated a hiatus of five years.

Oshima on Oshima
Oshima Nagisa

Filmmakers Should Not Rely on the
Conscience of the Masses

On November 12, 1960, the day that the showing of the film *Night and Fog in Japan* was suspended, I was in Osaka to write the script for *Seishun no fukaki fuchi Yori*,[1] at the request of the TV network Kansai Terebi. I did not hear the news through the company that employed me, but through a phone call from the newspaper *Mainichi* in Tokyo. The company (Shochiku) informed me thirteen days later when I went to give support to Morikawa Eitaro, a friend I knew from high school, who was then filming *Bushidomusan*[2] in the Kyoto studios. The reason given by the company for halting the public showing of *Night and Fog in Japan* was that the film was supposedly failing at the box office. But I couldn't accept that reason. In each of the downtown Tokyo theaters, the number of spectators varied between 1,300 and 1,800 on November 9, and between 600 and 800 on November 12. These figures were supposed to be slightly below average for the period, but there were films that had even fewer spectators. Even if one considers that the order to pull the film from theaters where it was playing was given in the evening of November 12, following the assassination of Asanuma, leader of the Socialist Party, earlier that afternoon, I feel compelled to trust my instinct and wonder if there were not reasons of a political nature behind this shutdown.

I therefore expressed my doubts openly in some articles published in the press, an action that seems only to have hardened Shochiku's position toward me. I was confused, and felt bad about the hard line they were taking. On the other hand, since requests for public resumption of the film were beginning to be heard from moviegoers and from theaters, I had no choice but to join them, and continued to ask the company to resume showing the film. The main point of my argument was this: if the film had been pulled from circulation only because it was not doing any business, the requests of moviegoers for it to be shown had to be addressed. But finally this argument was not considered valid (nor were others). Primarily because of this conflict, I left Shochiku the following summer (1961) and became an independent filmmaker, shooting *The Catch* (*Shiiku*).

The fact that *Night and Fog in Japan* was withdrawn from distribution in the above manner had and continues to have a strong influence on my work as a director, and also on young filmmakers working to bring reforms to Japanese cinema by creating works of personal and different content. It was an unfortunate event for us, and for the whole of Japanese cinema as well—an experience that I can summarize in one exact phrase: "painful spite."

Now that it has been decided to release the film again, should I forget my feeling of bitterness? No, no, indeed I should not. Of course, I am not going to speak of it now to Mr. X, who was one of the people in charge of the company at that time. However, I must nurture this "painful spite," and make it explode.

From *Night and Fog in Japan* until today, whether through haste or through inertia, it seems to me that I have not achieved the expected results. Since the film is in the domain of artistic endeavor, there is basically no need to ask whether it was a success or a failure. Personally, in my works which were to follow, I made the firm, unshakable decision to carry to complete fruition the effort to cultivate that painful spite and to make it explode.

As for certain unfavorable situations that I had to accept grudgingly because of the state of Japanese cinema after the conflict surrounding *Night and Fog in Japan,* I will allow myself to say something about the malicious view that "Oshima ignores the masses in the films he makes." I am going to speak clearly: I never made any film that ignored the masses. Moreover, it is unthinkable that I may have said I was ignoring the masses while making films. You, the individuals who have concocted such a rumor out of nothing, you, the individuals who are spreading it thoughtlessly, you have not just placed me in an unfavorable position—which does not matter since I am unshakable—you have also helped to debase the Japanese cinema at the most important period of Japanese cinema! Regarding the relationship between filmmakers and the masses, the two principles I believe in are as follows:

The first principle—and this goes without saying—is that while filmmakers must not be unaware of the masses, they must not depend on the masses for their support. The Japanese cinema of the past was almost entirely a cinema that relied on the spectators' conscience at base. As for us, we try to adopt the

opposite principle. A dialogue can emerge only from works in which the director is conscious of the masses and asserts his subjectivity as a director. This is
the necessary condition for art to be true entertainment. In the Japanese cinema
this dialogue between the director and the masses, which should be the most
natural thing in the world, was not taking place. All we did was apply the
"most natural thing in the world" to the Japanese cinema.

The second principle is that each cinema is intended for moviegoers interested in a particular type of film. This means that the spectators for whom a film
is usually intended represent one part of the masses, a defined part. It is nevertheless believed that there is a "general mass of spectators," but these words
refer only to those spectators who attend movie theaters where the current
Japanese films are being shown. Rejecting such an idea, we have also tried to
make films for those people who do not see the current Japanese films. Such a
film is *Night and Fog in Japan.* It was intended for a specific stratum of spectators; it was intended, in a general way, for students, the intelligentsia, unionized
workers, office workers, workers, and in particular all those who, in one way
or another, were part of such organizations or movements. All such spectators,
if they are rigorously conscious of themselves as constituent members of the
masses, will undoubtedly discover that the director is also vigorously searching
for his own self as a constituent member of the masses. From all this, as it
were, is born the prospect of future, concrete action in the struggle of activist
movements.

Regarding the re-release of *Night and Fog in Japan,* I feel somewhat overwhelmed by the emotion attached to it, and have several things to say. As for
the development of the film and the incident of its withdrawal, there already is a
tendency to forget it all. Therefore, if only for the process of its re-release, I am
going to limit myself to stating the facts. Since the journalists of modern Japan
have a short memory, and since they have lost the ability to get to the bottom of
the facts, I am going to be a substitute for them, so to speak. . . .

On the Subject of Uncalled-for
Political Criticism

The review *The Documentary Film* devotes a special column to "current modernism." I myself had written a piece entitled "Action in Art and Modernism,"
the larger part of which is an argument annihilating the quarrel sought by some
people with Hanada and me at the time we were still managing to survive. At the
end of the text, I stated the following provisional hypotheses:

1. The greatest obstacle to the influence of art in modern Japan, and within it, is the politicization which enslaves art. This is the result of a way of thinking that wants art to possess a direct political effectiveness, or believes, for instance, that a work is necessarily good if it is created by a laborer.

2. The greatest role for the avant-garde to play in the field of present-day art is to break down such a politicization; if this is not done, there can be no progress in the development of an art with a truly popular base.

3. There are some people who, while knowing the errors of politicization, fight it with inadequate vigor. Such people are found at the very heart of the action movement in the arts. On the one hand, they submit to politicization and political authorities, and for that reason cannot subjectively participate in the action movements of art with a truly popular base. On the other hand, for the same reason, they casually join up with a "modernism" which is totally outside the artistic action movements, and are the ones who, falling into this kind of "modernism," end up taking a slanderous position toward the true artistic avant-garde.

4. Such a tendency toward modernism in the framework of commercialism, which is the greatest obstacle to these artistic action movements, is reinforced by the fact that they are absorbed (by commercialism). The sheer urge to sell is their main goal, and in this case, if they are within action movements, being politically enslaved, they therefore do not participate in them in a personal way. Their spreading of utterly simplistic criticism ends up being their market value.

5. The avant-garde of the action movements of today's art must wage a radical fight against modernism's tendency to devalue and reject the subjective part of themselves, to repeat abstract and general arguments at each crisis of action movements, and to use their egos as a commodity for sale. All this becomes an obstacle to action inside the movement. By fighting this tendency deep in one's heart of hearts, one will truly be able to eradicate the politicization of art.

Today, two and a half years have passed since I wrote the above. I must stress that it was a strategic argument that came out of a court case and pertained to a situation which was circumstantial but is still valid now. I must also mention that *Night and Fog in Japan,* which once again is being shown in public and which is still timely, evokes in me a certain personal sadness. But one cannot live one's life being sad. In the text I wrote, to a certain degree I foresaw the state of Japanese art following the U.S.-Japan Security Treaty. But in fact this state has worsened beyond what I foresaw. This state, at least on the surface, is due to the fact that modernism and politicization are brutally, and each in its own way, destroying the art of Japan.

Excerpts from the book *My Idea of Evil and Cruelty* (*Ma to zankoku no hasso*) (Haga Shoten, 1972).

NOTES

1. *The Abyss of Youth,* directed by Hori Yasuo.
2. *The Cruelty of Martial Arts.*

Narrative Strategies in Ozu's Late Films

Kathe Geist

On one point, Ozu scholars are in complete agreement: the director's narrative strategies (his use of 360 degree space, his handling of causal continuity, and his reliance on "intermediate" spaces, or shots devoid of human characters) are very much his own, and radically different from the classical Hollywood model. But they disagree when it comes to how these narrative strategies function and what they actually signify.

The debate continues with Geist's essay, which examines Ozu's later films, concentrating in particular on *Late Spring* (*Banshun,* 1949), *Early Summer* (*Bakushu,* 1951), *Tokyo Story* (*Tokyo monogatari,* 1953), *Early Spring* (*Soshun,* 1956), *Equinox Flower* (*Higanbana,* 1958), *Late Autumn* (*Akibiyori,* 1960), *The End of Summer* (*Kohayakawake no aki,* 1961), and *An Autumn Afternoon* (*Samma no aji,* 1962). On the surface, Ozu's stories are simple—in David Bordwell's word, "banal." However, Geist argues that these simple stories are often told in a puzzling way: major story events are omitted; important characters never appear; inconsequential scenes take up substantial amounts of time; and upcoming scenes are frequently miscued in the scene before. One can read these peculiarities as disruptions to the surface narrative or as positive elements in a different, subtextual narrative. Geist shows how these apparent disruptions in Ozu's surface narrative work together to form a subtext that deepens, enriches, and at times counterpoints the surface narrative. In her view the "relentless" logic of Ozu's plotting and his "transgressions" (i.e., static scenes that only seem to be irrelevant) confound our expectations only to serve them more completely and sublimely.

For further reading, see David Desser, *"Early Summer,"* in *Magill's Survey of Cinema: Foreign Language Films*, Vol. 2 (Englewood Cliffs: Salem Press, 1985), pp. 898–902; *"Late Spring,"* in *Magill's Survey of Cinema: Foreign Language Films*, Vol. 4, pp. 1745–50; Dennis J. Konshak, "Space and Narrative in *Tokyo Story," Film Criticism* 4, 3 (Spring 1980):

31–40; Keiko I. McDonald, "A Basic Narrative Mode in Yasujiro Ozu's *Tokyo Story*," in *Cinema East: A Critical Study of Major Japanese Films* (Rutherford, N.J.: Fairleigh Dickinson UP, 1983), pp. 201–227; and Martin Rubin, "*Early Spring*," in *Magill's Survey of Cinema: Foreign Language Films*, Vol. 2, pp. 892–897.

From 1949 on, Ozu's films were dominated by the style and narrative format with which he is most readily identified: scenes made up of perfectly composed, relatively static shots with little or no camera movement; flat lighting; the use of frequently cryptic "empty shots"—empty of identified characters—as transitions between scenes and sometimes as interludes within them; and an even, stately, unhurried rhythm. The quiescent camera and cutting technique is reflected by narratives in which Ozu avoided drama, whose stories generally involve marriage and/or death, and whose plots take place over a fairly unified time period and in locales that are frequently predictable from film to film: the upper-middle-class house, the lower-middle-class apartment, the restaurant, the bar, the office, the train station, the temple, the scenic pilgrimage spot. Usually four generations are represented: underaged children, young adults, middle-aged parents, and senior citizens. In referring to several of these films, Ozu indicated that he was consciously striving to reflect the life cycle, mutability, and ephemerality.[1]

The style had, to be sure, antecedents in Ozu's previous work, particularly in his two wartime films, *The Brothers and Sisters of the Toda Family* (*Todake no kyodai*, 1941) and *There Was a Father* (*Chichi ariki*, 1942); furthermore, his writings indicate that his desire to avoid drama began at this time.[2] His concern with ephemerality is present in his early films, becoming increasingly important in the '40s and '50s; and the enigmatic "empty shots" can be found in his earliest surviving silent films. Nor do all of his post-1949 films fit the pattern I have outlined. *The Munekata Sisters* (*Munekata shimai*, 1950) and *Tokyo Twilight* (*Tokyo boshoku*, 1957) have heightened drama and depict an unhappier, more sordid world than is usual for the late films; they recall *Hen in the Wind* (*Kaze no naka no mendori*, 1948) and *Woman of Tokyo* (*Tokyo no onna*, 1933). *The Flavor of Green Rice over Tea* (*Ochazuke no aji*, 1952), *Ohayo* (aka *Good Morning*, 1959), and *Floating Weeds* (*Ukigusa*, 1959) are all in some sense remakes of 1930s films (*What Did the Lady Forget?* [*Shujo wa nani o wasuretaka*, 1937], *I Was Born, but . . .* [*Umarete wa mita keredo*, 1932], and *A Story of Floating Weeds* [*Ukigusa monogatari*, 1934] respectively), and their more free-wheeling plots feel uncomfortably constrained by the "static style" of the late period.

The films characterized by both the "static style" and stories dwelling on the life cycle constitute the majority of those made after 1948 and are those that I will be most concerned with here: *Late Spring* (*Banshun*, 1949), *Early Summer* (*Bakushu*, 1951), *Tokyo Story* (*Tokyo monogatari*, 1953), *Early Spring* (*Soshun*, 1956), *Equinox Flower* (*Higanbana*, 1958), *Late Autumn* (*Akibiyori*, 1960), *The End of Summer* (*Kohayakawake no aki*, 1961), and *An Autumn Afternoon* (*Samma no aji*, 1962). The evenness of their cinematic technique masks complex plot structures layered with meaning, which other critics have ignored and even denied. In this essay I will explore the nature of these structures and the meanings that can be inferred from them.

Noel Burch, dazzled by the spatial/pictorial inventiveness of Ozu's early films, has called the late films a "final fossilization" of his style, their imagery and diegesis "a senile mannerism."[3] David Bordwell admires Ozu's artistry in all its guises, but calls Ozu's subject matter "banal." Classifying Ozu as a "parametric" filmmaker, one whose "stylistic patterning splits away from the [plot],"[4] he writes:

> The parametric [plot] will thus tend to be recognizable by its deformities. . . .
> The films of Ozu and Bresson manage to be both elliptical . . . and repetitious.
> . . . Both severe ellipticality and repetition indicate that the constraints of stylistic patterning are imposing their will on the [plot], or at least that the narration limits itself to presenting events that display the style to its best advantage.[5]

Not only does parametric style deform plot, it invites stories with banal themes, presumably to limit the damage.

> Parametric filmmakers have tended to employ strikingly obvious themes. Not much acumen is needed to identify *Tokyo Story* as examining the decline of the "inherently" Japanese family. . . . It is as if stylistic organization becomes prominent only if the themes are so banal as to leave criticism little to interpret.[6]

Donald Richie states that Ozu frequently complained that plot bored him,[7] but the full text of Ozu's complaint qualifies this generalization. "Pictures with obvious plots bore me now. Naturally a film must have some kind of structure or else it's not a film, but I feel that a picture isn't good if it has too much drama."[8] Thus it was *drama*, not plot, that Ozu disliked, and *obvious* plots, not plot per se, that bored him. A film had to have some kind of structure to be a film. Was it a purely formal structure imposed on the plot, as Bordwell maintains, or was it a narrative structure designed to keep the plot from being obvious? If the latter, one cannot assume that Ozu's stories are banal because they are not entirely apparent. The so-called deformities contain information.

Ozu's style, far from existing alongside a plot contrived to show it off, is frequently, if not always, an integral part of the narrative process and a necessary guide to narrative and thematic meaning. His frequent uses of repetition and ellipsis do not "impose their will" on Ozu's plots: they *are* his plots. By paying attention to what has been left out and to what is repeated, one arrives at Ozu's essential story.

End of Summer has probably the most complex narrative structure of all the late films. It chronicles the demise of Kohayakawa Manbei, jovial head of a brewery clan, who, in his last months, renews his liaison with an old mistress, his wife having been dead for a number of years. While his married daughter, Fumiko, whose adopted husband will take over the brewery, fumes about his affair, his youngest daughter, Noriko, and his widowed daughter-in-law, Akiko, consider marriage proposals. His death frees the youngest to marry the man she really loves but forces his son-in-law to sell the brewery to a large firm, thus ending the family's independent status.

The film opens with two shots of Osaka at night. In the second of these, a large neon sign beams the words "New Japan." They prelude a scene in an Osaka bar where an uncle discusses a possible marriage arrangement for Akiko with a prospective suitor. Akiko arrives at the bar and, after being introduced, excuses herself to telephone home to see if her sister-in-law Noriko is waiting for her. Photographed from behind, she walks up the passageway between the bar stools and the booths. The camera holds on the empty passageway, then returns to the men waiting for her return. But instead of seeing her return through the empty aisle in the bar, we next see her walking down the hallway outside her apartment. She enters and chats briefly with Noriko, who is indeed waiting for her. Noriko wants to discuss a proposed *omiai,* the initial meeting between families contemplating an arranged marriage. The scene ends with a shot of Noriko from behind as she walks down the same hallway that Akiko came up at the beginning of the scene.

These opening scenes violate a number of narrative norms. First, Ozu suppresses the information that Akiko learned from her telephone call; only when she is already home do we realize what that information was. Second, because Ozu shows us the empty passageway in the bar, we anticipate her return through that passageway and are momentarily confused to see her in a different but similar passageway. Finally, Ozu includes a gratuitous shot of Noriko walking down the same passageway that Akiko came up. We seem to have both too much and too little, yet reading what we are given as *information pertinent to the narrative* instead of reading it as deformity allows us deeper insight into Ozu's story.

By eliding the information that Akiko has been called home, Ozu immediately establishes her rejection of the suitor, even though no formal proposal has been made. Politeness will have demanded that she return to the table and make her apologies. Not only do we not see this, we see nothing even leading up to it. Ozu does what the character cannot: he cuts out the suitor. The hold on the empty passageway in the bar, through which she never returns, signifies her position vis-à-vis the suitor: figuratively she never returns to him, a suggestion that becomes literal in another scene in the same bar, in which the suitor waits for her but she never shows up.

The closing shot of Noriko walking down the hallway outside the apartment functions thematically. First, it identifies the two women with one another, showing them in especial sympathy. Second, it creates a completed cycle. Like all the films under consideration here, *End of Summer* deals with the life cycle and is particularly rich in circle imagery, created through both editing and graphic patterning.[9] Finally, it allows Ozu to show the passageway once more. Passageways in houses, corridors in office and apartment buildings, and alleyways through neighborhoods abound in Ozu's films. They can be read as symbolic of the passages in human life from one stage to another; or, if that seems too literal, they can be seen in terms of the "go spaces" (*michiyuki, hashi*) in *ma*, the Japanese concept of time-space continuity, which connects one time to the next.[10] In either case, they belong specifically to Ozu's vision of an ephemeral world always in flux.

The confusion we feel when we expect to see Akiko in the bar only to find her at home contributes to one of the film's major paradigms: things never happen as expected. The film's main story event suggests this structure: Manbei becomes ill and is feared to be dying in the middle of the film but recovers, only to die suddenly and unexpectedly at the end.

Between the fourth and fifth scenes, another transition occurs in which Ozu deliberately misleads his viewers. Gathered in their living room, members of the Kohayakawa family discuss marriage prospects for both Akiko and Noriko. Brother-in-law Hisao remarks that Noriko's *omiai* will take place in the New Osaka Hotel. Soon after his remark, the scene ends, and a new scene begins with a shot of tall office buildings, an indication we are in Osaka, the business and industrial center of southern Honshu. To remove all doubt, Osaka Castle, an iconic landmark, appears in the background of the following shot, which has been taken out the window of a tall building. Surely Noriko's *omiai* will be the subject of this scene. Instead we next see an unknown woman talking on the telephone in an office; the previous shot was presumably taken from a window in this office. After hanging up, she sits down at a desk beside Noriko. The telephone call has been an invitation to a party for a fellow employee named

Teramoto, who will soon be leaving for a job in Sapporo, the capital of Japan's northernmost island, Hokkaido. Hearing the news, Noriko seems disappointed, and we soon learn that she is in love with Teramoto. Using a sound bridge, Ozu cuts to a restaurant where the farewell party is underway, showing first the hallway outside the party room and then the party itself. The next scene takes place in a train station, where Noriko and Teramoto converse awkwardly while waiting for their separate trains.

Earlier, Ozu had led us to believe that we would see Noriko's *omiai*. Instead he showed us Noriko at work. The substitution was not merely a trick, however, for instead of the *miai*-suitor, we meet the man Noriko really loves and will eventually marry. Although Noriko later reports on the *omiai*, Ozu does not waste time on the wrong man. But having promised us an *omiai*, he gives us one in the form of the train station scene. Although in love, Noriko and Teramoto are obviously not in very close contact, because she first learns of his final decision to move to Sapporo from her officemate. Thus the scene in which they sit on the platform bench speaking shyly to one another has the character of an *omiai*: each feels pressured by the impending departure and the distance that will separate them to reach a decision about marrying on the basis of relatively little familiarity. Here Ozu substitutes the unexpected for the expected, but in doing so he jettisons the unimportant for the important, thus keeping his storyline right on track.

The film climaxes when Manbei collapses from a heart attack. Noriko runs to telephone a doctor. From Noriko telephoning, Ozu cuts to two empty shots of the Hirayama Clinic, over which the phone keeps ringing. He then cuts back to the corridor, now empty, where Noriko had been telephoning, to the empty livingroom, to the empty passageway between the livingroom and the garden, and finally to the bedroom where the doctor is treating Manbei. Again we have been deliberately misled. The unanswered telephone ringing in the clinic suggests that the doctor is out and Manbei will die from lack of medical attention. Yet here again the narrative structure does not simply disrupt our conventional expectations; it tells a different story. In addition to the sound of the phone ringing over the shots of the empty clinic, we hear a clock ticking, and in the second of the clinic shots we see this clock. Over the shot of the empty corridor in the Kohayakawa house, we hear a train whistle; in the empty livingroom, a coil of insect-repelling incense sends up a plume of smoke: of the three shots inside the house, two are of passageways. Thus, at the moment Manbei appears to be dying, Ozu montages a series of visual and aural symbols of passage and transience. The empty rooms indicate the void Manbei will leave if he dies.[11]

The sequence following that of the doctor treating Manbei contains two brief scenes with Noriko cut between seven empty shots which show the livingroom, the brewery, and the cemetery at dawn. In this manner we wait with the family and view again the anticipated void. Bordwell has pointed out that the sequence echoes that in the earlier *Tokyo Story* in which the family waits by the grandmother's bedside through the night, and she dies toward dawn. Thus we are given every indication that Manbei will die.

The dawn sequence ends with a conversation between two clerks at the brewery. "Did the Old Master have a bad heart?" the younger asks. "No, a bad liver," the older man replies. Thus Ozu reminds us to expect the unexpected in this film, and, indeed, in the following scene Manbei astounds his family by getting out of bed fit and chipper.

In the next scenes Akiko comes to visit the family, tells Noriko that she does not want to remarry, and pries from her sister-in-law the secret of her love for Teramoto. Manbei plays hide-and-seek with his grandson and uses the occasion to sneak off to visit Sasaki, his mistress. We see them next at the bicycle races. Before showing Manbei and Sasaki, however, Ozu uses eleven shots to establish the location of the scene. The first three or four are typically cryptic; we have no idea where we are or where we might be headed until we finally see the stands and the racers and remember that Manbei and Sasaki, whose relationship underwent a fifteen-year hiatus, recently renewed their acquaintance at the bicycle races. Such a long uncharactered sequence is unusual even for Ozu. Part of the explanation lies in the associative and symbolic content of the shots. The cyclers race in a circle, again the completed cycle. Some win and some lose; Manbei's racers lose. So do those of an anonymous individual who throws his worthless stubs into the air in the shot preceding that of Manbei, who subsequently does the same. An empty shot after the dialogue sequence between Manbei and Sasaki shows torn stubs floating to the ground like confetti. Someone must have won this race, but Ozu tells us only about the losers and thus suggests Manbei's subsequent death. In fact, this scene is the last in which we see him alive. His conversation with Sasaki seems trivial enough, and we wonder why Ozu inflates the bicycle races to the status of a major scene by using such a lengthy introduction. Only later do we realize that the scene was important because after it Manbei would die; yet Ozu told us the scene was important at the time, just as he told us early in the film that Akiko would not marry her suitor and that Noriko would marry her lover and not her *miai*-suitor.

At the end of the short dialogue at the races, Manbei insists they go to Osaka. The shot of torn stubs falling behind the empty bleachers follows; then the shot of Osaka's night lights flashing "New Japan" is reprised. Using conventional logic, we anticipate finding Manbei and Sasaki in Osaka, but instead we return to the film's opening scene: Akiko's uncle and her suitor in the bar. Again Ozu has brought us to Osaka with the expectation of meeting one set of characters only to have us meet another. Formally, however, he is consistent, for the "New Japan" sign also preceded the earlier version of this scene. Thematically, too, the sequence makes sense. Manbei's loss at the races is followed by the suitor's loss of Akiko, for she doesn't show up at the bar this time and thereby signals her rejection of his proposal. Meanwhile, the suitor's loss of Akiko substitutes for Manbei's loss of life, which occurs in the story at about the same time as the second bar scene.

In short, the unfoldment of Ozu's plot in *End of Summer* is relentless in its logic. Although it confounds our expectations, it provides a rich and accurate description of the characters, themes, motivations, and events in Ozu's story and never deviates from or clutters that story with irrelevant information.

A similar logic operates in *An Autumn Afternoon*. A scene between the protagonist Hirayama and his friend Kawai ends with Kawai declining an invitation to dinner on the excuse that he cannot miss his baseball game. A shot out of Hirayama's office window is followed by six more uncharactered shots: three of the stands during a night baseball game, one of the game on a television set, and two of men we don't know watching the television in the bar section of a restaurant. Finally we are shown Hirayama, Kawai, and their friend Horie having dinner at the same restaurant. Again we have been deliberately misled. Kawai's comment, followed by the shots of the stands at the baseball field, suggests we will find him there. Instead he has changed his mind and joined his friends, information we are denied until we actually see the three men together. In an early article on Ozu, Bordwell and Thompson called this sequence Ozu's "most transgressive transition," one in which he moves "through spaces between scenes independently of any narrative demands."[12] Stephen Heath has objected to the suggestion that the transition is "transgressive" and forces a split between space and narrative. "Certainly," he writes, "there is a play of difficulty in finding the men, but that play—irony and revelation . . . is not transgressive of the terms of the narration it gives.[13]

In other words, Ozu narrates on his own terms, but *narrates* nonetheless. Moreover, what may seem like an elaborate joke on Ozu's part also points to a serious subtext in the film. By taking us to the baseball game, Ozu does not simply show us where Kawai is not; he shows us what Kawai is missing. Later in the restaurant Kawai protests Horie's early departure by pointing out that he gave up his baseball game for this meeting, thus underscoring his missed opportunity. Throughout the film, characters either have missed, do miss, or might miss a variety of opportunities. "Gourd," the old teacher, has neglected to marry off his daughter, and now it is too late. Kawai fears that Hirayama will do the same with his daughter Michiko. Having insisted she was not ready to marry, Michiko misses the opportunity to marry the man of her choice. Near the end of the film, Kawai teases Hirayama by telling him that since he waited too long to give an answer on the *miai*-match Kawai arranged for Michiko, the young man is no longer available, although this is only a joke. Throughout the film, Hirayama's son Koichi agonizes over a set of MacGregor golf clubs that his friend is selling at a bargain price, an opportunity not to be missed. Even Hirayama's former seaman speculates on the dubious opportunities Japan missed by losing the war.

An Autumn Afternoon is Ozu's third film on the subject of a daughter deciding to marry and leave a single parent, but neither of the others, *Late Spring* or *Late Autumn*, treats the subject in terms of missed opportunity. Neither exhibits the baleful example of a middle-aged old maid. In fact, in all of Ozu's "marriage films" except *Autumn Afternoon*, the heroine has an unmarried, highly independent female friend who is doing very well on her own. Although, as I shall argue below, *Late Spring* suggests that the heroine misses marrying the man she loves, she does so more because the two discover each other too late than because he was ready when she was not. Thus "missed opportunity" is uniquely central in *Autumn Afternoon*, and the baseball game is our first indication of it.

Late Spring is another case in which reading Ozu's "transgressions" considerably amplifies one's understanding of the film. The first of the marriage films, it begins with two shots of the Kita-Kamakura train station and proceeds to a tea house where Noriko, the heroine, learns tea ceremony with her aunt and a Mrs. Miwa, who will later be put forward as a possible marriage prospect for Noriko's father, Professor Sobiya. Noriko returns home to find Sobiya working with his handsome assistant Hattori. The next sequence begins with two shots of a station platform, shots of a train going through a tunnel, and views inside the train where we find Noriko and Sobiya. The presence of the train here, as in the opening shots, suggests the idea of passage, with which the film is concerned. Richie has noted that Ozu was careful that the locales through which we see the train pass in this three-minute sequence all occur in correct order;[14] such attention to detail is not gratuitous but sustains the parallel between a train journey and the life cycle insofar as each follows a fixed order.

However, the sequence also contains far more explicit references to marriage, or at least to coupling. The first shot shows an unknown woman standing alone on the platform. The next shot, taken farther down the platform, shows a man and woman standing together, and in the next shot the train goes through the tunnel. A coupling process seems to be implied here, as though Ozu were labeling this train sequence with the particular kind of passage with which this film will be mainly concerned.

For Ozu, station platforms seem to invite coupling. In *Early Summer, Early Spring, Ohayo, End of Summer,* and *An Autumn Afternoon,* would-be lovers wait together on station platforms. In films made prior to *Late Spring*, the young married couple in *There Was a Father* and the reunited couple in *A Story of Floating Weeds* are shown riding on trains in each film's final sequence, and the young lovers in *A Story of Floating Weeds* meet near the train tracks and watch a passing train. Given these associations, one is perhaps surprised to find Noriko and her father on the train in *Late Spring*. Yet the twist makes perfect sense, for the film's central emotional tension arises from Noriko's oedipal feelings for her father. The purity of these characters precludes any suggestion of incest, but oedipal psychology is straightforwardly described by Sobiya at the end of the film when he tells Noriko she must transfer her love for him to a new man because that is how life goes on.

The train ride ends in Tokyo, where Noriko accidentally meets Sobiya's friend Onodera. He suggests that they go to an art exhibit in Ueno, but Noriko says she has to buy needles. Ozu then cuts to a close-up of the poster for the exhibit, a shot of the same poster with the museum steps behind it, a close-up of a lantern outside a restaurant, then Noriko and Onodera sitting at the restaurant's bar. No mention is made of the exhibit, but Noriko says how much she enjoyed going to Ueno Park, implying that they went to the exhibit after all. Onodera tells her that he has remarried, which Noriko finds distasteful.

Instead of introducing a scene in the museum, the two shots of the exhibition poster stand in for the trip there, which seems to have little importance for the story and is never mentioned again. This elision indicates that Ozu indeed omits what is unimportant for *his* story and neither leaves out important events nor needlessly prolongs unimportant ones. (Kristin Thompson sees both the inclusion of the bicycle scene and the omission of Noriko's wedding as examples of these tendencies,[15] but both can and will be explained in terms of the narration Ozu is trying to give us.)

The bar scene functions rather like the twin bar scenes in *End of Summer*, for it is paired with another in the same bar at the end of the film, in which Sobiya confesses to Noriko's friend Aya that he never intended to remarry but lied about it to push Noriko into marrying. Thus the debate on the propriety of remarriage, which began in the first bar scene and over which Noriko has expended so much emotional energy, is closed in the second bar scene. (When one considers that both the elision of the baseball game in *Autumn Afternoon* and the twin bar scenes in *End of Summer* have their origins in the elision of the exhibition and the twin bar scenes in *Late Spring* and yet are used much more complexly, one is forced to conclude that far from "fossilizing" [Burch] in his late films, Ozu's narrative strategies continued to grow richer and more complicated throughout this thirteen-year period.)

Noriko brings Onodera home with her, and he remarks to her father that she should be thinking about marriage. The scene ends with Onodera, apparently on a whim, asking the direction of the ocean and making several incorrect attempts to point in the right direction. Cued by Onodera's question, the next shot pictures the ocean. It has nothing to do with Onodera, however, but begins a lengthy sequence in which Noriko and Hattori bicycle by the sea. They appear to be on a date. On the narrative rather than the associative level, not the ocean but Onodera's concern that Noriko should marry links this scene to the one before it. Later, hearing of the bicycle trip, Noriko's father asks if she wouldn't like to marry Hattori, whereupon she informs him (and us) that Hattori is already engaged.

At this point we wonder why Ozu has wasted so much time on the "wrong man." The scene by the ocean appears totally superfluous, yet a closer look reveals it as central to the film. For one thing, it establishes an important aspect of Noriko's character: she tells Hattori she is "the jealous type," a characteristic neither he nor we are inclined to credit to her since she appears a paragon of good nature. Subsequent events prove her right, however, for she reacts angrily to her father's admission that he plans to remarry. Her jealousy goads her into her own marriage and is thus the pivot on which the plot turns.

When her father suggests Hattori as a match, Noriko bursts out laughing. The joke is on him and on us and is reprised toward the end of the film when Hattori brings his wedding picture to the Sobiya house. Not finding the family at home, he leaves it with the maid, who remarks to the gardener, "I thought he was going to marry Miss Noriko." The humor has a darker side, however, because Ozu makes it clear that Hattori *should* have married Noriko. She admits to her father that Hattori would make a good husband, and subsequent to the bicycling scene, she meets him in a coffee shop, where he asks her to accompany him to a concert for which he has already purchased two tickets. Beginning to find their friendship awkward, she declines. He goes to the concert alone, placing his hat on the empty seat beside him. The camera holds on a close-up of the hat for about four seconds, then cuts to Noriko walking down the sidewalk alone and disconsolate.

The man Noriko marries never appears in the film, although he is "represented" by the meter man, whose voice we hear early in the film, for Noriko later tells Aya that her suitor looks like the meter man (*denkiyasan*). Significantly, however, it is Hattori who helps the man find a stool and Hattori whom we watch, while the meter man remains largely off camera. Noriko's actual wedding is elided, but as Sobiya's friend Hattori is present during the wedding preparations, standing in for the groom he will never be.

Ozu is not simply teasing by always showing us "the wrong man." Hattori is the "right man"; that he and Noriko miss each other because of the rigidity of Japanese marriage customs is meant to be seen as lamentable. Ozu was less subtle in *An Autumn Afternoon,* where both young people express deep disappointment at having missed the opportunity to marry one another. In most of Ozu's films, young men and women choose their own spouses; only in *Late Spring* and *Autumn Afternoon* do they resort to *miai* marriages. In this respect Ozu did not reflect the dominant trend in his society, in which *miai* marriage still predominated greatly over *renai* marriage.[16]

In pre-Meiji Japan, marriages based on individual choice and mutual attraction prevailed among commoners, but after the Restoration, the samurai code spread downward and *miai* marriage became an almost universal practice. *Renai* marriage came to be seen as a Western import. Significantly, Hattori's association with Noriko is often accompanied by references to Western culture: the Coca-Cola sign near the beach, on which the camera holds for ten seconds; the "Balboa Tea and Coffee" sign, which introduces the scene in the coffee shop; and the Western orchestral concert which Hattori attends.

Although all of Ozu's films reflect a synthesis between traditional Japanese and Western culture, *Late Spring* is the only one to set up so clear-cut a dialectic between them and by extension between *renai* and *miai*. Hattori, who represents the unclaimed possibility of *renai,* and Aya, the divorcée, are associated with the West. Aya lives in a Western-style house, and Noriko serves her tea Western-style. Noriko's father and aunt, who arrange the *omiai,* are associated with traditional Japan: the tea ceremony, the Noh play, the Zen garden at Ryoanji, the Kiomizu temple in Kyoto, and the Tsurugaoka Hachimangu shrine in Kamakura. These are appealing enough, but the father's justification of marriage on traditional terms, while full of wisdom, is rather grim. He not only states that one marries not for happiness but to keep human life going, he also confides that his own wife had a hard time adjusting to marriage and often wept in their early years. The film holds out the hope that Noriko may be able to synthesize *miai* and *renai,* for she appears charmed by her suitor, who plays basketball and may or may not look like Gary Cooper. But in the end we are brought back to an awareness of the relentlessness of the life cycle, which Western culture does not adequately acknowledge: we see Sobiya the night after the wedding, alone and desolate; the shot of the ocean is reprised. Symbolic of life's ebbing and flowing, it now assumes its proper significance.

Equinox Flower is the fourth marriage film, and in it a conflict breaks out between a father and daughter over whether she should be allowed to marry a man of her own choosing. Forced to concede, ostensibly because of a trick his daughter's pert friend plays on him, the father, Hirayama, is finally reconciled with his daughter in the film's last moments.

Ozu has said that the film is principally about the parents, and, indeed, the daughter Setsuko appears in only six of the film's twenty-five scenes, and in one of these she merely waves from a rowboat in extreme long shot. Young women as a group, however, constitute a major force in the film and counterbalance the weight given to Hirayama. Three in addition to Setsuko have major roles, and all play opposite Hirayama most of the time: Hisako, Hirayama's younger daughter, who, too young to marry, insists she will want to choose her own husband; Yukiko, Setsuko's friend from Kyoto, who seeks Hirayama's advice on marriage and tricks him into consenting to Setsuko's wedding; and Fumiko, the daughter of Hirayama's colleague Mikami, who, unable to obtain her father's consent to marry the man she loves, lives with him out of wedlock.

The film's title refers both to Hirayama and to the young women he must contend with. *Higanbana*, literally translated as "equinox flower," is a red amaryllis that blooms in September at the time of the autumnal equinox. As in *Autumn Afternoon* and *Late Autumn*, the season refers to the parents' generation. The color red, however, refers to the four young women. In Japan red is a color associated with festive occasions and with children, but most specifically with girls, whose holiday kimonos are red and pink, in contrast to the blue, green, and brown that boys wear. Young unmarried women continue to wear red and pink freely, and red appears in the headdress of the bride's traditional wedding garb and in the lining of the outer wedding kimono. At the time Ozu made this film, red was still considered inappropriate for married women to wear, however.

The color red crops up throughout *Equinox Flower*, particularly in the Hirayamas' red teakettle, perhaps in reference to the quartet of young women, two of whom (Hisako and Yukiko) are often costumed in red. It is hard to insist upon this, however, since Ozu was apparently very fond of red and used it extensively in both *Floating Weeds* and *An Autumn Afternoon*.

Like a number of Ozu's late films, *Equinox Flower* opens with references to trains. A shot of Tokyo Central Station from the front is followed by a long shot of the station from the back taken from across the many tracks that converge there. Next we see a close-up of one platform's time and destination sign as the numbers flip over to indicate that a train has just left, then an unidentified wedding party sending off the bride and groom on their honeymoon. Next, two station workers discuss the large number of brides they have seen that day. The connection between trains and marriage is made particularly obvious here. The train taking the bride on her honeymoon literally takes her into a new life, a journey from childhood to adulthood. (Equally obvious is the close-up which ends the sequence: a track sign reads "Warning Strong Winds Expected." The station workers comment on the predicted bad weather, but two scenes later a character says, "I'm glad the weatherman was wrong," indicating that the storm held off. The storm that comes, of course, is Hirayama's outrage at his daughter's engagement.)

The next scene begins with a view down a long corridor (passageway). A bride crosses the end of it on her way to another room, associatively connecting this scene to the last. Over the shots that follow, we hear a priest chanting and see the guests at the wedding, including Hirayama, his wife, and their friend Horie. A full shot of the priest follows and then one of Kawai, friend of Hirayama and father of the bride. As go-between, Hirayama is asked to make a speech. His acting as go-between was only a formality, it seems, since he notes appreciatively in his speech that the young couple actually made their own match.

The scene functions in several ways. It introduces Hirayama and his cohort and, by introducing them well before we meet the younger set, establishes them as the film's main focus. The wedding serves further as a substitute for Setsuko's wedding, which takes place at the end of the film, but which we never see. (The rural wedding procession at the end of Early Summer similarly substitutes for the heroine's wedding, which is never shown.) That the wedding we see in Equinox Flower has resulted from a love match links it even more closely with Setsuko's wedding and helps to set up Hirayama's hypocrisy, which is revealed later on.

Substitution works on other narrative levels as well in Equinox Flower. Yukiko substitutes for Setsuko, not in a metaphoric way but within the actual story. Hirayama has the heart-to-heart talks with her that he ought to be having with his own daughter, and at the end of the film she literally substitutes herself for Setsuko by representing Setsuko's problem to Hirayama as though it were her own—and getting, as anticipated, a much more sympathetic response.

Equinox Flower appears to climax when Hirayama, tricked into consenting to the wedding, also agrees to attend it, having vowed not to. Setsuko bursts into tears at the good news, but the scene does not end there. Rather, it ends with Hirayama still voicing his doubts: "I never thought she'd defy me," he says to his wife when they are alone. "She made this vital decision without letting her parents know. It's not right."

We then cut to Hirayama's class reunion at Gamagori, which Kawai has mentioned earlier in the film. The reunion scene is a long one, and several minutes of it are devoted to Mikami singing part of an epic poem. In his lengthy essay on Equinox Flower, Edward Branigan dismisses this scene as irrelevant to the plot,[17] while Donald Richie intuits that it "seems to suggest an importance beyond itself, as though it were somehow commenting on the film as a whole,"[18] but he fails to find the connection. In fact, this scene is the film's emotional center, the point at which we come to understand and sympathize with Hirayama.

Previous to this, our assessment of Hirayama has been largely negative. He seems distant from his family, unfair to Setsuko, hypocritical in his standards, and stubborn. His jocularity with Yukiko is appealing, but it further underscores his unfairness to Setsuko. When his wife accuses him of inconsistency, he fumes, "Then everyone is inconsistent, except God!"

The scene at Gamagori centers on the poem about Kusunoki Masahige that Mikami recites. In the fourteenth century, with Japan largely under the control of the Ashikaga shogunate, Kusunoki remained loyal to the emperor and won a number of important battles for him. In 1336, vastly outnumbered, the emperor insisted Kusunoki join battle with the opposing forces. His troops eventually vanquished, he committed suicide rather than face capture. The poem begins, "The precepts of my father lie buried deep in memory. The edicts of the emperor I'll follow faithfully." It then describes what the edicts are: to fight for the emperor and to die to the last man if necessary. Ancient though the poem may be, it describes the ethical standards with which this generation of schoolboys grew up. Remembering that during World War II most Japanese expected to die by suicide rather than surrender, one realizes that the inconsistencies Hirayama's wife accuses him of are embedded in the Great Inconsistency of twentieth-century Japan: after the bombing of Hiroshima and Nagasaki, the emperor reversed the centuries-old edict and told the Japanese that Japan would surrender but they should *not* commit suicide. Significantly, the young man Setsuko marries has been transferred to Hiroshima. Hiroshima changed Japan forever, and in order to be reconciled with Setsuko, Hirayama must travel to Hiroshima, i.e., acknowledge that Japan has changed.

David Bordwell sees the scene as part of an ongoing schema of nostalgia, eventually undermined, that is present in most of Ozu's postwar films.[19] While this analysis comes closer than any previous one to appreciating the significance of the scene, it fails to justify the scene's length or recognize its centrality to the film's story. After this scene, Mikami tells Hirayama that he has been reconciled with Fumiko. The reconciliation has taken place earlier in the story, but only after Gamagori do we learn about it. Subsequently, Hirayama is reconciled with Setsuko. It is as if by recognizing his own values as rooted in past, largely repudiated traditions, Hirayama is freed to accept and accommodate the present.

The Gamagori scene is nevertheless deeply poignant. When Mikami finishes his recitation, the group sings a popular ballad about Kusunoki: "Twilight is a time of sorrow and grief: the warrior ponders what the world is coming to."

The image here describes Hirayama, particularly as summed up by the previous scene's last shot, in which he ponders, confused and perplexed, Setsuko's flouting of his authority. Hirayama is entering his twilight (autumn) years and, played by Saburi Shin, best known for his samurai roles, he is very much the disillusioned warrior described in the song. Once again Ozu's apparent "transgression"—a static scene with little seeming relevance—turns out to be the pivot for the film's dramatic and thematic structure.

As we know, Tokyo Story is about the decline of the Japanese family, and since even Ozu characterizes it as such,[20] it must be so. Ozu's endorsement notwithstanding, however, this view requires qualification. For one thing, the film's family has, by traditional standards, disintegrated long before the film opens. Two sons have left home to work in large cities, and a third has been killed in the war. (Presumably he too had left home before his death, since his wife lives in Tokyo.)

Two female characters are contrasted in the film, the daughter Shige and the daughter-in-law Noriko. Shige finds her parents' visit burdensome and is insensitive and rude toward them. Noriko, who has far less means, welcomes them and treats them kindly. I believe that Ozu means us to read their different treatment of the parents as arising from their different characters. However, in some respects, their behavior corresponds with what was expected in the traditional Japanese family more than it deviates from it. Certainly Shige lacks filial piety, always deviant by traditional standards, but as a married daughter she is no longer part of her parents' family and has few obligations toward them. This is why a girl's marriage is (traditionally) so traumatic for a Japanese family, and why only girls' marriages are at issue in Ozu's films. When the father comments that "a married daughter is like a stranger," he is restating a cliché of traditional family life. On the other hand, a daughter-in-law, even a widowed one, is more obligated to her husband's family than to her natal family, and Noriko fulfills these traditional obligations. That the parents are truly touched by her kindness indicates that they really don't expect the standards of traditional family life to apply anymore.

More than the decline of the Japanese family, Tokyo Story is about the inroads time makes on human relationships, and finally on human life itself. Time and distance have caused the children to grow away from their parents. Ultimately they are as disappointed as the parents to find that the filial bonds have stretched so thin. "No one can serve his parents beyond the grave," mourns the youngest son, Keizo, at his mother's funeral. Their regret is not merely conditioned by a culture that has idealized these bonds, but is one most children who live far from their parents experience. Even Noriko cannot dam time with tradition. She tells the father, "Sometimes I feel that I just cannot go on like this. Sometimes at night I lie and wonder what will become of me if I stay this way [unmarried, faithful to the dead son]." She tells the unmarried daughter Kyoko, who still lives at home and can't understand her siblings' self-ishness, "I may become like that. In spite of myself."

The parents experience disillusionment not simply because they are victims of a particular social problem, the decline of the Japanese family, but because in Ozu's films, disillusionment is a condition of old age. In *Tokyo Story,* not only the protagonists Tomi and Shukichi are disappointed in their children; Shukichi's friend Numata is disappointed too. In *Early Spring* and *Ohayo,* retire-ment has disappointed the old men. The old teacher in *An Autumn Afternoon* has had neither a successful retirement nor a successful child. "Children don't live up to their parents' expectations," says Shukichi in *Tokyo Story.* "Let's think they are better than most." He echoes the parents in *Early Summer,* who insist that they have been happy and that their lives have been better than most and yet look sadly out over the fields surrounding the ancestral home to which they have returned.

Like many of the late films, *Tokyo Story* begins with a montage of symbols for passing time, but unlike those films, which generally use only one symbol in the opening montage—the train station in *Late Spring* and *Equinox Flower,* smokestacks in *Autumn Afternoon,* the ocean in *Early Summer*—*Tokyo Story* incorporates trains, boats, the sea, and smoke all in the film's five opening shots, which run as follows:

I: The sound of a boat chugging over a close-up of a stone lantern with Onomichi's harbor in the background.

II: Chugging continues over a shot of children walking to school.

III: A train moves through town across the bay, seen through the rooftops of Onomichi.

IV: The train close-up.

V: Long shot of the temple with the stone lantern: smoke comes out of a chimney; a train whistle sounds.

Finally we join Tomi and Shukichi, who are packing for a journey—by train, of course. They talk about the train schedule, and over the scene we hear a ticking clock, which they have packed with their belongings. The scene ends with a shot of smokestacks, a train whistle over it, and two shots of the station platform.

The symbols are insistent and seem to be most closely associated with Tomi's death, for the shots of the harbor recur just before and after her death. As she lays dying, Ozu cuts to a shot of the boats in the harbor, then to a moth fluttering around a light, an obvious symbol for impending death. In the scene that follows, the oldest son, a doctor, tells the family that Tomi will not live much longer. A montage paralleling the opening sequence follows:

- The empty boat landing in the harbor.
- The stone lantern from shot I.
- Sailboats tied up.
- The sidewalk from shot II without the children.
- The train tracks from shot IV without the train.

Back at the house, Tomi has died. Ostensibly the harbor, the tracks, and the sidewalk are empty and the boats are tied up because it is only daybreak; but their emptiness tells us that the transient life they signaled earlier has ended, at least for one person. Similar shots showing the harbor active once again are reprised at the end of the film, intercut with Noriko taking the train, perhaps to a new life, and Shukichi left to carry on alone.

As in most of the films I've discussed, train symbolism is central to *Tokyo Story* and is most prominently displayed in the scenes right before Tomi's death: when the family waits in the Tokyo train station with the old couple and in the sequence that follows when they stop over in Osaka. Ozu gives their youngest son a job with the railroad so that the stopover, occasioned by the onset of Tomi's illness, can be filled with references to trains. The trains associated with marriage in *Late Spring* and *Equinox Flower* are here associated with death (as was the train whistle in *End of Summer*).

Bridging the marriage and the death films, *Early Spring* describes the disintegration and resurrection of a couple's marriage. In contrast to the other films under discussion, the tension here is between the husband and wife rather than between parents and children. (In this respect it resembles *Hen in the Wind* [1948]; but whereas that film focused on the politics of betrayal, this one, like all the late films considered here, focuses on passing time.) In 1958 Ozu expressed disappointment in American critics who applauded *Tokyo Story* but failed to appreciate *Early Spring*. "Foreigners . . . only follow the story. They cannot understand the life of salaried men, ephemerality, and the atmosphere outside of the story at all."[21] The story of *Early Spring*, in which Sugiyama, an office worker bored with the monotony of his life, has an affair with a fellow commuter, is narrated more straightforwardly than is usual for Ozu, but the narration is filled with references to passing time: "ephemerality and the atmosphere outside of the story."

Many of the story events refer to disillusionment, old age, and death—uncharacteristically the death of the young. The Sugiyamas' only child has died some years before the film opens, war buddies recall fallen comrades, and a young man, Sugiyama's friend and fellow worker, dies after a long illness. Two older men, one who has retired and opened a bar and one who still works for the company, discuss the disillusionment that lifelong service to a big company brings. The Sugiyamas' resolve to maintain their marriage (which began as a love match) stems from their recognizing love and fidelity as their only hedge against ephemerality, the only possible constants in an inconstant world that brings mainly death and disappointment, even to the young.

As in his other films, Ozu makes many visual references to passing time: bridges, smoke, steam, and empty corridors. Again trains are central. The husband's girlfriend is one of a group of young workers who commute together. Thus the train is literally the vehicle which, over the course of time, erodes the marriage. At the end of the film, the husband is transferred to a small industrial outpost where tall smokestacks and the railway running past the factory are major motifs. His wife joins him there, and after explaining why she decided to come back to him, she points out a passing train. The next shots are their point of view of the train with a smokestack prominently in view, a two-shot of them standing and looking outside, a shot of them from behind, still looking out, a long shot of the smokestacks with the train disappearing in the background, and finally a medium shot of a single smokestack. Helpless against time's passing, they can at least help one another.

Ozu's symbols of mutability and passage have many implications. As the Sugiyamas watch the train here, they speak longingly of an eventual return to Tokyo: passing time can also bring good things. One young couple in the film is expecting a baby. However, the implications of passing time in this film are mainly negative and link it to the "death films"—*End of Summer* and *Tokyo Story*. The smokestacks at the end of *Early Spring* return at the end of *End of Summer* as those of the crematorium.

Balanced between the marriage and the death films, *Early Spring* is a reminder that Ozu connects marriage and death in obvious and subtle ways in most of his late films. One strategy is linking weddings and funerals. During the wedding scene at the beginning of *Equinox Flower,* the chanting of the priest dominates the sound track. Such chanting figures prominently in the funeral service in *Tokyo Story* and in the seven-year [after death] memorial service in *Late Autumn.* In *Equinox Flower* the priest is in the same room with the wedding guests, who are chatting until Hirayama is asked to make his go-between speech. Normally the go-between makes his speech at the wedding reception, not the ceremony, and the *bonze* chants only during the ceremony. Ozu has collapsed the ceremony and the reception together, probably to include the chanting and thus create a parallel to a funeral service. Later he underscores the connection when Hirayama tells his wife not to put away his formal clothes because he needs them the next day for a funeral. "Wedding one day, funeral the next," she says (so that we won't miss the point). Similarly, at the end of *Autumn Afternoon* the father enters a bar after his daughter's wedding and is asked if he's just come from a funeral. "Something like that," he replies. *Late*

Autumn begins with the seven-year ceremony for the dead father and ends with the daughter's wedding.

The comparison between weddings and funerals is not merely a clever device on Ozu's part, but is so fundamental a concept in Japanese culture that these ceremonies as well as those surrounding births have built-in similarities. Both new babies and corpses are dressed in pure white kimonos, and correspondingly a bride in a traditional wedding wears a pure white kimono under her heavily embroidered outer robe. The symbolism indicates that she dies to her natal family—the wedding *is* like a funeral for that family—and is reborn into a new family. Falling between birth and death, marriage, according to anthropologist Joy Hendry, is "the vital link in the sequence, at once associated with the birth of the next generation and the death of the previous one."[22] The elegiac melancholy Ozu evokes at the end of *Late Spring, Late Autumn,* and *An Autumn Afternoon* arises only partly because the parents have been left alone. The father in *Autumn Afternoon,* for example, is not entirely alone; his youngest son still lives with him. The sadness arises because the marriage of the younger generation inevitably reflects on the mortality of the older generation.

A deep identification with the life cycle inheres in Japanese culture as well as in Ozu's films and accounts, perhaps, for the "inherent Japaneseness" many viewers sense in them. But whether or not his late films are "inherently Japanese," they are deeply philosophical, built around an awareness of the give-and-take of the life cycle and man's inability to do anything about it. Their subject matter is not "banal"; nor are they empty of meaning and full of immobilized "codes,"[23] tabulae rasae on which Ozu performed artistic feats at the expense of narrative coherence. Rather, the narratives unfold with an astounding precision in which no shot and certainly no scene is wasted and all is overlayered with an intricate web of interlocking meaning.

NOTES

1. Donald Richie, *Ozu* (Berkeley: U of California P, 1974), p. 237; Yamamoto Kikuo, "Footsteps," in Paul Schrader, *Seinaru eiga* (Tokyo, 1981), p. 282.

2. Richie, *Ozu,* p. 248.

3. *To the Distant Observer: Form and Meaning in the Japanese Cinema* (Berkeley: U of California P, 1979), p. 276.

4. *Narration in the Fiction Film* (Madison: U of Wisconsin P, 1985), p. 200.

5. *Narration in the Fiction Film,* p. 288.

6. Bordwell, *Narration in the Fiction Film,* p. 282.

7. *Ozu,* p. 19.

8. Donald Richie, "The Late Films of Yasujiro Ozu," *Film Quarterly* 13, 1 (Fall 1959): 21.

9. Bordwell goes into the circle motifs in *End of Summer* in great detail but insists that their only interest for Ozu was their formal patterning. See *Ozu and the Poetics of Cinema* (Princeton: Princeton UP, 1988), p. 368.

10. See Cooper-Hewitt Museum, *MA: Space-Time in Japan*, exhibit catalog (New York, n.d.), and Gunther Nitschke, "MA: The Japanese Sense of Place," *Architectural Design* 36, 1 (March 1966): 143.

11. Ozu uses this void structure in *Late Spring* and *An Autumn Afternoon* when he shows the empty room of the daughter/bride after she has left for the wedding.

12. "Space and Narrative in the Films of Ozu," *Screen* 17, 2 (Summer 1976): 51.

13. *Questions of Cinema* (Bloomington: Indiana UP, 1981), pp. 61–62.

14. *Ozu*, pp. 165–166.

15. Kristin Thompson, *Breaking the Glass Armor* (Princeton: Princeton UP, 1988), p. 343.

16. Bordwell in *Ozu and the Poetics of Cinema*, pp. 307–308, argues that *Late Spring* depicts new, liberal views of marriage and is therefore reflective of the new, liberalized Occupation values. But in fact Ozu's position here, allowing Noriko a *miai* marriage, is much more conservative than that of both previous and subsequent films. Even in the wartime *There Was a Father*, the young couple know and love one another before they marry. (See also Thompson, *Breaking the Glass Armor*, pp. 320–326.)

17. "The Space of *Equinox Flower*," *Screen* 17, 2 (Summer 1976): 82.

18. *Ozu*, p. 44.

19. *Ozu and the Poetics of Cinema*, pp. 346–347.

20. "Ozu on Ozu: The Talkies," *Cinema* (USA) 6, 1 (1970): 4.

21. Yamamoto, "Postscript," in *Seinaru eiga*, p. 282.

22. *Marriage in Changing Japan* (London: Croom Helm, 1981), p. 235.

23. Branigan, "*Equinox Flower*," pp. 81ff.

The Inn Sequence from Ozu's *Late Autumn*

Donald Richie

Ozu Yasujiro's *Late Autumn* (*Akibiyori,* 1960) is in many ways a reworking of the director's earlier film *Late Spring* (*Banshun,* 1949). Both have to do with family relationships and the cycle of life itself, quintessential Ozu themes; both have to do with the subject of marriage, and a daughter's reluctance to leave her widowed parent. In the latter film the central relationship is between daughter and father; in the former, it is between daughter and mother. In both films the daughter ultimately marries, but her happiness, and that of her parent, is tempered by the knowledge that something has been lost forever. In analyzing the inn sequence from *Late Autumn,* Donald Richie focuses on one of the most moving episodes in the film: the last time that mother and daughter are together before the marriage takes place. Transcribing the sequence from the film, and illustrating it with stills, Richie takes us on a journey into the world of Ozu, pointing out how the director's articulation of space invariably emphasizes one thing: each shot as a pictorial unit in its own right. This notion of the shot acquires immediate and special meaning when later in the essay Richie recounts what he saw on the set when the sequence was shot. As Richie points out, Ozu's style of abstentious formal rigor is not meant to involve us in the emotions of the scene but to "inform" us of those emotions, and lead us to a deeper understanding.

For further reading, see Audie Bock, *Japanese Film Directors* (Tokyo: Kodansha, 1978), pp. 69–98; David Bordwell, *Ozu and the Poetics of Cinema* (Princeton: Princeton UP, 1988); Kathe Geist, "Yasujiro Ozu: Notes on a Retrospective," *Film Quarterly* 37 (Fall 1983): 2–9; John Gillett and David Wilson, eds., *Yasujiro Ozu: A Critical Anthology* (London: British Film Institute, 1976); Donald Richie, *Ozu* (Berkeley: U of California P, 1974); Donald Richie, "Viewing

Japanese Film: Some Considerations," *East-West Film Journal* 1 (December 1986): 23–35; Martin Rubin, "*Late Autumn (Akibiyori)*," in *Magill's Survey of Cinema: Foreign Language Films*, ed. Frank N. Magill (Englewood Cliffs, N.J.: Salem Press, 1985), Vol. 2, pp. 1739–1744; Paul Schrader, *Transcendental Style in Film: Ozu, Bresson, Dreyer* (Berkeley: U of California P, 1972); Kristin Thompson and David Bordwell, "Space and Narrative in the Films of Ozu," *Screen* 17 (Summer 1976): 41–73; and Don Willis, "Yasujiro Ozu: Emotion and Contemplation," *Sight and Sound* 48 (Winter 1978/79): 44–49.

In Ozu Yasujiro's 1960 film *Late Autumn* (*Akibiyori*), there occurs in the tenth reel a seven-minute sequence in an inn in Ikaho, a popular hot-springs resort. Here Akiko and her daughter Ayako have come for a few days' rest, staying at an inn run by Shukichi, the elder brother of Akiko's dead husband.

Earlier, in reel four, there had been talk of going on a trip together. Akiko remembered a last trip with her husband to an inn at Chuzenji. Then the talk turned to just the two of them, Akiko and Ayako, going to Ikaho. And Akiko added: "Moshi ii hito dekita" meaning, "Just before the daughter gets married." Now Ayako's marriage is arranged, and they are indeed on their last trip together.

The sequence is as follows:

The Script (Translation)		The Film (Description)		
Shot No.	Description/Sound/ Dialogue	Shot No.	Added Description	Plate
96	Entrance to the inn, people going in and out.	1	Entrance to the inn: Ryokan Tawaraya; people passing.	
97	Inside, a corridor: girl students running noisily past, some in uniform, some in *nemaki* sleeping kimono. Sounds, footsteps, masseur's footsteps, girls singing.	2	Corridor, people passing bathers, masseur, girl students.	1
98	Guest room, *genkan* entryway; interior, ten-mat room, *futon* already spread; in adjoining eight-mat	3	From second floor, looking across court, two floors of inn visible, girl students in rooms, etc.	2

room are Akiyo and Ayako. Sounds: tea-drinking.			
Shukichi. Sounds of girl students.	4	From farther away, bedding visible.	3
Shukichi: *Aya-chan, aren't you getting sleepy?* Ayako: *No, not yet.* Shukichi: *It's crowded today. Might be a bit noisy.*	5	Reverse. Bedding visible. Beyond, Ayako, Akiko, Shukichi.	4
Akiko: *Whenever we went to the Nikko inns, they were always full of school excursions.* (To Aya) *Isn't that so?*	6	Akiko.	5
Ayako: (Smiles and nods) *Someone even came into our room by mistake.*	7	Ayako.	6
Shukichi: *Is that so? Then you can't have gotten much rest.*	8	Shukichi.	7
Akiko: *But it was a nice trip.*	9	Akiko.	
Shukichi: *Well, that was nice.* In the corridor, the voice of the maid.	10	All three.	8
Maid: *Excuse me.* Sound: door being opened. Maid: *Master, the teacher in charge of the student group is waiting for you at the reception desk.*	11	Door. It is opened. Maid appears.	
Shukichi: *Really? All right, I'll come.*	12	Shukichi.	
Maid closes door. Sound: door closing.	13	Maid closes door.	
Shukichi: *Well, it's turned out all right. Ayako-san here gets a nice bridegroom and you* (to Akiko), *you'll be having some changes too.*	14	Shukichi.	
Akiko looks down at her hands.	15	Akiko.	
Shukichi: *Frankly, so far as I'm concerned, I've been more worried about you than about Ayako.*	16	Shukichi.	

	Akiko: *I appreciate your thinking of me.*	17	Akiko.	
	Shukichi: *Well, it turned out all right. You two, rest well now.*	18	Shukichi.	
	They bow in silence. He goes. Sound: *hayashi* music.	19	All three. Silence. Then the sound of distant festival music.	9
	Akiko: *Good night.* Ayako: *Good night.* Shukichi: *Good night.* Sound: door closing.			
	Akiko: *Shall we go to bed?*			
	Akiko gets up and goes to the next room. Ayako remains, opens her book. Sound: pages turning.	20	Reverse. Two of them. Balcony across court seen.	
99	Interior room. Akiko sits on the *futon*. She seems to be thinking. The sounds of the schoolgirls die away. Akiko: *Aya-chan, won't you come over here?*	21	Akiko.	10
100	Front room. Ayako puts down her book, stands up.	22	Ayako.	
101	Interior room. Ayako comes and sits on her *futon*.	23	The two of them.	11
	Ayako: *It's quiet, isn't it? The schoolgirls must already be asleep. School excursions were always fun, but when the last evening came and we had to leave the next day—that was never very nice. We used to think, well, it's all over. We felt awful. Mother, did you ever feel anything like that?*	24	Ayako.	12
	* * *	25	Akiko.	
	What is it?	26	Ayako.	13
	* * *			
	What's happened?			

Akiko: *Aya-chan, you once said that if I got married again it would be a dirty thing to do.*	27	Akiko.	14
Ayako: *Oh, let's forget about that. I'm sorry I ever said anything as awful as that.*	28	Ayako.	
Akiko: *But I think the same as you.*	29	The two of them.	15

Ayako: * * * *

Akiko: *I think I will not remarry.*

Ayako: *But, mother . . .*

Akiko: *No, father was enough for me. I'll just go on living with him. That is enough for me. To be starting all over again now . . . No, I've really had enough.*

Ayako: *But, mother.*	30	Ayako.
Akiko: *No, it's all right. You shouldn't worry about me anymore. You must marry Goto-san. If you are together with someone you love, then nothing could be better for you.* *Even if you were to forget all about me. That would be all right, too. I won't be lonely.*	31	Akiko.
Ayako: *But, mother. You all alone in that apartment.*	32	Ayako.
Akiko: *No. If the two of us continued living in that apartment. . . . That is no kind of life for you. You're still young. You don't know what kind of happiness is waiting for you. So, you must go and marry Goto-san. Mother is mother. She'll manage somehow.*	33	Akiko.

16

	Ayako: * * *	34	Ayako.	
	Akiko: *So you do that, and don't think I lied in order to make you go.*	35	Akiko.	17
	Ayako: * * * (sound of sniffling)	36	Ayako.	18
	Akiko: *You've understood? You've really understood?*	37	Akiko.	19
	Ayako covers her face with both hands. We hear her crying.	38	Ayako.	20
	Akiko: *What a nice trip we've had.*	39		21
	(She wipes her eyes.)	40	The two of them, Ayako crying.	22
	In the rooms the lights are out. The night continues. Festival music far away.	41	The darkened rooms across the court.	23
102	Outside the window, morning. Bright sunshine, mountain, covered with maple.	42	Morning, the mountain.	24
		43	The rooms across the way, girl students gone, a maid sweeping.	25
		44	Mount Haruna.	26

As in many of Ozu's sequences, space is articulated in series of shots by a typical movement which progresses into the area of movement and then away from it. Here, shots 1–3 indicate that the action takes place in a resort hotel (plates 1–2). Shot 4 (plate 3) is a transition between the general and the particular locations.

At the end of the sequence a similar movement, this time from particular to general, is usually to be observed. Here it is shots 41–44 (plates 24–26). After the shot of the two, Ayako weeping, the sequence continues with a shot similar in all ways to 3 (plate 2) except that the lights are now off. This is followed by a shot of the mountain near where the inn is located (shot 42, plate 24) and is followed by a further shot of the rooms across the way (shot 43, plate 25). This is in all ways similar to shots 3 and 41 except that it is morning, the guests are gone, and the maid is sweeping out. Then (shot 44, plate 26) the mountain is shown again, this time serving as transition to the location of the next sequence.

This movement (general-particular-general) is one which Ozu often describes, and it matches a like movement once the film has moved to the particu-

Plate 1

Plate 2

Plate 3

Plate 4

Plate 5

Plate 6

Plate 7

Plate 8

Plate 9

Plate 10

Plate 11

Plate 12

Plate 13

Plate 14

Plate 15

Plate 16

Plate 17

Plate 18

Plate 19

Plate 20

Plate 21

Plate 22

Plate 23

Plate 24

Plate 25   Plate 26

lar area of action. Here there is often a general view of the action area and its participants, and this is followed by various shots which bring one after another of these participants into fuller view.

In this sequence, after the shot linking outside and inside space (shot 4, plate 3), there is a reverse shot (bedding visible at the bottom of both frames), and the three characters are seen (shot 5, plate 4). This is followed by three shots of each, introductory as it were (shots 6–8; plates 5–7), followed by another of the protagonist (Akiko—shot 9), and then by another (shot 10, plate 8) of all three. Later Shukichi leaves during such a shot, and the other two remain (shot 19, plate 9). The sequence then continues with shots of the two (Akiko, Ayako), either separately or together. At the end of the sequence the shots are exclusively of the characters individually.

This articulation of space contains a general movement: the general to the particular, an "inward" movement which is "closest" during the heightened conclusion. The effect of such sequences is that viewers are introduced to the milieu and then enter it. After they have observed what occurs, they are, as it were, ushered out and taken to the next location. That they are being shown something, that they are being introduced—this impression is inescapable and perhaps accounts for comments concerning Ozu's formality, even his courtliness, that people behave like hosts and guests in the Ozu film, that so do the spectators.

To be sure, introducing the spectators and showing them something is the occupation of all film directors. Usually, however, not much is made of this. Indeed, the mechanisms are hidden. In Ozu, however, as in Japanese architecture, the structure is visible—intentionally.

If intentionally, then what was Ozu's intention? Or—a question easier to answer—what *didn't* Ozu intend?

He did not intend to draw us into his drama, to use techniques of camera placement and editing to heighten our emotional reactions. He did not intend to influence us in this manner. Rather, he wanted to influence us in another manner.

Ozu in this sequence insists that each shot be perceived as just what it is, a pictorial unit. These are all of near-identical length (longer or shorter, depending upon the length of each part of the conversation). They are further presented as shots in that there is an interval (usually 6 to 8 frames) after each line. Further, each line has its own unit.

We have been drawn closer, it is true, but we view a series of near-identical scenes which are in no overt way designed to involve us emotionally—though this scene is the emotional "core" of the film, and the only one in which the emotions of the principals are shown as uncontrolled (Ayako's weeping).

Critics of Ozu's dramaturgy have complained that sequences such as this are like lantern-slide shows, and the comparison is an apt one. We are shown one pictorial unit after another, and the very sameness of the presentation prevents just the sort of emotional "identification" that the movies are said to be good at.

Further, as in the "still" lantern slide, there is no accommodation. The camera is fixed. It refuses to accommodate. There is absolutely none of the reframing common to contemporary cinema, where the movement of an actor creates a movement of the camera.

(That shots which seem identical are not, that each set-up is really slightly different—compare the position of the striped towel in back of Akiko in plates 10, 14, and 16—is due not to accommodation but to the camera's actually having changed its position, for reasons which are examined in the final section of this essay.)

Characters are obviously not going to be accommodated. The actors must stay within the defined perimeters. Further, they are usually defined compositionally by the interiors they inhabit. Shot follows shot, usually at a steady pace, always photographed with the same lens (50mm, the "silent era" lens), each image looking much like the one before and the one after.

Those who complain about the "lack of freedom" in the Ozu films (director Imamura Shohei among them) are thinking of this effect—and what the actor had to go through to create it. Indeed, for the ordinary Japanese director—trained to think in terms of sequence, encouraged to improvise in realizing it—this kind of cinematic thinking, shot by shot, is baffling and seems to work against the very thing (some kind of "emotional involvement") that he has been taught film is about.

And, to be sure, film is indeed about this (as well as other things), and Ozu achieves this as well. It is that his method is different.

When we watch lantern slides, we give each one a similar degree of attention. They move past us at a fairly uniform rate and create a narrative rhythm which we come to expect. We feel that the photographer is not attempting to divert us (though this may occur as well), but that he is attempting to inform us.

The Ozu style (made of much more than I am imagining here) is that of someone rationally informing. He is not pleading or intimidating—he is informing. And it is through the very limitations of this style that the import is apprehended: low camera position, identical compositions in the frame, a standard rate of progress, large appreciable movements from "general" to "particular," music occurring in almost invariable positions within the sequence (beginning and end, usually), shot following similar shot. One thinks of a structural literary equivalent: the anecdote or even the essay.

Akiko and Ayako have gone off for their last time together. The daughter is going to be married; the mother will be alone. It is a situation fraught with emotion. And it is this emotion which Ozu communicates. Not despite this style, but because of it.

The narrational objectivity and externality, this style which consists of limitations, this right-angle universe—all contribute to emotional apprehension. Ozu, by refusing us the consolation of "naturalism," by insisting upon his own stylistically consistent presentation, returns to us much of the original emotional power of his anecdotes (daughter leaving mother alone), cleans situations, dialogue, character of our accumulated viewing habits.

He has, like a poet (particularly like a "modernist" poet, for Ozu, despite the traditional overtones of the subject matter, is a self-conscious stylist much influenced by popular "modernist" tenets of Japan in the 1920s and '30s), constructed a stylistic "text" which fits (like a glove) what he wants to show. As we read the one—daughter leaving mother alone—we must also read the other: scenes from the same low camera position, all of a length, all of steady rhythms, all similar one to the other.

In a way it is like reading the prose of Gertrude Stein; in a way it is like looking at a painting by Giorgio Morandi. The very apparent simplicity of subject matter, of means, of the very fact of its asking so plainly for no emotional involvement, has the effect of our drawing closer, as it were, of our lending ourselves, and experiencing as though new: a young black girl's life, an arrangement of bottles on a table, a mother being left alone.

The grid through which we see, the text through which we read, far from distancing us, has made us comprehend—not just understand but comprehend. And this is the business of art.

Although I had met Ozu several times, mainly at Shochiku parties, I had never been invited to watch him work. Then one day in early autumn in 1960, Kawakita Kashiko asked if I would like to go watch him film *Late Autumn*.

One of the Ofuna Shochiku studios was completely filled with the large, full-scale set of the Ikaho inn—two eight-mat rooms, beyond them a courtyard, and across the court, the full three floors of the inn wing. When we arrived, Ryu Chishu had already finished his part as Shukichi, the brother-in-law, in the inn sequence and was sitting at the side, watching, as he often did.

Akiko and Ayako (Hara Setsuko and Tsukasa Yoko respectively) were seated across from each other, and filming was continuing. When we arrived, Akiko's side was being taken. Quite literally, Ozu had divided this conversation into sides. The camera was between the two, and Hara Setsuko was facing it.

Ozu's method (at least in this sequence) was to do one side of the conversation, and then the other. Since the only alternate method would have been to turn the camera around for each cut, this method was logical—but Ozu's way of doing it was quite his own.

Each line of dialogue, each scene, was considered a unit in its own right. It was to be shot with reference only to itself. This is quite different from the way scenes such as this are shot elsewhere. While it is common enough for the two sides of a conversation to be filmed separately, usually the director does not stop his camera for each take. The camera records the feed-line and the replies, and the whole is edited for the finished picture.

Ozu, however, carefully recorded each line. His script lay open before him and he used it like a blueprint, constantly referring to it and to the sketches he had made in the margins, one sketch for each line of dialogue.

When he was ready, he nodded at Tsukasa Yoko, to one side, and she would deliver her line of dialogue. "Sutaato," said Ozu ("Start"), and his cameraman, Atsuta Yuharu, squatting behind his machine, would begin filming. The director would then nod at Hara Setsuko and she would say her line. "Cutto," Ozu would say, and Atsuta would stop filming. If Ozu had liked the delivery, he would continue on to the next shot. If he had not, it would be repeated until he did.

One scene finished, one line of dialogue completed, Ozu would begin getting ready for the next. It was, one would think, in all respects identical, but Ozu would nonetheless, often during this sequence, actually reframe. Hara had not moved, yet Ozu, looking through the view-finder, would insist upon half a millimeter to the right or left. The effect of this is often invisible on the screen (though it is sometimes to be noticed—as in Akiko's towel), and was perhaps visible to the director alone.

Then, the reframing completed to his satisfaction, Ozu was ready to go on the next line of dialogue. "You've understood? You've really understood?" Cut. The camera was fiddled with. In reply to a nod from the director, Tsukasa made crying noises. Start. "What a nice trip we've had," said Hara and then wiped her eyes.

This was the end of her side of the conversation. After a break for tea, the camera was reversed, Hara at one side, and all of Tsukasa's lines were filmed. This took the rest of the day. Everyone was exhausted. This way of making a film was, I thought, like climbing a face of sheer rock, one handful after the other, straight up.

When I later saw this sequence, all assembled, in the preview room, I marveled. Here was an assemblage of small segments made over several days at a speed so slow that any idea of tempo or pace or even performance was impossible. Here were scenes of two women talking to no one, reacting to nothing. And yet, up there on the screen, there was life itself—life with its own rhythm, its own pace, its own rarefied reality.

Ozu's calculations as to camera position, camera distance, delivery, timing—everything was there, but it was no longer apparent. It had been transformed. I thought of a pointilist painting—a Seurat I had seen at an exhibition a few days earlier. It was like that. When you view it up close, it is all dots of different colors. It is only when you step back and the dots disappear that the illusion of life is there, up on the canvas, up on the screen.

I remembered Ozu the carpenter, sitting there with his blueprint and fiddling with the camera, fiddling with the performances ("Don't even think about crying," he told Tsukasa. "Just suddenly put your face in your hands—that's quite enough.")

You step back. That is what you do in an Ozu film. And paradoxically it brings you closer. Through the maintenance of distance, intimacy is achieved. Perhaps consequently, the fewer the means, the greater the effect.

Two women, mother and daughter, sitting together in 1960 in an inn at a Japanese hot-springs resort. A five-minute conversation in which nothing much gets said. And it is as though one has comprehended filial affection for the first time, as though some deep, hidden pattern has been made visible, as though you have seen the great wheel of time slowly turning.

Part Two

Genre

The Samurai Film

Lisa Spalding and
David Desser

Beginning in the 1920s, when the Japanese film industry had organized itself into a group of major film studios devoted to the routine production of genre films, two major categories of films arose: *jidai-geki* and *gendai-geki*. These corresponded to the broad epochs in which the films within these classifications were set: *jidai,* or period films, denoting stories set before 1868 (the date of the Meiji Restoration), and *gendai,* or contemporary films, denoting stories set after this date. These two classifications followed a pattern of classifying types of plays in both the Noh and Kabuki/Bunraku canons, although the classifications used in the theatrical modes tended to be descriptive of characters and action rather than setting. Thus *jidai-geki* and *gendai-geki* did not stand as generic classifications, but did serve an industrial or commercial function. As Lisa Spalding points out, double bills were often organized around a *jidai-geki* and a *gendai-geki*.

Within the *gendai-geki* classification, there exist many types of films (or *mono*) which do have a clear generic basis: film types such as *nansensu mono* (nonsense stories) or the *haha mono* (mother film), among others. Fewer film genres, however, have been sifted out from the broad category of *jidai-geki*. This is a function primarily of the prevalence of either samurai or sword-wielding commoners (like gamblers) in the *jidai-geki* stories. The *jidai-geki* became synonymous with the immediate pre-Tokugawa or Tokugawa-era story of war lords, clan retainers, *ronin,* or other wandering swordsmen. In the postwar period, however, the *jidai-geki* was often used to promulgate an antifeudal stance, used to condemn the feudalistic basis of Japanese society which fed into militarism, which led to the destruction and tragedy of the Pacific War. It became necessary, then, for film scholars, at least, to distinguish more specific genres within the *jidai-geki,* to distinguish, for instance, between *Ugetsu monogatari* (*Ugetsu*) and *Shichinin no samurai* (*Seven Samurai*), films produced around the same time (1953 and 1954 respectively) and set within the same historical period (the era of civil war in the sixteenth century).

The period film of the prewar era tended to focus almost exclusively on swordsmen. Thus what David Desser calls the Samurai Film in his essay on the postwar era of *jidai-geki* is almost coterminous with the period film before 1945. If the *jidai-geki* of the prewar era has its own generic status, Lisa Spalding nevertheless isolates a series of subgenres from within the form. Spalding's essay is not only one of the few forays in English to deal exclusively with the prewar *jidai-geki* and its generic qualities, but it also goes a long way toward debunking one of the cavils that still haunt the Japanese cinema: the idea that the *jidai-geki,* or Samurai Film, was somehow a derivation or imitation of the American Western.

David Desser makes the point that the postwar Samurai Film (sifting out such a genre from within the *jidai-geki*) marked a break from the prewar form, but that, while influenced by the American Western (among other forms), it not only has great relevance for an understanding of Japanese culture of the postwar period, but it also has an artistic and cultural integrity of its own.

Period Films in the Prewar Era

Lisa Spalding

The term *jidai-geki*, or "period film," denotes the large body of Japanese films set before or during the collapse of feudal Japan. This broad category includes comedies, ghost stories, musicals, and the action-packed tales of heroism for which the period film genre is best known. Historically, the genre emerged from the practice of filming scenes from Kabuki plays, especially scenes of combat, which were considered best suited to primitive film techniques. Very quickly, this practice resulted in a preference for plays about the exploits of brave samurai or spirits possessing supernatural strength. As the genre developed, it was influenced by shifts in popular culture, the changing economic and political climates, and a growing sophistication on the part of film audiences.

Nearly six-thousand *jidai-geki* were made between 1908 and the end of the Pacific War.[1] By 1911 period films accounted for 39 percent of the total film production. Their production peaked at 60 percent in 1918 and fluctuated slightly around 40 percent between 1920 and 1925, dropping only once to 32 percent in 1923, the year the Great Kanto Earthquake devastated Tokyo. From 1926 through 1940, production ranged from 46 percent to 56 percent, with a yearly mean of 51 percent. Government regulations forced a drastic decline in general film production during the war years of 1941–1945, and the percentage of period films dropped from a high of 39 percent in 1941 to a low of 20 percent in 1943. In 1945, seven of the twenty-two films made before August 15 were period films.

In the years before the Pacific War, exhibition practices were responsible for the fairly equal production of *jidai-geki* and *gendai-geki* (films with a modern setting). A double bill consisting of a period film and a modern story formed the main body of a film program in first-run theaters. Second-run theaters drew audiences by adding a new low-budget feature in either genre to the original double bill. Slight imbalances in yearly production can be attributed to a number of small companies that cranked out cheap swordplay dramas for children, and the low-budget films made especially for second-run theaters. Very few of the vast number of period films made before the end of the Pacific War have survived, and even fewer survive in their original form. This is particularly true of silent films. The climate of Japan, numerous fires that plagued the cities, and the bombing during the war are partly responsible for this dearth. But also to blame are the film industry's policy of making only a few prints that were screened until they literally fell apart, and the practice of re-releasing a series of two or three films after editing them into a single print (often with little regard for continuity).[2]

Makino Shozo and the Early Period Film (1908–1922)

Makino Shozo was a central figure in the development of the period film form as a director and later as a producer. When he made his first film in 1908, many of the elements that shaped the course of the genre were already apparent. He used actors from a Kabuki troupe performing at a theater he managed, and selected a rousing battle scene from a play in their repertoire.[3] Makino's theater was located in Kyoto, and the film was shot outdoors on the grounds of one of the city's many temples.

Throughout the prewar period, *jidai-geki* stars, with rare exception, had previous experience in the Kabuki theater. The slow, stylized movements of Kabuki combat, or *tachimawari,* adopted by the early period film, were not replaced by a more realistic fighting style until the early 1920s. Outdoor locations added to the spectacle of the *tachimawari,* while saving the cost of building sets, as frugality was at the core of period film production. Among the economical measures employed by early filmmakers was the practice of cranking the camera at half the normal speed to save film.[4] Kyoto became the official center of period film production when the Nikkatsu trust was formed in 1912. Nikkatsu built a new studio in Tokyo for the production of contemporary dramas, and devoted the Kyoto studio where Makino Shozo worked to period films. A general trend followed for directors, actors, and crews to work in only one genre.

When Makino discovered Onoe Matsunosuke, an itinerant Kabuki actor with unusual grace and agility, he established a key element in the development of the genre: the star. Matsunosuke's reputation for *tachimawari* and acrobatic feats suited the early period film perfectly. Between his film debut in 1909 and his death in 1926, he appeared in close to one thousand films, enjoying unparalleled popularity during the 1910s. Today he is remembered not only as Japan's first film star but also as a children's hero, for his films were tailored to this group. In fact, until the early 1920s, children, shop apprentices, and young laborers are thought to have made up the primary audience for Japanese films. More highbrow audiences preferred imported films.

As Makino moved from filming excerpted scenes to storytelling, he realized Kabuki plays were not always the most suitable material for his films because of their typically complex narratives. In Kabuki, apart from wielding his sword, the brave samurai faced complicated situations and emotionally agonizing predicaments. These complexities were often beyond the scope of existing primitive film techniques, and above the heads of juvenile audiences. Makino therefore began to shift from Kabuki scenarios to the simplistic plots of *Kodan*, a narrative art popular in *yose*, or Japanese vaudeville.[5] *Kodan*, unlike Kabuki, focused on the daring exploits of historical characters in quick-paced, straightforward tales. Although *Kodan* is an oral tradition, its stories were transcribed, and enjoyed tremendous success as popular literature until the early 1920s. Children's versions of these books were read widely by the audience Makino sought to entertain. While the frantic rate of film production precluded the use of scripts, the stories were so well known to his audience that specific episodes could be extracted without concern for coherent plot structures. Requests poured in from theaters and distributors for films about favorite heroes.[6]

Major Narrative Patterns and Iconography

Based on materials drawn chiefly from Kabuki and *Kodan*, the early period film established thematic and narrative precedents that dominated the genre until the end of the Pacific War, and exerted considerable influence even after the war.[7] Although narrative patterns and hero types varied in early period films and in the mainstream tradition that grew out of them, their basic ideology was shaped by feudal values, which they confirmed, unlike the subgenres that developed subsequently.

The Meiji Restoration of 1868 marked the end of feudal Japan but did not entail a rejection of virtues central to the feudal value system. Honor, filial piety, loyalty, and righteousness continued to be held in high esteem, but were gradually manipulated to inculcate nationalism and ultimately to propagate militarism. These virtues, embodied by legendary samurai and plebeian folk heroes, formed the ideological backbone of the early period film. The young audiences were familiar with the stories adapted for the screen, and reared on the values the stories reflected. They were apparently satisfied with simplistic plots that drew clear distinctions between good and evil and offered ample opportunity for the righteous hero to display his superhuman strength through stupendous feats of swordsmanship.

One can isolate a handful of major narrative patterns established during the early stages of the period film's development. Prominent among these was that focusing on the theme of the vendetta. Honor was of the utmost importance to the samurai, and his code of ethics demanded that any slight to the reputation of his family or clan be avenged. Consequently, the virtuous intent of the participants elevated the vendetta from the base level of bloody revenge to a devout act of loyalty or filial piety. Two classic vendetta legends, the story of the Soga brothers and *Chūshingura*, were filmed repeatedly from as early as 1908. Inspired by incidents that occurred centuries apart, these legends reveal heroic and narrative archetypes that have endured from the early feudal period to the present.

The Soga brothers were still young boys when their father became an innocent victim of a family dispute. In 1193, after waiting nearly eighteen years, the two brothers fulfilled their filial duty by slaying the man responsible for their father's death. One brother died in the fighting that followed their attack, and the other was beheaded at the command of the shogun. *Chūshingura*, as is well known, recounts the vendetta carried out by forty-seven former retainers of Lord Asano of Ako in 1703. The shogun ordered Asano to commit *seppuku* (ritual disembowelment) after he drew his sword and attacked another lord in the palace. Asano's lands were confiscated and his retainers forced to live as *ronin* (masterless samurai). After almost two years of patient vigilance, a group of Ako *ronin* attacked and killed the man who had provoked their lord to behave so indecorously. The shogun allowed the *ronin* to commit *seppuku* to atone for their loyal but illegal act.

Neither the Soga brothers nor the Ako *ronin* were involved in the incidents that precipitated the necessity of a vendetta, but they assumed responsibility out of a sense of loyalty or filial piety. As righteous samurai, they placed honor above personal concerns and persisted until they accomplished their purpose. Although the death of the protagonist was not an essential element in the vendetta narrative, the fate of the Soga brothers and the Ako *ronin* is representative of a predilection in the period film for narratives that culminate in the hero's demise. On a mythological level, the posthumous hero can be seen as a vestige of *goryo shinko*, the religious practice of deifying the souls of men who met unjust deaths to prevent their return as malevolent spirits.[8] On a pragmatic level, however, the hero represents an unpardonable threat to authority. His death thus resolves the conflict between the demands of the samurai code of ethics and the obligation of the shogun to maintain political stability.

Other major narrative patterns first adopted by the early period film reflect a similar concern with the preeminence of authority. The *torimono* narrative offered simple accounts of the pursuit and capture of dangerous criminals by

Tokugawa-period detectives, highlighted by a battle between the criminal and the brave agents of the shogun's police force. Another popular pattern was *Oie sodo* narratives, which related legendary accounts of factional struggles within clans. These disputes commonly centered around the accession of an heir or rivalry among retainers for the favor of their lord, and presented ample opportunity for the samurai to perform filial or loyal acts. In extreme cases where violence undermined authority, the offense was expiated by the complete destruction of the clan. A popular subnarrative of this group focused on innocent female victims of the turmoil who returned to seek revenge as *bakeneko* (phantom cats).

Related to the ideals of lawfulness and the preeminence of authority, we find a narrative pattern which featured wise and benevolent officials who enforced the feudal precept of *kanzen choaku,* "promoting good and punishing evil." These heroes championed the weak against evil lords, greedy moneylenders, and corrupt local officials. The fictional adventures of Mito Komon, a grandson of the man who founded the Tokugawa shogunate, remain popular to this day. A model of the venerable patriarch, Mito Komon roamed the country in the disguise of a simple traveler accompanied only by a small entourage. Whenever he discerned wrongdoing, he cleverly exposed the evil perpetrator and then revealed his own identity to the astonishment of both victim and culprit.

The world of the occult was brought to the screen in another popular narrative pattern through the use of simple trick photography. Here we might find the tale of a brave samurai who challenged and defeated a legendary demon like the giant earth spider who emerged from his cave spinning long white streamers to ensnare his attacker.[9] Or we have heroes who vanquish their opponents through *ninjutsu,* a magic art that enables them to assume the forms of supernatural beings or render themselves invisible. Onoe Matsunosuke is best remembered for portraying such heroes who turned into huge fire-breathing toads or vanished in a puff of smoke.

Another major narrative pattern dealt with the deeds of legendary swordsmen. The frequent subject of early films, these narratives focused on exaggerated battles that pitted one invincible man against a host of adversaries. Miyamoto Musashi exemplifies this type of hero. He devoted his life to the sword, and traveled throughout the country in his quest for perfection. He challenged and was challenged by numerous swordsmen during his travels, but always emerged victorious.

Early filmmakers did not neglect the patriotic swordsmen who fought to restore the emperor to a position of authority during the turbulent years that preceded the fall of the Tokugawa shogunate. Assassinations, rampant during the final years of the last shogun's reign, figured prominently in such narratives.

One of the most popular of these national heroes was Sakamoto Ryoma, an accomplished swordsman and a leader in the imperialist movement. He presented a particularly dramatic figure as he intrepidly escaped one assassination attempt only to fall victim to another.

A last major narrative pattern employed by the early period film featured popular folk heroes who sprang from the ranks of the outlaw. These scrupulous thieves and *yakuza* flagrantly defied authority in their struggle to defend the oppressed, but their insubordination never went unpunished. On the contrary, the fact that the virtuous hero was expected to be captured reflects the extent to which respect for authority permeated the early period film. One such virtuous thief was Nezumi Kozo Jirokichi, a celebrated and honorable figure who stole only from the mansions of wealthy and evil samurai and passed the ill-gotten gains directly to the destitute. Stalked by the shogun's police and a network of vigilant spies, like all such outlaw folk-heroes, he was eventually captured.

Then there were the *yakuza*. Commonly depicted in period films as outlaws associated with the shady world of gambling, they were organized into territorial groups under patriarchal leaders, or *oyabun,* who commanded absolute obedience. The *yakuza*'s code of honor demanded not only that he protect the weak and oppose the strong, but that he also sacrifice his life for a virtuous cause, if necessary. Kunisada Chuji personified the noble *yakuza*. He was a powerful *oyabun* with a large following of loyal men and a reputation for rescuing victims of injustice and striking fear in the hearts of the wicked. Relentlessly pursued by the authorities, he was apprehended only after palsy left him incapable of wielding his sword. Although the *yakuza* hero, like the scrupulous thief, was admired for his virtuous character and his righteous acts, the jurisdiction of feudal authority was never questioned. Indeed, in films of the 1920s and after, a popular star would often play both the outlaw and his captor, thus resolving the conflict between the image of the honorable hero and the preeminent right of society to pursue and capture him.[10]

No discussion of the early period film would be complete without a brief acknowledgment of the iconography of the genre, a subject that deserves a detailed study of its own. The early period film employed simple props and costumes, but as the genre developed, a complex iconography evolved that distinguished both narrative patterns and hero types. Although the present essay can offer only a brief list of common images here, they are perhaps sufficient to indicate the breadth and function of iconography within the genre.

The image of the sword pervaded the genre as it was used to both precipitate and resolve narrative conflicts. The *daito,* a long sword worn by the samurai, was not only a deadly weapon but a symbol of the samurai soul. Loss of the *daito* was equivalent to spiritual castration. Alternately, in films which focused on the law pursuing criminals, the *torimono* narratives, we find an assortment of paraphernalia used to capture sword-slashing criminals: lanterns imprinted with the word *goyo* indicated an official manhunt was in progress; the detective was identified by his *jutte*, a pronged instrument used to catch the blow of a sword. Hoods or masks appear in the tales of thieves, assassins, ninja, and others who wished to act incognito. A character's coiffure and clothing immediately revealed his rank within the feudal hierarchy, so that the samurai was easily distinguished from the townsman or the unkempt *ronin*. Finally, there was the journey motif, which played a central role in many of the period film narratives, from the adventures of Mito Komon to the flight of the hunted outlaws, and which entailed its own unique iconography. *Waraji,* or straw sandals, present the most common image associated with the journey. The *yakuza* traveled on foot and was further identified by his straw hat and cape. Men of high rank rode in palanquins, accompanied by an elaborate parade of retainers. Occasionally, mounted samurai appeared, primarily in stories of clan intrigue or the shogun's court. While bigger budgets and changing notions of style influenced the overall appearance of the period film, the basic iconography remained fixed.

The Period Film between 1922 and the Pacific War

The Rebel Subgenre

By the early 1920s the period film was in a state of transformation. Makino Shozo had left Nikkatsu and established an independent production company. As a producer, he was attracting talented young men with new ideas and high expectations. Kabuki *tachimawari* was replaced by fast-paced swordplay that more closely approximated a realistic fighting style. Books of *Kodan* stories were eclipsed by novels that gave psychological dimensions to familiar characters and created new heroes who reflected the social unrest that marked the period. Such novels were widely read in serialized form in newspapers and magazines. The use of scripts, intertitles, and more sophisticated editing and camera work enabled the period film to reproduce the elaborate plots and complex characters introduced by the popular novel.

The narrative patterns and hero types established by the early period film flourished under these conditions, but at the same time a subgenre emerged that departed radically from the accepted ideology. The new period film, the rebel subgenre, attacked clear distinctions between good and bad as mere hypocrisy, rejected feudal values as ineffectual, and glorified the hero for rebelling against authority. Inspired by Nakazato Kaizan's serialized novel *Daibosatsu toge* (*The Great Boddhisattva Pass*), with its nihilistic hero, Tsukue Ryunosuke, Susukita Rokuhei, a young scriptwriter for Makino Shozo, introduced the rebel hero to film.[11] *Orochi* (1925) offers an extant example of a Susukita scripted film in the rebel subgenre. Directed by Futagawa Buntaro, the film was written for Bando Tsumasaburo, by then a popular new star.[12]

Orochi chronicles the tragic decline of a young samurai, Heizaburo, who is rejected by Namie, the girl he loves, and unjustly expelled from his clan. Forced into the lonely life of a destitute *ronin,* Heizaburo experiences a series of frustrating misunderstandings that lead to clashes with the authorities and frequent terms in jail. He falls in love with a young woman who reminds him of Namie, but his undeserved reputation as a depraved outlaw frightens her away. Although Heizaburo's values deteriorate as he becomes immersed in the corruption that pervades society, he remains an inherently decent figure. He is taken in by a reputedly noble *oyabun* who turns out to be a lecherous kidnapper. Heizaburo's disillusionment turns to despair when he finds the *oyabun* holding his old love, Namie, and her sick husband. He kills the *oyabun* and frees the couple. When the authorities arrive, Heizaburo faces them with reckless abandon, fighting furiously with no purpose but rebellion. He finally puts down his sword and is led off in ropes past crowds of people who line the streets to steal a glimpse of the "outlaw." Only Namie and her husband know he is not the criminal he is thought to be.

The rebel subgenre was popular from 1923 to 1931, a period of economic instability and social unrest.[13] World War I brought prosperity to Japan, but left in its wake inflation followed by a trade recession that affected both industry and agriculture. In 1925 the Peace Preservation Law (*chian iji ho*) was passed in an effort to curb farm and labor movements, and to suppress the spread of left-wing thought. Finally, the Great Depression hit Japan in 1930. Why the rebel hero was received enthusiastically is not hard to see. Contemporary audiences undoubtedly sympathized with an innocent victim of poverty and corruption who rises to heroic proportions through his defiant yet futile rebellion. Yet it is the very futility of the hero's rebellion that points to the ideological limitations of the period film genre. It was not capable of offering alternatives to feudal values: it could only refute them in an ambiguous manner.

Stylistically, the rebel subgenre did not differ from the more mainstream period film. First, the swordfight was of prime importance. Close to one-third of *Orochi* is devoted to swordplay, with the hero's final clash with the authorities claiming over two reels of film. Second, since the new generation of *jidai-geki* stars were admired for the speed and grace with which they wielded their swords, camera speed was freely manipulated to enhance the dramatic effect of swordfights (even though the overwhelming preference was for shooting at slow speeds so that the actors appeared to be moving abnormally fast). Third, dramatic angles and elaborate tracking shots came into vogue as the techniques for shooting swordplay were developed. Finally, despite the fact that the films were always presented with a *katsuben* (or *benshi,* the film narrator), extensive use was made of intertitles for plot development and dialogue. Intertitles, in fact, often employed distorted or exaggerated lettering to create an added visual impact. Budgets remained relatively low for the most part, allowing popular stars to establish their own production companies. These small star productions flourished from 1925 to 1937 and produced many of the era's most innovative films.

Shifts in the Mainstream Narrative Patterns

During the latter half of the 1920s the patriotic swordsman and the wandering *yakuza* assumed prominent positions among the hero types established in the earlier period of the genre. Although Sakamoto Ryoma and other historical figures dominated the patriotic swordsman narratives, fictional heroes such as Tsukigata Hampeita and Kurama Tengu were also popular. An emphasis on loyalty and patriotism made these films particularly compatible with the rise of nationalism and accounts for their importance during the war years. Kurama Tengu, a mysterious masked equestrian, presents an interesting deviation from the common narrative pattern. He fought with the imperialists against the pro-shogun forces, but abandoned the struggle to protect the defenseless from the injustices perpetrated by both sides. Kurama Tengu's debt to American films is obvious in his "nick-of-time arrivals" and his Zorro-inspired guise.

Matatabi mono, or films about wandering *yakuza,* combined the travel motif with swordplay and pathos. In the traditional pattern, a wandering *yakuza* would seek food, lodging, and often an opportunity to gamble from a local *oyabun.* In return for the hospitality he was strictly obliged to perform whatever act his host requested. As the '20s wore on, this narrative pattern increasingly focused on severe conflicts between *giri* and *ninjō.* For instance, in *Kutsukake Tokijiro* (1929) the hero must kill another *yakuza* out of duty to the *yakuza* code. But his own sense of compassion, of *ninjō,* forces him to assume responsibility for the dead man's son and pregnant wife. This brought a sophistication, comparable to much feudal-era literature and drama, to the period film.

| The Antihero Subgenre

In the early 1930s a subgenre began to emerge that rejected the two most deeply embedded elements in the *jidai-geki* tradition: the exaggerated hero and the swordfight. The new hero in this subgenre was portrayed realistically as a simple human being for dramatic or satiric purposes. Swordfights, when not eliminated, were at least used sparingly. Although these films account for a very small percentage of the period films made in the 1930s, they represent the last truly creative development in the genre until after the war. The two central figures in this subgenre were Itami Mansaku and Yamanaka Sadao; both men were accomplished scriptwriters as well as directors.

Itami Mansaku excelled at parodies of traditional narrative patterns, exposing the absurdity of vendettas, ridiculing the legendary swordsman, and treating the clan disturbance with humor.[14] In one of his most acclaimed silent films, *Kokushi muso* (*The Greatest Man in the World*, 1932),[15] a renowned swordsman is defeated by a humble impostor who has been using his name. The swordsman, Ise no Kami, retreats into the mountains to train while his daughter fawns over the impostor, who spends most of his time fishing. When Ise no Kami returns for another match, the impostor defeats him again, taking the swordsman's willing daughter as his prize. Although the film has been lost, the script survives as evidence of Itami's satiric wit. The following exchange takes place after the second match:

Ise no Kami [title]	I just don't understand it. There's no way a real swordsman could be beaten by an impostor.
Impostor [title]	Well, there's nothing you can do about it once you've been beaten.
Ise no Kami [title]	The real swordsman is in the right. The impostor is in the wrong. The person in the right was beaten by the person in the wrong.
Impostor [title]	Now wait a minute. The person in the right doesn't win; the person who wins is right.[16]

In another scene Itami cleverly avoids a typical swordfight while lampooning the conventional *yakuza* battle that pits a weaker group against a stronger one. The impostor happens by as Hachibei, an *oyabun*, prepares to lead three men against a force of fifty. The rival *oyabun* is angered by the impostor's suggestion that he lend Hachibei some men to make the fight fair. Borrowing a sword from Hachibei, the impostor disappears. He returns with a mangled sword to borrow another, and then another. Finally, the scene fades out on a shot of the entire gang of fifty dead.[17]

As for Yamanaka Sadao, unfortunately none of his silent films is known to be extant, but three of his talkies survive to confirm his reputation as one of the prewar period film's most brilliant directors. After five years as a scriptwriter, Yamanaka directed his first film in 1932 at the age of twenty-three. Although he worked with stock characters, and made use of traditional narrative elements, he transformed the *jidai-geki* into a new and more complex dramatic form. Yamanaka's realistic depiction of the thieves, *yakuza,* and poverty-level townsmen who populated the lower strata of Tokugawa society reveals the influence of American films and the films of Ozu Yasujiro that focused on the lower-middle class.[18]

Tange Sazen—hyakuman ryo no tsubo (Tange Sazen and the Pot Worth a Million Ryo, 1935) parodies the fierce killer Tange Sazen, known to film audiences through numerous adaptations of Hayashi Fubo's novel *Shimpan Ooka Seidan.*[19] Yamanaka portrays the one-eyed, one-armed swordsman as a congenial character who lives with his lover, Ofuji, and acts as a bouncer for her small archery parlor, an establishment geared to entertaining men with drinks and feminine charm. The plot revolves around the search for a pot that contains a map to a buried treasure, and an orphan whom Sazen brings home against Ofuji's protests. The search for the missing pot burlesques the search for a missing heirloom, a convention common to period film narratives. *Lady and Gent* (1932), an American film directed by Stephen Roberts, inspired the addition of a young boy to Sazen and Ofuji's strictly adult world.[20] By attributing contemporary sensibilities to realistically portrayed characters, Yamanaka goes beyond a simple parody of the period film to create a modern comedy in a *jidai-geki* format.

Although humor plays an integral part in all three of Yamanaka's extant films, *Kochiyama Soshun* (1936) and *Ninjo kamifusen (Humanity and Paper Balloons,* 1937) reveal the young director's move toward a fatalistic pessimism. Both films are loosely based on Kabuki plays by Kawatake Mokuami. In *Kochiyama Soshun,* Yamanaka expands on Mokuami's *Kumo ni mago ueno no hatsuhana,*[21] adding characters and developing a narrative that more closely resembles Ozu Yasujiro's *Hijosen no onna (Dragnet Girl,* 1933) than the original Kabuki play.[22] The film relates the story of a thief, Kochiyama Soshun, and a *yakuza* who attempt to save an innocent girl from being sold as a geisha to cover the debts incurred by her irresponsible younger brother. Kochiyama, his wife, and the *yakuza* are all killed in the swordfight that ends the film. This scene, the only extended swordfight in any of Yamanaka's extant films, places the work firmly within the *jidai-geki* tradition, but the careful delineation of characters and the natural manner in which they interact elevate the work to a position far above the typical period film.

In his last film, *Humanity and Paper Balloons,* Yamanaka reinterprets the characters and plot of Mokuami's *Tsuyu kosode mukashi hachijo*[23] and places them in a more complex narrative. The film depicts the daily lives of the inhabitants of a cramped one-story tenement building, focusing on Shinza, a barber in trouble with the local *oyabun* for running an unsanctioned gambling den, and a *ronin* whose wife makes paper balloons while he tries futilely to secure a position befitting his status as a samurai. The lives of the cocky barber and the humble, subservient *ronin* are presented in a parallel structure, but converge at a brief but disastrous point when Shinza enlists the *ronin*'s help in hiding the daughter of a pawnbroker whom he kidnapped to spite the *oyabun*. In the end, Shinza is killed for his flagrant insult to the *oyabun,* and the *ronin*'s wife kills her husband and herself when she realizes there is no chance of preserving their dignity as members of the samurai class.

The tone of the film is starkly pessimistic, although there are moments of great humor. Yamanaka avoids swordplay and heroics, aiming instead at a subtle tragedy that confronts the viewer with the immediacy of a contemporary drama. The day the film was released, Yamanaka received his draft notice. He died the following year in China at the age of 29.

NOTES

1. All calculations are based on *Nihon eiga sakuhin taikan* (*Comprehensive Dictionary of [Individual] Japanese Films [1896–1945]*), 7 vols. (Tokyo: Kinema Jumposha, 1960–61). The term *kyu-geki,* literally "old drama," was used to refer to the period film before *jidai-geki* came into use in the early 1920s. I have chosen to use only *jidai-geki* to stress the continuity of the form.

2. The nitrate stock on which films were printed was highly flammable to begin with, exacerbating the destruction of prints by fire and bombing. Nitrate also deteriorates over time, and so prints which survived earthquake, fire, and bombs needed special care which they rarely received—the situation was similar with many American films of the silent era. The recutting and reconstitution of films is an interesting case, revealing not only the commodification of film but, more significantly, also a revealing attitude toward questions of textuality and originality.

3. The scene was entitled *Hannoji gassen* (*The Battle of Honno Temple*).

4. Yokota Shokai seems to have begun the practice of shooting at 7–8 frames per second when 12 was considered normal for Japanese films. In 1915 Nikkatsu was still shooting period films at 7–8 fps. See Tanaka Jun'ichiro, *Nihon eiga hattatsu shi* (*The History of the Development of Japanese Film*), 2nd ed., Vol. 1 (Tokyo: Chuo Koron-sha, 1957), pp. 133, 209.

5. This discussion is indebted to Sato Tadao, "Nihon eiga no seiritsushita dodai" ("The Foundation of Japanese Film"), in *Nihon eiga no tanjo. Koza Nihon eiga* (*The Birth of Japanese Film: Lectures on Japanese Film*), Vol. 1 (Tokyo: Iwanami Shoten, 1985), pp. 19–20.

6. Tanaka, p. 162. Makino Shozo refers to a barrage of requests while he was working for Yokota Shokai before the formation of Nikkatsu.

7. A survey of popular Japanese period films made between 1926 and 1966, as listed in *Kinema Jumpo* 430 (1 Jan. 1967): 61–68:

TITLE	PREWAR FILMS	POSTWAR FILMS	TOTAL
Shimizu Jirocho	15	27	42
Yaji Kita	26	15	41
Mito Komon	20	20	40
Kunisada Chuji	27	8	35
Takadanobaba	20	6	26
Tange Sazen	15	11	26
Miyamoto Musashi	13	11	24
Chushingura	12	12	24
Nezumi Kozo Jirokichi	17	5	22
Araki Mataemon	14	6	20
Tsukigata Hampeita	12	3	15

8. The legends of the Soga brothers can be traced directly to *goryo shinko*. See Thomas J. Cogan, *The Tale of the Soga Brothers* (Tokyo: U of Tokyo P, 1987), p. xxxix.

9. *Shibukawa Bangoro* (1922) contains a scene in which Onoe Matsunosuke defeats the earth spider. His performance follows the Kabuki tradition closely and offers an example of the style in which this type of scene was played in films made during the 1910s. (Matsunosuke apparently never changed his acting style, so this film is seen as an example of what the lost films from the teens looked like.)

10. Okochi Denjiro played both Tange Sazen and Ooka Echizen no Kami in Ito Daisuke's three part series *Shimpan Ooka Seiden* (*New Versions of Ooka's Trial*, 1928), and Nezumi Kozo Jirokichi and his captor in Yamanaka Sadao's eponymous three-part series in 1933. None of these prints is extant, but they were extremely popular examples of this practice. See also Keiko McDonald's essay on *yakuza* films in this volume.

11. The novel was published in installments between 1913 and 1941. Although unfinished at the time of Nakazato's death in 1944, it runs to thirty-two volumes. There was one version of *Daibosatsu Toge* made in 1935 (by Inagaki Hiroshi), but no others in the prewar era. Adaptations of this story were quite numerous after the war, such as popular versions by Uchida Tomu, Misumi Kenji, and Okamoto Kihachi, whose 1967 version was released in the United States under the title *Sword of Doom*.

12. There is a 91-minute biographical documentary about Tsumasaburo entitled *Bantsuma: Bando Tsumasaburo no shogai* (*The Life of Tsumasaburo Bando*, 1988), written by Sato Tadao and directed by the late Matsuda Shunsui. Among the many film excerpts, there is one from *Orochi*, accompanied by director Matsuda's voice explaining the action *katsuben*-style. *Orochi* itself is available from Matsuda Eigasha in Tokyo. The company also has a video version for sale with Matsuda's *katsuben* soundtrack.

13. Sato Tadao, "Eizo hyogen no kakuritsu" ("The Establishment of Visual Images"), in *Musei eiga no kansei. Koza Nihon eiga* (*The Culmination of Silent Film: Lectures on Japanese Film*), Vol. 2 (Tokyo: Iwanami Shoten, 1986), p. 43.

14. It is worth noting that Itami Mansaku was the father of the contemporary satirical director Itami Juzo.

15. "The Greatest Man in the Land" is a literal translation of the term *kokushi muso*. Kitagawa Fuyuhiko feels that the title refers to a rare but theoretically possible play in *mah-jong*. See Itami Mansaku, *Itami Mansaku zenshu* (*The Complete Works of Itami Mansaku*), 2nd ed., Vol. 3 (Tokyo: Chikuma Shobo, 1973), p. 450.

16. Itami, p. 107.

17. Itami, pp. 99–100.

18. Yamamoto Kikuo, *Nihon eiga ni okeru gaikoku no eikyo—hikaku eigashi kenkyu* (*The Influence of Foreign Films in Japanese Cinema: Research in Comparative Film History*) (Tokyo: Waseda Daigaku Shuppanbu, 1983), p. 501.

19. The novel was first published as a newspaper serial from October 1927 to May 1928.

20. Yamamoto, p. 527.

21. This Mokuami play, which is made up of two parts, is commonly called *Kochiyama* (for part I) and *Naozamurai* (for part II). A more or less literal English translation of the Japanese title, *Kumo ni mago ueno no hatsuhana,* would be *Cherry Blossoms in Full Bloom against the Sky at Ueno.*

22. Yamamoto, p. 536. Mokuami's play also forms the basis of Shinoda Masahiro's *Buraikan* (*The Scandalous Adventures of Buraikan,* 1970). See David Desser, *Eros plus Massacre: An Introduction to the Japanese New Wave Cinema* (Bloomington and Indianapolis: Indiana UP, 1988), pp. 181–182.

23. A fairly literal English translation of *Tsuyu kosode mukashi hachijo* would be *The Old Story about the Wet-Wadded Silk Coat,* but this Mokuami play is commonly known in Japanese as *Kami yui shinza* (*The Hairdresser*).

Toward a Structural Analysis of the Postwar Samurai Film

David Desser

Throughout the prewar era, especially in the years 1927 through 1944, the Japanese cinema was dominated by the *jidai-geki*, or period film, particularly stories concerning samurai, or feudal swordsmen. In the immediate postwar period, the Samurai Film was basically banned by the American occupation army (SCAP). SCAP prohibited, for instance, films "favoring or approving feudal loyalty [and] direct or indirect approval of suicide."[1] Under such restrictions the Samurai Film was unlikely to prosper. Kurosawa's *Rashomon* in 1950 sparked a renewed interest in the *jidai-geki*, especially those which would similarly win favor in the West; Kurosawa's *Shichinin no samurai* (*Seven Samurai*) in 1954 (long after SCAP's departure) sparked a renewed interest in the Samurai Film and initiated a renaissance of the form. By 1961–62, the genre practically dominated native film production, with around forty new titles being released each year, or more than three every month. By 1970, however, this figure fell to about a dozen each year, and by 1980, the figure was down to two or three, mainly big-budget prestige pictures, or the lowest of the B's. We may conclude with some justification that sometime in the mid-'50s, the Japanese audience perceived a cultural need which the Samurai Film could fulfill, while by the mid-'70s that need had perhaps changed. Or, more likely, the structure of the form was passed on to a new genre, a new form, which carried on the mythic mission of the Samurai Film. What is proposed here is a structural outline of this renaissance Samurai Film to indicate something of the formal properties of the genre and some of its cultural implications. The Samurai Film, especially in the works of Kurosawa, Kobayashi, Inagaki, and Gosha, has achieved some popularity in America, an index of shared cultural similarities, and perhaps the presence of universal archetypes in the form.

Anderson and Richie offer a definition of the Samurai Film which begins to distinguish the form along narrative-structural lines:

> The hero in all these films was usually a samurai, masterless or not, or sometimes

a sort of "chivalrous commoner" who is allowed to carry a sword—or again, he might be a gambler. The plot usually turns upon his receiving an obligation, usually accidentally, which he must discharge by performing some dangerous or distasteful deed, often in conflict with other duties or obligations. Other plot movers are revenge and the protection of the innocent.[2]

This definition, put forth for the prewar Samurai Film in particular, has relevance for the postwar film. To this broad outline, I would add the frequent postwar plot of conflict between two feudal clans, or within a clan; such a plot reflects the postwar concern with the question of duty and loyalty to a society which may be in the wrong.

Just as the genre of the Western takes shape when we understand it not only by a series of narrative patterns but from iconographic clues as well, so too does the Samurai form, as distinguished from the mass of Japanese cinema. The key image in the genre is the samurai sword itself. The wearing, in full view, of the long killing sword (daito) immediately places one within the genre of the Samurai. And it is the use of this sword to bring the narrative conflicts into resolution that basically defines the form.

Naturally, this is grossly oversimplified. Some Samurai Films, as defined here, contain little killing; others seem devoted exclusively to the use of the sword; some focus on feudal society and politics, while others virtually ignore the historical setting. Four subgenres may be isolated to account for the difference in predominant patterns within the form. The differences between the subgenres articulate the changing mythic function of the genre as it tried to deal with cultural tensions of the postwar era. However, before the various subgenres are elucidated, some general comments about the Samurai Film are in order.

The Samurai Film is set in Japan's feudal past, which at its broadest can be considered from the years 1188 to 1868, encompassing the Kamakura, Muromachi, Momoyama, and Tokugawa eras. These years span the period from the rise of the warrior (samurai) class and its assumption of power from the emperor's court, to the disbanding of the samurai shortly after the Meiji Restoration of 1868. Yet, like the Western, the Samurai Film typically is situated in only a part of this spectrum. If the period of the American frontier (the Western's central concern) is the years 1750–1917, most Westerns confine themselves to the years 1830–1890 (and typically 1865–1890). The Samurai Film similarly occupies only a small span of the Japanese past, mainly the Tokugawa era (1600–1868). This is part of the great paradox of the Samurai Film: the focus of attention on warriors in a time of relative peace.

The obsolescence of the samurai as a warrior class is one of the key structural foundations of the genre. The audience viewing the film is forced to confront, at every moment the film is on the screen, both the tragic decay of the hero's traditions and the eventual outright destruction of his way of life. The samurai class is destined to be abolished in the wake of Meiji. Its spirit, its code, known as *Bushido* (the Way of the Warrior), will survive through World War II, but in the wake of defeat, it too will come in for revision and, sometimes, vilification. Thus there is in the Samurai Film a frontier of hopelessness, of a struggle by the hero foredoomed to failure. And it is this failed hero whom the Japanese prize so much, seeing, in Ivan Morris's term, a "nobility of failure."[3]

To the Japanese mind, the self-sacrificing hero is the most admirable hero of all. If Hollywood formula stories almost always demand that the hero be left alive at the conclusion, the classic Samurai Film usually ends badly for the protagonist. However, the nobility of failure extends well beyond this opposition of living and dead. It is not just the dying that the Japanese admire, but the hero who struggles for a doomed cause. What is demanded from the films is the hero's continued fight even when the cause is clearly lost, or rather, especially when the cause is lost. The hero must fight proudly until the bitter end. The very inevitability of the hero's defeat is precisely what is dramatic and uniquely Japanese about the classic Samurai Film.

The samurai hero, unlike his counterpart in the Western, is born into a rigidly defined system. If the Code of the West evolved spontaneously (as much in the pulp novels and in the cinema as on the real frontier), *Bushido* was actually codified. Simply by being born into a caste, the samurai inherited a host of obligations. In the Western, the gunfighter is not born, he is forged by the harsh climate and the times in which he lives. The samurai is not so much forged as molded, so that when he grows older, it is difficult to separate training, or acculturation, from his own humanity. This is expressed in the Japanese opposition *giri/ninjō* (duty vs. human feeling). To the modern Japanese, the *giri/ninjō* dichotomy is still very much present, but in the Samurai Film it occupies a more central, more highly dramatic place. The Samurai Film functions to mythicize the dichotomy by placing it in a cinematic past and alleviating the conflict through ritualistic acts of heroic violence.

The Nostalgic Samurai Drama

The first subgenre of the Samurai Film to emerge in the postwar era was the Nostalgic Samurai Drama. It, like the other three subgenres, should be understood as a paradigm, not a hard-and-fast category. These subgenres appear in a chronological fashion, but they may overlap. A number of films will have elements of more than one subgenre (even though every film can be satisfactorily placed in one of these categories). Each category is assigned a paradigmatic film, or director, or group of films which elucidate the mythic functioning of the various subgenres.

Kurosawa's *Seven Samurai* inaugurates the postwar Golden Age of the Samurai Film and ushers in the Nostalgic Samurai Drama. But this subgenre finds its paradigmatic films in the *oeuvre* of Inagaki Hiroshi. Inagaki's films are marked by the special Japanese propensity for *mono no aware*.[4] This feeling of sweet sadness, or an almost inexpressible sensation of life's mortality which is pleasantly painful, is one of the foundations of traditional Japanese aesthetic theory. From Lady Murasaki's classic novel *The Tale of Genji* to the more stylized forms of *yamato-e* (landscape painting in the Japanese style) to the highly prized films of Ozu Yasujiro and Naruse Mikio, *mono no aware* is a standard of aesthetic worth. Most familiar to Westerners, perhaps, is the structure par excellence of *mono no aware*: the haiku.

At an initial glance it might seem paradoxical, if not quite surprising, to claim a kind of aesthetic equation between, say, Ozu's *Bakushu* (*Early Summer*, 1951) and Inagaki's version of the Loyal Forty-Seven *Ronin* saga (*Chūshingura*, 1962). Yet such a comparison is not so strange. Ozu's characters struggle for a touch of happiness while rarely achieving their hearts' desire. When Ozu's people reflect on their lives past, as they so frequently do, they discover as much pain and dissatisfaction as they do pleasure. And yet they rarely grieve outright (not only publicly but privately, separately, as well). Rather, Ozu's protagonists savor the jumbled feelings of disappointment and contentment. So, too, the audience experiences for, and along with, the characters the sensation of *mono no aware*. Ozu's films are indeed a slice of life, but a slice of the emotive, interior, and aestheticized life.

The Nostalgic Samurai Drama similarly is devoted primarily to *mono no aware*. And, as in Ozu, it arises through thematic and stylistic devices. The Nostalgic Samurai Drama usually focuses on a *ronin*, a masterless samurai. The term *ronin*, meaning "wave man," not only indicates his status but can also suggest the feeling of *mono no aware*. The idea not merely of loss of status but of being buffeted about on the waves of fate, powerless yet proud, is a powerful symbol, to the Japanese mind, of humankind's eternal state. The films are typically situated in the Tokugawa era. Hence the *ronin* is unlikely to find employment as a true samurai. In times of peace and under the repressive Tokugawa shogunate, a lord (*daimyo*) is unlikely to need, or to be able to afford, a loyal retainer. The *ronin* then becomes a wanderer, a doer of good deeds in exchange for food and gratitude.

Sometimes *mono no aware* arises from the fact that the *ronin* hero does not help forge a new society. He never questions the moral right of the system which has given rise to his existence. Trapped in the way of *giri/ninjō*, he takes to the path of righteousness out of a sense of obligation, but he never (or almost never) attacks the system. About the only positive act the hero can perform is to try and sever his links with the feudal past by changing his name. As a sign with a material status of its own, his name calls forth his birth, his status, his link in a historical chain, and his sense of obligation to the historical present. By changing his name, the *ronin* tries to re-create himself. But in failing to help forge a new society, the *ronin* hero never does re-create, reconstitute, himself, and so he becomes a necessarily tragic figure.

Another of the modes of creating *mono no aware* is a formalistic approach. A good example of this can be found in Inagaki's *Yato kaze no naka o hashiru* (*Bandits on the Wind*, 1961). Filmed in black and white, *Bandits on the Wind* is one of Inagaki's most satisfying films, perhaps because it elicits *mono no aware* so completely. The plotline could just as easily have formed the basis of an Anti-Feudal Drama (see below), but Inagaki's special treatment of the material puts the film firmly in the Nostalgic Samurai Drama form.

The film focuses on a small village forced to accede to the unreasonable demands of a local *daimyo*. Into this volatile situation ride three *ronin*, who quickly become involved with the villagers against the specific advice of the *daimyo*'s retainers. At the end of the film, the *ronin* are killed in a fierce battle, but they have, in this instance, won their cause.

Inagaki's treatment of the heroes is both gentle and slightly mocking. These *ronin* are not the superb fighters found in Kurosawa's *Seven Samurai* or in Gosha Hideo's *Sambiki no samurai* (*Three Outlaw Samurai*, 1964). Rather, average men in every way, they grow into the roles of heroes as they become sympathetic to the villagers' plight.

But it is not simply in the tragic death of the likable heroes that we experience the nostalgia, *mono no aware*. Inagaki uses his camera and art direction to reflect emotional states. Although his treatment of action is grossly inferior to that of directors such as Kurosawa and Gosha, his graceful camera movements imbue this film with a great deal of sensitivity. Here we must first take note of the use of black and white cinematography, for Inagaki himself used color to marvelous effect in his *Samurai* (1954). The black and white becomes an aesthetic device, which in this case reflects the Japanese ideal of *wabi* (poverty, the prizing of that which looks simple). Like a monochrome painting, the film tries to capture a landscape without coloring in its details, details which might detract from the purity of its vision and the feelings it hopes to arouse. The camera movements tend toward horizontal tracking, which deemphasizes the illusion of depth within the frame. The relatively long takes employed combine with these lateral tracks in shots which link the village with the rural countryside which surrounds it, calling forth a clear association between nature and the villagers.

Nature, as such, is a common artistic mode which can, alone, be sufficient to elicit *mono no aware*. The final death scene here recalls the shot that closes Mizoguchi's *Ugetsu mongatari* (*Ugetsu*, 1953) wherein a gentle crane-up of the camera reminds one of nature's longevity compared to the transitoriness of individual humanity.

In addition to thematic and formalistic devices, the structuring of the *giri/ninjō* antinomy and its ultimate "resolution" is also a distinguishing feature of the Nostalgic Samurai Drama. To the Japanese of a very confusing modern world, the *jidai-geki* can offer a clear picture of good and evil, right and wrong. Doubtless today many Japanese are caught up in the kinds of existential crises previously unknown to the Japanese of an earlier age. (This goes some of the way toward explaining the cool reception the Japanese initially gave to *Rashomon*.) Whether or not the hero of a Samurai Film succeeds, and he usually does not, he moves in a world of clear-cut moral choices. When confronted by the *giri/ninjō* conflict, the hero of the Nostalgic Samurai Drama makes his choice knowing full well the price to be paid in social alienation and/or self-abnegation.

Of course, in life—in Japanese life—the *giri/ninjō* conflict is unresolvable. The mythology inherent in the Nostalgic Samurai Drama also can never resolve the tension. Rather, in true mythic fashion, it disperses the feelings of resentment and confusion and displaces them onto the sensation of *mono no aware*. The displacement is twofold. First comes the violent climax to which every Nostalgic Samurai Drama leads. The choice the *ronin* hero makes leads inevitably to violence, and usually to his own death. The cathartic nature of the violence, and the ritualistic way it is repeated by further entries into the genre, help resolve the anxiety created by the realization (or re-realization) of the ultimate insolubility of the *giri/ninjō* dichotomy. The hero thus functions as a sacrificial victim in the ritual of repeated formula (mythic) narratives.[5] Secondly, however, the violence gives way to *mono no aware* on the formal plane so that the viewer, instead of dwelling on societal causes, is left savoring life's ironies and its impermanence. The viewer is reminded of the bittersweet nature of existence and is asked to treasure that feeling.

| The Anti-Feudal Drama

The Nostalgic Samurai Drama arose out of a nostalgia for the form of the Samurai movie, as much as any other reason. Most of the films in this form followed quite closely the structural patterns of the prewar movies (with something of a deemphasis on the moral rightness of the feudal system). It can also be understood as a reassertion of the Japanese past—their unique past, denied to them by the strictures of SCAP. It soon became evident, however, that this form would not suffice. The Nostalgic Samurai Drama did not answer the questions in the minds of many filmmakers, filmmakers willing to deal with serious issues within an established filmic form. An altered form, a different subgenre, followed close on the heels of the Nostalgic Dramas: the Anti-Feudal Samurai Drama.

The Anti-Feudal Samurai Drama has produced, outside of Kurosawa's films, the best-known and most critically respected works within the Samurai Film. Two films by Kobayashi Masaki, *Seppuku (Hara-kiri,* 1962) and *Joiuchi (Samurai Rebellion,* 1967), demonstrated a creative vitality to the form that Inagaki's more contemplative works might have belied (again, with Kurosawa standing somehow outside the "mainstream"). Both films have received much acclaim in the West and in Japan: *Hara-kiri* was awarded the *Kinema Jumpo* #3 for the year, while *Samurai Rebellion* won the coveted "Best One" award from the critical journal. The stylish, often awesome films of Gosha Hideo have also contributed to making the Anti-Feudal Drama a form of great significance. Films such as *Goyokin (The Steel Edge of Revenge,* 1969) and *Hitokiri (Tenchu,* 1969), in which Mishima Yukio has an unfortunately prophetic role, testify to the powerful feelings just below the surface of the stereotypically serene Japanese facade.

It is surprising that the forceful Anti-Feudal Samurai Film did not arise earlier than the early 1960s. It is difficult to explain why, unless we accept the contention that a nostalgia for the form, as such, of the Samurai Film must necessarily precede the use of the form to deal with the past or the present in politically meaningful ways. Another possible reason is that filmmakers with virulent anti-feudal tendencies might have been unwilling to work in the form, especially following the militarist regime which gloried *Bushido.* As Lisa Spalding's essay in this volume makes clear, there were antecedents to this Anti-Feudal mode in the prewar years, especially those within the Rebel subgenre she isolates. Yet to find the return, and it is a return with a renewed vengeance, of this subgenre, we must briefly look at an explosive issue in the Japan of 1959–60.

The Japanese became a divided people over the issue of the renewal in 1960 of the Mutual Security Pact with the United States. Actual rioting broke out over the parliamentary debates, and in the ensuing violence hundreds of protesters were injured. These mass demonstrations were a response to the Diet's approval of the renewal pact in the absence of the Socialist Party, which had boycotted the debates in protest. Students, labor unions, and civil servants took

to the streets, their virulence causing President Eisenhower to cancel his sched-
uled visit to Japan to honor the new pact. Although the pact remained in force,
Prime Minister Kishi resigned.[6]

The renewal of the pact, the autocratic actions of Kishi, and the implications
contained within the pact served as a reminder of the militarist past and of the
possibility, at least, of becoming re-involved in militaristic politics. The Mutual
Defense Pact called for an increase in Japan's visibility in world politics and the
implicit siding with the U.S. in the still-sensitive cold war. To the left wing, such
an alliance was cause for bitter disagreement with the more conservative Liberal
Democrats then in power. Filmmakers in the intellectual forefront, like many of
their intellectual counterparts in other media, have typically harbored left-wing
tendencies, so that a seeming return to militarism, even at this rather low level,
was cause for concern.[7]

The Anti-Feudal Samurai Drama arose in the early sixties, then, as a possible
filmic reminder of the dangers of feudalism, of putting the system before the
welfare of the individual. It began both as a response to the current political
climate and as an attempt to redress the image of feudalism implicit in the
Nostalgic Samurai subgenre.

The plots of the Anti-Feudal Samurai Dramas are, in most respects, virtually
identical to those of the Nostalgic Dramas. A man of position (though not of
the highest) loses his status and becomes a *ronin*. He takes to the path of
wandering until he is eventually convinced to try and perform a good deed for a
weaker group of people. And, like his counterpart in the Nostalgic Drama, he
usually meets his death at the film's end. The differences in plot, in characterization, and in their treatment define the form.

The heroes of the Anti-Feudal Drama typically begin as men of position,
whereas the Nostalgic Drama often begins *after* their position has been lost.
They are ordinary samurai who have been born with a certain status they expect
to maintain. The society (almost always explicitly the Tokugawa era) expects
something from these men, and they expect something in return. When the
samurai hero, then, loses his position (the dissolution of his clan through no
fault of his own is typical, as in *Hara-kiri*), there is virtually no way he can regain
it. Tokugawa Japan, at the level of the samurai, is simply too stagnant to have
need for him. Becoming a *ronin* is his only alternative, a painful one since he has
always subscribed to *Bushido* and placed *giri* above *ninjō*.

The bleakness of the *ronin's* situation is made evident in the life of poverty
and loneliness which is his lot. This new position causes him to begin to question the moral rightness of such a system, a system which can simply rid itself of
valuable, loyal citizens without so much as a shrug. The *ronin* will then seek out
causes which will bring him into direct conflict with appropriately symbolic

representatives of the society's ruling class. Of course, his actions are inherently tragic, for he then actively works to bring about the destruction of the system which has given him his previously cherished beliefs.

The *ronin*-hero of the Anti-Feudal Drama is usually a far better swordsman than his counterpart in the Nostalgic Drama, as is displayed in at least one scene of spectacular swordplay and violence. (The committing of *seppuku* with bamboo swords, shown rather graphically, and the apocalyptic battle at the climax made Kobayashi's film of that name rather notorious in its day.) This, too, leads to a great deal of irony and the appreciation, once again, of the nobility of failure. The very skills the samurai so desperately wanted a *daimyo* or the shogun to put to use are turned against them. The hero struggles valiantly, spectacularly, but in a doomed effort.

Formally, the Anti-Feudal Drama relies on Cinemascope framing (a ratio of 2.33:1, width to height) and composition in depth (deep focus). These devices emphasize the space around the individual, thus deemphasizing him. Working in depth similarly contextualizes the hero. We should note, for instance, that while Inagaki favors horizontal pans and tracks, Kobayashi in *Hara-kiri* relies strongly on the dolly shot which actively explores the space within the frame.

The settings, too, are different. If the Nostalgic Drama leaned toward linking its heroes with nature, the Anti-Feudal Drama keeps them firmly within society. Courtyards and interiors of castles, or inns, are the predominant locales of the action.

The extreme virulence of the Anti-Feudal Drama, tending at times toward self-hatred, is too often undercut, however, by the tendency toward *mono no aware* caused by the nobility of failure. For while they undeniably denigrate the feudal system, the films inevitably allow the tragic *ronin* figure to dominate the emotional content. Again, the *giri/ninjō* conflict is central to the film, but again its ultimate insolubility is displaced via cathartic violence and the feeling of *mono no aware*.

Both the Nostalgic and Anti-Feudal Samurai Dramas share one important similarity which may be expressed by the following proportion: "the overvaluation of society and the undervaluation of the individual." This is, of course, another way of stating that the *giri/ninjō* dichotomy is either insoluble or weighted toward the side of society. In either case, the structuration of the conflict in this fashion causes tension and anxiety in the audience which the films must displace. However, a potentially "radical" solution is implicitly offered by these films, namely, that the corollary should be true: the undervaluation of the society and the overvaluation of the individual. But it is not the function of myth to foment change; it is, rather, to resolve tensions and ambiguities and to assimilate members of the audience into the dominant society.

Therefore, the potential anxiety that arises is dealt with via an "aestheticization" of the conflict. The feeling of *mono no aware* is an aesthetic response to a social issue. This helps point the way toward the mythicization process in which the Samurai Film engages. The Nostalgic and Anti-Feudal Dramas did not maintain their popularity very long because a more deeply mythic subgenre arose to take their place.

Zen Fighters

The third subgenre of the Samurai Film is termed *Zen Fighters*. In the postwar era, this subgenre arose concurrently with the Nostalgic Samurai Genre (and in the case of Inagaki's *Samurai* was literally simultaneous with it, being the story of Miyamoto Musashi) and continued after the Nostalgic Drama was all but dead. This subgenre deals with warriors of ancient legend or modern creation who explicitly invoke and evoke Zen. Zen's influence on Japanese culture in general, and on the military classes in specific, is, of course, well known. Yet the degree to which Zen precepts have become mythicized into the Samurai Film has gone almost totally unexplored.[8]

The Zen Fighters subgenre ignores, or perhaps transcends, the social contexts of its time. To understand this, we need only turn to any of a number of film versions of the life of famed Zen swordsman Miyamoto Musashi.

In films as radically different in characterization and technique as Inagaki's *Samurai Trilogy* (especially part I, *Miyamoto Musashi*, and part III, *Ketto ganryujima* [1955], known in English as *Musashi and Kojiro*) and Uchida Tomu's multipart series for Toei, *Miyamoto Musashi* (1962–1970), there is one commonality, namely, that Tokugawa society become merely a background for Musashi's ethical, moral, and "duelistic" impulses. And although Zen philosophy has it that the best swordsman never uses his sword, the Zen Fighters subgenre manages more than its fair share of spectacular duels. The Zen Fighters, like Musashi, remove themselves from the constraints of *Bushido* in order to achieve perfection in the art of swordsmanship. Thus the typical screen portrayal of Musashi unabashedly shows him as a man obsessed with testing his skills as a swordsman. Each feature in Uchida's series, barely longer than a television episode, builds up to a climactic fight scene detailing another of Musashi's legendary battles.

To the modern Japanese, still bound by the constraints of *giri/ninjō*, the Zen Fighters subgenre offers up an image of a figure who has transcended both forces entirely. The hero shows his disdain for life, his own and the life of others, by constantly engaging in fights to the finish. And, of course, in the paradoxical way of Zen, it is precisely in not caring if he dies that the hero manages to survive. Thus the Zen Fighters subgenre begins a move away from the nobility of failure, for it offers up an image of success.

Zen Fighters precepts have found their way into many other Samurai Films, particularly the Nostalgic Drama (where, in addition to the aforementioned Inagaki trilogy, we find two classic Zen swordsmen in the characters of Kambei and Kyuzo in Kurosawa's *Seven Samurai*) and the Sword Film, the fourth subgenre of the form. In fact, the utilization of Zen concepts in other forms has proven more interesting, overall, than any individual case in the Zen Fighters subgenre. In a sense, just as Zen has infiltrated all aspects of Japanese culture, including the cinema, it is difficult to isolate the specific mythic function of this subgenre, except to see it as a structural transition between the Nostalgic Samurai Drama and the Sword Film. The transcendence of historical specificity and of the *giri/ninjō* dichotomy, and the increased emphasis on violence within the subgenre provided an important stepping-stone toward the marvelous excesses and complex mythology of the Sword Film.

The Sword Film

The Japanese call swordfight films *chambara*, which is onomatopoeic for the sound of clanging steel. They also have a theatrical form known as *kengeki* (sword dramas). The category of the Sword Film, the fourth of the Samurai Film subgenres, should not be confused with either of them. The critical disparagement, or ignoring, of the Samurai Film in this country is matched by a similar underrating in Japan. Therefore, in the literature of Japanese film criticism, the separation between such vague terms as *jidai-geki*, Samurai Film, and *chambara* is not clear-cut. Basically, it seems that any period or costume film a particular critic likes is a *jidai-geki*; any film a critic doesn't like, or which appears overly formulaic, is a *chambara*. To avoid these confusions, the term *Sword Film* is utilized as a specifically definable subgenre of the Samurai Film.

The Sword Film is, in many ways, the most interesting and revealing of the subgenres within the Samurai Film. Films in this category are marked by huge commercial appeal in Japan (and, comparatively, in America) and by almost total critical deprecation, exceeding that greeting the other subgenres. By classical Western standards of aesthetic value, the Sword Film appears to be a vast wasteland of formulaic pulp. If originality is prized, as it is in Western art, then the virtually authorless, very similar Sword Films can never qualify as anything other than mere entertainment for the (Japanese) lowest common denominator. Too, the extremely violent nature of the films makes them, in the eyes of many critics, akin to pornography or rank exploitation and hence unworthy of attention.

Obviously, serious issue may be taken with such judgments. Not only are these films worthy of attention for what they reveal of the Japanese character, but there is great artistic merit in the best of them as well. Paying serious attention to the Sword Film is justified on cultural grounds; one might also be able to redeem the subgenre on aesthetic grounds.

The Sword Film, as defined here, begins with Kurosawa's *Yojimbo* (1961). Although typically described as a "Japanese Western," *Yojimbo* has much in common with American gangster films, hardly surprising (if ill understood) since it is strongly reminiscent in plot and setting of Dashiell Hammett's "hard-boiled" novel *Red Harvest*. The introduction of elements from the Western and gangster genres (with their very different mythologies) marks a change in the mythos of the Samurai Film.

The Sword Film, of course, has much in common with the other subgenres of the Samurai Film. As in the Nostalgic Dramas, the hero is usually a *ronin*. Or, as in the Anti-Feudal Film, he will begin as a clansman but then lose his status. The Sword Film is virtually without exception situated in the Tokugawa era, but, as in the Zen Fighters form, the society is often merely a backdrop against which spectacular duels take place. And, as in any (and every) Samurai Film, a duel, often of incredible proportions, inevitably provides the climax.

While the Samurai Film of the prewar era, as demonstrated by Lisa Spalding's article in this anthology, owes most of its particularities to Japanese specificities of culture, history, and aesthetics, Western critics have frequently commented upon the similarities between Samurai Films and Hollywood Westerns. In the case of the Sword Film, these comparisons are quite justified, for there are two important borrowings from American Westerns (and gangster films): the "gun for hire," and the pivotal role of an interestingly personified antagonist.

The hired gun is a popular formulaic protagonist in American action genres, no doubt a reflection of competitive capitalism. One perfects one's skills not in a Zen quest for transcendence through action, but in order to secure an edge in the marketplace. The fast draw and deadly aim become negotiable skills available to the highest bidder. There is often a proviso, namely, that the hero will reject the offer of money if the cause is unjust. This is, in fact, a standard way of distinguishing the hero from the villain: the former will switch his allegiance in the name of justice, while the latter remains merely an employee.

The transportation of the gun-for-hire, namely, the sword-for-hire, appears to a small extent in the Nostalgic Drama (for example, *Seven Samurai*), but the element of "hire" is deemphasized mainly by the small amount of money typically exchanged and by the relationship which subsequently develops between the hero and his protectees. In the Sword Film, on the other hand, it is not unusual for the hero to require and receive huge sums of money for his services—a significant break with *Bushido,* which specifically taught disdain for money.

The Sword Film also introduced an increased function for an antagonist. In the Nostalgic and Anti-Feudal Dramas, the antagonist was typically generalized into the system, and the climactic battle often featured massed armies against the lone hero (or very few). In both *Seven Samurai* and *Hara-kiri,* for instance, the heroes are attacked by nameless soldiers whom we do not know or care about in any way. The Zen Fighters film, of course, did require an antagonist, for the Zen swordsman had to face an opponent of considerable skill in order to communicate the palpable risk the hero was willing to face in his quest for perfection. The antagonist, however, was valuable for the most part insofar as he could wield a sword. The antagonist in the Sword Film plays a more central role.

In many Westerns the hero takes on significance in direct proportion to the villain he opposes. Moreover, the villain often shares some link with the hero—as hired guns, civil war veterans, former friends, etc. In the remarkable Westerns of Anthony Mann (such as *Winchester '73, Bend of the River,* and *The Man from Laramie*) and Budd Boetticher (*Seven Men from Now, The Tall T,* and *Ride Lonesome*), the villains and heroes are linked as family members or former friends who may be seen as structurally equivalent and psychologically paired. The Sword Film offers a similar pattern of matching oppositions. For the first time in the postwar Samurai Film, the villains are personified as viable, powerful enemies with personalities and motivations. Often the same actors portray hero and villain to further establish this linking. In Mann's *Bend of the River* and *The Man from Laramie,* James Stewart as the hero is paired with Arthur Kennedy as the villain. Kurosawa's *Yojimbo* sets Mifune Toshiro against Nakadai Tatsuya, and the two return, even more evenly matched and more closely linked, in *Tsubaki Sanjuro* (*Sanjuro,* 1962).

The Sword Film also acknowledges the Western and the gangster film by offering up an array of non-Samurai heroes, a kind of democratization of the genre. These heroes are not *ronin,* for they never were members of the Samurai caste. Two of the more popular heroes in Sword Film series exemplify this tendency: Zato Ichi, the blind swordsman, and Mekurano Oichi (the Crimson Bat), the blind swordswoman. (Why they should both be blind, and the significance of this fact from the point of view of cultural revelation, must await another study.) They both began life as humble masseurs but carved out, so to speak, a reputation for themselves via their swordplay and sense of justice. If one of the key factors in the Western or gangster film is that anyone can shoot a gun, so does the Sword Film seem to imply that a sword can be a great equalizer (as can a gun, which makes its appearance in this and the other Samurai sub-genres, on some symbolic occasions).

The underlying philosophy of the Sword Film seems to be a kind of nihilism. The rigid moral codes of Confucianism or *Bushido* are replaced in this subgenre by a world of meaningless death and destruction brought about by personal desires: greed, jealousy, revenge. The Sword Film delivers up a world of violence and chaos, a world in which people are mere objects for the cutting edge of a killing sword. The hero of the Sword Film often revels in the death and destruction he causes. The eponymous hero of *Yojimbo* ironically remarks at the film's conclusion that the town will be peaceful now; indeed it will, for almost everyone in it has been killed. A virtual slaughterfest climaxes every Sword Film.

The violence inherent in the Sword Film extends to both the numbers of deaths and the explicitness of their portrayal. The sight, often in color and usually in Cinemascope, of fountains of blood emerging from headless bodies, of severed limbs flying through the air, is common, and expected, in this subgenre. People are reduced to their components, becoming mere patterns of color and line. It is significant that in this respect one of the paradigmatic series in this subgenre, *Kozure Ookami* I-VI (known here as the *Sword of Vengeance* series), was adapted from a popular comic strip.[9] The characters in comic books are not real people but "essential people," people reduced to their defining graphic essence. If it has been the function of the cinema to make the fantastic seem credible, it is the purpose of comic books to make the fantastic seem incredible. The Sword Films, especially the *Sword of Vengeance* series and the later films within the Zato Ichi series, lose most of their realistic ties and enter a realm of magic and mystery.

An index of the ever-increasing sense of fantasy, or at least overly far-fetched extensions of reality, is the number of antagonists the hero is able to dispatch in a single battle. Ogami Itto, the "lone wolf with child" in the *Sword of Vengeance* series, kills perhaps two dozen combatants in the first film of the series, but by the fifth or sixth entry, he dispatches over a hundred, single-handedly.

Given the reduction of people to graphic elements, the extra prowess of the hero, and the removal of the historical/social context, the Sword Film begins to take shape as a subgenre of an order slightly different from the rest of the Samurai form. The Sword Film has a direct connection to folktales or myths, more so even than other Samurai Films based upon historical personages. And it does so because of its remarkable consistency as to narrative, character, and action. The films within this subgenre (especially the later films in the Zato Ichi series, along with the *Crimson Bat* and *Sword of Vengeance* series) seem to be mere variations of the same basic story. Critics have, in fact, complained that these films are almost indistinguishable. This is quite true, but there is significance in this truth.

Vladimir Propp, in his *Morphology of the Folk Tale*,[10] demonstrated that Russian children's stories had a remarkable consistency at the structural level. He outlined this morphology, demonstrating how each individual story was a variation of a more global story. Similarly, Lévi-Strauss has tried to show in his massive *Mythologiques* how myths become transformed over time, but that a coherent structural level can be isolated despite these sometimes large changes.[11] Similarly, the Sword Film can be shown to possess a narrative morphology, and a character or "actantial" morphology as well. The following outline does not purport to exhaust the form of the Sword Film, but rather to indicate that there is a high degree of sameness to the films in the form and that this sameness must be acknowledged and understood. This, then, is a schema of how the films are structured:

(1) A scene of battle is underway:
    (a) a battle in progress;
    (b) a duel in progress;
    (c) a quarrel in progress; or
    (d) a violent ritual in progress.
(2) The hero is identified:
    (a) the hero carries a sword which he uses successfully;
    (b) the hero carries a sword which he deigns to use; or
    (c) the hero uses some other weapon.
(3) The hero's circumstances are detailed:
    (a) the hero is a *ronin*;
    (b) the hero is a clansman; or
    (c) the hero, or heroine, is a non-samurai wanderer who carries a sword.
(4) The victim is introduced as:
    (a) a clan in need;
    (b) a peasant in need;
    (c) an errant child uncovered;
    (d) a town in need; or
    (e) the hero himself.
(5) The villain is introduced as:
    (a) a clan leader;
    (b) a clan scheme; or

    (c) an *oyabun* (gang boss).
(6) The hero comes in contact with the victim:
    (a) the wanderer-hero travels the countryside and becomes involved al-
    most accidentally;
    (b) the victim seeks out the hero because of his reputation and
        (1) the hero will be paid handsomely, or
        (2) the hero's morality is prevailed upon; or
    (c) the villain engineers the hero's destruction.
(7) The villain's henchman is introduced:
    (a) the henchman is given a separate narrative segment; or
    (b) the henchman is literally introduced by the villain in a separate scene.

These first seven "functions" I call the Basic Situation. This Basic Situation is
structured according to the following pattern:

(1)–(2)
(3) or
(3)–(4)
(5) or
(4)–(5)
(6)
(7)

   In detail, the typical Basic Situation is organized in the following manner:
   (1)–(2). The films usually begin on a note of confusion with a scene of
violence into whose midst we are plunged. This scene sets the tone of the action
to follow; it is a dynamic plunge into the filmic world. The chaos of the opening
scene also reflects the moral chaos of the diegesis. The hero can be isolated as a
result of his superior abilities and attitudes.
   (3) The hero's circumstances are revealed first indexically by the quality of
his kimono, how many swords he carries (one or two), how he wears his hair,
where he lives, etc. Often we get a quick glimpse of his circumstances in (1)–(2),
as the hero may be walking down a country road only to be attacked or to be
confronted by a quarrel.
   (4) Sometimes the hero is the victim, in which case (3) and (4) are linked.
Such is the case in *Kozure Ookami I* (the series I consider archetypal of the
Sword Film). Otherwise, a separate syntagmatic section will detail the victim,
or else the hero will witness the victim's treatment at the hands of the villain
(typical of the Zato Ichi series).
   (5) The villain usually receives his own syntagm in which he reveals his aims,
such as the hero's destruction or his intended victim's future plight. Alternately,

if the villain is an *oyabun,* he might not appear until later. This section will then allude to his existence.

(6) If the hero is not the victim, he will now come into intimate contact with him/her/them.

(7) The villain's henchman will often have his own syntagm by way of dynamic introduction; or he will be asked by his boss, the villain, or a more minor henchman to show his skill.

Once the basic situation is underway, the Sword Film proceeds toward the eventual meeting of the hero and villain according to the following functions:

(8) The hero and henchman sound each other out.

(9) The hero and victim form a relationship:

(a) romance (which is rare); or

(b) extreme sympathy and pity for each other's plight.

(10) The villain sends a minor henchman to attack the hero.

(11) The hero has an interlude:

(a) the hero engages in comic byplay and defeats the villain comically;

(b) the hero remembers his past life—relate to (3); or

(c) the hero comes into contact with a reminder of his past life.

(12) The hero engages in a slaughterfest of the villain's minions.

(13) The hero defeats the chief henchman:

(a) the two engage in a spectacular duel; or

(b) the henchman decides not to fight.

(14) The hero kills the villain.

It is possible for functions (12) and (13) to be reversed; that is, often the henchman is killed by the hero, causing the villain to send in the rest of his troops, who are then also killed by the hero.

Aside from the narrative movements, the relationships in the Sword Film can also be schematized:

hero	henchman
victim	villain

This relationship is to be read both horizontally and diagonally. There is a relationship between the hero and the victim similar to that between the henchman and the villain, mainly one of subordinate to superior. Too, the hero has a relationship to the henchman in that both share similar backgrounds and abilities. When there is no henchman, the villain and the hero share this function. And when there is no victim, the relationship between the hero and the villain is more direct.

The ritualistic repetition of these narrative and actantial functions causes any given Sword Film to be devalued in favor of the value of the form as a whole.

The films differ, of course, but they differ according to specific modes of action and types of antagonist. Too, as the Sword Film moved into the early '70s, each film simply tried to outdo its predecessor in number of deaths and their spectacular delivery. To achieve this differentiation, the films retreated from reality and entered the realm of fantasy. Their narrative similarities aided this movement, since the givens of each film would be known a priori. Similarly, elements of style, graphic design, and patterning enabled films to achieve their modest differentiation. The Sword of Vengeance series manifests this most directly, offering up some of the most interestingly composed shots and some of the most imaginatively staged fight scenes in the history of the cinema.

The nihilistic foundation of the Sword Film is not simply a function of the number of deaths, their graphic delivery, or the hero's relishing of them. It may also be seen by the degree of hopelessness to which the hero succumbs. There is no future for the wanderer-heroes in these films. They can take to the road of a moralistic hero, such as Zato Ichi, or of a paid assassin, such as Ogami Itto, but in no case will they find peace and contentment. Each of them has a tragic lot in life. However, this tragedy, unlike that of the hero in the Nostalgic or Anti-Feudal Drama, does not produce *mono no aware*. The reduction of people to graphic elements helps ensure that. Furthermore, the heroes, to a degree, relish their state, finding their life of hopelessness to be a positive one. As Ogami Itto himself states, he is on the road to hell. But it is not paved with good intentions. It is paved with the blood of countless other travelers along the same path.

We have seen that the Nostalgic and Anti-Feudal Dramas shared the following inverse ratio: the overvaluation of society, the undervaluation of the individual. The Zen Fighters subgenre simply reversed that: the undervaluation of society, the overvaluation of the individual. But in restructuring this relationship as the undervaluation of society, the undervaluation of the individual, the Sword Film exposes its nihilism. Neither society nor the individual possesses much value. Heroism is ultimately meaningless, as is a search for self-perfection. The Sword Film thus offers up a very bleak, though very stylized, view of the human condition.

The Mythicization of History and the Samurai Film

By the early 1980s, the Samurai Film became all but extinct. Even at its height in the '60s it gave way in popularity and industry (commercial) status to the *Yakuza* (gangster) film. Like the Western, though, the Samurai Film served, and continues to serve, an important cultural function helping to merge the past and the present and alleviate cultural tensions.[12] The mythos inherent in the Samurai Film took time to develop. A dimly perceived cultural need was felt: initially, a nostalgia which was followed by an anti-nostalgia. The Zen Fighters form struck other cultural roots, but it was the Sword Film, the most popular subform, which most clearly addressed mythic undercurrents. Simply put, the Sword Film mythicizes history by rewriting it. This rewriting, found in the ratio of society to individuality, or in the *giri/ninjō* dichotomy, reflects the postwar disjunction between the traditional, rural, family-centered society and the modern, post-industrial, work-centered society. With loosening traditional bonds and a deteriorating centrality of the family, increased societal tensions broke out. The dominant society, however, could not continue in the face of a deteriorating social structure. The Sword Film, by focusing on extremely self-contained, often acutely psychopathic heroes, rewrote the feudal past as an evolution toward personal freedom to be attained outside society. History was mythicized when it was ignored. "Myth deprives the object of which it speaks of all History. In it, history evaporates."[13] The sometimes glorious, sometimes shameful, sometimes disturbing Japanese past disappeared, giving way to violent men with swords roaming a land of chaos and heroism.

Of course, there is a "conservative" function to this mythicizing process. By transforming history into myth, the status quo legitimizes history in its own image; it transforms nature into culture. Myth, in the hands of a ruling class, through the industrial apparatus of the cinema, can transform "the reality of the world into an image of the world."[14] Myths can be used to blur the distinctions between the natural and the conventional, between the fact of history and the idea of history.

To a (conservative) Japanese ruling class, some of the potentially radical ideas inherent in the Samurai Film had to be displaced. The anger which could be built up over the continued re-recognition of the undervaluation of the individual could not be displaced merely through catharsis, but through a mythos which developed an alternative, albeit parallel, society—that is, an ahistorical sense of history. The great paradox of the Samurai Film is that it has nothing whatsoever to do with history and everything to do with myth.

NOTES

1. J. L. Anderson and Donald Richie. *The Japanese Film: Art and Industry,* Expanded edition (Princeton, N.J.: Princeton UP, 1982), p. 160.
2. Ibid., p. 64.
3. Ivan Morris, *The Nobility of Failure: Tragic Heroes in the History of Japan* (New York: New American Library, 1975).

4. For a discussion of the implications of this term, see *Sources of Japanese Tradition*, Vol. 1, compiled by Ryusaku Tsunoda, Wm. Theodore de Barry, and Donald Keene (New York: Columbia UP, 1958), pp. 172–174.

5. The concept of sacrificial victim is adapted from Rene Girard, *Violence and the Sacred*, trans. Patrick Gregory (Baltimore: Johns Hopkins UP, 1977), especially pp. 68–88, 250–273.

6. For an in-depth discussion of the anti–security treaty protests, see George W. Packard, *Protest in Tokyo: The Security Treaty Crisis of 1960* (Princeton, N.J.: Princeton UP, 1966). For a discussion of the significance of this protest movement with regard to a range of Japanese films, especially the growing New Wave movement, see David Desser, *Eros plus Massacre: An Introduction to the Japanese New Wave Cinema* (Bloomington and Indianapolis: Indiana UP, 1988), pp. 24–38.

7. See H. Paul Varley, *Japanese Culture: A Short History,* expanded edition (New York: Praeger, 1977), p. 196; and Desser, *Eros plus Massacre,* especially chapters 1 and 5.

8. A significant exception to this is Gregory Barrett's admirable *Archetypes in Japanese Film* (see bibliography for full reference), which discusses the film career, so to speak, of Miyamoto Musashi in rich detail. Barrett's discussion maintains that there is more continuity between the prewar and postwar period films than the present essay implies.

9. *Sword of Vengeance* is the English title for the series from Japan. Part III of the series was released by Columbia Pictures in 1973 in a dubbed version under the title *The Lightning Swords of Death.* The film was marketed in an effort to capitalize on the Kung Fu craze, as it was called, of dubbed films from Hong Kong (Bruce Lee, and the films of the Shaw Bros., for example). New World Pictures released an English-language version of part II (with some sequences from part I incorporated into it), replete with new music and sound effects, and a careful dubbing job, under the title *Shogun Assassin* in 1979. The increased popularity of Japanese comic books (*manga*) in the U.S. has led to an English-language version of the original comic strip, under the title of *Lone Wolf with Cub.*

10. Ed. Louis A. Wagner, trans. Laurence Scott (Austin: U of Texas P, 1968).

11. Under the general heading "Introduction to a Science of Mythology," this study has appeared in a multivolume series: *The Raw and the Cooked; From Honey to Ashes; The Origin of Table Manners; The Naked Man,* trans. John and Doreen Weightman (New York: Harper and Row, 1973–1981).

12. The death of the Samurai Film was aided, as was the death of the American Western, by its transposition to television. The Japanese film industry in general declined significantly in the 1960s, and has not yet recovered. See Anderson and Richie, pp. 254–256, 451–456. Samurai action dramas found a welcome home on television in the 1960s, but began to fade in the 1970s. A handful, however, can still be seen today in reruns. *Jidai-geki* (that is, period films which do not feature swordsmen), especially a kind of historical melodrama, still occupy a significant portion of the programming of NHK (the Japanese equivalent of the BBC and the U.S. PBS). It is significant that one *jidai-geki* series, *Mito Komon,* a combination of swordplay and melodrama, remains, even after two decades, one of the most popular Japanese television programs. A member of the shogunate family, Mito Komon roams the land, aided by his ninja-trained assistants, in search of wrongdoers. The show's simplistic ideology clearly reflects a desire for moral certitude and a benevolent, even magical, government ever watchful of its citizens' well-being.

13. Roland Barthes, *Mythologies,* trans. Annette Lavers (New York: Hill and Wang, 1972), p. 151.

14. Ibid., p. 141.

The *Yakuza* Film:
An Introduction

Keiko Iwai McDonald

For nearly a decade beginning in the early 1960s, the *yakuza* (gangster) film enjoyed tremendous popularity in Japan. Its hero invariably was a "good" *yakuza,* an honorable man who fought to preserve traditional values of loyalty and selflessness against the unprincipled opportunism of "bad" *yakuza.* Yet, as McDonald's survey of the history of the genre makes clear, the *yakuza* hero has undergone numerous transformations, both great and small. Contending that the *yakuza* genre "offers fascinating insights into the dynamic interplay between film, filmmaker, and culture," McDonald examines the areas of character types, iconography, structure, and theme for the generic elements they embody. Her method involves focusing on such representative prewar and postwar films as Ito Daisuke's *Chuji's Travel Diary (Chuji tabi nikki,* 1927), Makino Masahiro's *Adventures of Jirocho (Jirocho sangokushi,* 1952–54), Tadashima Tadashi's *The Theater of Life (Jinsei gekijo—Hishakaku,* 1963), and Fukasaku Kinji's *Combat without a Code (Jingi naki tataki,* 1973–74), among others. In the process she not only charts the subtle and ever-shifting demands of *giri* (obligation/responsibility), *ninjō* (personal inclination), and *jingi* (the code of honor in the *yakuza* world), but she also discusses the interaction of the *yakuza* genre and popular literature; the role of the Toei and the Nikkatsu companies in shaping the genre; the principal variations on the basic *yakuza* formula (including the introduction of the female *yakuza* Oryu); the contribution of superstars such as Takakura Ken, Okochi Denjiro, and Sugawara Bunta; and the decline of the genre in the 1970s and 1980s. Basically, McDonald sees the genre as important for two main reasons: (1) its inherent aesthetic worth, and (2) its reflection of Japan's changing social consciousness in nearly a century of radical change. In her conclusion she ponders what the future may have in store for this most durable of genres.

Little in English has appeared previously on the *yakuza*

film. The highly generic nature of the films, their association with working-class urban, male audiences (cf. Sato Tadao's *Currents in Japanese Cinema*), and the auteurist bias of most of the earlier work on Japanese cinema (e.g., Donald Richie's *Japanese Cinema: Film Style and National Character;* Joan Mellen's *The Waves at Genji' Door;* and Audie Bock' s *Japanese Film Directors*) has precluded serious study of the films. This bias has translated into a general lack of not only theatrical showings in the U.S., but also nontheatrical and video availability. We may also be faced with an instance where the popular tastes of one culture do not translate to overseas success, although this is a questionable thesis—that is, a hypothesis that precisely should be questioned. Keiko McDonald's essay is a good place to begin this discussion.

For additional English-language bibliography, see Gregory Barrett, *Archetypes in Japanese Film: The Sociopolitical and Religious Significance of the Principal Heroes and Heroines* (Selingsgrove: Susquehanna UP, 1989); Ian Buruma, *Behind the Mask: On Sexual Demons, Sacred Mothers, Transvestites, Gangsters, Drifters and Other Japanese Cultural Heroes* (New York: Pantheon, 1984); and Paul Schrader, "*Yakuza-eiga*: A Primer," *Film Comment* 10 (Jan.–Feb. 1974): 10–17.

The *yakuza* film is an excellent example of a genre taking shape, and changing shape, in response to popular culture. In fact, this responsiveness has existed for so long (sixty years to date) that the critic may well feel stymied by the complex interactions involved. Yet surely a constructive critical approach begins by recognizing that notions of genre themselves reflect sets of cultural conventions. As Andrew Tudor notes, "The crucial factors which distinguish a genre are not only characteristics inherent in the films themselves; they also depend on the particular culture within which we are operating."[1] Given this premise, the *yakuza* genre offers fascinating insights into the dynamic interplay between film, filmmaker, and culture. The formula characteristic of the genre relies heavily on "known plots," "recognizable characters," and "obvious iconography"—all aspects deeply rooted in the culture of the audience, and conditioned by it too.

My method here will involve choosing representative prewar and postwar examples from the vast array of *yakuza* films made. I will use them to illustrate significant changes in the given formula, showing along the way how the interaction of major cultural conventions contributes to the structural unity of individual films. I also hope to shed some light on the changing social consciousness these films reflect directly in a century of radical change for Japan and the world at large. (Since most of the films under discussion have not been shown in the West, I have included descriptive analyses whenever necessary.)

To begin with, let us bring the omnivorous lexicon of "the *yakuza* film" up to date. The genre it names, for example, is properly the *ninkyo* film, which translates as "film of a chivalrous nature," and which is about *yakuza*-gamblers (*bakuto*), con-artist vendors (*tekiya*), and dedicated gangsters.[2] As we shall see, most prewar films feature *bakuto yakuza,* as do most postwar films set in the feudal period. The two other kinds of *yakuza* have come into the genre more recently, since the 1950s.

Taking *jingi* (the code of honor prevalent in the world of *yakuza*) as his watchword, the *yakuza* experiences his own version of the characteristic Japanese tension between opposing values of *giri* (social obligation) and *ninjō* (personal inclination).[3] This conflict, internalized in a *yakuza* protagonist, forms a major plot convention, interacting with easily identifiable if often highly compressed icons. A typical plot climaxes in the hero's sword- or gunfight resolving the issue at hand. The plot advances by means of the clear-cut oppositions familiar in Westerns (and beloved of nimble structuralist critics). These good/bad, in/out, and individual/group polarities speak clearly of cultural values and ideals. Notably absent in the prewar *yakuza* formula, however, is the garden/desert opposition. Instead we shall see how the high/low dichotomy clearly reflects the vertical structure of Japanese society as a whole.

One Western critic sees the beginnings of most film genres as traceable to literary sources, most often "pulp" ones.[4] Interestingly enough, the uniquely Japanese *yakuza* genre derives from a somewhat richer cultural substrate. Its sources include not only popular literature but dramatic and oral-literary traditions as well.

One of the earliest and most fondly remembered *yakuza* films is Ito Daisuke's silent classic *Chuji tabi nikki* (*Chuji's Travel Diary,* 1927). The protagonist, Kunisada Chuji, was an actual historical figure who came to represent a kind of Robin Hood among *yakuza* bosses. He became a favorite subject of the *kodan* storytellers, who recited tales of derring-do from the Tokugawa period. Chuji also figured in the historical plays that were the specialty of the Shinkokugeki troupes. In all these sources Chuji, a young horse driver, changes from law-abiding citizen to hero with a price on his head. Outraged by injustice and sick of seeing magistrates tax poor farmers to death, he joins a *yakuza* gang and becomes its boss, leading his men in open defiance of the wicked magistrate, who—like the Sheriff of Nottingham—is a feared and hated oppressor of the poor.

Dependent on the audience's knowledge of such sources, Director Ito is free to shift his thematic focus so that *Chuji's Travel Diary,* interestingly enough, celebrates heroism in decline. A three-part study of a down-and-out heroic outlaw on the run, it has Chuji kill the wicked magistrate and hide out on Mount Akagi, only to become a star-crossed fugitive when he actually leaves the mountain.

The narrative pattern for the trilogy follows this outlaw hero on the lam. His adventures complicate but cannot change his destiny: having nowhere to go, he must inevitably fall into the clutches of the law. The solitary hero pitted against the group—society at large—thus forms the basic storyline, while issues of *giri* and *ninjō,* with various permutations, provide the moral tension and advance the plot.

Part one is titled *Koshu satsujin-hen (Swashbuckling in Koshu)*. Here Chuji has befriended the son of a distinguished family. A villainous uncle has joined a gang of *yakuza,* determined to cheat the nephew out of his inheritance by forcing himself on his niece. Torn between *giri* (his obligation to the son) and *ninjō* (his desire to survive), Chuji comes to the rescue, even though in doing so he reveals his true identity and makes himself a fugitive once again. Thus, following the ideal *yakuza's* heroic ethic serves only to hurry him into exile.

Simple as the storyline is, it illustrates a formulaic response to the demands of *giri* made on the footloose *yakuza.* In this case, the operative ideal of *isshoku ichihan* ("a night's lodging and a meal") means that the itinerant *yakuza* must repay his boss/benefactor with service even though it may involve him in gang warfare and put his life at risk.

That Chuji in part one has no boss of his own is important, since Ito's aim is to show a *yakuza* ostracized by his fellows, thus estranged from his own subculture. Moreover, by concealing his identity, Chuji puts himself that much more outside the pale, since it means he must count on the kindness meted out to one another by men *outside yakuza* society.

Part two, *Shinshu kessho-hen (Bloody Laugh in Shinshu)*, pits Chuji against his own band of men and shows how the solid vertical relationship established by *giri*—the boss-henchman relationship—dissolves. His mistress and most of his followers betray him, ruled as they are by *ninjō*—base and treacherous passions. Further, Chuji's sense of alienation is made worse by his failing health.

In part three, *Goyo-hen (Chuji's Arrest)*, the inevitable happens. As a prisoner being taken back to his home, Chuji is reduced to utter despair. Yet some goodness remains in the world. The restoration of the boss-henchman relationship advances the narrative as he is rescued by former followers still *giri*-bound to him; however, even rescue is humiliating for this now-ailing middle-aged man borne homeward on a stretcher. A devoted concubine nurses him back to health, yet Chuji runs away to become the trusted steward of a sake brewer in Niigata. Again, the *yakuza*'s sense of duty (*giri*) comes into conflict with the desire to live and be happy (*ninjō*). This happens when Chuji's actual identity is revealed during a fight with a villainous *yakuza* who threatens the brewer's son. Once again a wanted man, Chuji flees to his hometown. There he falls sick and is captured again. Clearly Ito labors to convey a sense of the pathos that lies behind the heroic destiny of the ideal *yakuza*. Unfortunately, the scenario is all that survives of this masterpiece of the *yakuza* genre.

This loss is all the more unfortunate because it is difficult to get a sense of this film's particular cinematic accomplishments. Specifically, as a subdivision of a broader genre (the *jidai-geki*), the film required a swordfight. Critics of the time were especially moved by the exquisitely fluid camera work in swashbuckling scenes, which were notable for their use of short takes captured by Ito's cameraman running among the fighters, literally swinging his camera. This tactic in particular serves to intensify the in/out and individual/society opposition,[5] for it expresses the anger and agony of the solitary hero fighting against overwhelming odds. Then, too, the superstar Okochi Denjiro, who played Chuji, was noted for his expressive power in face and body—important gifts in this era of silent film. Finally, there are the icons of the genre, most notably the attire. Chuji wears a cape, and hat and shoes made of straw. His vagabond status is defined by these properties in much the same way that the Western gunslinger is by his buckskin jacket and low-slung holster. It is important, too, that his getup be shabby. One particularly memorable, lyrical long shot finds Chuji so attired as he drags his palsy-ridden body through a field of pampas grass. Thus these icons provide a shorthand of mutually recognizable communication that neither filmmaker nor spectators need ponder: the uses of adversity more cogently expressed than any intertitle.

The immense popularity of this film might be traced to Chuji's own motto: "No human being wants to see his fortunes decline." Indeed, the acute economic depression of Japan in the late 1920s must have given a poignant immediacy to the troubles of this great man brought low.[6] However that may be, one critic sees genre films "made in imitation not of life but of other films."[7] If this is the case, then naturally we anticipate further explorations of Chuji's plight as solitary hero carried through a trilogy by Ito. Sure enough, Yamanaka Sadao's sound film, *Kunisada Chuji* (1935) leads the protagonist in a circle, describing escape from solitude to human involvement and back to solitude once more. Chuji, disguised as a peddler of medicines, comes in his wanderings to a country inn. There he meets three sets of guests, all victims of unkind fate: a couple forced to elope; a young samurai and his old retainers in need of someone to avenge their wrongs; and a father with his daughter soon to be sold to a brothel.

The shared uncertainty of all their lives brings Chuji close to these fellow travelers, but only for a single winter's day. He rescues no one, and at the end of the
film departs alone. The other guests also journey into uncertainty, but at least
they have the luxury of loving companionship.

In 1935 Itami Mansaku directed a sound film depicting the rise, not the fall,
of the ideal *yakuza*. In *Chuji uridasu* (*Chuji Makes a Name for Himself*), Itami's
first sound picture, the pattern, however, still shifts from "in" (society) to "out"
(social outcasts). Chuji, the law-abiding, lowly horse dealer, joins a *bakuto*
group, disgusted with the oppressive feudal system. He tries to kill a villainous
magistrate, but is foiled by a masterless samurai. Then, in a clash of factions, he
storms the enemy stronghold and single-handedly kills the rival *yakuza* boss.
Though famous overnight, he quickly becomes disillusioned with his own boss,
who does not follow the *jingi* code. Here, interestingly enough, we see a permutation of the classical *giri/ninjō* conflict. His absolute loyalty as a henchman—
one type of *giri*—is pitted against a larger sense of *giri*—obedience to the code
of honor. The second overrides the first. Once again, outlaw Chuji becomes the
odd man out, the suffering lone wolf.

The various images thus given Chuji indicate the response of directors to
an increasingly demanding audience. The glorified unreality of exploits told and
retold by the *kodan* storytellers no longer satisfied. The rise of popular literature
brought new demands to the attention of film studio moguls, who quickly fell in
line with trends in mass entertainment. Serial fiction in newspapers, in magazines, and on radio brought superheroes down to earth and made them real—
however outsized their exploits.

The cultural climate of the late 1920s favored yet another aspect of genre
development: interaction of film and popular literature. Two writers of popular
fiction were especially useful to directors seeking material for the *yakuza* genre:
Hasegawa Shin and Kobozawa Kan. While Hasegawa taught directors how to
humanize the *yakuza*, Kobozawa showed how to capture their charisma.

Beginning in 1929, something like a Hasegawa boom hit the cinema industry. In the next twelve years, seventy-six of his works were adapted for the
screen.[8] *Matatabi waraji* (*Yakuza on the Road*, 1929) was the first, and helped
establish a subgenre given the name *matatabi*, which translates as "traveling
everywhere." The travelers in this case are itinerant gamblers, and such icons as
the straw hat, cape, and gait all express the hero's plight. Significantly Hasegawa's writing provided a new type of vagabond for filmmakers: the prototypi-
cal *yakuza* who becomes a criminal outcast out of *sheer necessity* and who seeks
to free himself from the bondage imposed by his gang. Here the formula plots
out the *yakuza*'s shift from in-group (society) to outer group (social outcasts).

The corollary crisis results from his futile attempt to break the code of *giri* demanded by the group he has joined.

Mabuta no haha (*Long-Sought Mother*, aka *The Mother He Never Knew*, 1931), Inagaki Hiroshi's first screen adaptation of a Hasegawa novel, fits this pattern. The protagonist Chujiro, who possesses many attractive qualities, is a victim of unkind circumstance: his mother abandoned him as a child, so he had no choice but to live outside society. Even so, he grows up determined to reunite with her. Worried that she might be living in misery, he saves his money to help, only to find that she has married into wealth and social position and has no intention of seeing her outcast *yakuza* son.

True to the novel, the film ends by giving melodramatic form to the accepted view of the situation, according to 1931 standards. Chujiro blames himself, not his mother, for his becoming a *yakuza*. Though "somebody," he is nevertheless socially unacceptable, and therefore unworthy of a mother's love. Denied him is the ultimate male happiness of protecting the weaker sex or serving as head of a family. He cries out, "I don't want to be a *yakuza*!" Too late. His desire for respectability must remain a dream, a form of mere wish fulfillment.[9]

Since the director of a silent film aiming for melodrama could scarcely afford lengthy, sentimental dialogue rendered by subtitles, one way Inagaki solved this problem was by using two icons—one innovative, the other deeply rooted in Japanese literary tradition. Thus, at the beginning of the film, Chujiro is asked if he dreams of his mother. The camera cuts to a flock of birds in the sky, then to a solitary bird perched on a branch. Superimposed on this latter image is Issa's famous haiku: "Come here / To play with me / A motherless sparrow" (Ware to kite / Asobeya oya no / Nai suzume). This innovative icon is tied to a conventional one when the camera then cuts back to Chujiro in traveler's attire standing underneath a tree. The point is made.

The narrative pattern recording a shift from "in" to "out," for reasons beyond the hero's control, is used in another silent film by Inagaki: *Ippon gatata dohyoiri* (*Sumo Wrestler's Debut*, 1931). Here Mohei, an unpromising apprentice sumo wrestler abandoned by his trainer, is adrift and penniless. The prostitute Otsuta passes by and gives him what money she has. He promises that he will become a really good wrestler. Ten years pass. Mohei is on the road again, this time as a *yakuza*. He finds Otsuta and her family victimized by a local *yakuza* boss. Thus he is torn by conflicting loyalties: to his benefactress Otsuta on the "outside" and to his *yakuza* boss on the "inside." Conflict is resolved by a dazzling display of swashbuckling gallantry. Overcoming seemingly insurmountable odds, he tells Otsuta that this swordplay is his glorious debut as a wrestler. Here as elsewhere the woman figure symbolizes the hero's nostalgia for lost familial happiness.

Other Inagaki *yakuza* exhibit a contrary archetype: the optimistic hero who rejoices in his freedom and self-determination. The two-part silent film *Yataro gasa* (*Yataro's Travel Hat*, 1932) takes its bold outsider from a novel by Kobozawa. Having been a shogun's retainer—a position many masterless samurai would have been glad to occupy—Yataro rejects this fairly high social position to become an outcast. Yet his heroic spirit survives this loss of position with notable panache, for unlike the *yakuza* on the run, he is able to enjoy romantic involvement—and even indulge in displays of heroism for the woman he adores. Thus he is brilliantly prepared to avenge the death of the heroine Yuki's father. As such, the element of swordplay is masterfully realized in these films, with entertainment value balanced by the expected melodramatic romance.[10]

The heroes of two other Inagaki films also choose to be outsiders, and notably happy-go-lucky ones as well. In *Senryoraku* (*Lottery Jackpot*, 1935) and *Matatabi senichiya* (*One Thousand and One Nights of Traveling*, 1936), journey becomes a metaphor for the freedom enjoyed by outlaws. Asked by a woman which way he is headed, one of these scamps replies: "Better ask my horse." The woman says she envies him such freedom. Clearly these outlaws, exuberant in their optimism and freedom, offered escape for Japanese audiences from the harsh realities of the difficult 1930s.

Nevertheless, a few prewar directors did try to offer other perspectives in order to reflect the sufferings of ordinary people. Among these directors was Tsuji Yorihiro, whose many *yakuza* films explore the tensions felt by a *yakuza* caught in the *giri/ninjō* conflict.[11] In *Kaketoji Tokijiro* (1929), *giri* relates to the most basic necessities as a *yakuza* ponders his obligation to the boss who gives him food and shelter. As explained earlier, the *jingi* code has a name for this: *isshoku ichihan*, "repayment for a night's accommodation and a meal." Tokijiro is indebted for three days' lodging when he is asked to join a fight with a rival gang. Forced to challenge and kill, Tokijiro balks at a follow-up order to murder an enemy, his wife, and his child. In this case, *giri* expresses loyalty to a temporary boss and *ninjō* compassion for the innocent. He reconciles the two by telling his boss that the *jingi* code forbids the harming of innocent people. Still, *giri* makes its claims on Tokijiro, who feels guilty for not being able to satisfy his boss.

As in most *yakuza* films based on Hasegawa novels, the hero can never free himself entirely from these ties. To be sure, Tokijiro leaves the outlaw life behind and even assumes responsibility for the wife and child he was assigned to kill. But like him they are rootless now, the life of decent common folk is closed to them; all they have is a roaming, hand-to-mouth existence. In one emotionally charged shot, Director Tsuji provides an image of the fate meted out to a man ostracized from both "societies." Tokijiro is seen taking the samisen from an itinerant singer dead in the road. He silently prays for the singer's repose in heaven.[12] Even terrible poverty cannot force him to resume the gambling life of the *yakuza*. He prefers to resign himself to the lowly singer's life.

A critic eager to escape the solitary, pessimistic *yakuza* prototype must look to the films of the 1950s, when a more positive protagonist emerges. This change is easy to relate to an enthusiastic return to the *jidai-geki* (period film genre) in response to the lifting of the Occupation ban on feudal tales. The public was hungry for this source of cultural continuity, and a new type of *yakuza* emerged to satisfy new needs.

Given Japan's economic recovery in the '50s, it is scarcely surprising that the new *yakuza* is no longer an outsider, an outcast who must keep moving to survive. Instead he has become a charismatic *yakuza* boss, strong on leadership and gallant optimism. A convenient model was found in Shimizu Jirocho, who lived in the tumultuous period of transition from feudalism to modernism in the late nineteenth century. Although he died as recently as 1893, Jirocho had already been celebrated in popular *kodan* tales.

This new trend started with Makino Masahiro's nine-part *Jirocho sangoku-shi* (*Adventures of Jirocho*, 1952-54). Among the many spin-offs and remakes that resulted were Makino's two four-part series *Wakaki hi no Jirocho* (*Young Days of Jirocho*, 1960-62) and *Jirocho sangoku-shi* (*Adventures of Jirocho*, 1963-64). Other films about Jirocho were *Ninkyo Tokaido* (*Yakuza Front on the Tokaido Path*, 1958) and *Jirocho Fuji* (*Jirocho and Mt. Fuji*, 1959), both directed by Matsuda Shoji. In all of these films Jirocho is a full-fledged boss guarded by faithful henchmen. Interestingly, the "in/out" opposition is muted by the hero's charisma. Although still an outsider, he is nothing like an outcast. Quite the contrary, legitimate society gives him a measure of respect because of his power to effect justice and protect the common folk. In fact, his motives tend to be selfless, arising out of a sense of justice and loyalty to the group.

The *giri/ninjō* conflict in these films is directed outward, away from the individual and toward the group. Jirocho's good *yakuza* are untroubled in their loyalty to a benevolent boss. Conflict arises when rival gangs violate the *jingi* code for selfish gain. Confrontation is gang war, not a single hero's challenge to odds that must defeat him. As to the outcome, there is never any question. As in the Western, the struggle between "good" and "bad" is clear-cut, with the bad guys getting run out of Dodge. The only difference is that in the Japanese versions, business in Dodge picks up almost before the gunsmoke clears.

In short, the immense popularity of the various Jirocho series seems directly related to the prevailing mood of the times. Japan's status as a newly independent nation making great strides in the postwar economic recovery called for virtues such as charismatic leadership, group loyalty, and social harmony. The cinema industry was not slow to take its cue from the public, as even a cursory glance at *yakuza* genre films will show.[13]

The early 1960s brought a radical innovation in the genre. The seminal work was Tadashima Tadashi's *Jinsei gekijo: Hishakaku* (*The Theater of Life: Hishakaku,* 1963). Based on the popular Taisho fiction by Ozaki Shiro, this film established a new *yakuza* narrative formula that would be used in one variation or another in over three hundred films before the decade was out. It also furthered the cause of a revived star system.

This new formula updated the setting, bringing it out of the feudal period into a distinctly modern era: late Taisho to early Showa (1923–40). It was a period fraught with opportunities for *yakuza*. The Taisho democracy yielded to aggressive military expansion. This shift in political orientation put Japanese capitalism on the road to prosperity (with an interlude of depression along the way), so naturally *yakuza* were on hand to seize the advantage wherever they could.

Another distinctly modern touch was moving *yakuza* out of the feudal-period countryside into big cities such as Tokyo. There, the classical *yakuza* enterprise—organized gambling—could flourish as never before. Naturally, the higher the stakes, the wider the rift between competing groups of good and bad *bakuto*. The good are seen living up to the *jingi* code. The bad are interested only in the money—in cahoots with crooked politicians and businessmen, branching out into extortion, and even becoming hit men. Clearly, good and bad must fight it out in a kind of moral territorial war.

Unlike the typical prewar film, which developed its *giri/ninjō* conflict in a vertical relationship (boss-henchman bond), the new formulation extends the conflict horizontally, pitting peer against peer. This tends to put the antagonists on more equal footing, since both may suffer disgrace or defeat caused by *ninjō*—this time most often in the form of love for the same woman. Thus friction is caused by one *yakuza* who violates the *jingi* code by seducing a fellow *yakuza*'s woman. The hero's feelings translate into conflict between desire for personal revenge (*ninjō*) and the loyalties of brotherhood (*giri*). In short, romance thickens and complicates the plot, and as may be expected, the ensuing rivalry becomes a plot convention to be adopted in many *yakuza* films to follow. Only when the hero finds a way to resolve the classical *giri/ninjō* issues is the film's narrative pattern completed.

The formula worked out in *The Theater of Life: Hishakaku* is typical of this new trend. Hishakaku begins as an outsider. His heroic status derives from an issue of romantic interest; his pursuit of *ninjō* is a motivating force throughout.

He has eloped with Otoyo, another *yakuza*'s woman. This violation of *jingi* removes him from his gang and forces him into hiding with his lover. Unlike his prewar counterpart on the road, such as Chuji, Hishakaku—though ostracized—is not totally alienated from the world of *yakuza*. We become aware of this when the sympathetic boss of the Kokin gang takes the lovers under his protection, an act that puts him automatically at odds with Hishakaku's original gang. In a subplot that neatly complicates matters, the Kokin gang is further endangered by the villainous Oyokoda gang. This gang not only hotly pursues the lovers to protect Otoyo's former lover and his henchmen, but also tries to take advantage of Kokin's failing health to extend its territory.

In an interesting example of trying to reconcile *giri* and *ninjō* instead of choosing one or the other, Hishakaku volunteers to challenge Oyokoda's men— who include his own old comrades, now out to get him. His course of action reflects his love for Otoyo (and concern for her safety), as well as his sense of obligation to Kokin. But first Hishakaku must preface his decision with a *yakuza* ritual. *The Theater of Life* is among the first postwar *yakuza* films to attach considerable narrative significance to the sake cup, a familiar icon. The ritual of receiving a sake cup from the *yakuza* boss and keeping it signifies the henchman's pledge of loyalty to the group. Here Hishakaku returns the sake cup given him by Kokin, thereby signaling his departure from his benefactor's group so that he can become a free agent. As such, he, not the Kokin gang, will be responsible for the mayhem he plans to commit. This compromise, however, means that Hishakaku is completely isolated, both from society at large and from any *yakuza* group. This is why he turns himself in to the police after killing several enemies.

Hishakaku's imprisonment provides more circumstance for testing the power of the *giri*/*ninjō* conflict. This time a brother *yakuza*, Miyagawa, yields to temptation (*ninjō*) and becomes Otoyo's lover. When he learns that Hishakaku has been paroled, Miyagawa is conscience-stricken. Refusing to run away with Otoyo, he prefers to face the music. Director Tadashima uses this situation to express Hishakaku's attitudes toward *giri,* this time referring to another familiar icon, the ritual of fingercutting—the *yakuza*'s admission of guilt.[14] When Miyagawa offers to follow this ritual, Hishakaku says simply: "Don't be silly." The cultural implications are clear: Hishakaku considers himself free of any *yakuza* affiliation and therefore at liberty to criticize the traditional means of expiation. His long ordeal has turned him even more in the direction of *ninjō*. As might be expected, Director Tadashima invests his protagonist with humanistic traits to match this noble forgiveness—much in contrast with the dedication to revenge that would characterize a feudal counterpart. There is also more than a hint of the lone wolf image here.

Now it is Miyagawa's turn to experience moral enlightenment. His sense of *giri* reawakened, he attempts to restore the honor of the Kokin group by avenging its leader's murder. Single-handedly he breaks into the Oyokoda gang's headquarters, armed with a sword. This act of individual atonement leads to a predictable result: Miyagawa's death. But the Oyokoda gang is still intact.

Clearly, the long-awaited climax demands a showdown with the hero in charge. By this time even the long-suffering Hishakaku has had enough. He would prefer to live by *ninjō,* but the world outside is out of balance, and the deaths of Kokin and Miyagawa, boss and fellow *yakuza,* must be avenged.[15] Thus *giri* must be given its due by the lone wolf who sees his moral authenticity in terms of the *yakuza* code.

But first a touch of romance serves as a prelude to the drama. Hishakaku has recovered Otoyo, who represents his *ninjō* element. They are together on a beach. She tries in vain to dissuade him from undertaking his suicidal mission; nevertheless, he is determined. The moment for mellow sentiment is past. Buckling on his sword, he heads for Oyokoda's stronghold. There, of course, he overcomes his enemies in a climax rich in showmanship and gore—a combination that was the hallmark of the Toei Company, whose revival of the *jidai-geki* film was so successful in the 1950s.

Hishakaku returns to find Otoyo still weeping on the beach. A man of few words and noble sentiments, he forgives and pities her, saying: "You had better pray for the repose of Miyagawa's soul." A long shot shows Hishakaku moving away alone—giving up the life of love this *yakuza* has always dreamed of living.

The immense popularity of *The Theater of Life: Hishakaku* spawned other series featuring this hero, and a host of remakes and spin-offs as well. The *yakuza* image established at the outset by actor Tsuruta Koji was endlessly repeated, too: a lone wolf unwilling to be bound by the *jingi* code, which cramps his sense of moral authenticity and his need for *ninjō* self-assertiveness. Obviously, *ninjō* has lost some of its negative cultural implications here, since this *yakuza* is motivated not by greed or opportunism but by genuine humanistic impulses—pure love for a woman or a brother *yakuza.*

Even so, he remains a *yakuza,* and is part of that complex web of obligations. He stands apart chiefly by virtue of patience and long-suffering. His breaking point is slow in coming, yet he is pushed to his limit, and in the climax of the film he executes acts of virtuoso violence, most often in response to *giri* pressure to avenge lost comrades. As in the Western, his privileges of freedom and isolation are encoded in an obvious icon—the clothes he wears. This means a very informal kimono with a simple sash—no cloak or *hakama* trousers. An actor such as Tsuruta is shown dressed in this *kinagashi* style at all times, even on ceremonial occasions.

Another variation on this new style of *yakuza* appears in Yamashita Kosaku's *Sengo saidai no toba* (*The Largest Gambling Den in the Postwar Period*, 1969). Here the *yakuza*'s world is a complex and highly compromising blend of gambling and politics in which good/bad opposites virtually vanish. This is a world of gamblers and politicians in cahoots for reasons of unvarnished greed and cynical self-interest. What goodness there is resides in the few *yakuza* who retain some moral integrity, chiefly in the form of a sense of justice.

The *giri/ninjō* conflict adjusts accordingly. The individual *yakuza*'s loyalty to his corrupt boss (*giri*) runs counter to his own desire for personal integrity (*ninjō*). In this case, *ninjō* represents a genuine adherence to the code of *jingi*, while *giri* represents a corrupt and false interpretation of that code.

The resulting conflict is dramatized in the careers of two protagonists, not just one. These two represent opposing *yakuza* groups within a larger structure of *yakuza* organization allied with a conservative political party. This unholy alliance is called Dainihon Doshikai (United Federation of Japanese Comrades). Balance in this enormous amalgam of factions is maintained by carefully negotiated (and entirely corrupt) spheres of influence.

The element of discord is introduced by Honjo, one of the two heroes, played by Takakura Ken, a superstar veteran of many *yakuza* series. Honjo represents the Nagareyama group. His sense of justice outraged, he accuses his boss of corrupt self-interest. He pays for this breach of *giri* with his life—murdered by an obliging member of the other hero's Mauruwa group.

The other hero, Itsugi, is played by superstar Tsuruta Koji. He subscribes wholeheartedly to *giri* loyalty to the boss—a conviction easier to subscribe to, since his boss is also his father-in-law. Itsugi's bond of brotherhood with Honjo is broken by their vows of allegiance to different bosses. Yet when Itsugi learns that his boss/father-in-law has ordered Honjo's execution, his conscience is awakened, and he desires revenge (*ninjō*). Even so, he cannot dispense with his sense of loyalty (*giri*).

In the end the climactic showdown comes when this enduring type of hero reaches an impasse. His suffering conscience demands an affirmation of true *jingi* honor after all: he must choose between life and moral authenticity. Hiding a small sword in his kimono, he heads for the boss's gambling den, saying to himself: "My dear brother, see how I will avenge your honor."

Significantly enough, the film's "pseudo-familial bond" at both horizontal and vertical levels is most cogently encoded in iconography—the classical ritual of returning a sake cup. Itsugi and Honjo had marked the end of their brotherhood by throwing a cup to the ground. When Itsugi's group breaks up, the members throw their cups into the river. White cups slowly filling up and sinking in filthy water clearly symbolize a failure to cope with the course of corrupt events. At the climax of the film Itsugi, now firmly a man of principle, has no choice but to stab his villainous boss. He then breaks his sake cup with his short sword. Its white fragments stained with blood and scattering in midair provide a powerful image for this violent break of the surrogate father/son bond.[16]

While *The Largest Gambling Den in the Postwar Period* posits a horizontal relationship in its movement from solidarity to disparity then back to solidarity through one *yakuza*'s death, a different permutation takes place in *Showa zankyoden* (*The Story of the Last Yakuza in the Showa Period*, 1965–72). In *Karajishi shugi* (*The Tattoo of a Lion*, 1965), one of the ten-part series and Toei's biggest box-office hit in the *yakuza* genre, two heroes begin as opposites, then form a surviving bond defined by common purpose.

Again, superstars are used: Takakura Ken as Hanada, and Ikebe Ryo as Kazama. Hanada is an insider, thanks to his status as soldier in the Kuramae gang. Kazama is an outsider, a drifter with obligations to his temporary hosts, the Raimon gang. Because he owes them his *isshoku ichihan* obligation for food and shelter, he must fight the Kuramae gang. Thus he meets Handa at swordpoint right from the outset of the film. The two men like each other, but they have no choice. Kazama says: "I don't bear you any grudge. But I am bound by the code of the *yakuza,* and must force you to draw your sword." Hanada replies: "Win or lose, fate will decide for us. We must fight with a clear conscience."

Even so, one hero must change to unite the two. Hanada remains stubbornly *giri*-bound throughout. As a drifter, Kazama has been obligated to many *yakuza* hosts; yet he finally switches to *ninjō*, following his inclination to bond with his opponent, Hanada. That done, they have a common enemy in the boss of the Kabashima gang, who has wronged them both. The climactic showdown is therefore not a solo display of virtuoso swordplay but a sort of violent duet, as these heroes—one an insider, the other an outsider—join forces in the fight against evil. Yet this series is less concerned with questions of good and evil than with the comradeship of heroes and the affirmation of their moral strength.

In most parts of the series, the dramatic display of heroic manhood is provided by scenes of sentimental camaraderie. For example, *The Tattoo of a Lion* shows Hanada and Kazama meeting on a bridge in falling snow, then heading for the enemy stronghold, sharing an umbrella. It is as if the snowstorm must cover the final pathos of lives about to be lost in an act of suicidal heroism.

Significantly enough, the struggle between good and bad is used to develop an opposition between old and new. *The Story of the Last Yakuza in the Showa Period* is set in the 1930s, a time of sudden growth in Japan's "new" capitalism. The good *yakuza* still follow a traditional occupation as gamblers allied with established, "old" businessmen with strong ties to the locale. The evil *yakuza* are a thoroughly modern type. Not for them simple dealings with wholesalers and shopkeepers. They are allied to the new "shrewdocracy" of industrialists and money managers. Taking advantage of cozy dealings with crooked politicians and bureaucrats also swimming in this strong new economic tide, they do their best to transform the region. Theirs are the modern building complexes, amusement parks, and department stores springing up everywhere. The world is their "world-village," and they mean to profit by it.

The setting for this series is well chosen: the Asakusa district of Tokyo, where old and new clash on a really grand scale. This downtown area was developed in the mid-Edo period, the seventeenth century, and retained a vigorous tradition of old-style shops and markets, and even a licensed red-light district along with venerable temples and shrines. Even in the Showa period, the inhabitants were not middle-class white-collar workers, but lower-middle-class merchants and skilled laborers.

This contrast of values set in new terms was powerful enough to redefine the *giri/ninjō* conflict in another Toei Company *yakuza* series: *Nihon Kyokaku-den* (*A Story of Japanese Yakuza,* 1964–71). The first nine of eleven installments were made by veteran Makino Masahiro. Historical settings range from Meiji to early Showa. Accordingly, the in/out binary system becomes obscure, because these *yakuza* are no longer the gamblers of yesteryear. They run respectable businesses such as construction, transportation, and shipping. This shift makes it easier for them to form alliances with other social groups, especially politicians and bureaucrats.

The good *yakuza* are in fact law-abiding citizens—real converts, though of course they remain *yakuza* rooted in the *bakuto* tradition. It is as if they take seriously what the great feudal-period boss Jirocho is quoted as saying: "You may belong to the *yakuza* world—just don't lead a *yakuza* life." The bad *yakuza* are defined in terms of money. These hoodlums, gamblers, and *tekiya,* like the corrupt politicians and bureaucrats in cahoots with them, are out for profit, period. They are enemies of the innocent, and of respectable society.

The two groups are contrasted in other ways, as well. Take, for example, their costume. In the installment *Ketto Kanda matsuri* (*Bloody Festival at Kanda,* 1966), the good *yakuza* wear Japanese dress—informal kimono or *happi* (cloak)—while the bad guys sport Western suits. This contrast is presented almost as direct satire at the beginning of the film. Takakura Ken stars as the lieutenant of good *yakuza* firefighters. A large white car tries to push its way into their New Year's exhibition. Inside is a *yakuza* boss dressed to the nines in a Western suit—ditto his henchmen. Besides the contrast in costume, there are also the opposing attitudes of the two groups. The attitude of benevolent *yakuza*-ism is expressed by a boss who says: "We give the public the shady side of the street in the summer and the sunny side in the winter." The bad *yakuza,* of course, are not so neighborly. They take full advantage of political corruption, and expect a visiting *yakuza* to share their views and values. So a *giri/ninjō* conflict develops as the good guy is forced by group loyalty to fight on the side of the bad guys.[17]

As in the violent Samurai Films of the 1960s—e.g., *Yojimbo*—the protagonist in the *Story of Japanese Yakuza* series is matched with an equally notable antagonist. Sometimes this "showdown" formula yields the expected decisive confrontation between the two at the end. At other times the antagonist and protagonist unite and defeat the bad guys together—thanks, of course, to the antagonist's conversion along the way.

Another notable tendency is for villains to be easily provoked. It is as if the moral tenor of the genre demands a general rule: bad guys have temper tantrums; good guys keep their cool. In the end, however, traditional virtues of long-suffering and endurance reach their admirable limits—at which point triumph of virtue takes the form of bloody fray.

Finally, romance takes an appropriate back seat once *giri* is firmly at the wheel. Song lyrics in these pictures tend to spell the message out, as in "Leaving the pleading woman behind, the hero marches toward death to prove his manhood."

During the 1960s the Toei Company's commitment to the star system brought heavy and profitable promotion of this *giri*-bound macho imagery, as personified in Tsuruta Koji and Takakura Ken. In 1969 Sugawara Bunta joined them in the limelight, starring in a series, *Gendai yakuza (The Modern Yakuza,* 1969–71). The first three installments were directed by Furuhata Yasuo, the last one by Nakajima Sadao. Like Sergio Leone's "Spaghetti Westerns," this series offers a new type of hero, a lonely outsider-drifter; but unlike his prewar counterpart, the new hero is a dedicated materialist. The setting drifts closer in time—right up to the '60s, so this "with-it" *yakuza* can profit from Japan's new economic prosperity.

The hero's past is left out of the picture; suffice it to say that he had his brush with the law. Thus in the first part of the series, *Yotamono no okite (The Code of an Outlaw,* 1969), the protagonist has just been released from prison. Whatever he was before, he is a lone wolf now, and wants no part of any *yakuza* organization. The *jingi* code means nothing to him. Money is his sole concern and governs his actions, right or wrong. Hence in *The Code of an Outlaw* he has no qualms about passing a large bogus check. Nor is he encumbered by the suicidal anguish of traditional *yakuza* ideals of moral authenticity. Violence may serve a point of honor—but only at this *yakuza's* convenience. As for fights, his favorite grumble about overwhelming odds is: "I'm not going to get killed for this." Time and again the definitive shot of this hero shows him in silhouette, leather jacket and shirt encoding his tough, fight-me image, cigarette hanging out of his mouth as he walks away from the camera into a red sunset.[18]

The Nikkatsu Company challenged Toei with some star *yakuza* billing of its own, most notably Ishihara Yujiro and Takahashi Hideki. Most interesting from a structural point of view is *Otoko no monsho* (*The Crest of the Man*, 1963–66), a ten-part series starring Takahashi and directed by Matsuo Akinori, Takizawa Hideki, and Iida Tan. Like so much of the postwar *yakuza* genre, this series was set in the 1930s, the period of Japanese imperialist expansion. The horizontal relationship between *yakuza* groups is magnified, not by a good/bad dichotomy but by opposing family interests: husband/father/boss vs. wife/mother/boss.

The opening installment depicts the familiar pattern of conversion. Ryuji, the hero, is a medical doctor who happens to be the only son of a *yakuza* boss. Although he has chosen to remain outside *yakuza* society, he is drawn into it when the murder of his father prompts him to succeed as head of the Oshima Group. Then it turns out that his father's murder is protected by the Murata Group—headed by Ryuji's own mother.

The rest of the series is devoted to the hero's maturation. After his father's death, Ryuji has the old man's dragon tattooed on his back—an act of filial piety that challenges maternal authority. Ryuji does not want to be accepted as his mother's son, but rather as a "man in *yakuza* society." Indeed, one scholar sees the mother-son relationship in *The Crest of the Man* developing, not through ties of affection but in tension through struggle for power.[19] Nevertheless, it is a case of mother-as-enemy using her status to further the interests of her son. The two are reconciled only in the seventh installment, when Ryuji's group merges with his mother's, thus paving the way for her retirement. Once free from maternal protection, however, Ryuji still must perfect himself through adventure. Thus the seventh and ninth installments focus on the journey theme, with the outcome being his personal integration as boss and family man in the final installment of the series.

As we have seen, in the 1960s success in *yakuza* genre films meant variation on the given formula. It was only a matter of time (and still another variation) until a female *yakuza* took her place in the limelight—in Toei's *Hibotan Oryu* (*Oryu*, 1968), whose eight installments are set firmly in the middle of the Meiji era, toward the end of the nineteenth century.[20] Here Japan's push to modernize is symbolized by new types of theaters shown along with railroads and an expanded silk industry. All this provides up-to-date opportunities for *yakuza* expansion and conflict in defense of territorial rights as traditional gambling joins hands with modern business interests.

As elsewhere, good *yakuza* gangs stand for the values of community and genuine progress, while bad *yakuza* are unprincipled opportunists. Thus the second installment, *Isshoku ichihan* (*One Night's Lodging*, 1968), directed by Suzuki Norifumi, shows *yakuza* exploiting young girls working at a newly established silk factory. In Ozawa Shigehiro's fourth installment, *Nidaime shumei* (*Succeeding the Second*, 1968), *yakuza* try to block railway construction that threatens their horse-drawn carriage trade.

The heroine Oryu possesses all the assets displayed by her male counterparts. She exhibits deep respect for the *jingi* code, strong leadership, and even fighting ability. By the end of the fourth installment, she has inherited the top position in the Yano clan. Yet she suffers from a distinctly feminine pressure on the *ninjō* side. Thus, *giri/ninjō* assumes an interesting phase of permutation because the basic incompatibility between woman and *yakuza* boss becomes a point of tension expressed in some instances directly through conflict, and in others more subtly, as we shall see.

Each installment of the series puts Oryu on the journey quest familiar in *yakuza* films, a quest that tries her moral character through challenges to her honor and sense of justice. In the sixth installment, *Oryu sanjo* (*Oryu's Visit*, 1970), she travels from one gambling den to another, polishing her skills at the gaming tables and making contact with other bosses. The film opens with her search for Okimi, the blind daughter of Oryu's imposter killed in a *yakuza* battle. Her quest takes her to the Asakusa district of Tokyo, where good and bad *yakuza* gangs are fighting for control of a new theater with its popular drama troupe. The good *yakuza* boss means to use the theater to establish Asakusa as a center of popular culture. This would benefit the people of the district as well. A rival *yakuza* boss, however, is indifferent to cultural or community values. He wants to take charge and capitalize on the touring potential of the troupe.

A chance encounter with another *yakuza* also provides Oryu with an occasion for romance. As often is the case, the plot fosters increasing intimacy between heroine and stranger, usually in the form of mutual assistance. At the end of this episode, Oryu loses all her money gambling. Impressed by her style of losing, the stranger *yakuza* Tsunejiro lends her the money he has won. His generosity leads Oryu to discover his goodness, too, as she confides in him the purpose of her quest. It turns out that Tsunejiro himself is searching for a lost younger sister. Later Oryu is able to reciprocate his kindness by hiding him from the police. Of course, a permanent romantic connection cannot be made in such a series. Oryu's success places her beyond the pale of respectable society. As a female *yakuza* boss, she must forego the ordinary happiness in love that other young women enjoy.

Many critics have admired the scene of parting in *Oryu's Visit* as a classic illustration of the fate of a woman born into *yakuza* life. After learning that his sister is in fact dead, Tsunejiro leaves for his hometown to bury her remains. The scene is set on a bridge near Asakusa. It is night. Falling snow and icy winds add to the desolation of the scene. Oryu appears with the news that she has found the girl she was seeking. The girl now has a fiancé, in fact. Tsunejiro says simply: "You're such a good woman." Oryu does not reply. Seeking to hide her embarrassment, she hands Tsunejiro a lunch she has prepared for him.

Interestingly enough, rather than counting on a conventional icon, Director Kato introduces an icon more closely associated with other genres, such as melodrama and *shomin-geki* (films about lower-middle-class people). A tangerine falls from the bag. Both Oryu and Tsunejiro reach for it. This is the only time they touch, and their fingers touch for only a second. Yet the point is not lost on the Japanese audience. In Japan the tangerine, fruit of winter, suggests motherly love and solicitude. Here, too, the orange tangerine set against the whiteness of snow highlights Oryu's feminine kindness. Yet she must go without the everyday reward of fulfillment in love. Fond as Oryu and Tsunejiro are of one another, they must go their separate ways. He bows silently and walks toward the camera. A long shot shows her left alone. All that is said of her inner feelings is conveyed by the pathos of her figure merging with the wintry atmosphere.

Indeed, Director Kato emphasizes Oryu's self-sufficiency while insisting on her status as member of the weaker sex. In time of danger she is helped against overwhelming odds by two male cohorts, not just one. One of them, Torakichi, has merely sworn a comradely oath in her support, and appears in the scene of "intermediation," a common feature of many *yakuza* films. Here some influential *yakuza* bosses have arranged a banquet to patch up a feud between the evil Samesumasa gang and the good Teppomasa. Oryu attends as the latter's representative. Yet reconciliation proves impossible when she rejects the rival gang's unreasonable territorial demands. An attempt is made on her life, and she is rescued by Torakichi. The scene concludes with Samesumasa's ritual fingercutting—a *yakuza*'s admission of and punishment for wrongdoing.

Unsurprisingly, Oryu's second male cohort, and hero of choice, is Tsunejiro. He also serves as a foil to Samesumasa, who represents the very antithesis of *jingi* coded behavior. Cruel and unprincipled, this villain has ambushed and wounded his rival boss, Teppomasa, kidnapped innocent townspeople, and forced a member of a rival group to betray his oath of loyalty. No wonder, then, that when he challenges Oryu to a duel, he arranges for an ambush. Once again Tsunejiro proves his worth to Oryu. Not only does he second her and protect her, he also takes the blame for the men he and Oryu kill in the fight—and turns himself in to the police.

The moral quandary of the heroine outside society is underlined by her relationship to Okimi, the blind girl she set out to rescue in the first place. The girl's vision has been restored. Oryu has given her money, and yet no intimacy has developed between them. In fact, when the girl's fiancé is killed in a *yakuza* fight, she blames Oryu.

The end of *Oryu's Visit* reinforces Oryu's status outside society with emotional yet aesthetically controlled overtones. As Tsunejiro leaves to surrender to the police, Oryu calls out his name. The camera follows as she tries to run after him. Then suddenly it stops to study Oryu herself, a female *yakuza* emerging from a fight. Her hair is disheveled, her face expressive of great sorrow. A final shot of the deserted street offers all the comment that is necessary on the rootless Oryu's life.[21]

By the early 1970s the *yakuza* film genre had passed its prime and begun to share in the general decline of the Japanese film industry. The public had tired of its theme and variations on virtue rewarded. The stars themselves seemed on the wane, as Takakura Ken and Tsuruta Koji began to show their age.

Unwilling to let go of such a profitable commodity, the Toei Company took radical steps, putting Fukasaku Kinji in charge of sweeping changes in method, formula, and subject matter. Fukasaku had this to say about his part in changing the history of the genre:

> My contribution to the development of Japanese cinema was to abolish the star system. The traditional *yakuza* film depicted a clear-cut struggle between good and evil. Casting was entirely predictable. The odd thing was the good *yakuza* in these films were portrayed as being much better than your average law-abiding citizen. I was always puzzled by this. . . . I bucked this convention by playing up the negative aspects of *yakuza* life.[22]

Based on a novelist's version of a gangster's memoirs (written in prison), Fukasaku's series *Jingi naki tatakai* (*Combat without a Code*, 1973–74) offers a case-history approach to *yakuza* organization. Unlike its predecessors, it puts its subject in a broad social context: modern Japan in the twenty-five-year period ending in 1970. This is the story of individuals caught in a system, and rising and falling with it as one *yakuza* machine struggles with another in the quest for power. The gangs themselves are seen as victims of the social forces at work in their own anti-social background. In this series the classical *yakuza* struggle between extremes of good and evil is essentially meaningless. In place of simplistic polarities, there are complex realities of lawlessness, injustice, and irrationality. The *yakuza* here is no hero, but a pawn in a game played by warring powers themselves caught in forces far beyond their control.

Even so, Fukasaku invests his protagonist, Hirono (played by Sugawara

Bunta), with a certain degree of goodness. This takes the form of *giri* understood as obligation to a boss, though even that bond cannot hold in a world of escalating gangster warfare. Furthermore, the *giri*-bound Hirano is pitted against *yakuza* opportunists. Through a painful process, he comes to learn that he must adjust himself to the *yakuza* world, in which money is the be-all and end-all. Then, too, there is the opposition of good vs. bad as the innocent citizens and officials unite against a rising tide of gangsterism. Yet even this spirit of cooperation is not really successful.

Fukasaku is more concerned to depict extremes of violence and its consequences—the contagious, chaotic purposelessness of it. "All these are portrayed in *Combat without a Code*: violence perpetrated by the man in the street and the powerful *yakuza;* violence against violence; violence as an end in itself as well as violence directed against the weak and defenseless, and so on."[23]

Spanning as it does a full twenty-five-year period at a time of rapid and radical change in postwar Japan, this film has room to represent a comparable transformation in its subject, the Yamamori Group. In part one this group is a motley crew of hoodlums struggling to survive in the aftermath of war. By part four, set in the 1960s, the group has acquired a respectable facade of free enterprise engaged in tourism, trading, and transportation. The world of *yakuza* has bosses who are presidents of corporations—not just bosses of gangs. Yet modern structure takes money, and lots of it. Touching large sums takes power; power brings its own range of complexities and threats as bribes change hands inside and outside the sphere of law enforcement and law-abiding respectability.

Good/bad polarity in these films is found in parts four and five, in which townspeople and law-enforcement agencies unite in a challenge to *yakuza* organization weakened by escalating internecine strife. Even this alliance of the good, however, proves powerless against an overpowering drift into lawlessness.

The radical transformation of *yakuza* life in this postwar period is marked by an obviously symbolic growth in the power and purpose of money. Bribery is the lifeblood of this style of gangsterism, which has lost touch entirely with the group and community values of traditional *jingi*. The police themselves behave like gangsters when bribes from gangsters do not measure up to expectations.

The traditional vertical relationships fostered by *giri* have all but vanished. A boss is a top-dog tyrant, not a benevolent dictator concerned with the well-being of his henchmen. Yamanaka, boss of the Yamamori Group, is a master manipulator from beginning to end in this series. He is not above pitting one of his men against another if that removes obstacles to his ambitions.

Unlike *yakuza* bosses of days gone by, these high-level executives of violence are not directly involved in the mayhem they profit from. They merely administrate, monopolize, and control the agents of *yakuza* warfare. In a sense, *yakuza* combat has become cerebral, a matter of war games, not warfare. Boss Yamanaka is a gifted strategist for whom manipulation behind the scenes is as effective as a direct power play.

A key manifestation of this breakdown of group values is the growing importance of "saving face." Bosses cynically exploit the need of their men to salvage some vestige of personal respect, even when it costs them dearly. The boss himself is exempt from this game, and proves quite capable of creating situations deliberately calculated to put a subordinate in the wrong, sometimes even in ways that move against the interests of his group.

Importantly, the traditional icon of fingercutting is presented with an ironic twist throughout. The boss can substitute a punishment more expedient than the traditional expiatory sacrifice of the little finger. He can demand a sacrificial act to suit his own ambitions. Thus, for example, a man seeking to save face may kill to please his boss, then turn himself in for a prison sentence. The boss's power is consolidated by such a movement against the interests of the very man he traditionally would be expected to protect.

In part one of *Combat without a Code,* the protagonist Hirono shows how out of place he is in this modernized *yakuza* world. Having killed a man in a rival group, he goes to prison. There he has time to think and to see through his former boss. Once out of prison, he founds a small group of his own and tries to keep it neutral. This, however, is a significant departure from traditional *yakuza* practice, which demands that every group be allied with some other.

Neutrality, furthermore, proves vulnerable. In part four, *Kojo sakusen (The Climactic Operation,* 1974), Hirono's men are attacked by both gang factions. Realizing that "neutrality means nothing to ambitious, violence-prone youth," he has no choice but to dissolve his group and return to his former boss.

Part five, *Kanketsu-hen (Conclusion,* 1974), depicts a sorry triumph of *yakuza* modernization increasingly at war physically and economically. In this treacherous world, *jingi* is entirely forgotten. Hirono says to his friend Takeda—and it is rare to have such a friend in these days—"I can no longer trust what others think." Takeda and Hirono are now executives in the Yamamori Group, outdated remnants of a time whose notions of honor seem futile and absurd.

Yet Fukasaku makes it clear that he thinks the *yakuza* world and the "outer" world are headed in the same direction. The concluding part of his series shares a closing motif introduced by Yamanaka Sadao and Itami Mansaku four decades earlier in their *yakuza* films. This takes the form of a parting shot of the ruined atomic monument of Hiroshima, symbol of the defeat of imperialistic Japan. This image is accompanied by the narrator's voice-over: "When will fear for survival be over?" The viewer cannot help but register Fukasaku's nihilistic world view as symbolized by *yakuza* life.

Thus, it is almost a relief to turn to Ichikawa Kon's fiercely ironic parody of the postwar *yakuza* film in *Matatabi* (*Wanderers*, 1973). The object of Ichikawa's satire is the super-heroic, *jingi*-bound outlaw so popular in the 1960s. He achieves his effects chiefly by twisting good/bad, strong/weak, in/out polarities on their axes. As might be expected, familiar conventional icons such as the swordfight and the ritual of self-introduction are tinged with irony.

At the outset, the single/collective binary notion disappears. The solitary hero is replaced by a threesome of low-life peasant types whose commonplace wretchedness is apparent from our first glimpse of their shabby raincoats and battered traveling hats. Genta, Yamitaro, and Shinta are cut-rate desperadoes, worlds apart from such illustrious predecessors as Jirocho. The banding together of these anti-heroes, in fact, becomes an important structural device as the film focuses on how their camaraderie is established only to dissolve in the end. In one scene the camera even examines these three in such a way as to put them on a footing with beggars and prostitutes.

Heroes of 1960s films undertook journeys symbolic of freedom, quest, and challenge. They got their chance to prove strength, show benevolence, and acquire broad knowledge of human nature. Not Ichikawa's anti-heroes. Their shift from "in" to "out" is motivated by socio-economic forces beyond their control rather than by free will; poverty has put them on the road and on the outs with society. All they desire is to be the heavies of some powerful boss. Their standards of magnificence are exceedingly elementary: they rate potential bosses in terms of stacks of poker chips and bowls of noodles.

Exalted notions of brotherhood are also beyond their ken. The solidarity they know about is entirely happenstance. In their hopelessness they set out, and in their haplessness they form what bonds they are capable of. Genta and Shinta meet up and travel together five days before actual, real identities get straightened out. Even then, the film shows how weaklings must buddy up in a world ruled by more competent buddies—not that weakling plus weakling can ever add up to heroic strength.

Ichikawa is careful to exclude any hint of the benevolent *yakuza* boss from his parodic view. His bosses are strong, thanks to corruption, treachery, and cynical manipulation. The best that yokel hopefuls such as Genta, Yamitaro, and Shinta can do is resort to low cunning and hope to muddle through. Doing so, they break most, if not all, of the rules, including the ritual of self-introduction—an important icon in the genre. The traditional *yakuza* genre solemnly represents this ritual, since each wandering *yakuza* must formally declare himself to the local boss he wants to be his host. False identities are taboo, of course—the penalty being death, or ostracism at the very least. Yet both Genta and Shinta manage to pass themselves off as members of distinguished *yakuza* groups—with impressive success.

The *isshoku ichihan* obligation of service in exchange for a meal and night's lodging is also given an ironic twist. Asked by their host to help out with some swordsmanship, Genta and Shinta show themselves as adept inepts, skipping from opponent to opponent before parry-and-thrust gets too dangerous. Even so, Genta picks up a face-saving scratch.

Being, as they are, no better than dire necessity requires, Ichikawa's three anti-heroes oppress their own peasant class. Armed with their *yakuza* swords, they wade into an exceedingly small-time gambling operation, scatter the defenseless farmers, and scoop up the small change.

Genta even violates nature's most solemn bond between father and son. First, he competes for the attentions of his father's lover, Onami, and woos her away from the old man. Then, ordered by his boss to kill his father, Genta complies. Conflicting obligations—to father and to boss—have nothing to do with the outcome. Expediency wins the day. An opportunistic Genta cuts his father's head right off, telling himself it is no more than what the old man deserves for deserting the family when Genta was a child. Genta is not rewarded in any case. The boss who ordered the crime refuses to have a patricide among his henchmen, so the ultimate reward of the wandering *yakuza*—settling down—is not to be given to Genta.

When they turn against manipulative *yakuza* society, the three anti-heroes are joined by the vagabond woman Onami. Still, they are outcasts any way they turn, their insider/outsider sense of being lost voiced by Genta, who says: "I don't want to float anymore."

Sinking, of course, is the available alternative. Ichikawa suggests that the only moral strength accessible to these characters must derive from their camaraderie. Yet even that bond cannot hold in the context of parody. Here Ichikawa's trademark, black humor, comes to the fore. Shinta perishes as the result of an infected cut from a bamboo splinter. Genta sells Onami to a brothel, thinking that a "guarantee of room and board" there is better than life on the road.

In the final sequence, Genta's small portion of natural goodness comes to the fore. He has a chance to earn a boss's gratitude by killing someone they stayed with overnight. For the first time Genta displays a sense of *giri*, saying that he cannot do such a thing. Then in a mock-serious argument with his would-be co-assassin Yamitaro, Genta slips and falls to his death. His pal does not see him fall over the cliff, so the last we see of these heroic *yakuza* is the distracted Yamitaro running back and forth, calling Genta's name. The camera pans to Genta lying in the grass, dead of a broken neck. The camera cuts back to Yamitaro, who wonders if maybe Genta has gone to answer nature's call. The camera continues to study the lone unkempt figure of this man, standing exposed to a biting cold wind. We cannot but remember the opening shot of these three shabby figures set against surroundings equally uninviting. Thus, with fatalistic circularity, Ichikawa suggests that this sole survivor's time of roaming begins again—as the only means of survival.

That image may well serve to close this review of the *yakuza* genre. Given its long tradition in Japanese cinema, it is scarcely surprising that the genre has had its ups and downs. The 1960s witnessed a peak of popularity, followed by a decline shared by the cinema industry generally for the past twenty years.

Yet the *yakuza* genre is very much alive today. The two major studios—Toei and Toho—have made handsome profits and no doubt plan to continue making these films. The radical shift in pattern from idealism to realism has already brought fresh energy and topical thrust to scripts. Fukasaku's *Combat without a Code* has even given rise to the *jitsuroku* or true-account *yakuza* film. This subgenre may call into question the general operational principle that genre films are made in imitation not of life but of other films. Thus the title *Andogumi jitsuroku* (*The True Account of the Ando Group*, 1978–79), a series offering a case-history view of *yakuza* activities based on thinly disguised newspaper coverage. Another notable example is Nakajima Sadao's *Nihon no don* (*The Japanese Don*, 1981), a chronicle of two *yakuza* groups struggling for supremacy. Despite the director's disclaimer, the rivalry depicted obviously re-creates a famous war between well-known groups in eastern vs. western Japan.

No "world" of contemporary life is exempt from contact with *yakuza* organization, if cinema be verite, and beloved at all. Politicians, businessmen, and, yes, even academics are drawn into this world of underground struggle along an axis of in/out, gain/loss.

In 1987 and 1988 respectively, Toei came up with film adaptations of *Kabe no naka no korinai menmen* (*Tough Guys behind Bars*) and *Yakuza tose no suteki na menmen* (*Wonderful Men in the World of Yakuza*). Both films were based on autobiographical novels by former *yakuza* ex-con (now writer) Abe Joji. Toei may have to reassess past formulas if it hopes to capture its share of a market once so lucrative, now fallen on hard times. Other studios have reversed such a trend by developing new narrative patterns or discovering new stars. Another factor hanging in the balance is the downward shift in the age of the filmgoing audience. Will today's teenagers flock to see action-packed violence, *yakuza*-style—or will they prefer to watch their pop idols dancing and romancing?

NOTES

1. Andrew Tudor, *Theories of Film,* p. 139.

2. The name *yakuza* takes in two different groups, both with their roots in the seventeenth century, at the height of Tokugawa feudalism. One group, the *tekiya,* were gangs of peddlers banding together for self-defense. Eventually, the benefits of organization came to include monopoly of the portable booths at market fairs, temples, and shrines. The *tekiya* became in effect the con artists of feudal Japan.

The other group, the *bakuto* (literally translated as gamblers), were originally recruited by officials in areas not firmly under government control. These local toughs were hired to supervise the progress of public works such as irrigation and road building. Some of them were deputized. Authorized to carry swords and handle large sums of public money, these characters took a predictable turn toward outlawry. Their specialty was extortion in a system organized around gambling. Thus *yakuza* is also rendered as "gambler."

Only after the Meiji Restoration (1868) did the word *yakuza* come to include both types of underworld figure. Even today, *yakuza* organizations come under the headings *tekiya* or *bakuto*. The Occupation added yet another class, the *gurentai,* which has been compared to Al Capone–style gangsterism. This more ruthless newcomer recruited hooligans from the jobless repatriates of the postwar period, and footloose young men in that confusing time. For a more exhaustive account of the development of the *yakuza,* their interaction with modern-day politics, and overseas expansion, see David E. Kaplan and Alec Dubro, *Yakuza.*

3. Since *yakuza* got their start in the feudal period, with its complex mix of personal loyalties and political confusion, a code of ethics developed, taking its cue from Confucianism and *Bushido*. This code was called *jingi. Jin* expresses the Confucian virtue of benevolence; *gi,* the values of justice and rectitude. Needless to say, *jingi* came to express values modified to fit the *yakuza* way of life. Thus the element of rectitude yields the concept of absolute loyalty to the Organization, its boss especially.

4. Thomas Sobchack, "Genre Film: A Classical Experience," in *Film Genre,* ed. Barry K. Grant, p. 40.

5. Sato Tadao, "Ito Daisuke-ron" ("On Ito Daisuke"), p. 4.

6. Fujita Motohiko, *Nihon eigashi no shoshutsu: jidai o utsusu kagami (A History of Japanese Cinema in the Making: The Mirror Which Reflects the Era),* p. 166.

7. Thomas Sobchack, p. 40.

8. Sato Tadao, *Hasegawa Shin-ron (On Hasegawa Shin),* p. 276.

9. *The Long-Sought Mother* is interesting cinematically for the way it emphasizes lyrical, even sentimental, qualities at the expense of the expected swashbuckling. In fact, Chujiro wields his sword just twice. One scene exhibits swordplay in a gallant rescue caught by a notably versatile camera. Panning and shifts from long shot to close-up study his prowess from many angles. The other scene follows his mother's rejection. Chujiro is ambushed. The camera is fixed on his gradual raising of his sword in a flurry of snow. His anger and frustration explode when the camera cuts to his lowering sword and his opponent falling to the ground. See Sato Tadao, *Hasegawa Shin-ron,* p. 290.

10. Inagaki is careful to vary the dashing rhythms of derring-do with contrasting lyrical episodes. One comes after a subtitle reading "The autumn passes while Yuki weeps." A long shot shows the fragile heroine fetching water from the well. The wheel will not budge. Snowflakes light on her shoulders. The imagery is sentimental, yet it registers the pathos in her solitude.

11. In the hands of the right directors, working with first-class stars, the *yakuza* film could be a box-office hit and accomplished cinematic art. Thus Ooka Denjiro, working under the inspired direction of Ito and Tsuji, could use his famously prominent shining

eyes to great advantage in scenes of genuine pathos. Similarly, Kataoka Chiezo made his mark as a bright-eyed youth with a captivating smile in Inagaki's *Yataro's Travel Hat* and *The Long-Sought Mother.* The Inagaki-Kataoka combination helped bring the star system to the fore in the burgeoning *jidai-geki/chambara* market. The star system also lent itself to tireless elaboration of *yakuza* film themes before and after the war. Remakes proved profitable, as well. One outstanding example is provided by Kataoka Chiezo, who displayed undiminished prowess and unfaded charm in a 1954 remake of his 1931 film *Sumo Wrestler's Debut.*

12. Sato, *Hasegawa Shin-ron,* p. 290.

13. The studios had other motives, too, of course. The Toei Company had everything to gain by reviving the star system. Already the leader in *jidai-geki* ventures, Toei had the leading men for this new limelight. Kataoka Chiezo, as we have seen, was a veteran of undiminished power and charm, with experience going back to the early 1930s, and new talent such as Yorozuya Kinnosuke (then Nakamura Kinnosuke) had already risen to screen-idol status.

14. The highest price that a *yakuza* must pay for the breach of loyalty to his group is death. The second highest form of atonement is expulsion from his own group, and next comes the ritual of fingercutting.

15. Takizawa Eichi, "*Yakuza eiga kansho*" ("Appreciation of *Yakuza* Films"), in *Ninkyo eiga* (*The Yakuza Film*), ed. Kusumoto Kenkichi (Tokyo: Sanichi Shobo, 1971), p. 119.

16. Watanabe Takenobu, "*Yakuza no sekai: shi to shocho no kinko*" ("The World of *Yakuza*: Balance between Death and Symbolism"), in *Ninkyo eiga* (*The Yakuza Film*), p. 53.

17. In *The Story of Japanese Yakuza,* some installments feature Takakura Ken as a former gang member, while in others he is a drifter who happens along at just the "right" time to serve as focus for physical and moral conflict. Sometimes his relation to a group is renewed, as after military service, or when he contacts his old gang in order to reclaim the body of a younger brother killed in *yakuza* combat.

18. Takizawa, p. 113.

19. Watanabe Takenobu, *Nikkatsu akushon no karei na sekai* (*The Splendid World of Nikkatsu Action Films*), p. 191.

20. The Toei Company capitalized on the charms of Fuji Junko, groomed for this role by the studio. The Daiei Company responded with *Kanto onna bakutoshi* (*The Woman Gambler from Kanto,* 1968–69), and Nikkatsu with *Noboriryu* (*The Rising Dragon,* 1969). Nikkatsu cast a pop singer in the leading role. Neither rival studio invested as heavily in its series as Toei.

21. In the original script, the climax includes emotional shots of an embrace between Oryu and Okimi. But such sentimental reconciliation is absent in the film. See Kato Tai, *Nihon kyoka-den: Kato Tai shinario-shu* (*The Story of Japanese Yakuza: A Collection of Scenarios*), p. 127.

22. The author's interview with Fukasaku, New York, May 1979, when he was preparing for his film *Fukkatsu no hi* (*Virus,* 1980).

23. Ibid.

BIBLIOGRAPHY

Fujita Motohiko. *Nihon eigashi no shoshutsu: jidai o utsusu kagami* (*A History of Japanese Cinema in the Making: The Mirror Which Reflects the Era*). Tokyo: Goryushoin, 1983.

Grant, Barry K., ed. *Film Genre: Theory and Criticism*. Metuchen, N.J., and London: Scarecrow Press, 1977.

Kaplan, David E., and Alec Dubro. *Yakuza: The Explosive Account of Japan's Criminal World*. Reading, Mass.: Addison-Wesley, 1986.

Kato Tai. *Nihon kyoka-den: Kato Tai shinario-shu* (*The Story of Japanese Yakuza: A Collection of Scenarios*). Tokyo: Hokuto Shobo, 1973.

Kusomoto Kenkichi, ed. *Ninkyo eiga* (*The Yakuza Film*). Tokyo: Sanichi Shobo, 1971.

Sato Tadao. *Hasegawa Shin-ron* (*On Hasegawa Shin*). Tokyo: Chuo Koron, 1978.

———. "Ito Daisuke-ron" ("On Ito Daisuke"). In *Kantoku kenkyu: Ito Daisuke* (*Study of Directors: Ito Daisuke*), Vol. 40. Tokyo: Film Center, 1977.

Sobchack, Vivian. "Genre Film: Myth, Ritual, and Sociodrama." In *Film/Culture: Exploration of Cinema in Its Social Context,* ed. Sari Thomas. Metuchen, N.J. and London: Scarecrow Press, 1982.

Tudor, Andrew. *Theories of Film*. New York: Viking, 1973.

Watanabe Takenobu. *Nikkatsu akushon no karei na sekai* (*The Splendid World of Nikkatsu Action Films*). Tokyo: Miraisha, 1982.

Fires on the Plain:
The Human Cost of
the Pacific War

William B. Hauser

Historically, there are two separate but related groups of Japanese "war films": the "National Policy Films" (*Kokusaku eiga*) made between 1937 and 1945, and the pacifist films produced after Japan's defeat. With the beginning of the Sino-Japanese War in 1937, the government made the first of its demands on the film industry to turn out patriotic works to help mobilize and unite the country. By 1939 the industry was under the complete control of the Ministry of Home Affairs and the Media Section of the Imperial Army. By 1940 strict censorship was in effect. Scripts and finished films were inspected; Western-style individualism, foreign words, and phrases were eliminated; and women were not to be shown drinking in public or smoking. These were but a few of the new rules. Interestingly enough, unlike the propaganda films of many countries, the "National Policy Films" rarely sought to arouse hatred for the enemy; nor did they resort to racist stereotyping, as American combat films of the period frequently did. The enemy, in fact, was often not seen.

The emphasis was on the common bond of men, and the outlook was essentially humanistic. This pattern was clearly established in the first two important war films, both directed by Tasaka Tomotaka: *Five Scouts* (*Gonin no sekkohei*, 1938) and *Mud and Soldiers* (*Tsuchi to heitai*, 1939). Later films adhered to this pattern, while creating what Sato Tadao has called "a uniquely Japanese form of cinematic propaganda by treating war as a kind of spiritual training" (*Currents in Japanese Cinema*, p. 103). This is true of Yoshimura Kozaburo's *The Story of Tank Commander Nishizumi* (*Nishizumi sensacho-den*, 1940), and even more true of Yamamoto Kajiro's *The War at Sea from Hawaii to Malaya* (*Hawaii-Marei oki kaisen*, 1942), which has to do with the rigorous training and discipline of the aviators who attacked Pearl Harbor. None of these films discussed (or dared to discuss) the tragic ramifications of war. That had been done only once, in *Fighting Soldier* (*Tataku heitai*, 1940), and its director, Kamei Fumio, was not permitted to work again until the end of the war.

Following Japan's defeat, such discussions became the central preoccupation of the war film. This is partly because of the "democratization" of the country that began with the Occupation, but it is also because of the terrible suffering that many Japanese had experienced. Invariably pacifist, the postwar combat films not only condemned war on principle but excoriated the barbarous military authoritarianism that had suppressed freedoms and brought on the war in the first place. Although Japanese films continued to investigate into the 1960s and 1970s what the war experience had really been like for soldiers, the three most celebrated films were made in the late 1950s, at a time when the Americans had left, and the country was now ready to confront the demons of its recent past. These films are Kobayashi Masaki's nine-hour epic of the war, *The Human Condition* (*Ningen no joken*, 1958–61), and Ichikawa Kon's *The Harp of Burma* (*Biruma no tategoto*, 1956) and *Fires on the Plain* (*Nobi*, 1959).

In his close textual analysis of the last-named film, which he calls "one of the most graphic statements of anti-war and anti-military sentiment in postwar Japanese films," William Hauser shows how Ichikawa not only challenges the idealized values of the "National Policy Films" but forces viewers "to reconsider the place of nationalism, imperialism, and conflict in the human community."

For further reading, see Peter B. High, "The War Cinema of Imperial Japan and Its Aftermath: An Introduction," *Wide Angle* 1, 4 (1977): 19–21; Sato Tadao, "War as a Spiritual Exercise: Japan's 'National Policy Films,' " *Wide Angle* 1, 4 (1977): 22–24; Scott Nygren, "The Pacific War: Reading, Contradiction and Denial," *Wide Angle* 9, 2 (1987): 60–71; Max Tessier, "Les films de guerre: de Pearl-Harbour à Hiroshima" ("War Films from Pearl Harbor to Hiroshima"), in *Images du cinéma japonais* (Paris: Henri Veyrier, 1981), pp. 88–109; Oshima Nagisa, "Eiga ni totte senso towa nanika: Tasaka Tomotaka *Gonin no sekkohei* megutte" ("How War Is Depicted in the Movies: About Tasaka Tomotaka's *Five Scouts*"), in *Nihon eiga o yomu: paionia tachi no isan* (*Reading Japanese Film: Heritage of the Pioneers*) (Tokyo: Dagereo Shuppan, 1984), pp. 14–38; and John Dower, *War without*

Mercy: *Race and Power in the Pacific War* (New York: Pantheon, 1986).

Ichikawa Kon's *Fires on the Plain* (*Nobi*), produced in 1959, represents one of the most graphic statements of anti-war and anti-military sentiment in postwar Japanese films. As a portrayal of the degradation and dehumanization of the surviving Japanese forces in the Philippines in the last year of the war, it offers a set of images of military service and the struggle for survival which haunt viewers. It is a disturbing film, one which offends many who have seen it. Yet, if we analyze the most important themes which are included, we find that they are conventional in Japanese war films made during and after the Second World War. Some of the themes included are the nature of army life, relations between officers and men, comradeship, provisions and war materiel, relations with the enemy, and the sense of purpose and objectives of the fighting men. What makes Ichikawa's film a powerful essay against war and against the brutalization of the human spirit—even more powerful than the Ooka Shohei novel on which it is based—is its ability to force viewers to immerse themselves in the hardships experienced by the Japanese army, particularly in the struggle for survival by the protagonist of the story, Private Tamura (Funakoshi Eiji). This essay, in offering a narrative and analytical discussion of Tamura's struggle, will show how Ichikawa's film constitutes a major challenge to values championed in wartime Japan.

From the opening frames when Tamura's squad leader slaps him across the face, one gets a sense of brutal desperation. We are taken aback, stunned, and unsure of what to expect next. As the camera pulls back from the closeup of Tamura's gentle visage, reflecting his confusion and hurt, it is obvious that he is miscast in the Japanese army, is an innocent victim of the war and of military service. The squad's position is hopeless. Tamura is an embarrassment, and his squad leader expresses both his anger and the futility of the Japanese military situation in his assault on the helpless private. Tamura's failure in the eyes of his superiors is twofold. First, he has failed to die for the emperor and uphold the honor of the Japanese army. Second, his tuberculosis makes him unfit for continued service. Unable to help dig fortifications and scavenge for food, he is a drain on his unit. His duty is to persist in demanding admission to the military hospital and to stay there as long as his rations last. Failing that, his final duty is to die. His hand grenade is to be used to assure the attainment of this objective. Tamura's authorized choices are both self-destructive. He must gain admission to the hospital to better prepare himself to give his life for the emperor, or he must kill himself to remove the burden on his unit. Both alternatives offer death. Within the army, there is no provision for life, only a determination to achieve victory or die.

Tamura's dilemma is given visual power by the stark black and white photography used in the film. The heavy contrast reminds one of the paintings of George Rouault and adds emotional power. The desperation of the Japanese military situation is emphasized by the lack of gray tones in the film. Like the screen imagery, the choices offered Tamura provide no middle ground: they are matters of life or death. With death the overwhelmingly likely outcome, the photography is heavily black, accentuating the finality of Tamura's situation. He, and the Japanese army, suffer from terminal conditions. With death seemingly inevitable, it is a race between death by starvation or disease, and death by defeat in combat. With limited areas of white on the screen, the viewer gets a visceral sense that doom and destruction are unavoidable. The forces of darkness—death—dominate the forces of light—life. The heavily contrasted photography thus serves to reinforce the hopelessness which the material deprivation makes apparent. Tamura and the Japanese army are doomed.

The opening scenes of the film provide much evidence of the degrading conditions faced by the Japanese army in the final phase of the war in the Philippines. The men are starving and ill-equipped. They stand on guard duty and dig trenches, yet the squad leader admits they no longer even bother the advancing enemy. The unit's clerk dutifully fills out requisitions for food and equipment but has no place to send them, as the supply system has fallen apart and the squad is isolated and alone. Their situation is futile. Victory, which seemed so attainable early in the war, is now unimaginable. Surrender, a rational alternative when defeat is inevitable, is unacceptable, for it violates the Japanese code of military conduct. Survival instincts, the normal human responses to life-threatening situations, are inconsistent with the behavior expected from Japanese soldiers. The squad leader shouts at Tamura: "You don't want to be a burden, do you? Go back to the hospital and stay until they take you. If they won't take you, use your grenade. That is your final duty to the Japanese Imperial Army." Tamura's obligations as a soldier deny him the right to protect himself as an individual.

When Tamura salutes and prepares to depart, the squad clerk gives him his ration of sweet potatoes and advises: "Die only if you have to." Despite the anger and brutality of the squad leader, the clerk sympathizes with Tamura's dilemma. A scene of soldiers digging trenches with broken shovels, helmets, and sticks graphically illustrates their circumstances. They are exhausted, starving, and ill-equipped, yet they struggle to maintain their dignity as soldiers and mechanically perform the tasks to which they are assigned. Even the squad leader accepts the hopelessness of their position. After dismissing Tamura, he looks at his dejected troops, lies down in the grass, and stares through the trees with a look of resignation.

As Tamura prepares to march to the hospital, he is challenged by guards at the perimeter of the position. He tells them he is returning to the hospital, for he is no longer useful to the army. "This time I'll stick it out until they take me," he says. He has accepted the judgment of his commanding officer. He is weak, sick, and useless, a parasite on his unit. Saluting, he marches off to his fate. Stopping to rest, he dumps out the contents of his haversack. As the hand grenade rolls out, he eyes it with interest, picks it up, and seems to fondle it. This is the symbol of his redemption, the agent of his final obligation as a Japanese soldier. His duty is to recover his health and fight to the death, or to admit his failure and kill himself. As he repacks his haversack and prepares to leave, he overlooks the potatoes until after he stands up and is tying his bag. He pushes at them with his boot, unsure if what they represent—life—is an acceptable alternative. Unwilling to commit himself to death, he slowly picks them up and goes on his way. His options remain open, but the choice may not be his to make.

As an obedient soldier, Tamura accepts orders without question. His duties are to fight and to die. No alternatives are provided by the army. While death appears inevitable and his hand grenade seems more valuable than his rations, something spurs him onward. Army service has eliminated his right of self-determination, but he has not entirely conceded the issue. The focus of the film, while never explicitly stated, becomes the struggle between civil and military value systems, between duty to nation and duty to self, between the instinct for self-preservation and the demands for self-destruction. Will individualism or militarism win out in the end? Can Tamura, miscast as a warrior and caught in a desperate and hopeless conflict, preserve himself and his civilized values? Does the war environment necessarily restrict his choices, or can he transcend the hopelessness of his condition?

Tamura is no ordinary soldier. Throughout the film, clues are offered to his character and contrasts made between him and his fellow combatants. His use of polite language betrays him and illustrates his membership in the educated elite. In contrast, most of his fellow soldiers are from working-class or farming backgrounds. Whether or not he is Christian, he knows and understands Christianity. His concern with humanitarian values, and his ability to preserve an awareness of the possibility of personal choice, differentiate him from most of his comrades in arms. His sense of individual worth and his alienation from military values make him stand out from his peers. He is in, but not of, the army. Tamura is a cultured intellectual. He is the odd man out, for he represents a form of universal compassion suppressed by militarism and war. He is misplaced in the Japanese army.

The importance of human will and individual choice has many cultural implications in Japanese society. The capacity to transcend material limitations, the belief that determined efforts can overcome all odds, the conviction that the power of Imperial Will enabled Japan, alone among non-Western states, to attain equality with the industrialized nations of the West, are all basic themes in modern Japanese history. The uniqueness of the Japanese polity was for many wartime proponents of Japanese expansion both a justification for Japan's special rights in Asia and an explanation of how Japan would emerge victorious in conflict with larger and more powerful Western societies. Imperial Will would enable Japan to triumph, just as divine winds (*kamikaze*) had protected Japan against invasion in the thirteenth century. Now Imperial Will and the dedicated efforts of Japanese citizens would protect Japan from the debacle of defeat. Tragically, as illustrated by the images of desperation and deprivation in the film, Imperial Will was unequal to the tasks confronting it. Tamura is expected to dedicate himself to serving Imperial Will. Yet his struggle for personal survival forces him to question his obligations as a Japanese soldier. He faces a choice denied him by the Japanese code of military conduct. Which will dominate, individual will or Imperial Will? Faced with a perilous situation, can personal needs be given primary consideration when they conflict with military duties?

As the film progresses, this conflict dominates Tamura's responses to his plight. Ordered to fight and die by the army, he opts instead for life in a civil society. His choice is subtle and emerges slowly, for it takes time for his instincts to become conscious choices. Tamura's turmoil is presented as a struggle between military and civilian values and objectives. Implicit in the film is the conclusion that personal needs and personal objectives must transcend national or communitarian demands on the individual. Free will, free choice, and self-determination—all values associated with democratic societies—must triumph when faced with the brutal reality of militarism and war. It is not merely Tamura's survival which is at stake; it is the survival of civilized society and civil values.

This conflict is especially apparent in the relations between Tamura and his military colleagues. Life in the army is brutal. As conditions worsen, only the fittest and the most ruthless survive. Soldiers prey on each other, and Tamura stands out for his refusal to subordinate himself fully to military society. The rigid hierarchy of the Japanese army further complicates the lives of the enlisted men. At the hospital, the medical officers exploit their patients to gain control over their rations. Rejecting Tamura as a patient, they tell him he is too healthy because he is still mobile. He is too ill to fight, but not sick enough for medical attention. In fact, the medical situation is just as hopeless as the military situation. The army doctors can't adequately treat all the sick and the wounded. Given choices about how to utilize their limited resources, they pick the lost causes, rejecting those whose conditions might improve. Rather than look to the future and protect their patients for service to the postwar nation, they focus instead on assisting the helpless cases to attain their ritualized duty of death. Perceiving their situation as hopeless, the doctors focus on the dignity of death rather than the preservation of life. Militarism has perverted their sense of purpose. The only survival which concerns them is their own.

The futility of his situation confuses and disorients Tamura. Seeing a plume of smoke from the fires on the plain, he is shaken and hides. Yet he is not sure why he is hiding or just what he is hiding from. Frightened by a low-flying plane, he dives for cover and decides to bushwhack his way through the forest to avoid exposure on the trail. Yet, with no sense of purpose or objective, his reactions lack commitment and reflect instincts rather than a considered plan of action. If death is his only option, why struggle to live and prolong the agony? While unwilling to actively take his own life, he is unsure why he instinctively flees from death.

Reaching the hospital and rejected for admission, Tamura joins the stragglers camped in the trees on the edge of the hospital clearing. They are wounded, sick, and abandoned. Some are too well for admission to the hospital, others too weak to move. Most are on the verge of starvation. The exception is Yasuda, an older soldier who trades tobacco for food, his way to provide for himself in the face of adversity. When the next day American artillery destroys the hospital, the doctors steal the remaining rations and abandon their patients to their fate. Tamura and the other stragglers run for cover, their limited sense of community lost as they rush to save themselves. Fleeing from the hospital clearing, Tamura collapses on a stream bank, where he drinks hungrily and fills his canteen. Pondering his situation, he thinks: "I was told to die and intend to do so. Why am I running? Why did I fill my canteen?" He takes out and examines his hand grenade and laughs at the inconsistency of his actions. In the distance he sees the burning hospital with the dead and dying sprawled around it. He cries out: "I won't try to help you, even though some of you are probably alive. Soon, I'll be dead myself." Despite his own best instincts, he accepts the inevitability of death.

Tamura is left alone and wanders for days on end, unsure of where he is, where he is going, or why he is struggling to live. He is driven by craving for life. He is frightened by the war and by the signs of Filipino life around him. But he is even more frightened by the specter of death. As the film progresses, we see him acknowledge his reverence for life and his determination to survive. Tamura, unlike most of his fellow soldiers, recognizes that life without civilized values is life without substance. It is this growing awareness of the need for moral choice, not merely choice between life or death, that distinguishes this gentle yet determined Japanese soldier from those around him. He wanders aimlessly, unsure how to survive but unwilling to die. Sitting on rocks along a river bank, he removes his boots to soak his feet. Seeing an ant on the rocks, he gently picks it up and carefully examines it, only to have it bite him. His isolation is complete. Rejected by the army, chased by Filipinos and the advancing Americans, he now finds that not even a lowly ant will accept him as a fellow living creature. His only option is to fend for himself.

In the distance he notices the sun reflecting off a cross on a church spire. The symbol of Christian love and sanctuary beckons to him, suggesting redemption lies someplace off in the distance. Arriving in the deserted village surrounding the church, he not only discovers empty cigarette cartons and other evidence of an American presence in the area, but is attacked by a wild dog, which he kills, instinctively protecting himself. Hearing running water—the stuff of life—he walks to the village tap to cleanse himself and wash the bayonet used to kill the dog. His will to live is strong. This naive and gentle soldier is prepared to kill in order to assure his own survival.

Yet this is not the only, or even the most important, point of the scene, for Ichikawa shows us how quickly Tamura's humanity can be stripped away. Walking to the church after cleansing himself—a Shinto ritual of purification—he finds the steps and the sanctuary littered with the remains of dead Japanese soldiers. He is repulsed at the scene of a church transformed into a mausoleum. Crows are feasting on the decaying bodies, further despoiling the image of the church as a place of spiritual purity and repose. All the symbols of civilized society have been tarnished by the war: communities are abandoned, individuals left to their own devices, even religion is contaminated.

Hearing singing in the distance, Tamura hides and sees an open boat approaching the beach carrying a happy young Filipino couple. They laugh as they enter the village, holding hands and unaware of his presence. They look under the floor of the first house they enter, searching for food and salt. After spying on them through a window, Tamura attempts to befriend them. The young woman screams at his overtures, fearing his uniform, his rifle, and the brutal reputation of the Japanese army. His efforts rejected, Tamura raises his weapon and fires at the screaming girl. She falls, mortally wounded. The young man, failing to calm Tamura and frightened for his own life, abandons his friend and runs off toward the beach and his boat. Tamura chases and fires at him as he pushes the boat away from the shore. Threatened, he has reacted like a soldier.

His gesture of friendship denied, he becomes the killer they presume him to be as a Japanese soldier.

Returning to the hut, Tamura carefully arranges the dying girl's clothing and shows compassion for her suffering. But when he spies a salt cache under the floor, he rudely pushes her aside. The rapid oscillation between Tamura the desperate soldier and Tamura the concerned humanitarian reflects the severity of his struggle to survive. Filling his haversack with salt and relishing the taste of the large crystals, he walks away from the village and continues his quest. As he crosses over a stream, he looks down at the rushing water and his weapon, the agent of death and destruction as well as of his own salvation. Ceremoniously dropping his rifle into the purifying waters of the stream, he walks off, relieved of the hated symbol of his status as a soldier. While he has killed to protect himself, Tamura attempts redemption by discarding his weapon. Now more vulnerable, Tamura strips himself of the weapon which makes him a danger to others. In the conflict between military and civilian values, he rejects his rifle and the brutality it represents.

As he wanders on aimlessly, Tamura's haversack bulges with life-giving salt. His hand grenade—the symbol of the inevitability of death, and the salt—an essential ingredient for life, share the same satchel. Sweet potatoes and the hand grenade shared the haversack when he left his unit; now salt is carried together with this agent of death. The grenade was provided by the army, while the salt came from the deserted village, the remnant of civilized society in the Philippines. Unable either to abandon the army or to join with the natives, Tamura is isolated from both his fellow Japanese soldiers and the Filipino victims of the war. Undaunted by his loneliness, he is determined to survive.

Days later, seeing three Japanese soldiers, Tamura rushes up to them in search of companionship. He is greeted not as a comrade but as an intruder. The sergeant challenges his right to join them and asks why he wasn't killed with the rest of his unit, wiped out by the advancing Americans. In an instance of foreshadowing the future, the sergeant, who is prepared to survive by any means, jokingly tells him, "Better be careful, we might eat you." However, he shows no interest in Tamura's welfare until he discovers that he has salt in his haversack, something they need to assure their own survival. He feels no responsibility for Tamura as a Japanese soldier, but he lets him tag along once he has proven his value. Noting that Tamura has lost his rifle, he finds him a replacement. This symbolically transforms Tamura from a useless straggler into a combatant. When Tamura asks how he found it, he is cautioned by the other men not to ask questions. Once again the sergeant is shown to be a brute, confident of his right to dominate his men and prepared to survive at all costs. Tamura and the others, while followers, are also potential victims. The patron-client relationships which characterize Japanese society are replaced in the army by ties between the strong and the weak. In the army the weak get no guarantees. Military hierarchy is unidirectional. Those at lower levels are subject to exploitation and brutalization by those above.

This image of exploitation and brutalization within the army is in direct opposition to the messages included in wartime films. There the image was a family-style army with the officers and NCO's presented as father figures, taking care of and looking after their men. The camaraderie of army life and the communal satisfaction provided by military service to the nation were important themes for wartime audiences. Soldiers looked after one another, shared their rations and cigarettes, and treated each other with compassion. Soldiers were selfless and dedicated to watching out for their comrades. *Fires on the Plain* and other postwar films reverse many of the wartime messages in their effort to reject wartime values and the positive portrayals of military service. The brutality of military life is often depicted in postwar Japanese films. The NCO as the victimizer of enlisted men is a theme found in many films, such as Kobayashi Masaki's *The Human Condition* or Masumura Yasuzo's *Hoodlum Soldier* (*Heitai yakuza*, 1965). The dramatic contrast is striking with wartime films, such as Tasaka Tomotaka's *Five Scouts* or Yoshimura Kozaburo's *The Story of Tank Commander Nishizumi*, which present military life and training as a happy experience where all work together for the common good. In wartime films, officers and men share warm bonds characterized by sensitive interactions between the ranks.

While in his 1956 film, *The Harp of Burma*, Ichikawa offered a mixed view of army life, here he presents military life as brutal and dehumanizing. In *Harp of Burma* the viewer is shown the contrast between the sensitive, humanistic captain of Mizushima's singing company, which surrenders and survives the war, and the inflexible and domineering captain of the holdouts, who refuses to surrender and is exterminated with his men by the British. In both these companies, despite their different fates, there was a sense of solidarity among most of the men. While many of the holdouts would have surrendered had their officers allowed it, most seemed prepared to die for the emperor rather than admit the stigma of defeat. In *Fires on the Plain,* there is no sense of community or common interest among the Japanese soldiers, merely a desperate struggle to survive as individuals. Comradeship is replaced by constant victimization of the weak by the strong. Military discipline becomes brutal repression. The officer as father figure becomes instead a brutal overseer dominating his charges. Only the will of the master is valid. The servants must do as they are told, whatever the costs.

In *Fires on the Plain,* as in other postwar films, there is a remnant of fellowship among the enlisted men. Yet it is severely limited and extends only so far as self-interest is not compromised. Several scenes in the film reflect this. When the unit clerk tells Tamura: "Die only if you have to," one senses a bond of human feeling between them. Likewise, when Tamura talks with the guards as he is leaving the unit, they show compassion for him for the dressing down he received from the squad leader. Their human instincts have not yet been completely eroded by the war. Similarly, the two enlisted veterans show sympathy for Tamura and try to protect him from their sergeant. Yet, as the film progresses, one sees the fragility of these instincts. Desperate conditions force the Japanese soldiers to fend for themselves, whatever the costs to their fellows. Even Tamura is compromised. He, more than the others, struggles to protect his humanitarian instincts from obliteration. This struggle allows him to protect more than merely his life. It also allows him to sustain his sense of cultural values and his faith in the essential goodness of the human community.

Tamura's dilemma is similar to that faced by Kaji (Nakadai Tatsuya) in Kobayashi Masaki's *The Human Condition*. This nine-hour trilogy, made between 1958 and 1961, develops its protagonist to a degree impossible in a normal feature-length film. Kaji is a socialist-humanist, determined to better the conditions of the Chinese prisoners under his supervision at a Japanese mine. Like Tamura, Kaji finds that the war and the army make it impossible for him to make behavioral choices consistent with his personal philosophical principles. First as a labor supervisor, then in the army, and finally as a war prisoner in Soviet prison camps, his circumstances force him to commit actions which, while prolonging his survival, undermine his integrity as a civilized man. Both Kaji and Tamura are decent men, aware of the ethical implications of their actions, yet forced by the war to compromise their values to survive. Despite their best intentions, both are contaminated by their status as combatants. Neither is able to protect himself against the brutalization and dehumanization of war. In both films they struggle to preserve their moral integrity and civilian values, yet soon discover they must adapt to their situations in order to assure their own subsistence. The violence and degradation of war transforms both men. Neither is suited for normal civil society as a consequence. Both can be redeemed, returned to the human community, only by death. The human spirit cannot sustain such violent attacks on conventional moral values.

In the face of continuous threats to his survival, Tamura learns to assert his determination to survive. As he and his new companions march off toward Palompon and the promise of evacuation and safety, they join other stragglers on the trail. One of them points to a soldier passively awaiting death at the side of the path. He has given up and arranged his possessions neatly around him. Tamura refuses to look at him. "I won't look," he exclaims. "I won't look at death!" Death is no longer an acceptable alternative to life. Tamura will live. He refuses to acknowledge the dead and dying who surround him. Tamura has made a conscious choice for life.

Moving on, he meets his friend Nagamatsu from the hospital clearing and Yasuda, who have managed to survive, trading tobacco for food with the desperate soldiers. Because Yasuda is crippled by his wounds, Nagamatsu trades tobacco for him and collects food for both of them. Trading the tobacco is easy, he tells Tamura. But when he tries to do business with an officer coming down the trail, the officer takes the leaf and walks off without giving anything in exchange. When Nagamatsu objects, the officer's aide slaps him and tells him not to bother his superior. Status differences remain dominant, despite the fact that all are starving and struggling to survive.

It is at this point in the film that Ichikawa introduces a bizarre combination of humor and hopelessness to project a surreal quality onto the Japanese retreat and the soldiers' desperate struggle for survival. The troops slowly move onward and pass a man with his face in a puddle along the trail. "I'll be like that soon," one man jokes. Raising his head from the water, the dying man asks, "What?" and then his face falls back into the water. In an even more striking example of dark humor, farther down the trail, boots are exchanged by a series of soldiers for those left behind by others. This points up the inadequacy of Japanese supplies and the desperation of those marching to Palompon. In each instance, the boots taken are in better shape than those abandoned until Tamura completes the sequence. He pulls off his own torn and tattered boots and, pulling on those left behind, discovers his new boots have no soles. Briefly padding in place, he finds he likes the feel of the puddles on his feet. Discarding both pairs of boots, he walks off barefoot toward Palompon. A sense of absolute futility and impoverishment is projected by this episode. It adds a quality of cynical defeatism to the exercise of marching to Palompon to escape the advancing American forces. The whole effort seems both comical and pointless, yet the Japanese forces push on toward the promise of rescue.

Coming to a branch in the trail to Palompon, the disordered and retreating Japanese forces are confronted with a highway they must cross. American military vehicles are seen passing by, and GIs in one of the trucks randomly fire their weapons toward the jungles, shouting, "Hurry up, you Japs," illustrating their contempt for their opponents. The hidden Japanese stragglers exclaim: "They're all fat as pigs. They must get plenty to eat. First time I've seen them after being chased by their shelling. Ridiculous, isn't it?" Again, humor is included to emphasize the desperate plight of the Japanese forces. The sergeant Tamura has been following tells his men they have to cross a highway to get to the road to Palompon. Tamura, who had fallen behind, rushes up at the sound of the sergeant's voice, greeting him with enthusiasm. Still the naive, well-mannered follower, Tamura is contrasted sharply with the others by his language and his attitude. This contrast provides a stark reminder of how seemingly unblemished he is by his plight and by his army service. It also illustrates the degree to which he has isolated himself from his surroundings.

In fact, in contrast with the other soldiers fleeing toward Palompon, Tamura is free. One of the men in his group asks Tamura if he has any salt left, noting that the sergeant had taken his remaining supply. "He treats us like dirt," he tells Tamura. "Be careful of him." Despite the disarray of the Japanese forces, he has no control over his life. He is still bound to his squad leader by military discipline and is unable to extricate himself. Since Tamura's whole unit has been killed, he has no formal ties to any military superiors. Despite his uniform, he can respond to his condition as an individual. His innocence and his freedom to make personal choices distinguish him from the others.

The fact that these constraints still exist for the others is demonstrated when an American jeep drives by and Tamura reads the English lettering. He tells his companions that it holds a traveling chaplain. "So you can read English!" they exclaim. Suddenly the sergeant points his weapon at his men and admonishes: "Don't try to surrender. You're going to Palompon!" Despite their desperate situation, they are denied any rights to personal initiative or self-determination. Laughing, he lowers his weapon and giggles: "You look so scared." The sergeant is more frightening than the enemy. He is mad, yet determined to preserve his authority over his remaining men. The rumors of his cannibalism, his brutality, and his forceful assertion of his power over them reinforce their sense of helplessness. They are bound to serve the emperor until they achieve either victory or death. Military obligations compromise their struggle to survive.

In the evening darkness the Japanese troops wade through a deep bog and cross the highway. They struggle to get to the road and then crawl toward the apparent sanctuary of the jungle on the other side. As the vanguard closes on this goal, lights suddenly appear, and heavy vehicle engines are heard from behind the trees. American tanks have been waiting for them. As the tanks move out from the tree line with their searchlights beaming, the Japanese stragglers run in terror. Machine guns and cannons rip them to pieces. The brutal sergeant is hit in the stomach and falls face first into the muck, a look of startled disbelief on his face. Tamura, while losing his weapon, escapes unharmed and makes it back into the jungle. The innocent warrior has miraculously survived.

In the morning light, a scene of slaughter greets the Japanese survivors. The bog, road, and clearing across the highway are littered with Japanese dead and wounded. An American Red Cross truck stops, and medics examine the fallen Japanese, looking for wounded soldiers they might save. They find a survivor, load him into their truck, and drive off. The onlookers marvel that he is given a cigarette and treated kindly by his rescuers. Tamura decides the Americans look friendly and pulls off his loincloth to use as a flag of surrender. When a jeep approaches and an American officer gets out to smoke, a Japanese straggler rushes toward him with his hands up, shouting: "I surrender." A Filipino soldier quickly dismounts from the back of the enclosed jeep, raises her weapon, and fires at the defenseless Japanese. The American pushes down her weapon and admonishes her for killing an unarmed man. Her hatred testifies that for the Filipinos, victims of Japanese aggression, there will be no prisoners. In their eyes all Japanese soldiers deserve to die. Tamura understands that to surrender is to gamble on the humanity of the enemy. Dejected, he lowers his white flag and retreats into the jungle.

Through the mist and smoke of war, Tamura walks off across a field littered with bodies and moves up into the hills. His situation seems as hopeless as before. Now he has lost his companions and is alone among the retreating Japanese forces. As he wanders aimlessly away from the fighting, a soldier collapses in front of him and dies on the trail. Tamura strips off the man's boots and takes them for himself. There is no humor in this exchange, for Tamura is hardened and determined to ensure his own survival. Passing a wounded man leaning against a tree, he hears him calling to the Buddha to come and transport him to the Western Paradise. "A special plane will come for me," the crazed man tells him. "I will be saved." Convinced of his salvation, he offers himself to Tamura: "Eat me after I die. Take this flesh off my arm and eat it." Tamura turns away and runs off in disgust. As he walks down a lonely path, he tells himself, "Whatever happens, I won't eat human flesh." His survival instincts are strong, but his sense of humanity denies him this one mechanism for extending his life. Later, when he finds his friend Nagamatsu and is offered water and "monkey meat" as food, he is unable to eat it and loses several teeth as he tries to chew. When he drops the dried meat, Nagamatsu picks it up, brushes it off, and carefully replaces it in his haversack. For him, the meat represents a guarantee of life. For Tamura it is too tough, illustrating that both physically and morally, the eating of "monkey meat" is beyond his capacity. While not yet able to acknowledge the source of the meat, he is still unable to eat it.

Yet, in time, Tamura not only will acknowledge the source of "monkey meat," he will be the audience for the final confrontation between Nagamatsu and Yasuda. They are still together, still dependent on one another, even though neither trusts the other. Under no illusions about how the two have survived, Tamura asks Nagamatsu, who offers him assistance, "Did you mistake me for a monkey?" Nagamatsu's reply is telling. "Don't be foolish," he says, "I wouldn't shoot you. I know you have TB." It is not their friendship which has saved

Tamura from slaughter, but rather Nagamatsu's fear of his disease. It is this which makes him undesirable as food. Desperate for meat, Nagamatsu and Yasuda eventually confront each other, each determined to kill his companion in order to survive. In the end, Nagamatsu calmly shoots Yasuda and savagely butchers the corpse with his bayonet. Revolted, Tamura gets Nagamatsu's rifle and confronts him. Nagamatsu, his clothes and face grotesquely drenched with blood, tries to reason with him. Revolted, Tamura shoots him, disgusted by his cannibalism. Dropping the weapon, he walks off in search of a moral and civilized community. He has preserved his integrity but sacrificed his last remaining friend. He is now forever isolated from the remnants of the Japanese army.

Throughout the film, the fires on the plain have symbolized the enemy. Tamura has fled in fear from the plumes of smoke, a visual metaphor for the commonplace life of Filipino farmers and the agricultural cycle of harvest and renewal. Revolted by the desperate efforts at survival by the remaining Japanese stragglers, Tamura has come to see the fires as his only hope for a return to a civil society. Raising his hands in the air in a gesture of surrender, he calmly walks toward the burning cornstalks, the fires on the plain. Shots are fired toward him, and dirt is kicked up by the bullets hitting the ground around his feet as the voices of Filipino farmers are heard joking behind the smoke. Fearlessly pushing forward, Tamura falls, and appears to be dead. Titles announce that it is "February 1945, someplace on Leyte," and the film ends.

In the Ooka novel, Tamura writes from a mental hospital where he has confined himself following his repatriation to Japan. He cannot deal with the apparent normality of postwar Japan. In the film, he engages in a final act of self-sacrifice to preserve his integrity and reaffirm his humanity. Despite his best instincts and intentions, his ordeal has caused him to engage in the brutality associated with military service and war. While he has refused to eat human flesh, he has still crossed the boundary between civilization and barbarism. In each case of violent behavior, his own survival required that he take another's life. By killing Nagamatsu, his friend and protector, he allows violence to penetrate his own private community. He can no longer tolerate his own existence if it requires that he be excluded from normal civil society. He must be included in a civilian community and is prepared to risk death to achieve that. By walking toward the fires on the plain, Tamura is declaring that life without integrity, life without moral substance, life without the company of his fellows, is devoid of meaning. His survival as an isolated individual no longer can be justified. Despite the instincts which have preserved him from much of the contamination of the war, he has been irrevocably tarnished as a human being. It is only through the redemption offered through acceptance by others that his life can be sustained.

Death is now preferable to a meaningless life. He submits himself to his fate as he walks toward the fires on the plain.

Ichikawa's film transforms the message included in the original novel and takes it one step further. For the novelist Ooka, the horrors of war and the degradation of defeat make a normal life impossible for Tamura, the hapless victim of his fate as a survivor of the Philippines campaign. He can only retreat to a mental hospital where, isolated from postwar Japanese society, he can live out his remaining years in the company of his own private ghosts and terrors. In the film, even this is unattainable. Survival itself is unacceptable unless the victims of the war will accept him into their community. Only acceptance by those who were victimized and brutalized by the Japanese invasion of the Philippines can justify Tamura's continued existence. Only their reaffirmation of his humanity as an individual without nationality, without status as either victim or oppressor, can rationalize his continued survival. Doubts about his moral worth, about his personal integrity, about his right to life, have finally overwhelmed his strong determination to live. While he has rejected cannibalism, he has still so compromised himself that he requires absolution by the victims of Japanese oppression. All his civilian values have been contaminated and tarnished. Only through a willful sacrifice can he attain salvation. He must pay for his sins and for the sins of the Japanese army. His final rite of purification, the final cleansing of his guilt, will be at the hands of the innocent Filipino farmers. Just as the burning of the corn stalks represents the culmination of the harvest, so, too, does Tamura's death symbolize the culmination of the war.

Fires on the Plain is a major cinematic treatment of the need for all Japanese to purify themselves of the contamination of militarism and war. By illustrating Tamura's inability to accomplish this objective, it reaffirms the importance of moral values and civilized norms of individual behavior. By showing how the senses of community and nationality were destroyed, by illustrating the brutalization of the human spirit by military discipline and behavior, by presenting the human costs of overseas expansion and war, the film forces the viewer to reconsider the place of nationalism, imperialism, and conflict in the human community. The simple Filipino farmers represent a more traditional agricultural society than that of Japan. But in the film it is obvious that only they have preserved the essence of civilized community life. They work together, look out for each other's interests, and show sympathy for their fellows. Both in the final scene and elsewhere in the film, one gets a sense of communal solidarity among the Filipinos encountered by Tamura. The farmers are working together, and there are many voices talking behind the smoke of the fires on the plain.

In contrast, the Japanese are brutal, self-serving, and unable to sustain a sense of common interest or adhere to conventional norms of moral action. The sense of hopelessness which emerges from the film is emphasized by Tamura's willingness to offer himself as a sacrifice to the war in order to atone for his sins as a combatant. If even this kind and gentle man, this soldier who seemingly preserved his civilian outlook in the face of severe hardships and military discipline, was unable to maintain his personal integrity, what chance is there for the rest of us? Is war unacceptable, given its degrading impact on the human community? If so, how do we learn to resolve conflicts in a peaceful and less cataclysmic manner? Ichikawa offers no answers in *Fires on the Plain.* However, he forces his viewers to confront essential questions about the fragility of moral society and makes a major statement about the cultural impact and human costs of war.

WORKS CONSULTED

Anderson, Joseph L., and Donald Richie. *The Japanese Film: Art and Industry.* Expanded edition. Princeton: Princeton UP, 1982.
Benedict, Ruth Fulton. "Japanese Films: A Phase of Psychological Warfare." Foreign Morale Analysis Division, Office of War Information (RS53/2). Washington, D.C., March 30, 1944.
Bock, Audie. *Japanese Film Directors.* Tokyo: Kodansha, 1978.
Fires on the Plain [*Nobi*]. Dir. Ichikawa Kon. From the novel by Ooka Shohei. With Funakoshi Eiji. Daiei, 1959.
Manvell, Roger. *Films and the Second World War.* New York: Delta, 1974.
Mellen, Joan. *Voices from the Japanese Cinema.* New York: Liveright, 1975.
_____ . *The Waves at Genji's Door: Japan through Its Cinema.* New York: Pantheon, 1976.
Ooka, Shohei. *Fires on the Plain.* Trans. Ivan Norris. Rutland, Vt., and Tokyo: Charles E. Tuttle, 1957.
Richie, Donald. *Japanese Cinema: Film Style and National Character.* Garden City, N.Y.: Anchor, 1971.

Comic Targets and Comic Styles: An Introduction to Japanese Film Comedy

Gregory Barrett

Ian Buruma begins his essay "Humor in Japanese Cinema" (*East-West Film Journal* [December 1987]) with the following question and comment: "Do the Japanese have a sense of humor? There is a general feeling, among Westerners as well as Asians, that they do not" (p. 26). He then argues that indeed they do, while also analyzing the cultural reasons why their films have not been especially strong in ironical humor. Gregory Barrett's essay begins with an important assumption that in effect answers Buruma's question and takes it one step further: not only do the Japanese have a sense of humor, but we would be better able to appreciate it if we were more familiar with the nature and history of their film comedy.

Indeed, as Barrett says, Japanese film comedy has a long and rich history, one that has been shaped by traditional and Western influences. His essay charts the evolution of the genre by examining representative films, their comic styles, and the specific targets which they ridicule or poke fun at. First he takes a look at the *jidai-geki* (period films), such as Yamanaka Sadao's *Tange Sazen and the Pot Worth a Million Ryo* (*Tange Sazen—Hyakuman-ryo no tsubo,* 1935) and Itami Mansaku's *Kakita Akanishi* (1936), and shows how samurai were parodied, and what this signified in the cultural and political climate of the day. Then he turns to the *gendai-geki* (films set in the modern period), the mode in which comedy truly flourished. Beginning with the filming of skits in the 1900s and ending with the emergence of the present-day sophisticated comedies of Itami Juzo and Morita Yoshimitsu,

Barrett shows how "over the years the best of Japanese film comedy has turned increasingly to satire."

A thoroughly informed introduction, one that invites further exploration of its vast subject, Barrett's essay is also of interest in that it acquaints Western readers with important Japanese sources, such as Kido Shiro, Yamamoto Kikuo, and most of all Sato Tadao. For further reading on Japanese comedy, see Audie Bock, "Ozu Reconsidered," *Film Criticism* 8, 1 (Fall 1983): 50–53; Ian Buruma, "Humor in Japanese Cinema," *East-West Film Journal* 2, 1 (December 1987): 26–31; Keiko I. McDonald, "Family, Education, and Postmodern Society: Yoshimitsu Morita's *The Family Game*," *East-West Film Journal* 4, 1 (December 1989): 53–68; and Max Tessier, *Images du cinéma japonais* (Paris: Henri Veyrier, 1981), pp. 130–135.

Little is known about Japanese film comedy (*kigeki*) in the West. To be sure, Western critics have noted the humor in the films of Ozu and Kurosawa, and have praised the few isolated 1950s comedies that they have seen, such as Toyoda Shiro's *A Cat, Shozo, and Two Women* (*Neko to shozo to futari no onna*, 1956), about a henpecked married man who prefers his cat to the three domineering women in his life. But long before the recent wave of comic satires, initiated by Morita Yoshimitsu's brilliant dissection of the modern Japanese family *Family Games* (*Kazoku geimu*, 1983), comedy in fact was the staple of Shochiku Studios, where in the late 1920s and 1930s studio head Kido Shiro required his directors—among them Ozu, Naruse Mikio, and Gosho Heinosuke—to excel in the genre.

Japanese film comedy, then, has a long history—one that drew from both traditional and Western sources. It also is rich in variety. It encompasses slapstick, burlesque, parody, irony, black comedy, comedy of pathos, and comedy of manners. In addition it includes comic styles that are quintessentially Japanese. The first of these styles derives from Japanese performing arts, and includes *rakugo* (the traditional humor of stock characters in lowlife situations), *kyōgen* (short farcical pieces originally performed between plays on the Noh program), and *joruri* (a storytelling form with either a single narrator or a combination of narrator and mute performers, most often puppets). The second of these styles is the creation of Japanese filmmakers alone, and features *nansensu* ("nonsense") comedy and *ninjō kigeki* (comedy of human relationships).

No single essay can possibly do justice to the length and breadth of Japanese film comedy, but by examining its evolution we can provide a useful introduction to the genre. Here we will look at important representative films, noting their comic style and commenting on their particular comic targets, that is, what they ridicule or poke fun at. In doing so, we will see that over the years the best of Japanese film comedy has turned increasingly to satire, while *ninjō kigeki* (whether sentimental or humanistic in its treatment of human relations) was generally the most popular style.

Comedy and satire, of course, are never mutually exclusive terms. Still, for the purposes of this essay, comedy may be defined as a work that is primarily intended to please and amuse us; and while it may poke fun at characters, the fun does not ultimately engage our deep concern. Satire, on the other hand, is more serious business. It ridicules, castigates, and uses laughter to attack human foibles, stupidity, and hypocrisy. In Japanese film comedy, the proverbial satiric targets are individuals, class (e.g., commoners and samurai), institutions, social and political ideas, and even society at large.

Our discussion of the development of Japanese film comedy will follow the lead of Japanese film itself, which from its beginning at the turn of the century was divided into two main genres: period film (*jidai-geki*), dramas set in feudalistic historical periods, and contemporary film (*gendai-geki*), dramas set after the Meiji Restoration in 1868, when Japan began modernizing in earnest. We will begin with a consideration of period film.

There is usually some comic relief in most period films, but there are few pure comedies. This may be attributed in part to the impact on the genre of Kabuki, the traditional theater.[1] The main role (*tateyaku*) in Kabuki is the warrior from the samurai class, and the second role (*nimaime*) is an amorous man, usually from the merchant class. The role of the fool was called *sanmaime* because it was listed third on Kabuki programs. This hierarchy in billing suggests that fools came from the lowest social classes, but this was not always the case. In Chikamatsu Monzaemon's most famous play, *Double Suicide (Shinjū ten no Amijima)*, a clownish, rich merchant thwarts the true lovers. In *Kanadehon Chūshingura*, the best Kabuki play based on the tale of the forty-seven retainers who sacrifice themselves to avenge their dead lord, Moronao, the villain, has a comical retainer, Bannai, who is nevertheless a samurai. Such comical villains, however, seldom appear in period films. In fact, in most film versions of *Chūshingura*, neither Bannai nor anyone like him appears; therefore, the task of affording comic relief belongs to commoners.

Take, for example, the following scene from *Chūshingura*. On the night the forty-seven retainers plan to attack the residence of their dead lord's enemy, they meet in the second-floor dining room of a noodle shop. Their solemn demeanor as they make their preparations is contrasted with the confused expressions of the shopkeeper and his son down below, who cannot understand why they have so many customers on such a cold, snowy night. Then the loyal forty-seven come out of the dining room fully arrayed for battle. The timid shopkeeper and his son hide under the stairway, trembling as the brave samurai march majestically down the stairs above them.

This scene has appeared in most major film versions of *Chūshingura,* ever since Makino Shozo's between 1910 and 1912, and it never fails to produce chuckles among the viewing audience. Taken from *kodan,* "historical narratives," which rivaled Kabuki as a source of traditional materials for period film, it provides a contrast between timid commoners and loyal retainers that enhances the nobility of the latter group. It also illustrates a general truth in period film: that only commoners could play the role of the fool, and that even a comical villain such as the retainer Bannai would not be allowed to mar the noble image of film samurai.

Period film was very popular entertainment in prewar Japan. At the time old samurai values, such as loyalty to one's superior, were being disseminated among the masses through a modern, compulsory education system, and the modern version of the samurai code of *Bushido,* an imperialistic militarism, was on the rise. Most period filmmakers did not choose samurai as comic targets, perhaps because they were afraid that such ridicule might be associated with their contemporary military and political leaders. Instead they made the feudal commoner the butt of all the jokes; however, in doing so, they and their audiences were in effect laughing at their ancestors and themselves, since very few modern Japanese can actually claim descent from a samurai family. In fact, the main audience for period film came from the masses—contemporary commoners— while most prewar filmmakers either came from lower classes or were dropouts from the middle class, which did not consider filmmaking a respectable occupation until the late 1930s.[2] The audience, then, may have alternately identified with the samurai hero, wishfully thinking they could be that brave, too, and then with the foolish commoners, realizing that at heart they were timid. This "double identification" probably persists in the audience of the postwar era. Although most Japanese have become middle class, they probably identify even more with the feudal commoner than with the samurai hero, since *Bushido* values have been largely discredited on account of the defeat in World War II.

The commoner was not the only comic target in period film. Sometimes a foolish or frivolous *daimyo* (feudal lord) made an appearance. His prototype can be traced as far back as medieval *kyōgen* plays, where the foolishness of a haughty *daimyo* would be exposed, and he would be bested by his subordinates. This situation probably expressed the resentment of playwrights of outcaste or lower-class origins. In period film, however, the *daimyo's* prudent retainers either clean up his comic messes or cover up for him. In either case, he is clearly a far cry from a powerful feudal lord.

A good example of such a *daimyo* is Genzaburo, the young protagonist in *Tange Sazen and the Pot Worth a Million Ryo* (*Tange Sazen—Hyakuman-ryo no tsubo*, 1935). In the original story he had been a master swordsman, but director Yamanaka Sadao turned him into a frivolous fellow who would rather fool around with pretty girls than search for his missing family heirloom, a pot worth a million *ryo*. In fact, not only does this character seem a most unlikely samurai, but also during episodes when he is quarreling with or making up with his pouting wife, contemporary jazz music comes on the sound track, as it might in a Hollywood comedy, to further underscore his lack of heroic stature.

Sato Tadao has praised Yamanaka Sadao for changing master swordsmen such as Sazen Tange, the one-eyed *ronin* (masterless samurai) in the film, into lovable old neighborhood types.[3] By reducing samurai to the common level, Yamanaka erased class distinctions and produced a film in which all the characters are laughable. Human foolishness is not restricted to the lower classes, and audiences easily identify with common human foibles that exist in all social classes.

Yamanaka went even further in diminishing the status of samurai in his last (and perhaps his best) film, *Humanity and Paper Balloons* (*Ninjō kamifusen*, 1937). A tragedy, and therefore outside the scope of this essay, it is a tale of a destitute *ronin* who is just as pitiable as a commoner.

The best satire of the samurai class was probably Itami Mansaku's *Akanishi Kakita* (1936). Although Akanishi, the hero, is a samurai, he seems more like a comical commoner when he munches on jelly rolls and writes a love letter to a lady-in-waiting at a feudal castle. After he loses in love and flees the fief, the foolish *daimyo* and his prudent retainers have a big laugh at his expense in their meeting hall. While they are laughing, however, reports start coming in that reveal that the supposed fool was actually a spy for the shogunate, and that consequently their plot against the central government will be exposed.

Prewar critic Kitagawa Fuyuhiko has correctly observed that the *daimyo* and his retainers' ridiculing laughter, originally directed at Akanishi, is now heaped upon themselves.[4] Interestingly enough, Itami is careful to maintain class distinctions by presenting most of the samurai—particularly the chief retainers who hatched the plot—as brave and proud, as members of a warrior class should be. Yet these samurai are still funny, not because they have been transformed into foolish commoners but because they have been fooled by someone they consider beneath their dignity.

Itami's *Akanishi Kakita* is satire at its most subtle. Since the hero is a shogunate spy, Itami gives lip service to the maintenance of the social order. However, since the hero seems like a commoner *vis-à-vis* the scheming but orthodox samurai, his triumph in the end symbolically refutes samurai authority. It even questions by implication the authority of Japan's political and military leaders of the 1930s, for they adhered to old samurai values, particularly their prerogative to rule as the superior class. Thus, the comic target in *Akanishi Kakita* is ultimately the values of society at large.

Samurai were also being parodied in the 1930s by Enoken, then Japan's most famous comedian. As early as 1930 Enoken had spoofed *Chūshingura* on the Asakusa vaudevillian stage,[5] and in one of his first films, *Enoken's Kondo Isamu* (*Enoken no Kondo Isamu*, 1935, directed by Yamamoto Kajiro), he comically played the double role of Kondo Isamu and Sakamoto Ryoma, rival samurai who were also patriots. Kondo Isamu was considered a master swordsman, but in the film he becomes powerful only when the short Enoken can get into his high *geta,* wooden cloppers that here become equivalent to Popeye's spinach. In the midst of one melee, an old townsman calls for a time out and asks Enoken to have the swordfight elsewhere because it is disturbing the peace. When Enoken dutifully complies, the stereotypes of the timid townsman and the almighty samurai, time-honored conventions in period film, are both shattered.

Perhaps Enoken could get away with this because he was a comedian, a little guy with a funny face who made audiences laugh just by dressing as a samurai. His parody could be considered the form of tribute found in burlesque. Still, it seems that the authorities came to take Enoken's parodies as indirect criticism, for after *Enoken's Kondo Isamu,* he tended to spoof famous feudal outlaws rather than samurai; and after the outbreak of the Sino-Japanese War in 1937, samurai were neither parodied nor satirized in period film.

In postwar period film, parody was allowed, but intellectual satire like Itami's failed to reappear. Instead, the cruelties attendant with Bushido were exposed in such gripping films as Kobayashi Masaki's *Harakiri (Seppuku,* 1962) and Imai Tadashi's *Bushido—Samurai Saga (Bushido zankoku monogatari,* 1963), but there was nothing humorous in the directors' treatments.

As we have seen, there are few pure comedies in period film. Such is not the case in contemporary film (*gendai-geki*), where comedy began in the early 1900s with the filming of skits and acts from the Soganoya Brothers Theater of Comedy. Their comedy was called new then because it was set in the modern period after 1868, but its contents were quite traditional. Sato Tadao has concluded that it stressed the comedy of affinity, whereby everyone laughs together and recognizes common values, and that it had its antecedent in Kagura, dance dramas performed as far back as the third century A.D.[6] In one Kagura drama, the goddess Ame-no-Uzume performed a lewd dance that induced laughter among the gods and brought the sun goddess Amaterasu out of hiding. Evidently, even a Japanese goddess was not above making a fool of herself when it was for the common good—namely, returning the life-giving sun to heaven and earth.

Sato Tadao also sees a negative side to the humor of the Soganoya brothers, in that by making fun of themselves they recalled the old clowns from the lowest social classes, pathetic clown roles that had existed in *joruri* puppet plays since the seventeenth century, as well as in other traditional performing arts. Sato labels such humor "masochistic," in contrast to the "sadistic" slapstick from America, which often featured wholesale destruction of property and objects. Hence, in his view the comic artist "destroys" either himself or his environment. Sato much prefers the latter kind of "destruction" over the self-effacing former kind, because it expresses the vitality of the common people and could serve as a springboard for social criticism.[7] That is to say, a new society could be constructed on the ruins of the old. In this respect he seems to concur with American film critic Gerald Mast, who has stated that good comedy is bent on the destruction of the idols built by society.[8]

In fact, most prewar Japanese film critics also preferred slapstick. According to Yamamoto Kikuo, who has done extensive research on the influence of foreign films on Japanese cinema, critics at the time attacked the traditional, sentimental humor of the Soganoya brothers and encouraged Japanese filmmakers to take as their model the American comedies that had replaced the French ones in popularity during World War I. The reasons why critics did so were not merely aesthetic. American comedy was respected as the expression of a new civilization and mass culture, and its audacity could serve as a stimulus for a modernizing Japan which was rejecting, or "destroying," many of its old social idols.[9] At the same time, however, American comedy posed an economic threat to Japanese filmmakers. Thus, Kido Shiro, the head of Shochiku Studios, forced his novice directors to make two- or three-reel comedy shorts simply in order to compete with the American variety that was flooding the Japanese market.[10]

Thomas Kurihara's *Amateur Club* (*Amachua kurabu*, 1920) is considered the first good assimilation of American slapstick. Featuring the highjinks of an amateur theater troupe by the seaside, it set the parameters for future Japanese imitations. The Japanese could rival Mack Sennett's beach comedies, even supply their own version of the Sennett Girls; however, they could not afford to destroy a lot of cars in a chase and had no equivalent to the Keystone Kops. Japan was not materially affluent in the 1920s, and despite the influx of democratic and socialistic ideas, the police were above parody in their predominantly authoritarian society. Hence, a compromise was made, and *nansensu* comedy came into existence. It incorporated the Keystones' refusal to take anything seriously, while maintaining a hands-off policy toward authority figures; it thus became the most popular style of Japanese film comedy in the 1920s.

There is no extant print of *Amateur Club*. Unfortunately, as there are precious few extant prints of any Japanese films of the 1920s, a 1931 Ozu film, *The Lady and the Beard* (*Shukujo to hige*), will have to serve as an example of *nansensu* comedy. It mainly features embarrassing situations modeled on the humor of Harold Lloyd and jokes about a young nonconformist's beard, which he eventually shaves off in order to get a respectable job. In mood and denouement, Ozu skirted the serious problem of unemployment during the depression—which he would ironically treat in *Tokyo Chorus* (*Tokyo no gassho*, 1931)—and presented business executives (authority figures) who had the best interests of young men at heart, as long as they conformed. In this film Ozu amuses the audience with quite an array of gags and visual tricks, but his comic target, the beard, is as trivial as the one in Gosho Heinosuke's *The Bride Talks in Her Sleep* (*Hanayome no negoto*, 1933), a *nansensu* comedy predicated on the heroine's sweet nocturnal murmurs.

Yamamoto Kikuo has noted that Japanese film comedy eventually progressed from slapstick and *nansensu* to social satire, and cites the prewar films of Ozu.[11] Although Yamamoto does not give individual examples, *Days of Youth* (*Wakaki hi*, 1929) and *I Was Born but . . .* (*Umarete wa mita keredo*, 1932) come readily to mind. The former consists mainly of highjinks in the snow at a ski resort, and hardly takes anything seriously at all. The latter begins with children's games, moves into social satire, and ends with adult tragedy.

In *I Was Born but . . .* a father takes his two boys along for a visit to his boss's house, where they see home movies in which their father makes a fool of himself to please his boss. His comedy routine of rolling his eyeballs was probably borrowed from an American slapstick film, but his attitude simply expressed the contemporary version of timid, comical commoners in period film. Back at home the boys protest. In their neighborhood gang they are the leaders and the boss's son is their follower, simply because they are smarter than he is. Therefore, it is not that they are against hierarchy. Rather they feel that hierarchy should be based on ability, not social background.

With the boys' protest, Ozu's comedy moves into social satire, for their protest suggests that contemporary Japanese society in the 1930s is not basically different from the highly stratified feudal society it succeeded, *and* that this should not be so. When their father tells them that they would not be able to eat if he did not play up to the boss, they go on a hunger strike. But eventually, of course, they relent, and the film ends with a reconciliation between father and sons.

According to Sato Tadao, in contrast to the unrelenting confrontation in Chaplin's films, Ozu's prewar films generally end in resignation.[12] In *I Was Born but . . .* everyone is resigned to economic realities, and social satire becomes tragedy in that social reform is deemed impossible. Perhaps economic conditions in Japan in the 1930s could not be changed, and Ozu felt that his characters were simply resigning themselves to the human condition. This may very well be the case, for as Donald Richie has observed, in Ozu's later pictures, "the whole world exists in one family, the characters are family members rather than members of society. . . . "[13] Hence, they are shorn of social class, just like the characters in Yamanaka Sadao's period films, and all they can do is laugh at themselves as members of the human race. As such, the comedy in Ozu's later pictures can be considered *ninjō kigeki* (comedy of human relationships) at its very best.

There is a pathos in the films of Ozu and Yamanaka that is truly Chaplinesque. This is perhaps not surprising, since Chaplin was phenomenally popular in Japan. His humor made audiences laugh and cry, and that led many Japanese filmmakers to consciously imitate him.[14] These imitations, however, were not good at first because melodrama often outweighed humor,[15] something Chaplin usually managed to avoid by resorting to a joke when the sadness got too thick.[16]According to Yamamoto Kikuo, the only Japanese director who followed Chaplin's lead here was Torajiro Saito, and then only in his mature comedies such as *If We Don't Abandon This Child* (*Kono ko sutezareba,* 1935) and *Children—The Precious Disturbance* (*Kodakara sodo,* 1935).[17]

Both films present a Chaplinesque character who has to support a lot of kids, either his own or orphans; but the potential for melodrama and sentimentality in this subject matter is resolutely rejected by Saito. For example, in *Children—The Precious Disturbance,* the hero's children accidentally step on his wife's belly when she is undergoing birth throes, and after he helps another woman give birth, he casually tosses the newborn infant aside when he is reminded of the plight of his own children. The struggle of Saito's hero is made grimmer than any in Chaplin's films because his labor often comes to naught, and his attempts at crime are doomed to failure (a collorary to the hands-off policy toward authority figures in most prewar Japanese film). Unlike Chaplin's "Little Tramp," he is not particularly alienated; it just seems that the odds are so stacked against him that everything he does is futile. In the end, though, somehow he succeeds in getting a reward from a rich man or winning some prize. But these balms give him only brief respite before he has to continue his struggle for survival.

Saito's struggling character does not have time to question the social order or dream of utopia. Life for those on the bottom rung of society seems like a cruel joke, but nothing can be done about it in Saito's view except to laugh bitterly and to persevere. Such is the inevitable human condition. Ozu's middle-class office worker's response to it is sycophancy; Saito's character reacts with a desperate vitality. As the economic circumstances of Saito's characters improved in his postwar films, this vitality was replaced by zany antics, and a sentimental attitude toward family relations crept in.

The illusion that all social wrongs were only the result of inevitable human conditions, however, was rudely shattered after the defeat in 1945, when the Occupation authorities began jailing military and business leaders for war crimes and monopolies and encouraged unionization. Social satire of the vestiges of feudalism in contemporary society was welcome then, but ironically, the best film satires came out after the Occupation and were directed against a Japanese defense force being built with the approval of U.S. armed forces engaged in the Korean War. In *Carmen's Pure Love* (*Karumen junjosu,* 1952) Kinoshita Keisuke lampooned the widow of a naval officer, a militaristic mama who sang the national anthem whenever she could. In *Mr. Pu* (*Pu-san,* 1953) Ichikawa Kon showed how a pacifistic college professor could willingly take a job at a muni-tions factory during hard times. In both films the comic target was either the ignorance or timidity of the average citizen, who could still be manipulated by rightist leaders as in prewar days. The exposure of such manipulation, which was not permitted in the prewar authoritarian society, suggested that the recognition of such ignorance could lead to reform through education.

Kinoshita and Ichikawa were versatile directors who created fine films in various genres. The most significant postwar directors who specialized in com-edy, though, were Kawashima Yuzo and Yamada Yoji. Both began their careers at Shochiku Studios, the source of most prewar film comedies. In fact, Yamada served as Kawashima's assistant director for his last film there in 1954. Both had a strong interest in *rakugo,* the traditional anecdotal humor still popular on Japanese TV. However, while Kawashima successfully captured the audacious spirit of *rakugo* in some of his films in the late 1950s, Yamada failed to do so in his early attempts in the 1960s, but eventually found his own groove in *ninjō kigeki* and created Japan's most popular comedy series, *It's Tough to Be a Man* (*Otoko wa tsurai yo,* over 40 entries since 1969).

Kawashima's comic masterpiece is *Sun Legend of the Shogunate's Last Days* (*Bakumatsu taiyo den,* 1957). Set in old Edo (present-day Tokyo) during the 1860s, the watershed period between Japan's feudal past and modern future, the film revolves around Saiheiji, a resourceful commoner who works at a geisha house to pay off a big bill he ran up there with his cronies. Saiheiji takes up with a samurai patriot rooming there and makes a deal with him: if the samurai helps a young girl to escape from the geisha house, Saiheiji will obtain the floorplan of the British consulate, which the samurai's anti-Western faction wants to burn down. The films ends with all parties concerned getting what they wanted and Saiheiji escaping, too.

Sun Legend of the Shogunate's Last Days is an entertaining, thought-provoking film because it enables Kawashima to contrast the attitudes of the samurai and the commoner on the eve of Japan's modernization: the former lived by the sword and was concerned about the fate of the nation; the latter lived by his wits and was worried only about himself, his family, and his friends. Moreover, it warrants an unshakable position in Japanese film history because it is perhaps the only truly successful adaptation of *rakugo* materials to cinema.

Rakugo had been filmed during the silent period when the *benshi,* or narrator, read the comic anecdote that was illustrated on the screen rather than dramatized. Critics then generally felt that such treatments were static, wordy, and uncinematic in comparison with the speedy American silent comedies. With the advent of talkies and the appearance of the *rakugo* artist himself relating the tale, the results were not much better. As Sato Tadao has concluded, *rakugo* films before Kawashima were not successful because cinema's forte lies in the empathy induced by different players in each role, whereas in *rakugo,* empathy is lost because of the alienating effect of the artist playing all the roles himself.[18]

In *Sun Legend of the Shogunate's Last Days,* Kawashima solves this dilemma by inducing empathy for only one character, Saiheiji. All the others—the competitive geisha, the greedy husband and wife who own the brothel, their foolish son, their ignorant help (all *rakugo* stereotypes), and even samurai patriots—become comic caricatures as seen through Saiheiji's eyes, rather than sympathetic characters. Even the young girl whom Saiheiji rescues jolts the audience with her amusing frankness, which forestalls any sympathy for her plight. Saiheiji himself, played by the comedian Frankie Sakai, has a pathetic side, suffering as he does from tuberculosis, but Kawashima emphasizes his pluck and verve instead.

Kawashima's success in *Sun Legend of the Shogunate's Last Days* can be fully appreciated by a consideration of Yamada Yoji's failure to instill the audacious spirit of *rakugo* in his *It's Tough to Be a Man* series. The main setting of the series, Shibamata, a suburb of Tokyo, is a modern equivalent of an old Edo neighborhood where everybody knows everybody, and the sweets shop run by the main character's aunt and uncle, with the adjacent small factory where his brother-in-law works, resembles the old tenement house (*nagaya*) that provides lodging for most *rakugo* characters. In fact, the dumb owner of the small factory calls to mind the ignorant tenement landlord, the butt of many *rakugo* jokes. But there the resemblance ends. Yamada spoils the *rakugo* effect by inducing sympathy not only for the hero (a lovable itinerant peddler named Tora-san) but for all characters he comes in contact with, including the dumb factory owner.

At its best, Yamada's *It's Tough to Be a Man* series is good *ninjō kigeki*. *Rakugo* it isn't. After Kawashima, the only director to capture the *rakugo* spirit in film was Imamura Shohei, who worked as an assistant director on *Sun Legend of the Shogunate's Last Days*. Imamura did so by creating lower-class heroines (often the objects of pity in films by most Japanese directors) who are both ignorant and audacious. Hence, audiences both laugh at them and admire their pluck.

In *Sun Legend of the Shogunate's Last Days*, Kawashima also evoked *kyōgen*. His Saiheiji recalls the smart, cunning side to the *kyōgen* clown, Taro-kaja, rather than the pathetic *joruri* clown, who maintained only Taro-kaja's stupid, squeamish side and passed it on to comical commoners in period film and average citizens in contemporary film. In other words, Saiheiji survives by shrewdness rather than through the dogged effort of Saito's Chaplinesque character, or the quiet acceptance of his fate like Ozu's prewar office workers. By enjoying life as it comes, he demonstrates that even a commoner, an ordinary guy, can live with style.

Kawashima carried the shrewdness of the common people to extremes in *The Well-Mannered Beasts,* aka *Elegant Beast* (*Shitoyaka na kedamono*, 1962), a contemporary family drama that seems antithetical to a genre that usually features well-meaning people. The parents in this film have reared their children to take advantage of other people and use any means at their disposal to make money. Accordingly, the daughter goes from one sugar daddy to the next, while the son embezzles from his company. When the father attributes all their actions to the need to escape from the poverty experienced after World War II, he recalls the father in *I Was Born but . . .* , who excuses his sycophancy by telling his wife that at least they are better off than before. However, the characters' modus operandi in *The Well-Mannered Beasts* is not servility but cunning shrewdness.

The humor in *The Well-Mannered Beasts* comes from two sources: (1) the blatant hypocrisy of the parents, who feign shock and disbelief in front of accusers only to ask afterwards in private how much the suckers were taken for; and (2) the flippant attitude the son and daughter take toward their despicable actions. Such amoral behavior is not limited to the family, for we find out that the son's boss, an important executive, is also guilty of embezzlement, as, probably, are many other businessmen. Kawashima's comic target becomes social hypocrisy in general.

The Well-Mannered Beasts, which begins as good satire, may be the best example of black comedy in Japanese film. But midway through, it ceases to be funny. The only sincere character is a young man who embezzled office funds for the office beauty. After she laughs at him for being a fool, he atones for his crime by jumping off the roof of the apartment building where the amoral family reside. Kawashima's treatment of the suicide—an overhead shot of the dejected young man in the rain before he jumps, followed by a long shot of the unconcerned family seen through their windows, and then a close-up of his briefcase on the roof—suggests that the cause of the suicide is pathetic weakness rather than a guilty conscience. Thus, Kawashima's theme in *The Well-Mannered Beasts* seems to be that human beings are only beasts with some manners, and that while the weak perish, the strong survive by shrewdness and cunning. With this nihilistic view, satire vanishes because there is no possibility of reform.

Other examples of black comedy in the 1960s are Ichikawa Kon's *Ten Dark Women* (*Kuroi junin no onna*, 1961) and Okamoto Kihachi's *Age of Assassins* (*Satsujinkyo jidai*, 1965). The most popular film comedies in the 1960s, however, were those based on the lives of office workers (*sarariiman* in Japanese): the *Company President* series (*Shacho*, some 30 entries between 1956 and 1971), starring Morishige Hisaya, and the films of Ueki Hitoshi and the Crazy Cats band and comedy team, beginning with *The Age of Irresponsibility in Japan* (*Nippon musekinin jidai*, 1962). Ueki's films started out as satires of big business, but soon confined the discontent of office workers to drunken grumblings after work, which actually provide a release valve that psychologically contributes to office efficiency. Ueki's "Irresponsible Salaryman" was at heart loyal to his work gang, and thus his comedy series stressed affinity among office workers, as did the *Company President* series. The humor in these office comedy series would be considered situational by Western standards. Since their directors concentrated on delicate human relations, though, these films would belong to the *ninjō kigeki* genre by Japanese standards.

The most popular film comedy from the 1970s on is, of course, Yamada Yoji's *It's Tough to Be a Man* series. In fact, Yamada's series became so popular in the 1980s that anyone who was anybody in the Japanese entertainment world had to appear in at least one of them, and they eventually were labeled *kokumin no eiga*, meaning films for the whole Japanese nation. In the early entries, despite quarrels and misunderstandings, the affinity of everyone in Tora-san's old neighborhood was emphasized. As the series wore on, elite members of Japanese society, too, including college professors, famous authors, and business executives, came in contact with Tora-san, and he always succeeded in getting them to reveal their own human failings. In some respects, Yamada's humor here recalls Yamanaka Sadao's feat of reducing samurai to the common level. But

Yamanaka's humor was usually ironical and never sentimental. In contrast, the *It's Tough to Be a Man* series can sometimes become *ninjō kigeki* at its stickiest. For better or worse, *ninjō kigeki* is comedy of affinity, the affinity of people in a family, in a neighborhood, in a nation, and even the affinity of the whole human race. Nevertheless, while it is sometimes enjoyable to see the elite in any society taken down a peg or two, Yamada's comedy series sometimes degenerates into hymns in praise of the mundane.

True satire, which is always socially critical and thus the antithesis of the comedy of affinity, triumphantly returned to Japanese film with *Family Games* (*Kazoku geimu*, 1983), directed by Morita Yoshimitsu. Morita's first film, *Second-Rate Comedian*, aka *Something like That* (*No yo na mono*, 1981), which is about a young, inept *rakugo* comedian, has some satire—e.g., it spoofs the greed of young Japanese housewives looking for a bargain. But on the whole, the depiction of the camaraderie among young comedians places the film in the *ninjō kigeki* genre.

Family Games, on the other hand, is satire from beginning to end. It is about a young private tutor who straightens out a problem teenager, but quits in disgust during a family celebration when the demanding father starts picking on the older son for falling behind in *his* studies. The film ends with the oldest son watching a karate team in training, and the indolent mother falling asleep in the afternoon while a helicopter buzzes over their house.

The Japanese entrance examination system, which determines what schools a young person can go to and thus his future career, had been criticized before *Family Games,* but most Japanese felt it was almost impossible to change, and that a young person's career might as well be decided by that means as any other. Morita, however, places the blame on the parents' attitude toward study as the only road to success, no matter what the emotional and psychological cost to their children. While systems may be hard to change, attitudes are more flexible. The father could be less demanding and the mother less indolent, and both of them could make an attempt to try to understand their children, rather than continue to put pressure on them. Although the film ends with the ultimate failure of the tutor because of the parents, one can still hope that at least some parents are capable of reform.

Family Games is not simply a satire of bad parents. When the oldest son watches a karate team in training, Morita seems to be suggesting that frustrated youth may turn to violence, for among Japanese liberals the martial arts call to mind *Bushido* and prewar militarism, rather than the spiritual training they are associated with in the West. Moreover, the ending, which has puzzled many critics and viewers, becomes clearer if we assume that the helicopter, a primary weapon during the Vietnam War, represents postwar Japanese militarism, for at the time of the film's showing, the then prime minister was advocating increased military spending. The indolent mother falling asleep, then, could represent apathetic Japanese citizens who could once again be manipulated by political leaders of a militaristic bent.

Other young film satirists, such as Ishii Sogo, followed in Morita's wake. The greatest Japanese film satirist currently, though, is the middle-aged character actor who played the father in *Family Games,* and who began making his own films only quite recently. He is Itami Juzo, the son of Itami Mansaku. Itami's first film, *The Funeral* (*Ososhiki,* 1984), began as a comedy of manners of sorts, for it concerned a middle-class couple whose ignorance of traditional customs for wakes and funerals leads to a comedy of errors upon the death of the wife's father. As the plot develops, however, we find that the husband and wife have a wonderful, understanding relationship whose depiction turns the film into intellectual *ninjō kigeki.* Itami's second film, *Tampopo* (1986), was about a woman who runs a *ramen,* or noodle shop, and a stranger who comes into the shop one day and eventually turns it into a successful business. It was both a parody of *Shane* (an immensely popular film in Japan) and a spoof of the current Japanese food fad which has spawned countless cooking *and* eating shows on TV. (Itami himself writes and directs commercials for a brand of mayonnaise.)

With *A Taxing Woman* (*Marusa no onna,* 1987), Itami created one of the best satires in Japanese film history. It concerns a woman tax investigator from Japan's equivalent to the IRS who relentlessly tracks down some comical tax evaders. The wife of one of them criticizes her for investigating only small businessmen, and when she thereby vows to go after the fat cats, she not only redeems herself for comically picking on small fry but also demonstrates that Itami's ultimate comic target is none other than the upper echelons of Japan, Inc.

The heroine eventually manages to expose a big businessman with underworld connections and make him confess to tax evasion by appealing to his love for his son. But here Itami may have weakened his satire by humanizing the unscrupulous entrepreneur in the end. By making him a sympathetic character, Itami seemed to be reverting to the *ninjō kigeki* of his first film. Even intellectual *ninjō kigeki* is still comedy of affinity. When we *feel* for the entrepreneur as a fellow human being, he *and* Japan, Inc., are no longer being satirized.

Such a complaint, or reservation, cannot be made about Itami's next film, *A Taxing Woman, Part 2* (*Marusa no onna 2,* 1988). In this devastating exposé of tax evasion through a sham religious organization and ruthless real-estate speculation involving Japan's underworld and political leaders, Itami even satirizes the Japanese tendency to humanize or sentimentalize just about everyone. When an investigator gets a politician to confess to taking bribes by feigning sympathy for the excuse that he did so because he has to give big, expensive parties in his home prefecture, the audience does not empathize with the politician but instead laughs at his blubbering. When a hoodlum is gunned down and dies with tears in his eyes while listening to children singing, we remember the touching ending to Kurosawa's *Stray Dog* (*Nora inu,* 1949), in which cop and thief lie down together exhausted after the chase, while a children's song plays on the soundtrack. In short, we also laugh at Itami's spoof of maudlin scenes.

A Taxing Woman, Part 2 ends with the sham religious leader hiding out in a shellproof mausoleum from hitmen seeking to kill him and his young, pregnant mistress because he has confessed to the tax investigators. Overjoyed at the prospect of becoming a father at his age, he seems almost as human as the villain in *A Taxing Woman* had become because of love for his son. Unfortunately, this sudden outburst of human feelings in *A Taxing Woman, Part 2* seems too far-fetched. We are unable to sympathize with him and view the denouement with only a strange sense of horror. When such a sudden show of humanity appears grotesque, perhaps satire has gone too far.

Itami's films well illustrate the relationship between the two main styles in Japanese film comedy, that of affinity (*ninjō kigeki*) and that of satire. We have considered these two styles antithetical. Such is definitely apparent when both styles appear within a single film, such as *A Taxing Woman*. However, in the context of the whole genre of film comedy, they can be considered complementary, in that each style is needed to combat excesses in the other. Satire counterbalances sentimentality in *ninjō kigeki,* just as *rakugo* and *kyōgen* counterbalanced sentimentality in the other traditional performing arts. Moreover, *ninjō kigeki* that affirms the humanistic value of affinity (for example, comedy in the films of Ozu and Yamanaka and even Itami's *The Funeral*) probably evolved in part from a subliminal awareness of the cruel, dehumanizing possibilities in satire (for example, in *A Taxing Woman, Part 2*). This interaction between the comedy of affinity and satire through almost ninety years of Japanese film comedy not only enriched the film genre itself but advanced the development of Japanese comedy in general.

NOTES

1. A notable exception is *Narukami,* which was made into a film by Yoshimura Kozaburo, *The Beauty and the Dragon* (*Bijo to kairyu,* 1955).

2. Sato Tadao, *Currents in Japanese Cinema,* trans. Gregory Barrett (Tokyo: Kodansha International, 1982), pp. 7–9.

3. Ibid., p. 222.

4. As quoted by Sato Tadao, "Kigeki no nagare"("Currents in Comedy"), in *Nihon eiga shiso-shi* (*History of the Intellectual Currents in Japanese Film*) (Tokyo: Sanichi Shobo, 1970), p. 222. This essay was not included in the English translation, *Currents in Japanese Cinema*, but it has strongly influenced my own views on Japanese film comedy.

5. Sato, "Currents in Comedy," pp. 213–214.

6. Ibid., p. 200.

7. Ibid., pp. 200–202.

8. *The Comic Mind: Comedy and the Movies*, 2nd ed. (Chicago and London: U of Chicago P, 1979), p. 338.

9. Yamamoto Kikuo, *Nihon eiga ni okeru gaikoku eiga no eikyo—hikaku eigashi kenkyu* (*The Influence of Foreign Films in Japanese Cinema: Research in Comparative Film History*) (Tokyo: Waseda Daigaku Shuppanbu, 1983), pp. 279–382. Most of my background information on prewar contemporary film comedy comes from the chapters on slapstick, Chaplin, and Lloyd (pp. 279–342). For more information on the worldwide popularity of French film comedy before World War I, see David Robinson, "Rise and Fall of the Clowns: The Golden Age of French Comedy, 1907–1914," *Sight and Sound* 56, 3 (Summer 1987): 198–203.

10. Kido Shiro, *Nihon eiga den—eiga seisakusha no kiroku* (*The Story of the Japanese Film: A Movie Producer's Record*) (Tokyo: Bungei Shunjushinsha, 1956), p. 166. American silent comedies exerted such a strong influence that even prewar period films about traditional comic figures such as Yaji and Kita featured slapstick instead of the ribald humor of the original novel, *Tokai dochu kizakurige* by Ikku Jippensha (1765–1831).

11. *The Influence of Foreign Films in Japanese Cinema*, pp. 294–295.

12. "The Comedy of Ozu and Chaplin: A Study in Contrast," *Wide Angle* 3, 2 (1979): 51–53.

13. *Ozu: His Life and Films* (Berkeley and Los Angeles: U of California P, 1974), p. 1.

14. Joseph L. Anderson and Donald Richie, *The Japanese Film: Art and Industry*, Expanded edition (Princeton: Princeton UP, 1982), p. 99.

15. Yamamoto, pp. 315–316.

16. Mast, *The Comic Mind*, p. 15.

17. Yamamoto, p. 313.

18. "Currents in Comedy," pp. 227–231.

Part
Three

History

Some Characteristics of Japanese Cinema before World War I

Komatsu Hiroshi

Translated by Linda C. Ehrlich
and Yuko Okutsu

The business of writing film history is never complete. Each new generation of histories strives to correct inaccuracies or oversimplifications of past works and to incorporate new research, new findings; each new generation also has its own particular goals and methodologies. Currently gaining favor among the new generation of film historians are approaches which view film as "not just a set of components forming a whole, but an *interrelated* set of components [e.g., technological, economic, aesthetic, and cultural] that condition and are conditioned by each other" (Robert C. Allen and Douglas Gomery, *Film History: Theory and Practice* [New York: Alfred A. Knopf, 1985], pp. 16–17). The end result is not so much a definitive or even a near-definitive history (if either is possible) as a shedding of new light on an area, however large or small, that before was not so clear or discernible.

Komatsu's essay gives us a fresh and satisfyingly full look at one of the most neglected periods of Japanese film history: its very beginnings. The years covered are approximately 1897 (when the first camera was imported to Japan) to 1914–1915 (when Japanese cinema, under the influence of American film, adapted the Western mode of narration).

Drawing on contemporary newspaper accounts and reviews of the day, as well as on traditional scholarly sources (e.g., Tanaka Jun'ichiro's history of Japanese cinema), Komatsu explores the complex creative process of the Japanese cinema that came into being in the 1910s, and which became dominant. This was a mixed process in which Western and Japanese representational modes at times conflicted, but mostly coexisted. The Western mode was what it remains today: an illusionistic mode in which cinema undertakes narration in a self-sufficient manner. The Japanese mode, on the other hand, was one in which cinematic narration was not self-sufficient, but operated in conjunction with either *katsuben* (aka *benshi*: individuals who narrated, commented upon, and interpreted the film) or actual stage performance, or both.

Komatsu's essay covers a wide range of topics: the series of geisha dances and Kabuki films that formed the first Japanese films; the role of the Russo-Japanese War in helping develop the Japanese film industry; the importance of the Yoshizawa and the Yokota companies; and the impact of imported films. (Interestingly enough, the first influential group, which came in 1905–1906, was mostly from France; American films made no real impression until 1914). What Komatsu makes abundantly clear is the richness, complexity, and excitement of these early years, and the fact that more work needs to be done here.

For further reading see Joseph L. Anderson and Donald Richie, *The Japanese Film: Art and Industry*, Expanded edition (Princeton: Princeton UP, 1982), pp. 21–34; Iijima Tadashi, *Nihon Eiga Shi* (*A History of Japanese Film*), 2 vols. (Hakusuisha, 1955); Hiroshi Komatsu and Charles Musser, "Benshi Search," *Wide Angle* 9, 2 (1987): 72–90; Sato Tadao, *Currents in Japanese Cinema* (Tokyo: Kodansha, 1982); and Yamamoto Kikuo, *Nihon eiga ni okeru gaikoku eiga no eikyo* (*The Influence of Foreign Film on Japanese Cinema*) (Waseda Daigaku Shuppanbu, 1983).

In the Meiji era, Japan imported a large amount of knowledge and scientific technology from the Western world. Just as there was a conspicuous coexistence of new knowledge and already existing traditional culture during this period, so was there a coexistence, and a conflict, in the field of cinema between Western systems such as the "fake documentary" or trompe l'oeil and indigenous Japanese systems which resisted this pretense and artificial representation. This coexistence and conflict of Western and non-Western modes in Japanese cinema has been cited as a characteristic of the later period of its history, but it actually originated in the earlier period.

In Japanese art, Japanese modes and Western modes tend to be completely separate, based on the modes imported from the Western world during the Meiji era. For instance, in the field of painting, there are Japanese paintings and Western paintings. In music, there is Japanese music (*hōgaku*) and Western music (*yōgaku*). Furthermore, dance is categorized into two very different forms, and so far each form has developed within its own framework. As for painting, just as the quality of the canvas and the modes of representation of Japanese paintings and Western paintings are different, so is the medium itself different.

In the case of cinema, however, the medium used by the Japanese and non-Japanese is the same in every respect, because cinema is created through the same optical and scientific processes, by a camera of the same construction. Of course, there is a distinction similar to that between plays derived from traditional Japanese drama (*kyūgeki*) and plays influenced by Western drama (*shimpa*), but this is a difference only of genre, like the distinction between tragedy and comedy. Therefore, "Japaneseness" and "Westernness" in the Japanese cinema lie not in the medium used but in the representational mode, and the coexistence and conflict of these different qualities should be understood within the framework of that representational mode. From this point of view, there was a mixture of native and Western ideas and modes in the early Japanese cinema. These views had to coexist, yet they also tended to counteract each other.

The Japanese term *wayō sechū* (a compromise between a Japanese and Western style) was coincidentally born about the same time as Japanese cinema. This kind of mixture of different qualities is conspicuous in the Japanese cinema of later years. In the history of cinema, it can be seen around 1904 or 1905, when films on the Russo-Japanese War were made as fake documentaries. After that, the process by which the content of films was compromised was facilitated by the appearance of *shimpa* comedy. In terms of the representational modes used in Japanese cinema, a state of coexistence, rather than contention, became dominant by the mid-1910s.

This stage paralleled the establishment of the classical Western cinema, but in the Japanese cinema, this mixed stage of development was stabilized through a different procedure from that occurring in Western cinema. This system established in Japan is a composite form which is also different from the classical Western cinema. In this paper, we will look at the creation process of the complex system of the Japanese cinema which was formed in the mid-1910s (i.e., in the context of European cinema, by World War I) and which became dominant throughout the 1910s. The title of a *shimpa* comedy, *Semi-Japanese Semi-Western Wedding* (*Wayō sechū kekkonshiki*), released by the Yoshizawa Company (an important cinema company in early Japanese cinematic history) on

October 17, 1908, symbolizes this process of being Japanese but at the same time Western.

Nineteenth-Century Japanese Cinema

The Japanese did not contribute to any invention which could be related to cinematic technology. Rather, all cinematic equipment was brought from foreign countries in an already completed form. For the Japanese people, cinema was both the imported fruit of the science and technology of more advanced cultures and, at the same time, a strange Western display.

Movie projectors were being produced at the Yoshizawa Company in 1900. However, the projectors made in the Yoshizawa factories were simplified models of ones by Lumière and Edison. They were designed by the chief engineer of the Yoshizawa Company, Osawa Yoshinojo, and produced by Seki Hisakichi at a subcontract factory of the Yoshizawa Company store in the Kuruma section of Shiba ward.[1] Thus they apparently were merely imitations of foreign products.

In fact, cameras made by the Gaumont Company were used in shooting the earliest Japanese films. The camera was imported in 1897 by the Konishi photography shop, located in Nihonbashi ward in Tokyo, and the first Japanese to use one was Asano Shiro, who shot scenes of Nihonbashi, Asakusa, and Ginza. For Asano, this filming was only a means of gaining experience in operating the camera. Nevertheless, he chose scenes of the busiest streets in Tokyo as his first filming motif, rather than unknown, nameless streets. If this filming had been only for the purpose of gaining practical experience, it would have been enough for him just to shoot the scene outside his window. Asano probably chose these typical, picture-postcard scenes of the city with at least some artistic concern and with the intention of showing them to other people.

Asano's next filming motif was geisha dances. In 1899, he shot popular geisha dancing such works as *Matsuzukushi, Kappore,* and *Tsurukame,* this time with the clear intention of showing his films to the public. This geisha motif also followed the most typical picture-postcard motif of late nineteenth-century Japan. Asano himself said: "You can understand how popular geisha were in those days from the fact that geisha postcards sold better than any other postcards."[2] For the two years from the summer of 1897, when he filmed the scenes of Nihonbashi, Asakusa, and Ginza, until the early summer of 1899, when he filmed geisha, Asano shot nothing at all. Apparently there were enough foreign films to meet public demand, because of the underdeveloped nature of Japanese cinema production. During this period, however, François Constant Girel, who brought Lumière's Cinématograph from France, filmed a performance of Kabuki actors in Osaka in May 1897, prior to Asano. Gabriel Veyre, also from the Lumière Company, filmed in Tokyo in December 1898. In 1899, the famous Francis Doublier filmed in Yokohama. As for Americans, James H. White filmed in Tokyo and Yokohama in 1899.

There is little difference between the subjects filmed by foreign cameramen and those filmed by early Japanese cameramen. In other words, the subjects in the cinema of those early years were all treated like painterly photographs, which in those days were considered artistic scenes. On the other hand, the series of geisha dances were exotic for foreigners, but they were merely picturesque for the Japanese. On June 20, 1899, at the Kabukiza in Tokyo, Japanese cinema was shown to the general public by Komada Koyo's Association of Japanese Motion Pictures (Nihon Sossen Katsudō Shashin Kai). Most of the films shown at the time were about geisha dances.[3]

When we think about the content as well as the representational mode of early Japanese cinema, it is significant that geisha dances were chosen as a dominant subject matter. These films record dancing, but they are not necessarily documentaries. Even though the camera faced the geishas to film their dancing, the subjects were definitely performing without making any accidental movements and without throwing even one curious glance at the camera. Moreover, in some cases, tatami mats were set up outside in order to catch natural light, or curtains or folding screens were put up artificially. It could be said that this was stage apparatus for the sake of performance. In a different manner from the early documentary films, which shot streets full of people who viewed the camera curiously, the geisha dance motif became a kind of genre through repeated filming.

This borderline between documentary and fiction can be seen in the films shot in the Black Maria by the Edison Company. The denial of documentary's arbitrariness by the necessity of a performance is exemplified in the filming by Louis Lumière in 1895. This denial is caused by the repetitious shooting of a particular motif. This has something to do with the structure of the primitive nineteenth-century cinema, which is generally regarded as lacking structure.[4] In any case, the series of geisha dances formed the first type of Japanese film and was the origin of the unique Kabuki cinema style which continued until the mid-1910s.

In addition to Asano Shiro's work, the Japanese cinema series released on June 20, 1899, was shot by Shibata Tsunekichi and Shirai Kanzo. Asano and Shirai soon quit shooting films, so the geisha dance motif was not developed by these two cinematographers. On the other hand, Shibata Tsunekichi shot *Lightning Burglar* (*Inazuma goto*) in September of the same year; *Viewing Scarlet Maple Leaves* (*Momijigari*) in November, and *Two People at Dojō Temple* (*Ninin dojōji*) in December. This opened the way for the narrative cinema (*monogatari eiga*) and the Kabuki cinema. For Shibata, however, these films probably did not need to be categorized into different genres, since there was no clear distinction between fiction and documentary in Japanese cinema at that time.

Lightning Burglar was a one-scene film about the arrest of a burglar based on an actual burglary which had happened at that time. In this film, which resembles *Burglar on the Roof* by the Vitagraph Company, a burglar is first shown hiding behind shrubbery. A policeman and a detective (played by Yokoyama Unpei) find the burglar (played by Sakamoto Keijirō) and capture him after a struggle. These seventy feet of film could have been the record of a real incident for the Japanese audience, which was not familiar with the idea of fiction in cinema. As Eileen Bowser states, in early cinema it is difficult to define, or to distinguish, fiction from nonfiction.[5] In Japanese cinema, the role of the film interpreter (*benshi*) was already important, even in the nineteenth century. Therefore, this film, in which the burglar (called a "lightning burglar") was captured, could have been disguised as nonfiction reportage. Depending on the *benshi*'s explanation, the same hero of this cinema could have become Shimizu Sadakichi, who was an actual armed burglar. This principle did not necessarily apply only to Japanese cinema. Francis Doublier, for example, showed a combination of reportage films, accompanied by his own explanations, to a Jewish residential area in southern Russia and disguised them as films about the Dreyfus Affair.[6] In this way, the fiction represented by cinema can be distorted or wiped out with the help of language.

Viewing Scarlet Maple Leaves, in which Ichikawa Danjūrō IX and Onoe Kikugorō V appear, crossed back and forth over the borderline between fiction and nonfiction without the mediation of language. This film was certainly intended as a performance record of Danjūrō and Kikugorō. In that sense, it is a documentary. On the other hand, the actions and stage apparatus have a diegetic quality, owing to the nature of Kabuki narrative. Since Kabuki cinema is usually made as a substitute form of Kabuki stage performance, audiences are well versed, on a narrative level, with the meaning of the actions and the stage apparatus. This narrative nature is reinforced by the voice of the person reciting the *gidayū* (ballad drama) during the performance. Before 1908 (i.e., at a time when films were very short compared with stage performances), films contained only a few scenes excerpted from a Kabuki play. Therefore, in Kabuki cinema, the audience expected to see how the familiar story was represented by the actors in its divided and excerpted form, rather than to watch the development of the story (as was common in Western cinema). In short, the form of representation by the actors or the stage apparatus was more important than the narrative nature. Thus, the fictive quality resided in the object which was given meaning by the film itself, and at the same time, the nonfictive quality existed in the process by which the cinema created meaning.

The story of *Viewing Scarlet Maple Leaves*—Taira no Koremori conquers an ogress who has disguised herself as Sarashina-hime (Princess Sarashina)—unfolds, emphasizing the kind of dance with formal mime unique to Kabuki. This film was shot primarily to preserve the performance of Danjūrō. Therefore, it intentionally indicated that the object being filmed was on stage. This led to the later Kabuki cinematic mode, which tried to reduce the frame of a film to the size of a proscenium stage. In Western illusionism, in order to enhance the credibility of a narrative film, cinema tended to proceed along the same path as naturalistic theater. In the case of Kabuki cinema, the credibility required of a narrative film did not matter because its representational mode hardly depended on the story itself. Whether or not the thing which a film represented was realistic did not matter. What mattered was to make the audience conscious of the fact that there was a stage. *Viewing Scarlet Maple Leaves,* which succeeded the geisha dance motif and initiated the motif of making Kabuki into cinema, had both a fictional and a nonfictional nature. The fictional nature was derived from the original Kabuki theater as a story, and the nonfictional nature was caused by the nonillusionism, which clearly indicated that what was happening in front of one's eyes actually was taking place on stage.

We cannot say, however, that distinguishing foreign fake documentaries from documentaries is as difficult as distinguishing the fiction from the nonfiction inherent in Kabuki films. This is because the problem of the nature of Kabuki cinema is a matter of the representational mode itself rather than of the viewer's identification of what is represented in the film. This mode continued as one of the genres unique to Japanese cinema until the mid-1910s.

Because of the need for light, *Viewing Scarlet Maple Leaves* was shot on a temporary stage on location. At that time, Shibata's camera was set at a higher position, looking down onto the stage so as to emphasize it, and so the wooden floor of the stage was always in the frame of the camera. For Shibata, the notion that the actors were on the stage was important. That would have been an inappropriate style of framing from the standpoint of Western illusionism. For example, in *A Trip to the Moon* (*Le Voyage dans la lune,* 1902), when Georges Méliès showed scientists from Earth on the moon, he covered the wooden floor of the stage with some stage apparatus so it could not be seen. In the Pathé Company's film of the same name, made by Ferdinand Zecca, the wooden floor is clearly seen. This is considered a mistake in terms of the process of imitation.

Contrary to Shibata's emphasis on the stage in *Viewing Scarlet Maple Leaves,* the Kabuki film *The Floating Nest of the Little Grebe* (*Nio no Ukisu*), shot by Tsuchiya Tsuneji in July 1900, was filmed right on the ground. Moreover, the very low position of the camera, a rarity in cinema of this period, contributed to its unusual image. As shown in *Viewing Scarlet Maple Leaves,* as a rule, people in Kabuki films move horizontally on stage, and the actors form a kind of facade facing the camera. This facade seen in Kabuki cinema is a typical kind of frontality.[7] However, in Tsuchiya's *The Floating Nest of the Little Grebe,* a procession of courtesans comes toward the camera from the back, just like the rushing train in Lumière's *Arrival of a Train* (*Arrivée d'un train à La Ciotat,* 1895). In contrast to typical Kabuki cinema, which took notice of the surface, in Tsuchiya's cinema depth became important. In Tsuchiya's film, while the courtesans are approaching the center, two attendants play the fool in the rear of the shot. The geishas' image becomes larger until it fills the camera frame, and then it disappears into the right side of the screen. One of the attendants (played by Nakamura Ganjirō), who is left on the screen, recedes into the depth of the screen as he walks along the road, away from a grove of trees, while glancing at the camera.

In this case, depth of field is not the only problem. The procession of courtesans approaches the camera, then appears to pass the position of the camera and go beyond it. The direction of this procession and the glance of Nakamura Ganjirō imply an imaginary and invisible domain behind the camera. For example, the emblematic function of a close shot of a man can be seen in American films such as Edwin S. Porter's *The Great Train Robbery* (1903) or G. W. Bitzer's *The Fire-Bug* (1905), in which a character in the film faces the camera lens (that is to say, the film audience), and their eyes meet. After the procession withdraws beyond the camera in *The Floating Nest of the Little Grebe,* however, the attendant left on the screen (Nakamura Ganjirō) looks at the place where the procession is supposed to be at that moment, i.e. beyond the camera. In the normative montage of post-1915 American cinema, this glance would have been received by a match cut following this shot. In this one-shot cinema of Tsuchiya Tsuneji, however, the place where the glance is received is in an imaginary domain in the audience's mind.

Documentary

As in the early films of other countries, there were street scenes in Japan's first films. They functioned mainly as picturesque displays, rather than as something shot for the purpose of reportage about real events.

The Yoshizawa Company in Tokyo made the first documentary, or reportage cinema, in Japan. It imported and showed a film on the Spanish-American War in 1899, and another one on the Boer War in April 1900. Since these were great successes, the Yoshizawa Company sent Shibata Tsunekichi and Fukaya Komakichi to China during the Boxer Rebellion to make reportage films. These two men boarded with the fifth division of the Japanese army on the twenty-eighth of July and filmed the embarkation of soldiers and horses. In China, they moved with the Japanese army and filmed the rebellion until its settlement in Beijing in August. This is considered to be the first news film shot by a Japanese. Early "picturesque" cinema which filmed streets or geisha, or the *sumō* cinema shot by Tsuchiya Tsuneji in April 1900, was not made for the purpose of reporting events. On the other hand, the Yoshizawa Company's reportage cinema on the Boxer Rebellion, called *Grand Motion Picture on the Boxer Rebellion* (*Hokushinjihen katsudō daishashin*), reported an incident in China in the same style as did the newspapers of that time.

Grand Motion Picture on the Boxer Rebellion was first released on October 18, 1900, at the Kinki-kan in Tokyo. After that, it was shown successively in many cities throughout Japan. This cinema, with other imported reportage films on the same subject, became part of the repertoire of films shown in Japan for several years. However, Japanese film producers never took up the Boxer Rebellion as a form of fiction, as, for example, some of their British counterparts did. In addition, even though this reportage film by the Yoshizawa Company was successful, few similar films based on the actual reporting of events followed. At this time in Japan, domestic cinema production was still on shaky ground, a result of both economic and personnel problems. Of the documentary films made between 1901 and 1902, none exceeded *Grand Motion Picture on the Boxer Rebellion* in scope. Even the Yoshizawa Company depended on imported cinema, except for one small documentary called *Bicycle Race* (*Jitensha kyōsō*), which was shot in Japan in 1902.

In 1903 the Yoshizawa Company, probably imitating a motif seen in American cinema, released three films on funerals. They were also documentaries with the character of contemporary news films. The first film was on the funeral of Myōjoshonin, a monk of Nishi-honganji temple; the second, of Imperial Prince Komatsunomiya Akihito; the third, of Kikugorō Onoe V, who acted in *Viewing Scarlet Maple Leaves*. The reportage film of the funeral of Imperial Prince Komatsunomiya was the first Japanese film on the imperial family. In Japan, even after this, the relationship between the imperial family and cinema was not close. Neither the Meiji emperor nor the Taisho emperor ever appeared on the screen.

Besides these funeral films, the Yoshizawa Company produced various documentary films in 1903, including *The Actual Scene of the Kobe Naval Review* (*Kobe kankanshiki jikkyō*, May); *The Actual Scene of the Fifth Osaka Exhibition* (*Osaka daigokai hakurankai jikkyō*, May), *The Actual Scene of the Kyoto Gion*

Festival (*Kyōto gion matsuri jikkyō,* May), and *The Actual Scene of the Asakusa Flower Garden* (*Asakusa hanayashiki jikkyō,* August). While these films reported each event as an event, they also employed the early documentary cinema technique of showing each event's picturesque beauty. In short, these films combined several characteristics which documentary cinema had developed before this time.

The Russo-Japanese War, which began in 1904, helped the Japanese film industry make a large leap forward. Immediately after the outbreak of this war, the Yoshizawa Company (which had successfully filmed the Boxer Rebellion) sent a cameraman, Fujiwara Kozaburo, assisted by Shimizu Kumejirō, to the Russian continent. Several other independent production companies also dispatched cameramen to the continent. At least twelve Japanese cameramen documented the Russo-Japanese War. Among the cameramen who went to the front, Ito Kyutaro and Kuboi Shinichi invaded Russian territory so deeply that they ended up as Russian prisoners of war. When the Kinki-kan exhibited the reportage film on the Russo-Japanese war, it used this fact as a form of advertisement.

> A film shot with so much hardship is unprecedented. After its inspection, this film received special permission for its exhibition from the imperial headquarters of the Japanese Army. Up to now, films on the Russo-Japanese War made by foreign countries have been deceptive. We strongly recommend that you see this film, which is different from those other commonplace films.[8]

From May 1904, many foreign-made reportage films on the Russo-Japanese War were imported and shown along with those made by Japanese cameramen. The advertisements of the Kinki-kan emphasized the risk Japanese cameramen ran in shooting scenes which could not be seen in the films made by foreigners. In this way, the patriotic trend of those times could be seen even in the domestic cinema. This trend reached its zenith upon the release of foreign-made fake documentaries. In September 1904, reporting the release of a Russo-Japanese War film shot by seven Japanese cameramen sent to the continent by Hakubun-kan (including Shibata Tsunekichi), *Yorozu Chōhō* included the following comment: "Most of the recent motion pictures on the Russo-Japanese War are foreign-made fakes. They are so ridiculous that they are unbearable to watch. The film shot by the Hakubun-kan cameramen is probably different from those fakes. I have been deceived so many times, however, that I can't say anything before I actually see it."

During this period, any film dealing with the war was a great success, no matter what its entertainment value. However, new films on the war soon became scarce. At first, the only Japanese films on the war were those shot by Japanese cameramen on the continent. After many foreign-made fake documentaries were released, fake Russo-Japanese War films were made in Japan itself, in order to compensate for the lack of new films. Extras were dressed in military uniforms, and fires were built to produce smoke, in order to create the atmosphere of an actual battle. This kind of cinema was made after 1904, and it introduced the Western mode of providing the audience with an illusion of reality. Because these fake documentaries increased in number, starting later in 1904, advertisements for films on the Russo-Japanese War included the statement "Shot in the real setting."

Fiction

The repertoire of Japanese cinema from 1904 and 1905 seems to be very different from that of other countries. This is because 80 percent of the films released were on the Russo-Japanese War. Of course, not all of them were documentaries. Films such as *The Hero of Liao Yang,* shot in New York by G. W. Bitzer, were shown as Russo-Japanese war films. Until some films on the Russo-Japanese War were made by Japanese independent production companies as fake documentaries, the concept of fiction based on illusionism did not exist in the Japanese cinema. Only the dualistic concept of fiction and nonfiction existed. However, the fake documentary gave the audience an impression of nonreality which clearly differed from this duality, and which was typically seen in Kabuki cinema. It continued even up to 1908, when nonfiction in cinema had already been established in Japan. The reaction of a Japanese audience member after seeing a war film made by the French Pathé Company can be gathered from the following excerpt from an article published at the time:

> White smoke rose, and Japanese and Russian soldiers scrambled in confusion for the regimental colors. It was absurd that a few soldiers brought out the regimental colors, which looked as clean as a piece of pure white paper. An audience member sitting in front of me said: "People don't do this kind of thing in a war. What is that commotion? It looks like a kids' game." Someone sitting behind me said: "The regimental colors should not be carried like that by two or three people. They're making fools of us. This is artificial. This is a fake." While they were saying this, the scene changed and a rush between the Russian and the Japanese armies started. The audience took great interest in backing up the Japanese army, but in vain. The Japanese army started to withdraw. Shouts of "Damn it! Stop it!" rose from all corners of the audience.[9]

In 1899, *Lightning Burglar* had already shown Japanese audiences the concept of nonreality in cinema. For the Japanese, who attributed to the event of the Russo-Japanese War a realistic significance, the sense of nonreality found in the Pathé Company's fake documentary was significant for the development of fiction in the cinema of 1904 to 1905 (at least within the context of Japanese cinematic history). The significance was that the audience knew that what was represented was a fake. In the case of *Lightning Burglar,* depending on the skillful explanation of the *benshi,* it could be an actual report of a burglar's arrest, or it could be a completely different story of a burglar from what the producers intended. This was due to the multivocality unique to the cinema of that period. However, the audience's awareness that the content of a film was not necessarily true meant the awakening of a sense of fiction in Japanese cinema.

It is difficult to pinpoint the first fiction film in Japan. If we consider a genre such as Kabuki cinema, with its dual character, to be fiction, then *Viewing Scarlet Maple Leaves* would be the beginning of fictional cinema. If the depiction of a represented event was the beginning, then it had already occurred in *Lightning Burglar.* Among existing films, *The Floating Nest of the Little Grebe* is one in which the actors' performances can be recognized in a modern sense, rather than through formal gestures or dancing, as in *Viewing Scarlet Maple Leaves.* It is probably accurate to say that these works showed the signs of a budding fictional cinema.

This Japanese fictional cinema was clearly different, however, from European or American cinema of this same period, which tried to create a dramatic illusion cinematically. In the case of Japanese cinema, the dramatic nature of the film depended either on the fact that the audience already knew the plot of a play such as *Viewing Scarlet Maple Leaves,* or on the freely created story of a *benshi,* as in *Lightning Burglar.* The courtesan procession and the antics of the attendants shown moving from the back of the screen in *The Floating Nest of the Little Grebe* are also just one scene from a stage play (in the new Kabuki [*Shin-Kabuki*] style) filmed on location, and are subordinate to the plot of the play. In short, these films do not narrate for themselves. Responding to meanings always provided from the outside, the narratives freely attach themselves to the images in these films. This open-ended early Japanese cinema kept the Western concept of fiction at a distance.

If we accept that fiction in early Japanese cinema had a diverse reality (based on such things as an awareness of familiar Kabuki plays or *benshi* explanations) which attached meaning from the outside and which could not be found in Western cinema, the unusual activities of Takamatsu Toyojirō would be an example of an intentional use of the meaning-application feature of Japanese cinema. Takamatsu (1872–1952), who was involved in the socialist movement until the mid-1910s, quickly recognized the educational value of cinema and thought that cinema would have a strong effect on the audience when combined with speech. As he was also a comic storyteller (*rakugoka*), he purchased a projector and films in 1900 and showed films in a variety hall (*yose*) accompanied by his own comic stories. His stories were on socialistic topics, and even foreign films shown at that time were transformed beyond their original content by Takamatsu's explanation. He dragged foreign films into the context of his own ideology. Thus, films which were subordinated to the discourse were compelled to have diverse meanings, divergent from their original meaning. Cinema, no matter what its original content, had become a tool for communicating ideas.

In 1901, Takamatsu traveled around the country with his gramophone, projector, and films, making speeches on the labor movement to listeners, and interpreting the film on the screen from a socialistic perspective. In 1903, he began producing his own films. These were a series of allegorical short films which were later named "Society Puck Motion Pictures" ("Shakai pukku katsudō shashin"). Among this comic series were *Riding on a Ball in Real Society* (*Katsu-shakai no tamanori*), *A Maroon Wooden Drum* (*Ebicha no mokugyō*), *A Grievance about Public Morality* (*Kotoku no nakigoto*), *The True Character of Gentlemen Nowadays* (*Tosei shinshi no shotai*), *The Failure of Overconfidence* (*Unubore no shippai*), *National Boarding House* (*Kokuyu no Geshukuya*), *The Surface and True Feelings of People's Minds* (*Jinshin no ura-omote*), *The Education of Old Ideas* (*Kyu-shiso no kyōiku*), and *The Dandyish Procession* (*Haikara no gyōretsu*).

Morality plays included *The End of the Role of the Schoolgirl* (*Jogakusei no matsuro*), *Tragedy: The Self-Immolation of the Captain* (*Higeki: sencho no junshi*), *The Prison Breakout in Saghalien* (*Karafuto no hagoku*), *The Drinking Habit and the Family* (*Inshu to katei*), and *The Successful Love* (*Ai no seikō*).

Professional acrobats appeared in *Riding on a Ball in Society*, which was shot on location in Mukojima and Hibiya Park. In this allegorical dramatic sketch, these acrobats played the part of university students. In the film, they compete for successful careers in the "real world" (*katsu-shakai*) while walking on balls on which the names of various universities are written. Chiba Yoshizo, a cameraman of the Yoshizawa Company, shot these films.

Takamatsu Toyojirō went to Taiwan in 1904 and, using it as his base, continued to work in the entertainment industry (both cinema and theater) until 1915. After Takamatsu went to Taiwan, his films were sold to a comic magazine publishing company, Tokyo Puck Company. Three years after they were shot, these films were shown in September of 1906, under the name "Society Puck Motion Pictures," at ordinary movie theaters. They were accompanied by the usual narrative explanations by a *benshi* rather than by the kind of socialistic explanations Takamatsu had provided.

As a comic narrator, Takamatsu satirized the dishonesty of contemporary society and tried to raise the social consciousness of the townspeople and workers who came to listen to his comic stories. Just as these stories were caricatures of society for Takamatsu, so was cinema one of the means to allegorize societal systems. However, these comic films never developed the nature of fiction running along a narrative thread which characterized Western cinema. Dramatic sketches symbolizing contemporary society became the illustrations of Takamatsu's own speeches. Therefore, even if he showed foreign films imported from France or the United States to people in rural towns, their content was subordinated to the context of Takamatsu's stories, and they were altered to support his thought. Thus, the series of films which Takamatsu made in 1903 not only were different from both Kabuki cinema and early Japanese cinema in which an event was represented, they also were different from the Western fictional cinema of that same period. In terms of supplementing ideologies, they resemble films of passion plays, but they also differ from passion plays, because in the latter, a familiar story is arranged in a linear order. Takamatsu's films differed from Western fictional cinema in which the style of the film was motivated by the narrative nature; rather, they were icons used for expressing thoughts. They also had a nature which could be understood only by the explanation of what was happening on the screen, rather than being sufficient in themselves. In this regard, it could be said that Takamatsu's films were quite typical of early Japanese cinema.

The Period after the Boom of the Russo-Japanese War Films

From 1904 until 1905, 80 percent of the films shown in Japan were about the Russo-Japanese War. Because of the timely nature of that subject, as soon as 1906 began, the number of such films rapidly decreased. The only new film about the war shown in 1906 was released in January, a news film of field marshals Oyama and Togo returning triumphantly to Japan. Chiba Yoshizo of the Yoshizawa Company had shot this reportage film of the triumphal return in December of the previous year.

There were only a few non-war-related films made in Japan from 1904 until 1905. These were all documentary films which were shown in addition to the war films during public film screenings. They included scenic films (*fukei eiga*) such as *Tokyo Snowscape* (*Tōkyō no sekkei*, June 1905), *A View of Nikko* (*Nikko no kokei*, June 1905), and *A River Fête at Ryōgoku* (*Tōkyō Ryōgoku no kawabiraki*, October 1905), and dance films such as *The Genroku Dance of the Yoshimachi Dancers* (*Yoshimachi geigi genroku odori*, June 1905). This was a repetition of the picture-postcard images that the cinema entertainment industry had specialized in up to that time.

After November 1896, when Edison's Kinetoscope was introduced into Japan, and February 1897, when Lumière's Cinematograph arrived, the majority of films shown in Japan were imported from foreign countries. Most were from France: works of the Pathé Company, Gaumont, Méliès. A smaller number were from the United States and England. Among the French films, the most successful all over Japan were historical dramas such as Pathé's *L'Epopée napoleonienne* (*The Napoleonic Epic*), shown at the Kinki-kan theater on July 1, 1904, and fantasy films such as those of Méliès. On the other hand, there were no large-scale historic drama films or fantasy films produced in Japan which were influenced by those Western films. One reason for this was the scarcity of capital in the Japanese cinematic world, but another was that the representational mode in those films was just too different from the traditional Japanese kind of visual exhibition. Even as the unusual representational forms of foreign films were being enthusiastically received in Japan, the idea that those forms could not be successfully combined with traditional Japanese representational modes surfaced rather quickly. When *Viewing Scarlet Maple Leaves* opened again in 1907, one newspaper critic wrote: "The motion pictures at the Kinki-kan include a smattering of Western films, which conspicuously reveal a sense of unnaturalness, but, in general, the films are interesting. *Viewing Scarlet Maple Leaves*, with actors Danjūrō and Kikugorō, is, as expected, a special feature."[10]

The unnatural look of foreign films was, of course, not limited to trick films (*torikku eiga*). Foreign-made dramatic films were probably treated as a subject in the above-quoted account in comparison with *Viewing Scarlet Maple Leaves*. That the average film viewer received foreign films favorably is evident in the fact that many movie theaters of that period showed films imported from abroad.

In terms of film production, however, it was almost impossible to imitate a style which did not exist in Japan. For example, there was nothing in Japan like the case of Edwin S. Porter making a movie such as *Jack and the Beanstalk* (1902) after having been influenced by George Méliès. When Takamatsu Toyojirō made his allegorical film, he may have borrowed the idea from dramatic sketches of early French films. However, as I stated previously, it would be difficult to say that even Takamatsu's films had a self-sufficient Western-style narrative quality, because they were used mainly to illustrate his speeches. Takamatsu's works were shown at the Kinki-kan on September 7, 1906, with the usual *benshi* interpretation. Based on the success of that film showing, four French films, similarly entitled "Society Puck Motion Pictures," were shown at Kobe's Daikokuza in December of the same year.

The Japanese titles of these four French films were *The Law of the Newly Invented 20th-Century Puck* (*Niju seiki shinhatsumei pukku o hakurai kuinige no ho*), *Clear Skies Avenge* (*Tenhare adauchi*), *A Three-Man Collision* (*Sannin otoko no shototsu*), and *The True State of Parisian Coeds' Depravity* (*Danjo gakusei daraku no shinso*). Just as Takamatsu's works conveyed an allegorical meaning to the film viewers, according to the *benshi*'s interpretation, these French films also had the full potential to transcend the actual content of the film being interpreted allegorically by the *benshi*. Along with these French films, the Daikokuza also showed two Japanese documentaries entitled *Japanese-Made Social Puck Moving Picture* (*Nippon-sei shakai pukku katsudō shashin*). Even though those two films—*Girl Students' Military Arts* (*Jogakusei no bugeitaiso*) and *A Group of Japanese Men Swimming* (*Danseito no suiei*)—could be called documentaries, they were included in the context of the allegorical social drama called "society puck."

As the Russo-Japanese War ended, the popularity of films based on that theme declined. Instead of discovering new subjects, Japanese film production cut the number of indigenously made films and once again tried to supply the entertainment industry with films imported from abroad. Most of the small number of new Japanese productions were documentaries, scenic films and *sumō* films. On the other hand, there were some experiments with incorporating the subjects of Western-style films on a different dimension from fiction. For example, there was a film of a magician's conjuring tricks, and another film entitled *The Feather Cloak Dance of Miss Tenkatsu* (*Tenkatsujo no hagoromai*), released on August 1, 1906, which imitated the *Butterfly Dance* and *Serpentine Dance* of dancers such as Loie Fuller and Annabelle.

If one looks at the entire entertainment industry, however, there were few new Japanese productions at that time, although film viewers had a strong interest in Japanese-made films. In order to get the viewer's attention in a 1906 film screening report, advertisements stressed some Japanese films included among around ten screened works. From 1906 to 1907, however, there were no attempts to model foreign films in the Japanese cinema, which had lost the war theme.

During the war period, several independent production companies temporarily joined in making war films, but after the end of the Russo-Japanese War, the Yoshizawa Company and the Yokota Company monopolized film production. These two companies primarily made documentaries, but after the reopening of *Viewing Scarlet Maple Leaves* in 1907 proved such an unexpected success, they felt an incentive to try to film dramatic stage performance. The Osaka branch of the Yoshizawa Company, with cameraman Konishi Ryo, filmed performances of *The Fifth Scene of the Loyal Forty-Seven Retainers* (*Chūshingura godanme*) and *Benkei of the Bridge* (*Hashi Benkei*), with leading actor Kataoka Nizaemon and *Bell Forest* (*Suzu ga mori*) and *Stone Bridge* (*Shakkyō*), with Ichikawa Udanji as the leading actor. The Yokota Company made Kikuchi Yuho's best-seller *One's Sin* (*One ga tsumi*) into a film. *One's Sin* was one of the first experiments with *shimpa* film, and the story was subsequently used as the basis for many other films. This Yoshizawa Company's work, including *Viewing Scarlet Maple Leaves*, was filmed on location on a specifically constructed Kabuki stage. Konishi Ryo recounted the following memory of the filming of *The Tale of the Loyal Forty-Seven Retainers*:

> I filmed the three actors' quick costume change [*hayagawari*] just as in a play. With location filming, we don't construct a real stage or backdrop but, because everything was supposed to be just like in a play, we purposely spread a scenic curtain or made a temporary stage. In order to fit in everything happening on stage, I put the camera at about ten meters' distance and, using the method of *idokoro-utsushi* [setting the camera and filming], I would leave the camera as it was, and turn aside only during the *hayagawari*. In this way, I was able to get everything onto about 450 feet of film. Each magazine [of film] was about 150 feet, so this meant I had to change it twice. While I changed film, the actors stopped just where they were and waited.[11]

Following in the same Kabuki film tradition, *Benkei of the Bridge* used six hundred feet of film and was shown with traditional narrative chanting and musical accompaniment (*jōruri narimono iri*).[12]

These were, however, rare examples. There was resistance among Kabuki actors toward Kabuki films, so the films could not be made easily. This was one reason why there were few dramatic films in early Japanese cinema. Most famous Kabuki actors refused to stand in front of the movie camera. For that reason, subsequent Kabuki films gave up on the idea of showing the most famous actors' performances and decided to use second- or third-rate *kyūgeki* actors. Only a little time was needed for Kabuki actors to relax their prejudice against cinema. From 1909 until mid-1910, starting with Onoe Matsunosuke, *kyūgeki* actors became movie stars and Kabuki cinema no longer needed to use real Kabuki actors. Until that time, however, with the insufficient number of Japanese theatrical performances in Japanese cinema after the Russo-Japanese War, Japanese cinema had no other way to satisfy viewers' desires but with *shimpa*-style films such as *One's Sin*, produced by the Yoshizawa and Yokota companies, or the old-style Kabuki cinema made before and after 1900, or the revivals of the (rarely produced) newer Kabuki films.

The Beginning of Westernization

Until 1907, Japanese film production was sporadic and small-scale, but after the Yoshizawa Company built a glass studio in Tokyo's Meguro area in January

1908, production gradually proceeded in a more systematic, orderly manner. The first film shot at the Yoshizawa studio was Hibino Raifu's sword dance *The Art of Shinto-Style Sword Drama* (*Shintō-ryū kenbujutsu sugekimi,* released on May 1, 1908). When this film was screened in the Denki-kan (which became the first permanent movie theater in 1903), a famous *benshi,* Somei Saburo, gave an introduction before the screening. During the actual screening, Hibino stood in front of the screen and recited Chinese poems in time to the sword dance.[13] Because musical performance with dramatic speech in imitation of famous actors (*kowairo narimono*) was already used during the screening of Kabuki films, it naturally also became necessary to include a kind of chanted recitation in the case of sword-dance films.

Even in a Western movie theater, there is an aural aspect of imitation in addition to the visual aspect. In other words, the musical accompaniment for silent films is regarded as an essential element of cinema. At the early stages, as illustrated by, for example, the French Gaumont Company's phonoscene, there were even times when visual images depended on the songs. In Japan's case, however, as illustrated in the traditional *Kabuki gidayū,* the drama, song, music, and voice were of an indivisible importance in the performance art, and therefore such a dependent relationship did not exist. When Nakamura Kasen's troupe performed *Dawn at the Soga Brothers' Hunting Grounds* (*Soga kyōdai kariha no akebono,* released on September 30, 1906), there was a special event during which one member of the movie theater came and, while watching their performance on the screen, recited the dialogue, but this was actually a natural course of events. It might appear that this characteristic (of feeling no necessity to provide their own narration) of early Japanese dramatic films would be totally refuted in the stage of adopting foreign cinematic forms. On the other hand, after touring film studios in the United States, Yoshizawa Company's head Kawaura Kenichi, who then constructed a glass movie studio in Tokyo, started producing *shimpa* films along with Kabuki films. As for *shimpa* melodrama, the Yokota Company had made *One's Sin* the previous year. However, the Yoshizawa Company did not make a Japanese *shimpa* melodrama, but rather first tried a Western-style narrative film, a comedy. For that purpose, the Japanese theatrical revolutionary Kawakami Otojirō was invited to have his troupe perform *Semi-Japanese Semi-Western Wedding.* That period saw the budding of Westernization in Japanese cinema. For example, at the same time as *Semi-Japanese Semi-Western Wedding* (the first half of 1908), in Osaka, the Yokota Company made a comedy, *A Charred Water Lizard* (*Imori no kuroyaki,* released on June 25, 1908), in which a Western-style structure can be seen. The cameraman for this film was the Yokota Company's Fukui Shigeichi, who had gone to Korea the previous year to film a documentary. The three-scene *Charred Water*

Lizard used as its climax a scene like those in French chase films which were often shown in Japan at that time.

In the first scene, an elderly female beggar is begging near the bridge of a shrine. A beautiful woman passes by. A young man sees this woman and buys a love charm made of charred water lizard powder from a nearby store. He tries to throw the powder at the woman from behind, so she will turn around and fall in love with him. By mistake, the powder is thrown on the elderly female beggar. The second and third scenes show a chase between the old woman and the man, in which, as the man escapes in a boat, the old beggar chases him in another boat.[14]

Chase films were popular in the United States from around 1904 and were soon imitated by the French. Until 1908 such scenes could be seen in many comic films; as a result, the number of shots in a film increased.[15] In Japan, however, until 1908, there were absolutely no indigenously produced films with chase scenes (which did not require the interpretation of the *benshi* for their meaning), although such foreign films were frequently exhibited. (The *benshi* even tried to embellish the chase scenes of foreign films with language, using various kinds of rhetoric during all of the shots.) After *A Charred Water Lizard,* even up to the heyday of chase scenes influenced by the French movie *Zigomar* (1911, seen in Japan in 1912), there were sometimes climactic chases in *shimpa* films. For example, the Yoshizawa Company's eight-scene *Pheasant in a Burnt Field* (*Yakino no kigisu,* released May 27, 1909) includes several shots of a chase between a policeman and a man who has kidnapped a child.

In the same way, from around 1908, a kind of *shimpa*-based Japanese film was made which incorporated some of the Western representational modes and which clearly differed from the usual Kabuki films. Even among the *kyūgeki* of this period, Kabuki film remained the oldest mode and, as filmed Kabuki theater, was consistently of a quiet style. M. Pathé's film *Ehon Taikoki,* starring Nakamura Kasen and Ichikawa Sakiji, released on December 10, 1908, was also known by the title *The Tenth Scene of Taikoki* (*Taikoki jūdanme*). As this film shows, in the case of Kabuki films, the film image does not give an illusion of the present as the diegesis; rather, it makes one aware of the stage performance. This new concept of cinema as theater is notable in the mode of Kabuki films made until mid-1910, but another kind of film, also born from a similar concept, was made for chain-drama (*rensageki*).[16] *Rensageki* devises its total dramatic storyline from the union of cinema and actual staged performances. Filmed scenes, such as location scenes, are shot as part of the drama within the film, rather than as actual performances. Tanaka Jun'ichiro wrote the following about his memory of seeing a *rensageki* performance:

I recall seeing *rensageki* at Torigoe Asakusa's Chuo Theater, run by Kobayashi Kisaburo, around the beginning of the summer of 1917. While four or five actors performed a kind of verbal exchange on stage, a screaming woman fled into the curtains. Then two or three men and women chased after her, also going behind the curtain. At that point, the stage grew dark and a white curtain descended smoothly in the downstage area. It became the scene of a park, into which the previous woman was fleeing. A fight broke out between the woman and the people following her. A passing car gave the woman requesting help a ride, and then drove away. The men began to run after her even harder. The car arrived at a wealthy mansion, and the woman accompanying the male driver went with him inside the grounds, up to the reception area. At that point, as the film disappeared and the white curtain was raised, the stage became the same reception room scene as in the movie, and the play between the man and the woman from the movie continued.[17]

The Yoshizawa Company attempted this kind of *rensageki* from 1908. When actors such as Sawamura Gennosuke and Nakamura Kangoro performed plays such as *Otomi Stabbed* (*Kirare Otomi*), *Woman Samurai* (*Onna samurai*), and *Demon Thistle* (*Oni azami*), one section was filmed and mixed with the play. On the other hand, one could say that the concept of *rensageki* was older, originating as one scene of the Kabuki films. Because early Japanese cinema did not automatically try to maintain a self-sufficient narrative function, it was not necessary for the entire play to become to a film. The 1899 film *The Floating Nest of the Little Grebe* by Tsuchiya Tsuneji was one such example. The procession of courtesans actually filmed was a part of the longer stage drama. The same was true of *The Fifth Tale of the Loyal Forty-Seven Retainers* and *Ehon Taikoki*.

Because the practice of viewing a film as only one part of the whole began rather early in Japan, a documentary on the Russo-Japanese War was filmed as one scene of the play *The Imperial Army on an Expedition for Russia* (*Seiro no Kogun*), performed by Ii Yoho's theatrical troupe at the Masagoza theater in 1904. In later periods, however, the films themselves became more autonomous. The Yoshizawa Company's 1908 films mentioned earlier were the first films intended as part of a *rensageki* performance, but these works were not just part of *rensageki* but were also shown as independent films. *Otomi Stabbed* was released on October 17, 1908, *Woman Samurai* on October 31, and *Demon Thistle* on November 18.

In addition to the previously mentioned productions, the Yoshizawa Company also made *kyūgeki* films such as *The Scene of Miyamoto Musashi's Elimination of the Baboons* (*Miyamoto Musashi hihi taiji no ba* (released November 22, 1908), with a mechanical doll of a baboon; the Kabuki film *The Kumagai Fan Store* (*Ogiya Kumagai*), starring Ichikawa Sadanji (released November 18); and *Hosokawa Covered with Blood* (*Hosokawa no chidaruma*, released December 12), starring Ichikawa Saben. In addition, they made *shimpa* films such as a new version of *One's Sin,* starring Nakano Nobuchika's troupe (released November 11), and *Ghost Mirror (Yūrei kagami,* released December 10). Both the *shimpa* and the *kyūgeki* films cinematized only one section of the original novel. For example, in the case of *One's Sin,* only two seaside scenes of the novel were filmed. The scenes following those were made into a sequel or into a separate film. In this way, these *shimpa* films comprised one scene of the novel. Moreover, because the filmed places were of one specific location, it was difficult to develop an autonomous narrative scene. Therefore, as in the case of *kyūgeki* films, a *benshi*'s detailed explanations were needed during the actual showing of these Japanese-style *shimpa* films. Once they were put into actual *rensageki* stage performances, these films, serving as one section of the play, secured a discourse on theater through the words of the actors performing in a play.

Various Experiments in Filmmaking

After 1909, the number of films in Japan increased. Because each of the film companies combined foreign and Japanese films in their screenings, the exact number of films made by each company is unknown. However, even if we count only those which can clearly be judged Japanese films, in 1909 the Yoshizawa Company released thirty-one films, the Yokota Company twenty-five, M. Pathé thirty-nine, and an unknown company twelve. In addition, there were about eighty films which could not be distinguished as either foreign or Japanese. This figure shows a remarkable increase compared with the figures for 1908, when fewer than fifty Japanese films were made in total. In 1910, the total number of films made by all of the companies rose to more than three hundred.

As the number of films increased, various technical experiments were attempted. Filmgoers also began to pay attention to these new experiments, and the critical ability of the audience suddenly matured. For example, the following review was written about the Yoshizawa Company's *New Katsura River (Shin-katsura gawa,* released on August 12, 1909):

> Since Sakie's room was filmed in its actual location, there was some unnaturalness in the framing; however, the fact that this gave a feeling remote from that of the theater was good. The use of the image of Tamadare Waterfall for the background of Ogami's villa was refreshing, and it worked as a sign of summer. However, since this waterfall is well-known, it could be misunderstood as showing that Ogami's villa was located in Hakone. In the scene of Hell, Fukushima's performance as Tsuneda made the demon who confronted him look frail in comparison. In order to create a nighttime atmosphere, Sakie's bedroom in Ogami's villa was filmed under a weak light. This seemed an overly elaborate approach. In the films

of Pathé and Gaumont, night scenes are splendidly represented with the help of stage machinery and props. I wonder if the figure of Kawara [performing as Sakie], leaning on a column, was filmed as a very thin and tall figure because of the curvature of the lens. In the scene of Inubo-saki, the background was magnificent. Without the use of a dissolve, the ghost of Sakie was not as skillful as that of a magic film [*majitsu eiga*]. It was a shame that the director did not use this method unique to motion pictures because, if he had done so, the ghost would have become even better than those seen in staged theater. The scene in which Tsunada staggers under a big wave could never be seen in any other theatrical form.[18]

The noteworthy point in this review is its comparison between scenes filmed in a studio and those filmed on location. Until 1908, when the Yoshizawa Company started using a glass studio, filmmakers shot ordinary Kabuki cinema on a temporary stage out in the field, trying to give the audience the impression of a stage by putting up a background curtain. As for drama which used actual natural objects as a background during filming, during the early days of cinema there was *The Floating Nest of the Little Grebe* and *Lightning Burglar,* and the works of Takamatsu Toyojirō. Except for those cases, films in which indoor scenes and location scenes were arranged in a comparative way started to be made after 1908. After studios existed, there was no need to construct temporary stages on location, as in the early days. In other words, filming on location was limited to when natural objects were used as background or when streets were used as stages.

This system, which was taken for granted in the West by that time, was not adapted in Japan until after 1908. This slow adaptation was due to the principle of abstracting natural objects used in traditional Japanese theater. This principle was maintained even when drama was made into film. When the open field became a stage, the impression of reality intensified. During this period, shooting a film on location, instead of representing the open air by means of an actual stage, was given the name *deutsushi* (literally, "to go out and film"). The Yoshizawa Company's *One's Sin* and the Yokota Company's *The Battle of Honno Temple* (*Honnoji gassen,* released on September 17, 1909) took advantage of these outdoor scenes in filming. The images framed by the *deutsushi* method could also be excerpted from the entire film. In accordance with the methods of Western cinema, these scenes could be one film combined with indoor scenes filmed in a studio, or they could be combined with a stage drama into a *rensageki* performance.

After 1909, the number of films made in Japan increased markedly. However, a film in 1909 rarely exceeded one reel in length. One of the major works made by the M. Pathé Company, *Shadow Figure* (*Kageboshi,* released August 8, 1909), took up twenty-five hundred feet of film. Almost all of the other films showed some famous scenes from novels, theater, or folk stories (*mukashi-*

banashi). These famous scenes, interpreted and explained by a *benshi*, generally illustrated familiar stories, and in most cases, they served the purpose of supplementing the *benshi*'s monologue. (In other words, it was the opposite of what one might expect, i.e., that the *benshi*'s descriptions would supplement the story of the film!) This phenomenon—that a film, as visual supplement, became subordinate to narration instead of becoming the center of attraction—was unique to many Japanese films from 1909 to 1910. The following passage appeared in a review of a *rensageki* play:

> The Opera House in Asakusa Park, which opened last August, is a novelty. There, theater and motion pictures are combined. When an actress starts dancing *Takasago Tanzen*, a motion picture shows the waves in the background. Kusunoki Masahige's parting scene at Sakurai station is performed to Satsuma lute (*biwa*) accompaniment. The film of the Battle of Minatogawa is used as background. In front of that background, Masashige and Masasue stab each other.[19]

Here, cinema's only role was to add a sense of illusion to the drama. Its effect was on the same level as that of stage lighting. Cinema itself was only one element of a narrative, with the stage drama in its entirety controlling all of the elements. Even when a film was shown alone, it might be just one element of the general storytelling mode (*kodan*). This is because the cinema of the period did not aim only at achieving a narrative sense in a self-sufficient manner.

The president of the Yoshizawa Company, Kawaura Kenichi (who was very much aware of the fact that cinema not only existed as a narrative art in itself but could also be used to provide effects for a *benshi*'s narration, or for stage drama or "cinémathèque"),[20] had seen *Hale's Tours*[21] in 1904 at the St. Louis Exposition. That experience inspired him to construct Luna Park in Asakusa in September 1910, where he showed "steam locomotive motion pictures" and "*sumō* wrestling motion pictures." "Steam locomotive motion pictures" give the audience the illusion of boarding, and traveling on, a train, while "*sumō* wrestling motion pictures" give the illusion of watching *sumō* wrestling matches. In this case, another mode of cinema, besides the narrative mode found in films shown in movie theaters, was found. Even though the films shown at Luna Park did not assume the same modes as films shown in movie theaters, there was no doubt that they were films. The difference was that these Luna Park films relied mainly on conveying the impression of reality instead of exploiting cinema's fictive or narrative capabilities. The same could be said for the early *rensageki* films shown at the Asakusa Opera House.

Indeed, the fragmentary nature of most Japanese films of this period—which allowed the *benshi*'s interpretation to dominate—is illustrative of typical early Japanese cinema, which (unlike Western cinema of the same period, with its spontaneous, self-sufficient narrative) was subordinate to other discourses, such as novels, the theater, folktales, travel, and sports. In fact, when we view this kind of subordination from the perspective of traditional Japanese art, the cinema and other discourses coexist without either resisting or absorbing each other. This need not be understood as cinema being the tool of those other discourses. During this period, cinema was used experimentally in various ways. In the process, cinema did not develop its form by itself; instead, various outside forms influenced it and facilitated new discoveries of cinematic effects.

The 1910s

It is surprising that there were very few American films among the foreign films released in Japan between 1908 and 1911. When Japan started importing foreign films, most of them were French films, and even in 1910, there were only a small number of imports from the United States. Many of the American films that were shown were made by the Vitagraph Company, and works by D. W. Griffith were almost unknown in Japan until *The Lonedale Operator* (1911) was released on October 21, 1913. Thus the Westernization of Japanese cinema which was apparent by the early 1910s was brought about not by the American cinema but by the influence of French cinema. When Griffith's *The Lonedale Operator* was released in Japan, one critic wrote: "Since this is a chase film, it was a tremendous hit with the audience of the Kinryu-kan in Asakusa Park. However, the essence of American cinema only lies in films about war, cowboys and chases. There is no substance at all."[22]

In Japan, chase films had already passed their zenith by 1913. If this film had been shown immediately after it was made in 1911, it might have conveyed a fresher impression to Japanese critics. However, since 1910, many films by Griffith imitators had shown in Japan, and the chase films had already been decisively revealed to the Japanese audience and critics two years earlier, on November 11, 1911, when a French film, *Zigomar,* made by Victorin Jasset, was released at the same Kinryu-kan.

In 1910, the number of Japanese films measuring two or three reels began to increase. Among them, *The Life Story of Saint Nichiren* (*Seishō Nichiren Daishi goichidai-ki,* released on August 27, 1910, by the Yokota Company) was a monumental work ten thousand feet (ten reels) long. This was unprecedented anywhere in the world at this time. This film, clearly influenced by French films such as *Passion Play* or *La Vie de Moise* by the Pathé Company, consisted of sixty-seven scenes chronicling the life of Saint Nichiren, from his birth to his pilgrimage to Mt. Minobu. In other words, one reel had an average of six or seven scenes, which was a standard number in the Japanese cinema of this period. That was also the standard number of scenes per reel for pre–World

War I Japanese cinema. (The number of scenes, of course, does not necessarily match the number of shots. Dividing one scene into several shots had already been attempted in *Japanese Cherry Blossoms* [*Nihon zakura,* released May 23, 1909], a forerunner example made by the M. Pathé Company. In the 1910s, this kind of experiment became conspicuous because of the Westernization of Japanese cinema. *A Woman Aviator* [*Onna hikoka,* released November 15, 1913] by the Komatsu Company was one such example.)[23] However, because chase films such as *Zigomar* were imitated with great success in Japan, and because the heyday of Japanese chase films had passed, the standard number of scenes in those films had decreased. The phenomenon that the number of scenes and shots in chase films tended to increase had already been seen in the United States and France.

In Japan, this phenomenon was seen later, during the early 1910s. *Japanese Zigomar* (*Nippon Jigoma,* released August 25), made by the Yoshizawa Company, was fifty-five hundred feet long, with ninety-six scenes. That is an average of seventeen to eighteen scenes per reel. Such an increase in the number of scenes—which was twice as many as in a standard Japanese film—was the characteristic of other "Zigomar films" made in Japan. Among them were *New Great Detective Zigomar* (*Shin Jigoma Dai-tantei,* released September 29, 1912), made by the M. Pathé Company, and *The Amended Record of Japanese Zigomar* (*Zoku Nippon Jigoma kaishin-roku,* released October 1, 1912) by the Yoshizawa Company.

The increase in the number of shots was proportionate to the Westernization of Japanese cinema. By the increase of shots, the self-sufficiency of cinema, i.e., its ability to make its meaning clear without depending on other discourses, was acquired. Explanations or interpretations by a *benshi* were unnecessary in order to indicate the chasing detective and the villain being chased in *Japanese Zigomar.* This was quite different from the dominant mode of Japanese cinema in those days, in which a *benshi* was an absolute necessity. In fact, the Fukuhodo theater chain, which imported Victorin Jasset's *Zigomar,* did not release this film immediately but rather kept it in a warehouse for some time because it was so different from the standard foreign films being shown at that time. This film was shown as a stopgap measure because films were in short supply at the Kinryu-kan. The amount of explanation given by the *benshi* for those chase films was in proportion to that of an ordinary film in which every action was verbalized; moreover, the language used was full of strange figures of speech. Although cinema itself does not call for any explanation, the customary way of showing films in Japan did not allow for any films without accompanying explanations. Thus a conflict arose between the Westernization of Japanese cinema and the customary Japanese modes.

Japanese cinema in the early 1910s initiated a conflict between the Western mode and the Japanese mode which continued throughout the 1910s. In terms of content, *shimpa,* which tried to deal with modern subjects in the theater, came to the fore in the cinema as well. If we take Japanese films made in 1910 as an example, the ratio of *shimpa* to *kyūgeki* had become almost even. The appearance of Westernization was recognized in one kind of *kyūgeki* which tried to eliminate the Kabuki form, but the most obvious case was found in *shimpa.*

In the Japanese cinema of this period, which received its baptism of Westernization mainly from French cinema, subjects for *shimpa* drama were almost clearly divided into two genres, comedy and tragedy, just like the films made up to 1910 by companies such as Pathé or Gaumont. In *shimpa*-inspired Japanese cinema, Western-style subject matter appeared more strongly in comedies than in tragedies. This was because comedies, whose effects are produced with movements and actions, naturally lessened the dependency on the *benshi*'s language. In contrast, tragedies, which increased their effect through the *benshi*'s exaggerated language, did not have as much of a dynamic nature as comedies. Therefore, in tragedies, there were few of the kinds of effects to be found in comedies influenced and altered by Western-oriented content. However, according to the general view of Japanese performing arts, tragedy was traditionally considered superior to comedy. In the case of cinema, this prejudice also existed for a long time.

In any case, it can be said that the process of Westernization of Japanese cinema differed according to the genre of the film. In comedy, the genre that represents a world somewhat remote from the real world, the imagination of cinema in Japan was not much different from that of Western comedies of the same period. Therefore, a traditional Japanese form of comedy called *kyōgen* was not introduced into cinema. On the other hand, tragedy remained popular throughout the 1910s, because of its very close ties to the theater, and also the fact that tragedy, like *kyūgeki,* depends on other discourses. There were certainly some *shimpa* tragedy films with Western concepts, such as *The Cuckoo— New Form* (*Shin hototogisu,* released on June 25, 1909) by the M. Pathé Company, which experimented with the use of flashbacks, or *The Green of the Pine* (*Matsu no midori,* released on January 15, 1911) by the Yoshizawa Company, which used a film-within-a-film *deus ex machina* kind of construction, in which the heroine finds her separated lover in the movie projected on the theater screen. However, such experiments never became a dominant trend.

The characteristic form of Japanese cinema in the first half of the 1910s was an image which was easy for a *benshi* to explain or interpret, i.e., one which had a small number of shots and relatively static action and yet, at the same time, could be interpreted in many ways. In Kabuki films, this characteristic was faithfully preserved. For example, among many Kabuki films made between 1908 and 1915, almost no change or progress was seen in the mode of representation, except in terms of the length. Since 1910, the Yokota Company's version of *The Tale of the Loyal Forty-seven Retainers* (*Chūshingura*), starring Onoe Matsunosuke, has been remade many times. In the early 1910s, the entire long Kabuki play was not filmed at one time; rather, each part was filmed and shown separately. As with the *Passion Play* by the French Pathé Company, sometimes the individual small parts were collected and later shown as a long film. For example, the following was written concerning *The Loyal Forty-seven Retainers:*

> *The Loyal Forty-seven Retainers*—starring the Onoe Matsunosuke school of Kyoto—is a highlight of this show. This is the same popular *Chūshingura* (shown from November 15 of last year for one month) to which many parts have been added. The episodes of "Quick attack of the samurais Kayano and Hayami," "Oishi's merrymaking at Ichiriki-tei in Gion," "Takei Kinuemon remonstrates with Oishi," "Daimongai," "Oishi goes to the east," and "Pulling up the Ryogoku Bridge" are left intact, just as they were shown last year. Excellent parts in this new version are "Disgrace at the Geese Room (*Kari no ma*)," "Bloodshed at Pine Corridor (*Matsu no roka*)," and "A desperate fight of royal retainers." The use of props in the far rear of the set is good. The scene of the noodle-shop from last year's production is not bad, but the background for the final scene "In front of the tomb of Takuminokami" is too stagey. Moreover, it lacks a total effect of freshness as a newly-released film. Probably this is a shortcoming of the former Yokota company. I'm definitely not saying this for the sake of faultfinding. Matsunosuke's performance of Oishi was really effective on stage. I was a little troubled by Kitsuraku's portrayal of six roles but, among those roles, that of Takei Kinuemon was really striking. In the end, I will mention the running time for your information, although this is the schedule for the second day and they might change it according to the movie theater's convenience. From "A command of a banquet by the Imperial messenger" to "Takuminokami commits harakiri"—about 50 minutes. From "Quick attack by the samurais" to "Daimongai inu-bushi"—about 75 minutes. From "The separation at Nanbu-zaka" to "Royal retainers' long-cherished desire"—about 45 minutes.[24]

The oldest extant *Loyal Forty-seven Retainers,* starring Onoe Matsunosuke, is a composite of several films made between 1910 and 1913 (including a part of the work mentioned in the passage above). It is difficult to judge which parts were filmed during which year, because almost no changes took place during this period in terms of representational modes. However, it is at least easy to confirm here a representational mode unique to Japanese cinema, i.e., a non-Western mode of traditional Japanese cinema which was practiced with hardly any changes until the mid-1910s.

In the first five shots (which constitute the bloodshed sequence at Edo Castle), the actors who performed in front of the sliding doors (*fusuma*) were viewed in terms of a concept of frontality which, from the Western point of view, can be seen in films of the early part of this century. However, in terms of the relationship between the actors and the sliding doors in the back, the visual field of these five shots was joined exactly in an alternating order of front, diagonal, front, diagonal, front. The effect produced by this orderly arrangement of shots, and the very low position of the camera, lets us feel the kind of static beauty and pleasant slow rhythm unique to Japanese cinema.

When we look closely at the fifth shot, we can see that the picture painted on the sliding door is different from that in the preceding four shots. After the fifth shot, we can recognize the insertion of a short bust-shot in which the face of Onoe Matsunosuke can be clearly seen for the first time. This short shot is very much out of proportion. Probably this was filmed in 1913, or it was a segment of a film which was made much later.

In spite of its composite form, the oldest *Forty-seven Loyal Retainers* starring Matsunosuke does not necessarily show the same kind of unnatural joining of sequences as a whole as does Pathé's *Passion Play*. This is proof, after all, that the non-Western quality of Japanese cinema, typically represented by the Kabuki cinema, remained homogeneous for a relatively long period (until the mid-1910s). Like the performance in front of the sliding screens in the first few shots, the static performance in front of the sliding screens in the harakiri scene of Asano Takuminokami becomes an "ensemble" performance, combining the actors and the decorations placed in the back of the scene. Because these performances face the camera directly (or, in some cases, diagonally), they give the film a sense of frontality, and they also determine the depth of scene.

In 1912, the Yoshizawa Company, the Yokota Company, the M. Pathé Company, and the Fukuhōdō theater chains amalgamated into one company, Nikkatsu. That year the Emperor Meiji died, and the name of the era changed from Meiji to Taisho. It is relatively easy to understand why the history of early Japanese cinema was divided into two parts. One is the cinema of the Meiji period, prior to 1912, before the Nikkatsu trust was established, and the other is the cinema of the Taisho period, in which the trust was established. However, even after Nikkatsu was established, old films by each of the four companies were shown for a while, until 1913, when companies outside Nikkatsu, such as the Komatsu Company, the Shikishima Company, and the Tōyō Company, started making films in competition with Nikkatsu. Tenkatsu was established in 1914; M. Kashi started filmmaking in 1915. One could say that this rivalry between Nikkatsu and other films companies became apparent about the time of World War I.

From 1914 to 1915, the number of foreign films shown in Japan shifted from a predominance of European-made films to films made in the United States. Along with this shift, changes appeared in Japanese films themselves. Even in a genre such as *kyūgeki*, dynamic action (as in Westerns) became required, and the earlier mode in which the audience was asked to view the acting statically was altered. For example, the following critique was written about the *Daimyō Saburo-maru* (1914) made by Nikkatsu Kyoto (i.e., the Yokota Company before the establishment of the trust): "If critics who value dance posturings and poses see this film, they might speak ill of it. However, we should see this film as a *kyūgeki*. Moreover, it was filmed by Nikkatsu Kyoto. This film is full of life, has interesting scene changes, and even uses trick filming."[25]

On the one hand, a genre such as the theatrical *kowairo narimono Kabuki* (the stage mode which included voices and music) never completely disappeared. Even while it was absorbed into dynamic *kyūgeki* films such as *Daimyō Saburo-maru*, it continued until the late 1910s. However, the establishment of Nikkatsu and new trials in filmmaking by rival film companies became a power which was able to alter the whole Japanese cinematic world, and the main mode of film-making changed drastically after 1914. Japanese cinema decided to take the direction of adapting the representational mode of Western cinema in which cinema undertakes its own narration. The release of many American films also became a big factor in the alteration of Japanese cinema.

In terms of narrative, the history of Japanese cinema up to the early 1910s was unique for its lack of self-sufficiency. Even after the mid-1910s, when cinema started to supply its own narration, the *benshi* remained a remembrance of the mode of early Japanese cinema. From this period, the very existence of the *benshi* certainly helped Japanese cinema retain its own Japanese-style modes (for example, the use of the long take and of few close-ups). However, the fact that the existence of the *benshi* helped Japanese cinema preserve its form is due to the fact that the Japanese cinema originally was not self-sufficient. The subsequent character of Japanese cinema was established on this foundation built up during the pre-World War I period.

NOTES

1. Tanaka Jun'ichiro, *History of the Development of Japanese Film 1* (*Nihon eiga hattatsu shi*) (Tokyo: Chūo Kōrōnsha [chuko bunko version, 1975]), p. 104.

2. Tanaka, p. 74.

3. *Hōchi Newspaper* (June 20, 1899).

4. Komatsu Hiroshi, "What Is Meant by Primitive Structure?" ("Primitivu na kozo ni yori nani ga imi sareru ka"), *Modern Philosophy* (*Gendai Shisō*) (August, 1987): 252–259.

5. Eileen Bowser, "Preparation for Brighton—The American Contribution," in *Cinema 1900/1906: An Analytical Study* (FIAF, Brussels, 1982), p. 4.

6. Jay Leyda, *Kino: A History of the Russian and Soviet Film* (London: George Allen and Unwin, 1973), p. 23.

7. Noel Burch, *To the Distant Observer* (Berkeley: U of California P, 1979), pp. 117–122.

8. Advertisement published by Kinki-kan (October 1904).

9. *Kobe Newspaper* (September 28, 1908).

10. *People's Newspaper* (May 12, 1907).

11. Tanaka, p. 133.

12. *Osaka Current Events Newspaper* (December 31, 1907).

13. Tanaka, p. 136.

14. Tanaka, p. 144.

15. Komatsu Hiroshi, "Supplementing the Lack of Quality" ("Kessei o hōjō suru koto"), *Modern Philosophy* (*Gendai Shisō*) (October 1987).

16. The name *rensageki* was first used in a film starring Yamazaki Chonosuke in 1913.

17. Tanaka Jun'ichiro, *A Shower of Ballads* (*Uta shigure*), Act 5, Scene 8 (Separate volume of *Kinema Jumpō*, October 1966), p. 29.

18. *Miyako Newspaper* (August 15, 1909).

19. *Miyako Newspaper* (May 16, 1909).

20. "Cinémathèque" means one of the attractions practiced in 1905, when many films about the Russo-Japanese War were shown. A water tank was placed on the stage, and a toy warship was set on the water and moved around. In order to heighten the warlike effect, a documentary film of war was shown in the rear.

21. Raymond Fielding, "Hale's Tours: Ultrarealism in the Pre-1910 Motion Picture," in John L. Fell, ed., *Film before Griffith* (Berkeley: U of California P, 1983).

22. *Film Record*, No. 3 (1913), p. 13.

23. Komatsu Hiroshi, "Shot or Plan—Phylogeny of the Concepts" ("Shot naishi plan—gainen no keitôhassei"), *Modern Philosophy* (*Gendai Shisō*) (April 1987).

24. *Kinema Record*, No. 5 (1913), pp. 18–19.

25. *Kinema Record* (September 1914), pp. 28–29.

Spoken Silents in the Japanese Cinema; or, Talking to Pictures: Essaying the *Katsuben,* Contexturalizing the Texts

J. L. Anderson

Katsuben (or *benshi*) were performers who provided live dialogue, narration, and commentary whenever pre-talkie films were shown in Japan. They remained the dominant element of the Japanese viewing experience until replaced by the sound film. Anderson's illustrated summary essay discusses the following aspects of the *katsuben.* First, the pre-talkie film experience in Japan was not a new, autonomous entertainment but an extension of tradition-based vocal story-telling venues; in other words, the *katsuben* performance extensively incorporated major elements of literary, painterly, and vocal performance traditions. Second, *katsuben* film, Japanese drama, and many narrative forms are commingled media, i.e., two or more co-equal media are integrated into a single narrative presentation. Third, the *katsuben* film performance demonstrates Japanese indigenous dramaturgy in which the primary structural base is a tension between the teller of a story and the story rather than conflict between protagonist and antagonist within a story. Finally, the ubiquity of *katsuben* was related to critical economic factors in the pre–World War II Japanese film industry.

One of the most comprehensive discussions in or out of Japan of the theoretical implications of the *katsuben,* Anderson's essay also boasts especially full and flavorsome explanatory notes and a superbly helpful bibliography. Finally, Anderson touches on a number of topics that warrant further study. Among these are the seminal influence that the *katsuben* had on subsequent vocal media and, perhaps most intriguing of all, an in-depth examination of women *katsuben*.

This essay appeared in an earlier version as "Spoken Silents in the Japanese Cinema: Essay on the Necessity of *Katsuben*," in *Journal of Film and Video* 40, 1 (Winter 1988): 13–33.

Katsuben in performance at movie theaters.[1]

We all know there was no silent movie experience. Throughout the world, when you went to a "silent" movie you heard live musical accompaniment. In Japan during this "silent period," there was not only live music but also a live talking *katsuben* who performed with the movie. In full view of the audience, the *katsuben* stood or sat to the left of the movie screen for all those films that, only after the coming of 100 percent talking pictures, were called silent films. Most other foreign-language discussions call a *katsuben* a *benshi*, which is a vague term meaning speaker or orator. *Katsuben* clearly denotes the person who performed with motion pictures. It is a portmanteau word which telescopes *katsudō shashin* (moving pictures, literally "moving photographs") and *benshi*.[2]

The *katsuben* gave a vocal performance which involved dialogue, narration, an interpretation of content, and incidental comments while the movie was

Interior of mid-1920s first-class theater.[3]

being shown. What the *katsuben* did was called *eiga setsumei*.[4] The literal translation of this is "film explanation." It is well documented that—with almost no exceptions—silent films had *katsuben*[5] when they were shown in Japan, in the colonies of Korea and Taiwan, and in Japanese neighborhoods in Hawaii, in Brazil, and on the West Coast of the United States.[6]

Although other countries had "talkers," "explainers," and "spielers" to accompany early films,[7] the use of these live performers did not become a common practice in the West, and eventually they disappeared. In Japan, there was always somebody, male or female, performing by the side of the screen. Women *katsuben* were apparently restricted to working with shorts and imported love stories, and occasionally performing dialogue for female characters in domestically produced *shimpa kowairo* films, which are discussed later in this essay.[8] A 1920 police registration of *katsuben* working in the Tokyo area listed 750 male, 90 female.[9]

Because *katsuben* were so important to movie audiences and the movie experience, they often got billing larger than the stars of the movie. Indeed, *katsuben were* the show for many people.[10] There are old people today who, when they recall their silent movie experiences, remember a *katsuben*'s performance as much as any film.[11] One author, in a book about his pleasant memories of old movies, entitles a chapter "Eloquent *Katsuben* Words from Chaplin Films."[12]

Unlike spectators in other countries, the Japanese did not come to view motion pictures as a new, different, modern, mass-produced, machine-driven, autonomous entertainment. What they experienced with the *katsuben* at the movies was (1) *an extension of an indigenous narrative practice which I call commingled media,* and (2) *a modern variation of vocal storytelling traditions.*

Commingled Media

While Japanese art may be best known abroad for its simplicity and reduction (as in poems complete in seventeen syllables and paintings finished in a few black brush ink strokes), an opposing aesthetic tendency is extreme complexity with heterogeneous, often redundant, elements brought together to form a work. The result is a commingling or a mixing of media rather than adherence to a rigidly defined pure and narrow medium. Commingling as artistic practice arises, in part, from traditional Japanese concepts about how "all the arts are one in essence."[13]

One manifestation of this commingling tendency is the combining of written words with narrative painting. In these works, neither words nor pictures alone present the whole story. The words are not captions for the pictures; the pictures are not illustrations for the words. Both elements share the same surface. Both are read altogether as the story unfolds through multiple narrative means. The most familiar commingling picture-and-written-word forms are certain narrative *emakimono* (horizontal picture scrolls). While many East Asian painting traditions incorporate caption, poem, or artist's signature into the pictorial composition, these narrative *emakimono* expand the graphic mix to present a complex story with extensive literary text combined with many successive pictures.[14]

Detail from a commingled narrative *emakimono*
(scroll).[15]

Pictorial novels of the Edo era (seventeenth to mid-nineteenth centuries) present another kind of Japanese read-word and see-picture commingling. While the primary discourse is literary, many pictures add essential story material that is not explicit in the words. The reading of these works is more complex than single-track reading of a novel that has only scattered, incidental illustrations.[16] Iharu Saikaku,[17] the best known of the novelists who worked in this commingled form, occasionally drew his own pictorial material.

In addition to these commingled graphic narratives, there is another fundamental word and picture commingling tendency known as *etoki*. This is a broadly descriptive term that covers vocal storytelling traditions in which a performer talks with still pictures. The origins of *etoki* go back to Buddhist priests who used paintings of hell in their proselytizing sermons.[18] Barbara Ruch described this commingled form as an event in which "painting, story, chanter, and even the sounding of musical instruments (often pure sound rather than music) combine to create a total audio-visual experience rare, if not unique, in the pre-modern history of world literature."[19] She suggested that "this combination of the visual aid, the audio accompaniment, and the chanter/narrator . . . represented the mainstream of nonpoetic, non-Chinese literature in Japanese literary history."[20]

A secular *etoki* performer performs before an audience of three.[21]

Although some *etoki* performers recited a memorized text or read from a book, it is likely that a performer more often improvised his or her personal variation of a familiar story. When something was written on the picture, the performer read it aloud.[22] This commingled narrative tradition was contemporary with a highly developed nonpictorial written literature as well as with storytellers and text readers who worked without pictorial materials. *Etoki* storytelling with pictures combined with the *etoki* performer's *reacting to those pictures* offered an analogue for what *katsuben* did. As with twentieth-century *katsuben,* the vocal virtuosity of the *etoki* performer often surpassed the content of the pictures shown and the words spoken. Religious *etoki* is still performed today in Japan in a few Buddhist temples.[23]

International scholarship dealing with narrative and dramatic forms has largely ignored vocal and picture commingled media, of which Japanese *etoki* is but one local example. Although precursors of *etoki* performers worked more than a thousand years ago in China and India, this commingled narrative form of the storyteller who works with still pictures is not an isolated Oriental phenomenon. Vocal performance with pictures appears in different ways in different cultures over two millennia up until the present.[24] This performance art may not have received its scholarly due because its surviving texts are not considered to have literary merit, or, as in many picture performance traditions, there is no fixed text to survive.[25] Similarly, the surviving pictures of picture performers have most likely been ignored because so few have high painterly merit. Moreover, picture performers are usually[26] part of popular culture, and throughout history they have been at the lowest end of social and artistic scales. It is also possible that picture recitation has been ignored because it fits no established notion of highly demarcated narrative means, such as Northrop Frye's "radicals of presentation."

A German picture performer in the eighteenth century.[27]

Verbal performance commingled with pictures is an alternative practice to the more familiar traditions of vocal storytelling without pictures. It is an alternative practice to most actor-based dramatic forms and to most puppet and shadow plays because the characters are not directly enacted or impersonated by actor substitutes. Instead, the story is *performed* by a narrator, and characters are indicated by various pictorial devices. *Katsuben* are a modern manifestation in one culture of this international narrative form of commingled verbal performance and pictures.

Theatrical Connections

In addition to *etoki* and the picture-and-written-word forms, the Japanese traditional puppet theater, now called *bunraku*, suggests an obvious third type of precursor of the *katsuben*. The puppets of *bunraku* are silent artifacts like a film. They (and their silent human manipulators) occupy center stage. A *jōruri* chanter or two and *shamisen* musicians sit on stage to the audience's right. Unlike the Japanese dramatic forms of Noh and Kabuki, which mix speaking narrators[28] with speaking actors, the entire vocal burden in *bunraku* rests on the *jōruri* artist who narrates the drama and performs all of its dialogue. The most significant differences between *jōruri* and *katsuben* are that (1) *jōruri* performers work from canonized texts, and (2) the vocal techniques of *jōruri* are a difficult mix of singing, chanting, and speaking, while those of the *katsuben* are more easily performed conversational and declamatory modes.

Bunraku in performance.[29]

Although *jōruri* originated and is still performed as a vocal narrative art without picture, puppet, or actor accompaniment, its history suggests just how commingled Japanese storytelling forms can be. Both before and after *jōruri* joined with puppets, *jōruri* performers, seeking to make spectacle, sought out other kinds of mute actors to enhance their stories. The nonpuppet *jōruri* commingled form with the longest history was *sarushibai*[30] ("monkey play"), in which monkeys acted out the story as the *jōruri* artist performed. *Sarushibai* often staged excerpts from classics such as *Ichinotani, Dōjōji,* and *Chūshingura.* Five or six *sarushibai* troupes were still touring rural areas during the 1920s, but there are probably none today. In earlier centuries, *jōruri* commingled with other animals to produce dog plays (*inushibai*), cat plays (*nekoshibai*), and rat plays (*nezumishibai*).[31]

Early nineteenth-century
sarushibai (monkey play).[32]

The classical Noh and Kabuki are commingled dramatic forms in which the storytelling of narrators is joined by actors' enacting scenes on stage. In Noh and in most Kabuki plays, major vocal passages focus on narrators when the aural emphasis converges on their *description* of characters' emotions rather than on the actors' *enacting* of those emotions.[33] Even dialogue of characters on stage is sometimes spoken by the narrating chanter rather than by Noh or Kabuki actors.

In this essay I am not proposing precise causal connections between these commingled precursors and the *katsuben.* I am describing the narrative and show business environments in which the *katsuben* appeared. The closest candidate for the *Ur-katsuben* show is a form of *etoki* known as *utsushie* (projected pictures). This narrative entertainment developed after Dutch traders first brought the magic lantern to Japan in the early nineteenth century.[34] While magic lantern shows are increasingly studied in the West as precursors of motion pictures, the seminal connections between *utsushie* and *katsuben* movies have long been recognized.[35]

Utsushie performed in a *yose* (variety theater).[36]

In *utsushie,* separate pictures of major characters in a story were painted with transparent colors on glass slides and back-projected onto a paper screen. Each character—only two or three appeared at one time—had its own separate projector which was hand-held by an operator who moved the projected image across the screen to give movement to the character. Slides changed as the attitude of a character changed. Characters were further animated with slides that had movable body parts or by successive slides that presented key poses of a broad gesture. Two stationary projectors at the extreme left and right sides of the screen showed scenic elements.

An *utsushie* operator hand-holds two projectors.[37]

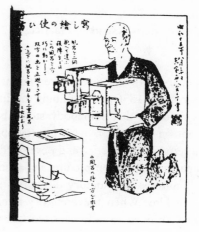

The *utsushie* repertoire was largely composed of abbreviated puppet play and Kabuki standards. A *jōruri*-like storyteller performed with the pictures, although the projectionists sometimes yelled out dialogue. *Utsushie* performers put on their shows in tiny huts at festivals, or they worked as one of the standard non-storytelling acts in small variety halls called *yose*. *Yose* was and is the principal venue for traditional storytellers. During the Sino-Japanese War of the mid-1890s, *utsushie* achieved its greatest popularity with timely patriotic stories based on the latest news from the front. A few years later these shows were wiped out by the higher technology of the Cinématographe and Vitascope as photographic moving pictures replaced the painted slides of *utsushie*.[38]

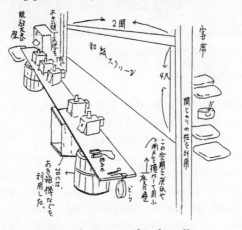

Set-up for an *utsushie* show.[39]

Early *Katsuben* Practices

Forerunners of the *katsuben* were present at the first exhibition in Japan of the Kinetoscope in 1896 and the Lumière Cinématographe in 1897. Japanese newspapers reported that somebody stood beside the machines or the screen to comment on how the moving photographs worked.[40] This, of course, was an early international practice and developed elsewhere into an occasional lecturer accompanying a motion picture. In Japan, these technical explanations turned into ubiquitous introductory discourses about people and things about to be seen in a film. When the prefatory remarks ended, the film started and the speaker continued to talk. This worked well for documentary and travel subjects as well as for story films from abroad.[41]

The didactic inclinations of these speakers decreased as the number of foreign-made narrative films increased. The early *katsuben*'s talk before a film was shown resembled the forepart of a *rakugo* performer's act.[42] *Rakugo* is a solo vocal narrative tradition centered on comic tales of everyday life. *Rakugo* performers were—and are—the principal acts of *yose*. During his forepart or warmup, the *rakugo* performer explains what his story is about, suggests what the audience should pay special attention to, and tries a few jokes to assess what kind of audience he is facing.[43]

Apart from its formal relation to *rakugo* practice, the early *katsuben*'s pre-talk had an economic determinant. Film rentals and print prices were high compared to the wages of the earliest *katsuben*. Japanese movie shows, like drama and *yose* performances, tended to be long. With a talented *katsuben* doing amusing introductions, managers in the early days could get by with fewer films and still be competitive with a long, entertaining show. The pre-talk disappeared when feature-length films became the dominant movie format.[44]

When foreign films were shown in Japan, they were shown with their original intertitles intact. *Katsuben* functioned seemingly as translators of these titles. They actually relied on little books of Japanese translations that came with each print of a foreign movie.[45] No money had to be spent to prepare new titles in Japanese. Prints—and they were often used prints—were imported directly from abroad and shown without change. Because so few prints were required to service Japan, the savings in preparation for distribution were large.[46] Even during the late 1920s and most of the 1930s, a print order for only the most popular Japanese features was fifteen. Most films, including imported products, were distributed with half or less that number of prints.[47] The origins of the *katsuben* must be seen, in part, as a product of the economic marginality of the Japanese movie business.

While the single *katsuben* appeared with foreign dramatic films and with documentary and scenic subjects, Japanese story films required something else. The domestically produced story films of the 1900s and 1910s have been described as "photographed stage plays," which suggests that they were direct recordings of actual stage productions. That was not the case. These productions[48] were staged for the camera in studios.[49] They were filmed mostly in long shot with minimal editing: usually one scene, one shot. Exterior scenes were often shot on location.[50] In his autobiography, Kinugasa Teinosuke, who began his career in these films as an *onnagata* (an actor who plays female roles) before becoming a director, described how they were usually shot without a director. The cameraman was totally in charge, and a prompter read the script aloud as the actors performed in synchronization with the spoken narration and dialogue. A copy of this script accompanied prints of the film.[51]

During this same period, most American and European story films were made with increasingly complex multiple shots within a scene and with continuity editing gradually determined by matching action. Foreign directors made films to function as autonomous vehicles for presenting a story. They were complete, fixed texts that came in cans. All that had to be done to show a foreign movie was to open a can and put the product on the projector.

Japanese story films were not autonomous. They were created and viewed as imitations of live theater with extensive dialogue and narrated passages. They were shown in theaters with a group of four to eight *katsuben*-actors lined up on the left and right sides of the screen to do the voices of the characters in a manner that we might now call live dubbing.[52] This staging replicated Kabuki and doll drama (*bunraku*), in which the stage is shared by moving actors or dolls who perform the action and chanting artists who perform some or all of the vocal elements.

Although similar kinds of live dubbing appeared elsewhere in the world, it is unlikely that this practice was imported into Japan. A significant difference is that the speaking actors appeared in full view of the audience in accordance with Japanese traditions of commingled media and visible artistic process. In foreign countries, actors were usually hidden behind the screen in an attempt to create a unified, transparent illusion of characters on the screen talking.[53]

Almost all Japanese costume films of this early period were highly abbreviated adaptations of stories taken (1) from the solo, noncommingled vocal narrative tradition *kōdan*, (2) from printed popular literature derived from *kōdan*, and (3), to a much lesser degree, from Kabuki and *jōruri* plays. Although Kabuki was only a minor source for stories, it provided the foundation for the acting and staging techniques of period films. *Shimpa*, a modernizing theatrical movement, which sought to put contemporary Japan on stage in a way that Kabuki could not do, was the source of the acting style and most of the stories for films with contemporary settings. Many of the *shimpa* plays adapted to film were, in turn, stage adaptations of contemporary novels.[54]

This dominant practice for the production and exhibition of Japanese-made films prior to 1920 was in large part based on *kowairo*, an established non-commingled performance tradition whose practitioners imitated famous Kabuki actors. *Kowairo* originated in the early eighteenth century when special performers stood in front of a Kabuki theater barking the merits of the show, reciting the bill and cast for the day, and doing imitations of the stars inside. They were not Kabuki actors but were a separate and subsidiary theatrical trade.[55] Subsequently divorced from shilling for Kabuki, *kowairo* became one of the standard acts of *yose* with impressions of famous actors in famous scenes. *Kowairo* techniques were borrowed and commingled with movies from the earliest production of Japanese story films around 1906.[56]

In keeping with standard Japanese theatrical practice, the acting dialogue elements of moving picture *kowairo* were usually accompanied by a separate narrator who chanted in imitation of *jōruri* and other Kabuki narrator styles. *Kowairo* films required both *shamisen* and *narimono* (the musically stylized sound effects of Kabuki) because of their direct relationship to established Japanese theatrical practice.[57] *Kowairo* with *narimono* was a practice restricted to Japanese story films. In contrast, foreign movies got only a single *katsuben* and a small orchestra of foreign instruments.[58]

Chained Drama

So tenuous was the hold of the moving picture on its small portion of Japanese show business that in the 1910s regular movies (*kowairo* and foreign films) began to lose their share of the market to yet another commingled form.[59] This third form was *rensageki*, chained drama. In this commingled dramatic medium, dialogue scenes of a *shimpa* melodrama acted live on stage in an interior set alternated with exterior scenes of spectacle and physical action seen on film. Live performance was "chained" to film. In the typical chained drama transition from stage to screen, actors ran down the *hanamichi* and exited at the rear of the auditorium as the movie screen was brought on stage. The *hanamichi* is a narrow extension of the Kabuki stage that runs from downstage right through the audience to the rear of the auditorium. Used for important entrances and exits, the *hanamichi* extends the playing area into the audience space and decenters focus from the main stage. During the scenes on film, chained drama actors usually lined up in full view of the audience, as in *kowairo,* to deliver their lines for the filmed scenes. They were often accompanied by a *katsuben*.[60]

Chained drama troupes on tour sometimes reshot a few of their action scenes on the busiest streets of the city where they were playing. The actors and camera attracted public attention to the show while the shots they made in familiar landmarks gave the plays specific local appeal. Film was processed and printed with portable equipment. Sometimes the shooting on a local street was staged without film in the camera. Just the sight of a chained drama company at work generated extensive word of mouth and was an effective alternative to the more familiar parade of actors through the streets before a performance.[61]

Chained drama disappeared rapidly after 1917, when the government outlawed this commingled form on the grounds that the exhibition of motion pictures in small wooden theaters was too great a fire hazard. The secondary historical record is unclear about the logic behind this curious ruling.[62] Theaters playing chained drama were seldom different in basic construction from those that played only motion pictures, and they could all be equally crowded. Why was one form of film presentation so dangerous and the other not?

While mixtures of film and live performances similar to chained drama occurred in other countries,[63] I find no evidence that foreign practice influenced the Japanese in this mode of film production. The significant difference was that the commingling of film and live drama was a theatrical novelty in Europe and America. It did not become a threat to regular movie business as it did in Japan. A 1915 poll designed to name the most popular Japanese movie stars revealed that one-third of the nation's movie favorites worked *only* in chained drama.[64]

Twenty-five years after the introduction of motion pictures in Japan, three separate modes prevailed for the production and presentation of movies. First, there were the foreign films, which were autonomous vehicles accompanied by a single *katsuben* whose performance was derived from *etoki* and other traditions of Japanese commingled storytelling. In the second and third modes of production and exhibition, story films made in Japan were either (1) photographed, direct replications of conventional dramatic performances which required a group of *kowairo katsuben,* or (2) integral parts of theatrical productions chained to live performance.

Business Conditions

Movies of all forms remained a minor part of show business in Japan during this period. In 1920, there were only 470 movie theaters throughout the Japanese empire, along with several dozen traveling exhibition companies. With only twice the population of Japan, the United States at this time had more than fifty times the number of movie theaters. Movie attendance in Japan was far below one visit per year per person.[65]

The marginality of the Japanese film business during the 1910s is, in part, demonstrated by various recycling practices for the film segments of chained drama. The movie materials used for one production could be integrated into other plays or sold to another chained drama troupe doing the same play. Because scenes were filmed in long shot, matching the actors on the screen with those on the stage was hardly a problem if, indeed, matching appearances between stage and screen characters was of any importance at all. In addition, scenes that were originally performed live on stage could be filmed after the chained drama closed. These new shots were edited into the existing footage to put all of the story on film. There was yet another alternative: the original film segments could be strung out without any additional footage or actors' performance on stage. The visual gaps in the story were filled by the *katsuben*'s words.[66]

Sensing a business opportunity by broadening the appeal of films made in Japan, larger-scale capital entered the movie business after 1920. Writers, modern theater (*shingeki*) pioneers, and assorted intellectuals caught up in the intellectual fervor of the post–World War I era called for broadening the range of stories, emotional possibilities, thematic material, and techniques beyond the established domestic movie forms.[67] These modernizers wanted Japanese production based on international movie styles. They sought reform not unlike that which was already transforming Japanese literature and drama. They wanted reform that would be "modern" yet Japanese. The fundamental call was for films that would stand by themselves as self-sufficient artifacts and not be dependent on any kind of mix with live performers.[68] The principal theorist of this *jun-eiga* ("pure motion picture") movement, Kaeriyama Norimasa, insisted that narrative motion pictures had to change if Japan was ever going to be able to export its motion pictures.[69]

After 1920, *kowairo* films began to disappear as new filmmakers moved away from theatre-analogue cinema to make autonomous works with more elaborate *mise-en-scène*, editing, and intertitles. The historians' consensus is that, among other things, these pioneering directors sought to restrict the range of *katsuben* interpretation.[70] Although these new Japanese films could stand alone without live performance, the popularity of the *katsuben* and their collective strength as an integral part of the exhibition system assured that all motion pictures continued to be shown with *katsuben*. Thus, the single *katsuben*, which was the presentation method long established for the showing of foreign films, became the exclusive practice. The 1920s evolution (some called it a revolution) in Japanese filmmaking killed *kowairo* cinema and invigorated the *katsuben*.[71]

First-class theaters in larger cities required a staff of seven or eight *katsuben* along with their apprentices. Most second-class theaters had three or four.[72] When a loud bell signaled that a film was about to start, the designated *katsuben* made his entrance on stage. Like a bus driver climbing on board to take over a bus, the *katsuben* made his entrance and placed a large card with his name on it in an illuminated sign. He might also display the title of the film he was about to perform.[73] Many *katsuben* dressed in formal kimono. Those who worked foreign films often preferred a swallowtail frock coat and striped black trousers in imitation of the formal dress of Japanese diplomats and politicians. Others wore pseudo-military uniforms with braid or the formal black robes of Japanese judges.[74] *Katsuben* were important people.

Most *katsuben* were under contract to specific theaters or to shows that toured the provinces. Sometimes a *katsuben* with a reputation big enough to precede him toured major cities with his hits.[75] While *katsuben* in a small theater or in a traveling show might be called upon to work every kind of film, most specialized in one of the three lines of *katsuben* business: *jidai-geki* (Japanese period films), *gendai-geki* (Japanese films with contemporary settings),[76] and foreign films (*yōga*). The most versatile *katsuben* were, of course, often eager to show off their talents in all three genres.

The common practice was for one *katsuben* to work one film on a bill. But if a film was long or if a theater chose to show off its gaggle of *katsuben,* the person who started a film might be replaced midway by another *katsuben* who, without interruption, would pick up where the former left off.[77] Instant replacement such as this is a common practice of *jōruri* chanters in *bunraku* and Kabuki. Until the late nineteenth century, different Kabuki actors also alternated playing the same role during the same performance so that the audience could compare their respective talents. Sequential replacement further suggests the practice of *renga* poetry, in which several writers alternate in the composition of a poem. Their shared writing is an arena for the contesting of rival talents.

Some enthusiasts followed a film around as it played various theaters in order to catch what different *katsuben* did with the same movie.[78] The competitive aspects of *katsuben* performance were similarly emphasized when *katsuben* took turns doing the same film at different shows so that their abilities could be readily compared. These and similar competitive performance practices are called *kyōen* ("rival performances"). As in other Japanese performance arts and in sports such as sumo, *katsuben* were ranked in a national hierarchy as they strove for top positions in widely published *katsuben* popularity charts called *katsuben bansuke*.[79] The higher you were in the charts, the stronger your bargaining position with a theater manager.

Occasionally, *katsuben* assembled in "tournaments" (*taikai*) where each performed a small part of a program so that the talent of all could be readily judged. In some tournament performances, as many as fifty *katsuben* appeared at one theater during a week's run of a multiple-feature bill.[80] Such unrestrained matching of one's skills against those of one's peers was also common among directors. Two to four directors, each working for a different company, would make their respective film versions of the same popular novel for release around the same time. The appeal to audiences of these multiple versions was in contrasting the skills of the respective directors and the *kyōen* of their actors.

A 1931 *banzuke* which rates *katsuben* in the Tokyo area.[81]

In working out what he wanted to do with a film, a *katsuben* might decide to have a projectionist vary the speed of a scene to accommodate his feeling for proper pace or to move swiftly through something he found boring. Sometimes projection speed was varied because the *katsuben* wanted more or less time to speak.[82] In many theaters the *katsuben* had a button on his podium which he pressed to sound a buzzer in the booth. A typical instruction by buzzer was an order for an immediate change in projection speed. Two buzzes: crank faster. One long buzz: slow down. In jargon-prone show business, the term for this coordination of projection speed between *katsuben* and projectionists was *kokyū awase* ("breathing in unison").[83] In his definitive book on motion picture projection published in 1932, Kaeriyama Norimasa further suggested that the projectionist might vary the speed of the projector on his own initiative in order to reinforce the effect of a scene. Kaeriyama also advised that scenes of the imperial family should be projected slowly to show respect. He stated that the standard speed for taking and projecting films produced by major Japanese companies was sixteen frames per second. He implied that films from minor companies should be shown at less than this speed because they were shot at a slower frame rate to save money on film stock.[84]

Movie Theaters and the Industry

While precise documentation about who went to the movies in Japan is hard to find, anecdotes, theater addresses in directories, and vague statistics suggest that most movie audiences came from the Shitamachi[85] sections of urban and small-town Japan. This was where artisans, petite bourgeoisie, their families, and employees lived. Most movie theaters were in Shitamachi or in public amusement areas near them. Movies played to a smaller number of white-collar workers and even fewer proletarians and farmers. Foreign films attracted a large percentage of students and intellectuals.[86] As many of those who went to the movies tended to go frequently, the overall audience base was very narrow. Clearly one restraint for many people was the high cost. Adult admission at first-class movie theaters ranged from one-half to one-fifth of a white-collar or skilled workman's daily wages. Yose admissions were lower; live theater admissions, higher. Tickets to second-class movie theaters were half that of first-class.[87] Movies in Japan were not the entertainment of the poor.

Japan was a small exhibition market that devoured product. In terms of sheer output during the late 1920s and early 1930s, Japan's production of five hundred to seven hundred features a year was occasionally greater than the corresponding American output.[88] From the mid-1920s, the market share of foreign films continued to decrease even as total movie attendance was increasing. Japanese movies became dominant in the domestic market by 1925 and held on to their major share until the 1970s.

Many theaters, both first and subsequent run, played three features in shows that were four hours or more in length. Although total show time was less than that of a yose bill or a traditional six-hour theatrical performance, the long movie program allowed a large number of katsuben to appear.[89] A precedent (but certainly not the model) for this expansion of performing opportunities is found in the gradually increasing length of early jōruri shows, which was necessitated in part to show off the expanding number of members in many jōruri troupes.[90] Once again, text was subordinate to performer perquisites and inspiration.

The standard exhibition practice was two shows a day in major theaters and one show a day in smaller houses. By shortening the length of the show, they could run three shows on holidays.[91] Rather than drop a few reels from the bill, the often preferred practice on crowded holidays was to crank the projector faster to make the show time shorter.[92] A chart used for adjusting projection speeds to accommodate the number of reels that had to fit into a given show time indicated that films might be speeded up to almost twice "normal" projection speed, but it is doubtful that holiday speed-ups ever went to this extreme.[93] There were also exceptions to the widespread multiple feature policy when some theaters ground out six shows a day with only a double bill.[94]

Half of the movie theaters in Japan had officially rated capacities of 500 to

800 persons. One authoritative source shows that during this period Japan had very few theaters with a capacity under 200.[95] Looking at their floor plans and counting the seats, it is obvious that standing room was included in these computations. The standees who could be accommodated in the wide aisles next to the side walls of a theater were frequently equal to the number of seats in a theater.[96] Capacity figures did not include the additional standing room available to those who were sold full admission tickets that allowed them to stand *outside* the theater and look at the screen through open exit doors.[97] During the same 1920s, almost 50 percent of the movie theaters in the United States had *fewer* than 350 seats.[98]

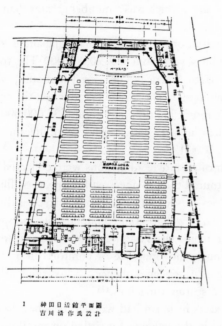

Architect's floor plan of a typical mid-1920s theater.[99]

1   神田日活館平面圖
     吉川清作氏設計

One reason why smaller-capacity theaters were not feasible in Japan was the relatively high expense of the essential *katsuben*. Star *katsuben* earned as much as top film directors and many movie stars. The ratio of other theater employees to theater capacity was also probably higher than in America. The overall high costs of exhibition relative to net film rentals and film production negative costs suggest an inefficient distribution-exhibition system that was and is typical of the Japanese retail economy. The film business could not take full advantage of mass-production economies inherent in the ability to make multiple cheap copies from the negative of one picture. The structure of the American industry allowed thousands and thousands of low-cost, low-admission small theaters to survive with only fair or marginal business. This broadened the dissemination of motion pictures even if the net return to the studios at this final end of the market was not great. With comparatively high ticket prices and few theaters, movies in Japan could not consistently attract audiences large enough to spread the cost of production over many bookings and thereby provide greater profit to studios or even larger production budgets. For maximum mass-production economy, better to have one film do 1,000,000 admissions than five similar films do a total of 1,000,000 admissions.[100] Instead, Japan in 1926 produced 855 features (films four or more reels in length), which was a number greater than all of the theaters in the country.[101]

By the late 1920s the total capitalization of the four major Japanese film companies, including their theater holdings, was about $19–20,000,000. This total was only two-thirds the value of the large American company Paramount, with its studios and extensive theater holdings.[102] The overall production-through-exhibition investment in the Japanese movie industry was about $30,000,000.[103] Movies in Japan became a more efficient industry with a high level of investment, receipts, and profits only after World War II.

During the 1920s about one-fifth of all movie admissions were collected by traveling exhibition companies that toured the provinces with projectors, films, katsuben, and orchestra. These troupes of six to twelve people played in Buddhist temples, Shintō shrines, and tents, as well as in hired public halls and small general-purpose theaters.[104] Although major cities had a few first-class theaters, even a trip to the best of these brought no opulence or comfort on a scale like that which attracted European and American audiences to luxurious urban movie palaces with multiple-thousand seating capacities.[105]

Most of the principal movie theaters in Japan had wooden benches downstairs and sometimes matting (tatami) in the balcony for sitting on the floor.[106] The architecture of the typical wood and stucco movie house duplicated that of old-fashioned live drama theaters known as shibaigoya ("play shacks").[107] Japan did not construct fancy theaters until several years after the advent of talkies. Most Japanese movie houses were closer in hovel comfort to their third- and fourth-class counterparts abroad. By 1930, the number of theaters had increased to 1,392, and annual attendance was up to almost three visits per capita. In the same period, the United States had sixteen times as many theaters and a much greater number of annual admissions.[108]

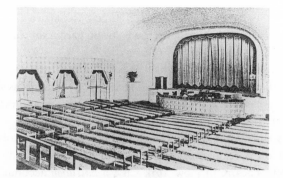

Interior of a first-run theater in Tokyo,
1924.[109]

The Golden Age

Few of the earliest *katsuben* had any prior performance experience. They entered the business without any special preparation for the job. Although theater chains controlled by the studios set up short-lived *katsuben* schools, the preferred training for *katsuben* was the individualized master-pupil system of Japanese traditional arts. When pupils were ready to debut, they were first assigned to newsreels, then worked up to short "interest films" and on to comedy shorts before they got to perform with a feature.

During the 1920s, the performance level, the literary standards, the quality of people in the profession, the wages, the opportunities, the social standing, and the future prospects of *katsuben* all improved. The Golden Age of the *Katsuben* (in a history as generalized and conventional as this, we must have a golden age) came between 1927 and 1931. I have found no *Katsuben* Golden Age director who acknowledged that he made his films dependent on *katsuben* performance. Looking at the writings of critics and at the recorded impressions of directors of the era, I am surprised by the large number who, although by no means unanimous, liked and even passively supported what the *katsuben* added to the film experience.[110] The Shōchiku company's leading senior director, Nomura Hōtei, boasted that he paced his 1929 hit film *Haha* (*Mother*) to the speaking style of his favorite *katsuben*.[111] Director Kinugasa Teinosuke wrote that he was impressed by what Tokugawa Musei, a specialist in foreign films and the top *katsuben* of all time, added to his *Kurutta ippeiji* (*A Crazy Page/A Page*

Out of Order) on its initial release in 1926. He felt Tokugawa's "excellent explanation" (*"meikaisetsu"*) matched his own avant garde *shinkankakuha* ("new sensibilities" or "neo-impressionist") film style.[112]

When director Katsumi Masayoshi went to Berlin in 1933 to investigate German sound film production and was asked to show one of his silent pictures, he himself performed as a *katsuben*. A German critic was impressed by "the extraordinary art of the speaker [and] the persistence of the transparent use of different kinds of elocution."[113] Earlier, in 1929, when a Gosho Heinosuke feature played on a regular double bill with a Harry Langdon comedy at the Fifth Avenue Theatre in New York City, a *katsuben* accompanied the film in Japanese, even though it was aimed at local American audiences and had English-language intertitles.[114]

During the Golden Age, *katsuben* turned to other venues to develop their art as solo performers *unaccompanied* by movies. Record companies sold many records of abbreviated star *katsuben* performances.[115] After 1925, *katsuben* began to be heard on radio with their movie interpretations.[116] These *katsuben* programs, called *eiga monogatari* ("film stories"), remained popular until the mid-1930s. Broadcasts of the traditional storytelling arts were also popular and easily outnumbered dramas patterned after Western radio forms. Silent film stars also performed on radio programs known as *eiga geki* ("film dramas"), which were full-dialogue versions of their current silent film hits. With the coming of talkies, NHK (the Japanese Broadcasting Corporation) developed a commingled radio form known as *tōkī chūkei* ("talkie remote broadcasts"). These were live broadcasts direct from a movie theater where a foreign film was being shown. The *katsuben*'s performance in Japanese was heard over the original foreign-language track, which was played as background at a lower volume level.[117] Star *katsuben* also published anthologies of transcriptions of their most popular film interpretations.[118] These were called *eiga setsumeishū* ("anthologies of film explanations") and followed the established *rakugo, kōdan, shimpa,* and Kabuki practices of publishing partial or complete scripts of performers' most popular pieces.

| *Katsuben* and Traditional Storytelling

Because *katsuben* did not come from any established storytelling tradition, their vocal styles were eclectic. What they needed for their peculiar modern art, they adapted from the traditional noncommingled storytelling arts: *kōdan, rōkyoku,* and *rakugo*.[119] All three of these forms have a solo performer who works without pictures and who offers personal variations of mostly familiar stories. All of these storytellers have a repertoire of gestures, facial expressions, and a fan or other props that are essential visual elements of their performances.

Kōdan evolved out of the public reading of epic texts during the fourteenth and fifteenth centuries. The principal book text was *Taiheiki* (*Chronicle of the Great Peace*), which was derived from oral storytelling traditions and composed of episodic stories about fourteenth-century civil war. Such written canon was gradually abandoned as *kōdan* evolved into a vocal narrative form with its own distinct repertoire of often-told tales. The oldest *kōdan* stories were about samurai in battle or the equally heroic deeds of *rōnin* and nonsamurai swordsmen. Two hundred years ago, the *kōdan* narrative world enlarged to include stories of love, crime, and ghosts among the common people.[120] *Kōdan* is a spoken prose medium with occasional descriptive sections done in rhythmic speech patterns. Major portions of *kōdan* stories are dialogue passages during which the storyteller performs the voices of his characters. Because *kōdan* with its focus on sword-carrying characters was the principal story source for early Japanese costume films, *katsuben* readily borrowed elements of its vocal style.[121]

Symbiosis in the world of Japanese narrative is well illustrated by *kōdan*. During the eighteenth century, *kōdan* expanded its unwritten repertoire by borrowing from widely published contemporary novels. Subsequently, in the mid-nineteenth century, many *kōdan* stories became the basis for new Kabuki plays. Several decades later, *rakugo* performers who were losing audiences to *kōdan* took *kōdan* tales and adapted them to create a new and less humorous *rakugo* genre known as *ninjōbanashi* ("tales of human nature").[122] Around 1885, transcriptions of *kōdan* performances captured in shorthand began to be published in small books. These were soon widely sold as a new form of printed popular literature "written" in the contemporary vernacular. In turn, these *kōdan* books became not only the principal story sources for *kowairo*-based costume films[123] but also the inspiration for the original writing of new kinds of swashbuckling novels that served as the foundation for modern popular literature (*taishū bungaku*).[124] The widespread success of these *taishū bungaku* novels made them a good story source for the thrilling action plays created by the Shinkokugeki ("New National Drama") troupe in its efforts to create a new dramatic form that would be truly Japanese, modern, and popular. One of the newly created staging techniques of Shinkokugeki was the spectacular, realistic swordfighting style called *chambara*. Young film directors adapted *chambara* to the swordfighting scenes of their new, post-1921 action-filled costume movies (*jidaigeki*).[125] While this summary oversimplifies developments, it presents an accurate historical outline that merits detailed investigation by scholars interested in Japanese film or popular culture.

Rōkyoku (also called *Naniwabushi*) is a vocal narrative tradition dating from the nineteenth century that is related to *kōdan* and has an overlapping repertoire of stories. Dialogue scenes are performed in a manner similar to *kōdan*, but passages descriptive of characters' emotions and fates are sung to the accompaniment of a *shamisen*. The distinctive *rōkyoku* singing style, with its thick, nasalized voice production (*hanagoe*), influenced the vocal style of many *katsuben* who specialized in period stories.[126] Unlike *rōkyoku*, traditional *kōdan* and *rakugo* have no singing or chanting passages and no musical accompaniment.

Rakugo is a comic vocal narrative tradition dating from the sixteenth century. A major element of its appeal is how well a performer comes across with his own distinctive version of a story drawn from a large repertoire of stories without definitive versions.[127] Most of these stories, along with the basic *rakugo* topoi, are passed along aurally from master to apprentice. Spontaneity, or at least the appearance of same, is a fundamental requirement for *rakugo* artists. In addition to extensive dialogue scenes, the pieces include many stand-alone humorous observations about everyday life which interrupt the central story line for plot-and-diegetic-effect-be-damned diversion.[128] *Rakugo* provided *katsuben* with a delivery style for comedy films and a conversational idiom for everyday dialogue. Even more important, it provided a precedent for the close *katsuben* and audience relationship.[129]

A *katsuben* kicks out his storyteller competitors and other *yose* rivals.[130]

The *katsuben* and the movies that accompanied them were the principal competitors of these traditional storytellers. Box office receipts for all three of these performing arts declined as they lost audiences to *katsuben* movies. Live drama was not quite as quickly affected.[131] The *katsuben* had no professional relationship with the older vocal narrative professions because the latter were closed professions that required long periods of apprenticeship to masters, although some lesser lights quit traditional storytelling ranks to became *ka-*

tsuben.[132] The early film exhibition business also attracted many street showmen and vendors from the outer fringes of entertainment and commerce. All over the world, these Barnums of the byways have distinctive ways of crying out to attract and sell to customers. In Japan, their pitches—commonly called either *shōnin yūbenjutsu* ("merchant eloquence") or *shōnin oshaberi* ("merchant prattle")—became yet another influence on eclectic *katsuben* vocal styles.[133]

Contemporary writers divided *katsuben* vocal techniques into two general types. The most prevalent style was *kataru,* which in this context meant "speaking voice." *Katsuben* of this type relied largely on conversational syntax and tone. The other approach was *utau,* which literally means "singing."[134] Those working in this style incorporated touches of *rōkyoku* and *jōruri* as they often performed narration in songlike rhythms.[135] *Utau katsuben* were usually specialists in swordfighting films.

Regional styles among *katsuben* were important and distinctive. In the Kamigata (Osaka) area, *katsuben* were said to be more oratorical and dramatic, while those in the Kantō (Tokyo) area were conversational.[136] The traditional performing arts also made sharp distinctions between Kamigata and Kantō styles, although not of the same kind. Following the national obsession with taxonomy, different critics created their own idiosyncratic classifications of *katsuben* styles. Ike Toshiyuki recently defined the basic Tokyo styles as *riarizumu* ("realism," meaning "conversational" in this context), *roman* ("Romantic," suggesting melodramatic tendencies), and *koten* ("classic," which meant the *katsuben* borrowed phrases and images from classical literature). He posited four schools for Osaka: *kochō* ("bombastic" or exaggerated style), *senchi* ("sentimental," or enough to make you cry), *shōjokageki* ("girls' operetta," which was sweet and rhythmical and based on a modern theatrical form born in the Osaka area), and *ogosoka* ("solemn" and homiletic like a Buddhist sermon).[137]

Another recent writer, Misono Kyōhei, found the styles of *katsuben* in Tokyo related to the geographical areas of the city. Those in Asakusa, the largest and oldest amusement area, tended toward *shichigochō* (traditional 7-5 poetic meter) because most of their audiences came from the old-fashioned petite bourgeoisie who were also patrons of traditional storytellers. In Yamanote, a ring of new residential areas inside the city limits, *katsuben* drew more up-to-date white-collar audiences, and so they preferred a conversational *kataru* style.[138]

While traditional storytellers perfected a personal repertoire through repeated performances over the years, *katsuben* could view a film only once or twice before they had to go on. They worked with notes or a rough script which they put together before the first performance. They also ad-libbed when the spirit moved or when lack of time for preparation compelled them.[139] The following week, there would be another new film or two to do. Surviving examples of *katsuben setsumei* reveal occasional high levels of literary talent and prove that quite a few had a fair education in the classics. Some could instantly compose lyric passages in the *shichigochō* syllable structure that dominates Japanese poetic composition and incorporate the conventional figures and intertextuality of traditional literature.[140] No one suggested that *katsuben* explanations were equal to the work of the best poets, although fans repeated parts of a *katsuben's setsumei* ("explanation") like music fans repeated the lyrics of a song.[141] Sometimes film interpretations were so successful that *katsuben* kept them alive in their personal repertoires long after the pictures were out of circulation. Tokugawa Musei performed his *Cabinet of Dr. Caligari* for half a century—usually without the film.[142]

Katsuben Functions

In my search through writings about *katsuben,* I discovered no elegant unified theory of *katsuben* performance. There was sufficient consensus in 1920s texts to suggest that *katsuben* performance had three major functions. Not that every *katsuben* could adequately handle all three. Or even attempt all three. My summary of this consensus is this: the ideal *katsuben* should be a (1) narrator and voice actor; (2) commentator-reader; and (3) audience representative.[143]

In the first and universally acknowledged of these roles, the *katsuben* was held to be essential to the movie experience in order to enhance the voiceless film with his vocal art. By appealing to senses other than sight, he made the movie a fuller sensual experience.[144] As narrator and voice actor, the *katsuben* read the intertitles aloud. Because almost everyone in the audience could read, *katsuben* were not required at movie shows to help illiterates comprehend the intertitles. There was no need for this. Japan's literacy rate was already higher than that of the United States. Of course, as few Japanese could read foreign languages, a *katsuben,* ignoring the intertitle pony in front of him, could be much freer in his translation and creation of dialogue for a foreign film.[145]

The *katsuben* not only read the spoken intertitles but also added additional talk to make scenes of apparent conversation on screen work more like full theatrical dialogue. Because the *katsuben* was an interpreter and not a ventriloquist, there was no need to read every title verbatim or to match lip movements of the actors.[146] While the *katsuben* used various voices to designate who was speaking, consistent delineation between characters was not always practiced. Most *katsuben* worked with a few stock voices. They indicated characters rather than imitate them. As in *jōruri* and the traditional storytelling arts, it was not always clear which character was speaking. Sometimes the audience could not be certain if the dialogue heard was the direct voice of a character speaking or the narrator's indirect report of what a character said. Japanese written literature, including modern novels, also has this tendency to elide the speaker as well as not indicate what is direct or indirect speech.[147] Despite the immediacy of the moving image on the screen and its illusion of events happening now, most *katsuben* treated a film as a recording of past events rather than as events now unfolding. A film was more of a document of the heretofore and less an illusion of an event happening now before our eyes.

In narration (nondialogue) passages, the *katsuben* gave exposition, bridged scenes, created additional narrative details about things not explicit on screen, and reported on characters' emotions and motives.[148] At a *katsuben* performance, there was a continuing tension between what the audience saw on the screen and what it heard from the *katsuben*. Novelistic irony was a possibility. Feelings and thoughts of characters were either omnipotently described or expressed obliquely through conventional poetic imagery. Interior monologue and psychological description were apparently seldom used. Because *katsuben* narration practices were similar to those employed in traditional drama, in certain major scenes the emphasis was on the narrated *description* of the emotions of a character rather than on *enactment* of those emotions.[149]

By locating the film experience within the Japanese vocal narrative tradition, the *katsuben* repudiated film as a Western-based dramatic form. Recent Japanese drama scholarship finds concepts based on Aristotle of the *Poetics* almost useless because the historic European concepts of drama are inapplicable to Noh, Kabuki, and other indigenous theatrical forms.[150] In this view, Japanese traditional theater is fundamentally a visual expansion of storytelling. Unlike European drama, traditionally based Japanese drama is a presentation in which (1) actors do not autonomously enact events for spectators; (2) dialogue spoken by actors is not the primary speech modality; and (3) basic plot structure is not based on conflict, crisis, climax, resolution, and dramatic unity.

In ways that resembled similar epithet devices in both Japanese and non-Japanese storytelling traditions, *katsuben* developed formulaic phrases which they occasionally repeated for subsequent films. The most familiar of these *katsuben* formulas was "*haru ya haru*," which could be employed to close scenes of young love blooming in vernal seasons. "*Haru ya haru*" has the meaning of "spring, ah, spring" and suggests "youth, ah, youth." This phrase, relentlessly repeated in nostalgic writings about silent movies and *katsuben,* came from an ending created by *katsuben* Hayashi Tempū for *Southern Justice,*[151] an American film of great seminal influence on the Japanese cinema.[152]

> Out of the misty darkness
> Spring radiating
> Throughout every village
> Stars all scattered
> Across a lavender sky
> Blossoms blown like snow
> Over the green earth.
> Spring, ah, Spring. Youth, ah, youth. Spring:
> Romance in the South.
> [As the final scene fades out and "The End" appears:]
> The title of this film: *Southern Justice*. In five reels.[153]

The last line was the second most frequent formula for ending a performance. The most common phrase would have been "The film *Southern Justice* has ended."[154] Endings in Japan often come with such simple prorogue expressions rather than with structural closure.

Commentator and Explainer

In the *katsuben*'s second function as commentator and explainer, the task was "to interpret and analyze a film."[155] This required the *katsuben* to move beyond narration of a story. On its most obvious level, this function derived from the early days of *katsuben* when they were explainers of exotic things seen on screen. With foreign films especially, it was felt necessary to talk about strange customs and offer discourse outside the story.[156] Such material did not have to be relevant to the development of the plot. Indeed, anything in the film could be an invitation to digress, but the discussion had to be interesting and in aesthetic balance with other elements of the total presentation. This kind of sidebarring is a prominent trait of Japanese literature, where plot itself can be decoration. Similarly, many classic anthologies of poetry give more space to background about the poems than to the poems themselves.

As in traditional storytelling, what mattered was turning a given story into a personal interpretation. Carping critics commented on the divergence of *katsuben* interpretation from the intent of the filmmaker.[157] But to most audiences, the film was an open text and one element in a complex, mixed-media, live entertainment. A large part of the pleasure for the audience was in the *katsuben*'s creative and critical reading of the film. But certainly that was not the pleasure for everyone in the audience. Some film viewers preferred the pure film unadorned by commingled vocal performance. They felt the *katsuben*'s pleonastic art was an intrusion on the primacy of the images. One author of a *katsuben* textbook warned that the *katsuben*'s words could easily distort the work of actors, writers, and directors. Then he noted that a talented *katsuben* might also enhance their efforts and cover up their deficiencies.[158] While friendly to *katsuben* but not dependent on them, director Inagaki Hiroshi acknowledged that a *katsuben* could "make a bad movie good."[159]

Other 1920s writings about *katsuben* suggested that a film, unlike the typical literary composition, had three authors (*sakusha*): scriptwriter, director, *katsuben*.[160] Like those Japanese poetry traditions based on multiple, successive authorship, the finished work became a kind of palimpsest in which the poet took an existing poem and superimposed his or her own composition on the original. The original remained but was transformed by another's vision.[161]

A *katsuben* who felt that a picture was uninteresting might choose to work against it and turn bad melodrama into comedy.[162] One example of the possibilities was a popular, libidinous Tokyo *katsuben* who found and exploited sexual innuendo in even the most innocent scenes on screen.[163] The dominance and apparent reality of the photographic images on the screen could be deconstructed by the *katsuben*'s words and demeanor.[164] Indeed, the presence of the *katsuben* attacked the ontological status of the film. Was truth in the photographic images or in what the *katsuben* said?

Katsuben argued about what their *primary* purpose should be. This division of opinion can in part be attributed to various matters of social status. Poor as school teachers might be, they were honored with higher social status. Entertainers such as *katsuben* were near the bottom of the social scale regardless of their success and wealth.[165] A small minority of *katsuben* saw themselves first as teachers and their work as an occasion to amusingly convey information about the world. Some accented this mission by using elevated language and difficult words. Government officials continually called for better-educated *katsuben* who would instruct audiences in the moral lessons to be drawn from films. Similar uplifting demands were not made on traditional storytellers. Despite the pressures to make a movie teach, the majority of *katsuben* saw their primary role as entertainers whose success could be measured only in terms of how well they entertained audiences.[166]

| Audience Representative

The third function of the *katsuben* was to perform as the "chosen representative of the audience."[167] Movies required a communal response under the leadership of the *katsuben*.[168] Part of the *katsuben*'s job was said to be to react to the film as a viewer and convey his or her reactions to the audience. One critic described this as the necessity to "intoxicate the audience" and "induce . . . mass emotional response."[169] Even novels written for individual reading require this kind of palpable reaction. J. Thomas Rimer concluded that "in the Japanese tradition the climax of any sequence lies not in the event itself but rather in the genuineness and spontaneity of the human response to that event. . . . The strategies of so many of the great narrative works in the Japanese tradition lie in an ability to ease us into that realm of feelings."[170]

Several writers proposed that the words spoken by the *katsuben* were less important in moving the audience than the emotional expression *in* their voices and *on* their faces—even though you could hardly see a *katsuben*'s barely illuminated features during the movie.[171] Like other Japanese performers, *katsuben* objectified the act of performing to make their performances transcend the meaning of their words. The process was what entertained. It was what made the event art. For instance, the Kabuki actor accents his apartness from the role he plays because actors must have a simultaneous dual identity on stage: self and character. In Kabuki, there is a continuing tension between creating and eliminating the distance between the work/performer and the audience. The *katsuben*-audience relationship was no different. As in Kabuki, enthusiasts cheered on favorites at their entrances or before virtuoso passages with cries like "*Matte imashita!*" ("We've been waiting for you!") and "*Daitōryō!*" ("President!").[172] These cries (*kakegoe*) for *katsuben* were much more informal than those heard in drama theaters. They lacked the traditional precision and insider knowledge common to those who yell out from the audience at Kabuki performances. And not all cries from the movie audience were complimentary. *Katsuben* who were too torpid, droll, or drunk might be greeted with, "Get serious!" or "Give up the sake and talk straight."[173]

As this essay at this point has turned into rhapsody, I may have pushed beyond the limits what *katsuben* were, could be, and might have been. I confess that at rare postwar revivals of *katsuben* performances,[174] I have personally witnessed *katsuben* (and heard about many others) whose talent and ambition limited them to the perfunctory reading of intertitles. But I have also been in the audience at transcendent *katsuben* performances when the movie experience did become much more than a look at moving pictures.

The new medium of motion pictures first appeared throughout the world at a time when much of modern European theater was distancing itself from direct interplay with audiences to move toward further realistic illusions. The fourth wall of the new realist theater was more than an imaginary conceit. It was a real barrier that kept those in the audience apart from performers in order to make them more passive observers of the proceedings. Moving pictures, formed only of intangible photographic images, further distanced audiences from direct human contact with the show in front of them. What movie audiences beheld overseas were moving shadows on a flat surface. Meanwhile, Japanese storytelling and nineteenth-century Kabuki continued the ancient intercourse between audience and artists. The *katsuben* brought this live, reciprocal relationship to the movies. The *katsuben*'s presence denied film as a depersonalized, mass-produced object and made every show a unique, human-crafted experience. It was more than a coincidence that many of the Japanese calling for the autonomous film and the abolition of *katsuben* were the pioneers of modern, European-originated theater in Japan.

Film Music

Each of the three *katsuben* divisions (*jidai-geki, gendai-geki,* and foreign films) developed its own form of musical accompaniment.[175] As narrative films from abroad became popular in the mid-1910s, theaters added small Western-style ensembles to play in a style derived from the European martial music adopted by the Japanese military. As previously described, films made in the theater-analogue *kowairo* manner were accompanied by *shamisen* and *narimono* borrowed directly from Kabuki. When this early type of Japanese film began to disappear after 1920, the *shamisen* and sometimes the other principal *narimono* instrument, the *taiko* (large drum), were incorporated into Western-style ensembles to produce a unique syncretistic musical form for *jidai-geki,* those Japanese period films done in the modern manner. Many of the tunes used for *jidai-geki* music were adapted from traditional folk and theatrical music by transposing them into a European-flavored idiom.[176] A musical tradition related to the *katsuben jidai-geki* music survives today in the simple tunes played by *chindonya,* who are street performers engaged by Shitamachi shop owners to publicize the opening of stores or bargain sales.[177] Only a store that wants to emphasize traditional values employs the old-fashioned *chindonya.* The generic name for this kind of music is *jinta,* which comes from its rhythm: *jin-ta-ta jin-ta-ta.* Foreign films and most *gendai-geki* used European-style program music.[178]

Even the smallest movie theaters employed an ensemble whose principal Western instruments were piano, violin, and clarinet or coronet (or trumpet). This was augmented with *shamisen* for *jidai-geki.* The higher-class urban movie theaters employed larger orchestras with eight to sixteen musicians in the pit. The best of these movie theater musicians became pioneers in the promulgation of Western classical and popular music in other venues in Japan. The solitary piano and the massive pipe organ, so common in the United States for pre-talkie films, were not popular in Japan.[179]

As elsewhere, prints often circulated with prearranged music cue sheets. A very special foreign film might come with a full score. After 1928, Japanese silent films were often distributed with a specially composed theme song that was sung live by a guest singer or, on rare occasions, by a *katsuben*. A film and the record of its theme song arrived on the market simultaneously to cross-plug each other. Because many movie theme songs became top hits, they played an important role in the development of modern Japanese popular music. Most of these original theme tunes were based on the Japanese pentatonic scale scored for Western instruments or were standard fox-trot idiom. After the coming of sound-on-film, movie theme songs flourished to a degree that did not occur in the United States until twenty-five years later.[180]

After Silents

The first sound-on-film and record-synchronized films in Japan were imported shorts. These, as well as feature-length musicals, were initially shown in a few major city venues without *katsuben* and without any kind of translation other than the plot summaries that always appeared in the printed programs that Japanese theaters handed out free to their patrons. During this transitional period, sound-on-film and record-synchronized features that had little or no dialogue but full musical accompaniment allowed *katsuben* to continue their regular movie interpretations without interference.[181] But the arrival of 100 percent talking films from abroad threatened *katsuben*. One form of resistance—or adaptation—was to turn off the sound track and do what *katsuben* had always done.[182] One of the biggest 1931 hits in Japan was Josef von Sternberg's German talkie *The Blue Angel*. On its initial release, it was usually shown silent with a *katsuben*'s live performance. Marlene Dietrich's songs were sung live in Japanese language versions by Japanese singers.[183]

This total replacement of the sound track by the *katsuben* was not necessarily good for business. When talking pictures were the scientific and entertainment rage of the world, theaters had to show talking pictures. Because these 100 percent talking pictures had to be heard to be believed, a new commingled form appeared. The sound track of a foreign film was turned down a bit so the audience could still hear the original synchronous dialogue and music. The *katsuben* then spoke over this subdued sound. This was tried with minor success with films such as Lewis Milestone's *All Quiet on the Western Front* (1930), which had relatively little dialogue, and with René Clair's "100 percent French

Talking and Singing Film," *Sous les toits de Paris* (1930). Enough of the original track of the latter came through to make its theme song a major hit in Japan.[184] Unfortunately, most foreign releases were too full of dialogue for this commingled form to work well. One critic described the Babel as "the movie talks and the *katsuben* yells."[185]

In 1931, von Sternberg's English-language *Morocco* was the first film to be subtitled in Japanese. Following the impressive box office success of *Morocco*, subtitling eventually became the standard practice for foreign talkies, but not before a few *katsuben* tried turning off the sound track and reading the superimposed subtitles.[186] There were, of course, strong precedents for the dubbing of foreign films into Japanese. The inescapable example was the ever-present *katsuben*. And earlier, theatre-analogue *kowairo* films had required live dubbing. Although dubbing of imported films became an established practice in several European countries during the early 1930s, dubbing did not become popular in Japan until after television made it the standard for that medium's imported programs and feature films. Subtitling remains the dominant practice for the theatrical release of foreign films in Japan.

Japan slowly increased its own sound-on-film production after 1931. Because Japanese films held two-thirds of the domestic market share, the conversion of the domestic industry to talkies was an even greater threat to *katsuben*. Faced with technological unemployment, *katsuben* went on strike. In 1932, there were 203 *katsuben* strikes against talkies. A decade earlier there had been concerted protests by *kowairo katsuben* against the introduction of intertitles in Japanese films.[187] Musicians began to lose their jobs before *katsuben* because (1) many early sound films had recorded musical accompaniment but little or no dialogue, so there was still a place in theaters for *katsuben*; (2) musicians were anonymous employees without specific box office appeal, so there was much less risk that audiences would be offended by their disappearance; and (3) unlike the *katsuben,* musicians had no strong union to offer cohesive resistance.[188]

Despite their attempts to halt the spread of talkies, *katsuben* by the hundreds began to lose their jobs. A few eventually became radio announcers, film narrators, actors, comedians, film critics, theater managers. Two later made it as major studio executives. Many more *katsuben* became traveling salesmen, office workers, shopkeepers, janitors, and day laborers.[189] Director Kurosawa Akira's elder brother, who was a *katsuben,* committed suicide.[190] A few *katsuben* recycled their vocal talents to create a new but minor act for *yose* halls called *mandan*. *Mandan* was essentially a routine in which two comedians (ex-*katsuben*) commented randomly on social foibles and events in the news.[191]

Katsuben had excellent preparation for this kind of act. They had to be good at improvisation in order to cover themselves when they didn't have time to prepare a script, or when the film broke, or when electrical power failed, or when a bicycled reel didn't get back to the theater on time.

Throughout the 1930s, minor companies which specialized in very low budget four- and five-reel *jidai-geki* features continued to make silent films for limited release. They also produced *setsumei tōkī* ("explanation talkies"), which were shot silent but released with recorded *katsuben* tracks.[192] A *setsumei tōkī* could also be shown silent if a live *katsuben* was available. At the height of the Golden Age in 1927, the National Police Bureau, which had the responsibility for licensing *katsuben,* reported that there were 6,818 *katsuben* throughout the Japanese empire. Of these, 180 were women.[193] In 1937, two years after talkies became the dominant form of domestic production, one-fifth of all new Japanese films were still silent. There were still 3,695 active *katsuben*.[194] Finally, in late 1941, the government prohibited the making of all minor studio silent films on the grounds that they had no redeeming social or moral values and that their swordfighter heroes were subversive of official ideology. A military procurement agency denounced these cheap movies as a waste of precious resources because the raw materials used to manufacture nitrate film stock could be used to make explosives.[195] The silent film in Japan literally ended with a bang.

Old prints of silent films continued to circulate. In 1940, 1,295 people still claimed they were professional *katsuben*.[196] It is not clear how many venues remained open to them.[197] No doubt most of those *katsuben* were sustained only by the peculiar, abused, and eternal hope common to all show people: the business will pick up, just hang in there. They were just like their American show business contemporaries—those tap dancers, animal acts, and song-and-dance men—who survived only because they believed in the second coming of vaudeville.

In contrast to the situation in the United States, talkies caused little displacement of filmmaking talent in Japan. The studios signed on very few people from the theater. Director Hiroshi Inagaki claimed that Japanese silent film directors had fewer problems with film dialogue than their counterparts abroad. He concluded: "Although movies were made silent, the Japanese cinema had something from the earliest times called *katsuben*. Because of them, we directors were aware that when you went to a movie theater, voices came out of the characters on the screen. Shouldn't we really say that Japanese movies never had a silent period?"[198] Several actors did have a hard time making it to the talkies. Bandō Tsumasaburō, the greatest movie swordfighter of all time, had a weak voice which did not record well. Working with a speech teacher, he adapted a *katsuben* declamatory style for his new voice and went on to twenty more years of stardom.[199]

Katsuben were another story. Most were forced to leave show business at a time when it was difficult to find employment of any kind. Some struggled to make a living by performing *kamishibai* ("paper play"), which was a modern form of *etoki.* In *kamishibai,* the performer showed successive pictures painted on fifteen to thirty sheets of cardboard while reading aloud a text written on their reverse side. If he was really good, he ad-libbed. A *kamishibai* performer traveled around residential areas on a bicycle. When he saw a likely spot, he set up his picture frame stage, announced he was in the neighborhood, and first sold cheap candy to children. When enough had assembled, the kids got a short *kamishibai* show with their sweet. The stories were usually full of violence. *Kamishibai* was a direct precursor of the television cartoons and comic books of today's Japan.[200]

A *kamishibai* man sells candy before his show, 1956.[201]

Kamishibai originated less than a century ago and was always an economically marginal street trade that blossomed in hard times. After the Tokyo earthquake of 1923, many jobless persons (not *katsuben*) took up the trade. Although there were several thousand *kamishibai* performers during the depression years of the 1930s, activity exploded in the decade immediately after the end of the World War II, when 30,000 people tried their hands and voices at *kamishibai*. Few of these had the artistic competence of a good *katsuben*. Even fewer made a decent living.[202] But in their crude performances one could find hints of the *katsuben* art long after the Golden Age ended. As Japan began to prosper in the sixties, television replaced *kamishibai*.[203]

Kamishibai performance, Tokyo,
1988.[204]

Last Sunday, I took the above photograph of a man who claims to be "the last of the professional *kamishibaiya*" (paper play performers). Right now, I am again trying to rewrite the difficult final paragraphs of this essay. How do I get out of this? All I want is an ending, not closure. Why did I take this unfinished manuscript with me on a short visit to Japan? I am now seated at a little writing table in Kitazawa. It's a rainy weekday. Early morning. I hear a television program coming from somewhere. It's "Renzoku terebi shōsetsu" ("The Continuing Television Novel"). I've finally figured out that "Renzoku terebi shōsetsu" is both the title of this series and the label for its genre. Broadcast by NHK every morning six times a week since 1961, "The Continuing Television Novel" consists of daily quarter-hour installments of home dramas that run for several months to a year. Tokyo and Osaka still take turns producing the novels in this series. As far as I know, the current story is not an adaptation of a book but, like most of these television novels, an original work written for broadcast.

I begin to listen. From what I hear coming from the other room, I can catch most of what's happening. If there's a problem, it's with my comprehension of spoken Japanese. Voice-over narration not only recaps previous episodes but every so often talks about things that are happening right now on the tube. I don't have to look at this television drama. I hear it. Anybody who tunes in can follow the story and still get ready for the day without having to watch the set. Of course there are actors to be seen acting on the tube (at least they were there the last time I looked three days ago), but the mix of dialogue and a little narration tells me all of the story. If I went to the TV set, I'd see the characters in this fully produced drama. And they'd be doing what the narration says they're doing. I'd also notice the digital clock numbers that are continually superimposed (commingled?) over the image throughout the entire program. Even if you just listen and don't watch during your morning haste, you always

A *katsuben* greets his audience.

TEREMENTE

know where to glance for the correct time.[205] Depending on the appeal of a particular story, ratings for "Renzoku terebi shōsetsu" are sometimes as high as those for primetime shows. What survives after the *katsuben* is a continuing propensity toward vocal storytelling and commingled media.

NOTES

1. The sketch on the left is a caricature of Matsuda Shunsui, "the last of the *katsuben*." The word in Japanese above his head is *katsuben*. In the drawing at the right, two musicians in the pit are seen with a *katsuben* behind his podium. The illuminated sign on the left shows the title of the film now being performed.

2. Furuta, 135; Kata, "Taishū," 338; Kishi, 12.

3. The theater is the Kyōbashi Nikkatsukan in central Tokyo. The size and layout are typical of first-class movie theaters during the 1920s. The decor is atypically *moderne*. An empty *katsuben* podium is on stage at the left. The orchestra pit accommodates ten musicians. Horizontal banners at both sides of the proscenium announce current or coming attractions. (Kenchiku, *Katsudō shashinkan*, 1924:10.)

4. The term *eiga kaisetsu* was used in the Osaka area. It also means "film explanation." A *katsuben* was also called an *eiga setsumeisha* ("film explainer").

5. As Japanese nouns do not normally indicate number, *katsuben* is used in this essay as both a singular and a plural form.

6. An, 29–35; "Eiga jiji," 170; Furuta, 28–37; Kishi; Kobayashi, Victor; Mikuni, 306; Wade, 176–177.

7. There are many references to this practice scattered throughout the international literature of film. See Berg reference in Works Cited section. This description by actor Neil Schaffner of a job he took in 1907 sounds like a *katsuben*'s work: "I soon had an opportunity to do a single as an 'announcer' at the Delight Theater, a new movie house in Fort Dodge. . . . At the Delight I stood on a platform to one side of the screen and described the action as it unfolded, calling attention to more subtle aspects of the picture" (Schaffner, 25).

8. Yoshida, "Katsuben," 9:82.

9. Yamaji. Details about women *katsuben* (who no doubt played a larger role than I have indicated in this essay) will require discovery of sources other than those I found.

10. Furuya, 24; Kinugasa, 19; Kurosawa, 75; Ōta, 142; Tanaka, *Nihon*, 1:211–212.

11. Anderson, Research; Furuta, 124, 191–192; Itami, 244, 250; Yoshida, "Katsuben," 7:49.

12. Ōta, 146. Ōta calls his chapter "Chapurin eiga no meichōshi," and his text establishes the context for my more than literal translation.

13. Ueda, *Literary*, 225.

14. Mason; Okudaira, 64–67.

15. The illustration is a detail from the sixteenth-century *Dōjōji engi* (*The Legend of Dōjō Temple*) *emakimono*. The writing on the scroll is primarily dialogue and is roughly equivalent to dialogue found in the balloons of twentieth-century comics. This scroll is kept at Dōjōji in Wakayama Prefecture, where the story is supposed to have taken place.

16. Hibbett; Morris, 44–48; Tsubouchi Shōyō; Ueda, *Literary*, 27.

17. Saikaku wrote the semi-erotic novel which became the basis for Mizoguchi Kenji's 1952 film *Saikaku ichidai onna* (*The Life of a Woman by Saikaku*, known abroad as *The Life of O-Haru*). See Morris reference in Works Cited section for an English-language translation. This version omits many of the original pictures, which leads me to suspect that somebody has forced the translation to conform to the dominant Eurocentric tradition of literary purity and isolation of literary forms from other media. On the other hand, the relatively few pictures may be due less to aesthetic decorum and more to a parsimonious publisher.

18. See Sekiyama.

19. Ruch, 288.

20. Ruch, 289.

21. The illustration shows only one kind of *etoki* performer. A *Kumano bikuni* (nun from Kumano) talks and unrolls her narrative scroll as her entertainment affects an intimate audience of well-to-do women. *Kumano bikuni* were also known as *etoki bikuni* (*etoki* nuns). They were neither pious nor celibate. (From *Kinsei kiseki kō* [*A Treatise on Recent Marvels*] by Santō Kyōden, 1804.)

22. Ruch, 298–301.

23. One of these is Dōjōji, where priests perform with the *Dōjōji* commingled *emakimono* shown in the previous illustration.

24. These include the Chinese *pien-wen*, Indian *śaubhika* and *paṛ*, Tibetan *ma-ṇi-pa*, Indonesian *wayang bèbèr*, Iranian *parda-dār*, Arab *tamāthīl*, Czech *krámarský*, Swedish *marknadsångere*, German *Bänkelsänger* and *Moritat*, Italian *cantambanco* and *cantastorie*, French *chanteur de foire*, Spanish *cantor de feria* and *retablo de las maravillas*, and American and British moving panorama reciter and magic lantern lecturer traditions. (Altick, 198–202, 208–209; Mair, 1, 19, 57, 93, 116, 119–131.) Contemporary practice of picture performance in the United States could be seen on the "Prophecy Marches On" television program carried by one of the religious cable networks during the 1990–91 season. Minister John G. Hall preached in front of a gigantic painting which showed the fulfillment of biblical prophecies. Everything in his sermon was reinforced by some part of the painting, to which he made frequent reference. As he glanced frequently at the painting, its many images suggested to him additional topics even as they inspired him to greater ecstasy.

25. Mair, 12.

26. The word *usually* in this essay indicates that there is (1) additional evidence for a variety of minor different practices, or (2) a lack of definitive evidence to support non-qualified generalization.

27. A *Bänkelsänger* ("bench singer") tells a commingled story with pictures in 1765. Under his arm are broadsides that he sells after his performance. *Bänkelsänger* in a more modern form could be found in Germany as late as the 1960s. (See Eichler.)

28. I employ the term *narrator* in this article for a person who tells or reads aloud a

story in conjunction with other story-related elements such as actors or pictures. I use *narration* as a broad term for all nondialogue parts of a storyteller's story.

29. A *jōruri* chanter and *shamisen* musician perform downstage left (to the audience's right-hand side). Puppets and their manipulators occupy center stage. The play is *Tsubosaka reigenki* (*The Miracle at Tsubosaka Temple*).

30. *Sarushibai* should not be confused with *sarugaku*, one of the human actor forerunners of Noh.

31. Furukawa, 176–178; Kawatake, 3:13–14; Tsubouchi Hakushi, 460–461. For an extensive exploration of various kinds of monkey performances in Japan, see Ohnuki-Tierney.

32. A *sarushibai* roadside show with two monkey actors, a handler, and a *shamisen*-playing storyteller (probably a *jōruri* performer). They are apparently performing a *michiyuki* ("road traveling"/journey) piece in which two lovers flee—often to the place of their double suicide.

33. That most famous of all Japanese dramas, *Chūshingura*, provides ready examples. In an early scene of confrontation between two principal characters, the narrator begins by saying of one of them: "So sure is he of his own lordship's favor that without restraint he pounds in his abuse arrogantly, unconcerned that he may be exposing himself to attack." And only then does the character speak in that manner. (Takeda Izumo, 31.)

34. The magic lantern arrived in Japan soon after its appearance in Fantasmagoria (or Phantasmagoria) shows in Paris during the 1790s. Fantasmagoria also spread quickly to other countries in Europe and North America. Descriptions of the techniques that produce the projected moving images of Fantasmagoria indicate that they were similar to those of *utsushie* but were employed for different theatrical ends. The Japanese preferred to adapt the devices to replications of traditional dramatic fare, while the Europeans exploited them primarily for ghost illusions and other tricks. (Altick, 217–219; McKechnie, 176.)

35. See Matsuki.

36. Two projectionist-performers work from the floor with hand-held projectors. Stationary projectors at each far end project scenic elements which are arranged according to conventional Kabuki staging, with the principal entrance on the left (stage right). In the lower right corner of the illustration, the insert shows an articulated slide of a sword-carrying character. The three consecutive attitudes shown in rapid succession suggest the movement of a sword thrust. The illustration is a recent drawing.

37. The boxlike extensions on the front of the *utsushie* projectors support small lenses and are slid back and forth to adjust focus. The hole in the top of a projector is a vent for its kerosene lamp. The drawing was made at a twentieth-century performance. (Kobayashi Gentarō.)

38. Ei, 88–90; Fukuda; Furukawa, 240–243, 304–306; Kata, *Kamishibai*, 15; Kobayashi Ayako, n.p.; Kobayashi Gentarō, n.p.; Ozaki, 224–226.

39. To the right, under the large heading *yose*, are cushions for the seated audience. The dimensions of the screen (which is made of sheets of Japanese paper pasted together) are two *kan* (twelve feet) across and four *shaku* (four feet) high. A *doro* (gong) hangs from the right side of the table. Next to the *doro* are two *hyōshiki* (wooden clappers) connected by a short rope. Both *doro* and *hyōshiki* are used for nonrealistic sound effects. The boards which form the top of the projector table rest on empty boxes and barrels. At the far left is a cushion for the vocal performer. A support to hold his script is attached to the wooden box in front of his cushion. In this alternative set-up, the projectors are worked by projectionists who stand in back of the tables rather than kneel on the floor as shown in the two previous illustrations. (Kobayashi Gentarō, n.p.)

40. Katō, 140–141; Yoshida, *Mō*, 11–12.

41. Furuta, 34; Ike, 247; Kishi, 12; Masumoto, 12; Nishimura, 422.

42. The term for the *katsuben* pre-talk was *maesetsu* (prefatory comments). The *rakugo* forepart is called *makura,* whose literal meaning is "pillow." The *katsuben*'s performance during the film was termed *nakasetsu* (middle comments).

43. Morioka and Sasaki, 26–30; Novograd, 190–191; Ōnishi 106–107.

44. Misono, "Mukashi," 4–5; Yoshida, "Katsuben," 9:85.

45. Ishimaki, *Katsudō,* 180.

46. Takeda Akira, 28.

47. Negishi, "Hompō," 62; Tanaka, *Nihon,* 2:244–245, 270. The small number of prints struck for each title is no doubt a major reason why so few pre–World War II films survive.

48. Only a few of these early films—largely fragments—have apparently survived. The most accessible are *Chūshingura,* Yokoda Company, ca. 1910; *Jiraiya,* Nikkatsu, 1914; *Genroku Chūshingura (The 47 Loyal Rōnin of the Genroku Era),* Nikkatsu, ca. 1914; *Ninomiya Kanejirō,* Makino Kyōiku, 1920; *Gōketsu Jiraiya (Jiraiya, the Hero),* Nikkatsu, 1921; and *Yaji Kita Kikōji mairi (Yaji and Kita on a Pilgrimage to Kikō Temple),* Nikkatsu, 1921. Most of these films were made by Makino Shōzō, the major film producer-director of the 1910s. For a biographical account of the production of these theater analogue movies and early efforts to expand the filmic means of the moving picture form in Japan, see Makino, 27–85.

49. Shimaji, 11.

50. Kaeriyama, *Katsudō shashin geki no sōsaku to satsueihō,* 8–9; Tanaka, "Eiga," 98–99; Yoshida, "Katsuben," 4:45.

51. Kinugasa, 17–18.

52. Ōta, 142; Tanaka, *Nihon,* 1:215.

53. Berg; Schaffner, 26.

54. After the elimination of *shimpa*-based theater analogue films in the early 1920s, *shimpa* continued to be the strongest theatrical influence on the Japanese cinema. Its pervasive effects are found in the evolution of melodrama forms, female protagonists, and the uses of pathos and sentimentality, as well as more directly in film adaptations of *shimpa* plays and, conversely, *shimpa* dramatic adaptations of films. An important example of this affinity is the work of Mizoguchi Kenji. His work has many symbiotic and synchronous relationships with developments in *shimpa* drama.

55. These male performers were called *kido geisha* (theater entrance talents), and their art was known as *kageshibai* (shadow plays). Their imitations were sometimes straight and sometimes parodical. *Kowairo* was also known as *kagezerifu* (shadow dialogue).

56. Katō, 177–189; Ozaki, 222–224; Takahashi, 179–181; Tanaka, "Eiga," 98–99; Tokugawa Musei, *Musei,* 1:144; Tsubouchi Hakushi, 458.

57. *Narimono* is also known as *hayashi.* Its principal instruments are various-sized drums, small percussion, and Japanese lateral flute. The sound effects of *narimono* are seldom representational but are rather semantic signs for both aural and *visual* phenomena. For instance, flowing water and falling snow, which are major motifs in Japanese drama, are indicated by different kinds of beats on a large drum.

58. Ōi, 8; Ōta, 142; Tanaka, *Nihon,* 1:215; Yoshida, "Katsuben," 2:8–10.

59. Ishimaki, "Eiga," 41–42.

60. Furuta, 37–42; Shibata, *Jitsuen;* Tanaka, "*Uta*"; Yoshida, "Katsuben," 3:34–35.

61. Furuta, 40–42.

62. Masumoto, 16; Tanaka, *Nihon,* 1:232.

63. See, for instance, Pratt, 18. He indicates, among other things, that both D. W. Griffith and Cecil B. DeMille appeared as actors in American stage and film mixtures similar to Japanese chained drama before they entered mainstream movies. Similarly,

director Kinugasa Teinosuke's very first work in films was in chained drama in *onnagata* roles. (Masumoto, 56.)

64. Okamura (page reference lost).

65. See *Zenkoku.*

66. Furuta, 39–44; Muramatsu, 92–93; Tanaka, *Nihon,* 1:224–228.

67. Kaeriyama, *Katsudō shashin geki no sōsaku to satsueihō;* Shimaji, 22–30.

68. Hazumi, 119–122; Masumoto, 13–15, 41.

69. Kaeriyama, *Katsudō shashin geki no sōsaku to satsueihō,* 9.

70.Iijima, "Nihon," 108–111, 121–123; Kaeriyama, *Katsudō shashin geki no sōsaku to satsueihō,* 5–13; Tanaka, "Eiga," 100–103; Yoshida, *Mō,* 77–90.

71. Ishimaki, *Katsudō,* 181; Tanaka, *Nihon,* 1:262; Yamamoto, 42; Yoshida, *Mō,* 81–84.

72. Misono, "Mukashi," 3.

73. Mifune, 194.

74. Kishi, 12.

75. Tokugawa Musei, *Musei,* 2:178.

76. Conventionally defined as post-1868.

77. *Kurashikku,* 203:4; Yoshida, *Mō,* 109.

78. Misono, "Mukashi," 6.

79. Furuta, 47; Yoshida, *Mō,* 180–181, 186.

80. Nihon Eiga Terebi, 101–102.

81. The heading at the top of the *banzuke* reads "Kantō setsumeisha ichiranhyō" ("A Listing of Kantō [Tokyo-area] Explainers [*katsuben*]"). Running across the top of the chart in large print are the names of ten major *katsuben* who are given the highest rank of *tōsui* (the supreme command). Running down the extreme right- and left-hand sides are the names of eighteen lesser *tōsui*. Next in rank are the *bekkaku* (extraordinary), whose names in vertical smaller print flank those of the lesser *tōsui*. In somewhat descending order in boxes going down the middle of the chart are *ryūko* (heroes, literally "dragons and tigers"), *chūken* (the stalwarts), *shinshin hanagata* (up-and-coming stars), and *rōrenjukutachi* (old masters). Of the 925 *katsuben* listed, 806 are unranked. The military terms in this chart were only one way to structure a *banzuke* hierarchy. Ranking by sumō titles (such as *yokozuna, ōzeki*) was the most common. It is unlikely that this *banzuke* is a complete listing of all *katsuben* in the Kantō area. Recordings of three of the *katsuben* rated here as the top *tōsui* are found in the Works Cited and Consulted section (Kunii; Matsuda, *Natsukashi* [with Tokugawa Musei]; Tani).

82. Furuta, 122; Ichinohe, 411; Nishimura, 423; Yume (page citations lost).

83. Ichinohe, 411.

84. Kaeriyama, *Katsudō shashin eishahō,* 235. Until the coming of sound-on-film, directors were also interested in varying camera speeds as an expressive device. For instance, in 1931, Ozu Yasujirō and Shimizu Hiroshi discussed their respective interests in slightly "overcranking" (which produces slower motion). ("Eiga jiji," 159–60.) See also Yanagi, 16.

85. Literally "low town" or "down town," the location of small stores and work-shops which also housed the living quarters of their owners. See also Edward Seiden-sticker, who in *Low City, High City* (New York: Knopf, 1983, 8–11, 85–86, 349–351) makes a related distinction between the "low city" and "high city" areas of Tokyo.

86. Relevant data are contained throughout the following: Mifune, 193–195; Narusawa; Shibata, *Ōsaka;* Tachibana Takashirō; Yanagi, 17–20; *Zenkoku.*

87. Ishimaki, *Katsudō,* 193; Mifune, 193; Shōji, 271.

88. Ishimaki, "Eiga," 28.

89. Furuta, 35; Nihon Eiga Terebi, 39–46 passim, 111–172 passim; Takahashi, 191.

90. Yūda, 20–21.

91. Ishimaki, "Eiga," 28; Nihon Eiga Terebi, 42, 45, 57; Ōta, 136–137; Sudzuky, 22.

92. Takeda Akira, 234.

93. Tachibana Takashirō, 92–93.

94. Amari, 422.

95. *Zenkoku.*

96. Ishimaki, *Katsudō,* 175–176; Kenchiku, *Katsudō shashinkan,* 1924:1–36.

97. Until 1931, theaters were required to segregate seating for women and men. It is not clear whether this division was maintained in standing-room areas. Theaters also had to provide special seats for police officers from the censorship bureau. (Mifune, 193–94.) A uniformed policeman had to be present at all shows to oversee the live and possibly unpredictable performance of the *katsuben.*

98. Ishimaki, *Katsudō,* 175–176; Koszarski, 24–26 (in manuscript).

99. This shows the layout of the ground floor of the Kanda Nikkatsukan (Nikkatsu Theater in Kanda), a first-run theater in central Tokyo. It is typical of major theaters built in Tokyo after the 1923 earthquake. Note the wide aisles to accommodate large standing-room audiences and the many exits along the sides of the theater. (Kenchiku, *Katsudō shashinkan,* 1924:1.)

100. Only in the early 1940s did Japan began to produce fewer films (with larger average print orders per film) which were shown to increasingly larger national audiences. (Tanaka, *Nihon,* 2:244–245.) This move to a more economically efficient production-distribution-exhibition system was the result of government-enforced consolidation of the industry to conserve and control resources for the war effort rather than the result of market forces.

101. Ishimaki, "Eiga," 28.

102. Negishi, "Tōshi," 58–59. The Paramount calculations are based on Negishi's data.

103. "Filmdom," 24. This may not be an accurate source.

104. Furuta, 30–31; Ishimaki, *Katsudō,* 164–166; Itō, 51; Kokusho, 34–35.

105. Kenchiku, *Katsudō shashinkan,* 1924 and 1926; Kokusho, 5–43 passim.

106. Mifune, 193.

107. Furuta, 29, 36; Takeda Akira, 206.

108. Alicoate, 106; Ishimaki, *Katsudō,* 163; Shimaji, 66.

109. The Kanda Nikkatsukan specialized in premiere releases of the Nikkatsu Company, one of the two largest movie studios of the era. Benches with padded seats and no backs like those shown in the photograph were the standard for first-run theaters. Benches in lesser houses had no padding. The plan for the ground floor of this theater appears in the preceding illustration. The Kanda Nikkatsukan was renovated and enlarged in 1929. (Kenchiku, *Katsudō shashinkan,* 1924:4. Also see Kajita.)

110. "Eiga jiji," 161–162, 170–171; Furuta, 163; Kinugasa, 20; Nishimura, 423; Takeda Akira, 228–235.

111. Nishimura, 423.

112. Kinugasa, 78–79.

113. Koch, 297.

114. Hall.

115. Furuta, 124–125; Katsumura, 190.

116. Ōta, 143.

117. Nihon Hōsō Kyōkai Hōsō Shi, 1:51–52, 94–95, 209, 220–221.

118. Furuta, 122, 125; Katsumura, 130.

119. Tokugawa Musei, *Musei,* 1:184; Yume.

120. Aritake, 9–24.

121. Tachibana Takahiro, 72–75.

122. Morioka and Sasaki, 5, 157–159.

123. Even in the late 1920s, Kawai Tokusaburō, head of a studio that made many cheap *jidai-geki* features, could proclaim, "All I need is a collection of *kōdan* stories and I can make movies." (Quoted in Arai, 414.)

124. Enomoto, 259–264.

125. Nagata, 38–69.

126. Kasu, 56–57; Matsuki.

127. Published transcriptions of *rakugo* stories taken in shorthand became another important influence on the Japanese novel during the late nineteenth century. (Enomoto, 253–259; Novograd, 189.)

128. Kata, *Rakugo*, 242–258; Morioka and Sasaki, 8–10, 21–27, 32–45.

129. While *jōruri* as a solo art (without puppets or actors) has a long tradition of women performers, only recently have women been admitted into the highest ranks of *kōdan* and *rōkyoku* professionals. Professional *rakugo* remains largely resistant to women performers.

130. This newspaper editorial cartoon from the *Asahi Shimbun*, 8 August 1908, is entitled "Moving Pictures, the Big Hit: The Moving Picture Man's Moves." A *katsuben* kicks a *yose* manager into oblivion while a *yose* performer cringes at lower left. The figures above the *katsuben* represent, right to left, *kōdan*, *rakugo*, and *Naniwabushi* (*rōkyoku*) performers.

131. Ishimaki, *Katsudō*, 163.

132. Narusawa, 233–293; Yoshida, *Mō*, 157, 162–168; Yume.

133. Katō, 139–145; Muramachi.

134. The distinction made here between *kataru* (or *katari*) and *utau* (or *utai*) *katsuben* should not be confused with the same two terms used in music and literature. In music, *katarimono* are narrative songs and *utaimono* are lyrical songs. In literature, the terms broadly distinguish between narrative prose and poetry.

135. Furuta, 132; Kishi, 13.

136. Ike, 16, 249–250.

137. Ike, 250–251.

138. Misono, "Mukashi," 5.

139. Furuta, 122; Iijima, "Nihon," 107–112, 122–123; Yoshida, "Katsuben," 6:36–37.

140. Ike; Kunii; Matsuda, *Natsukashi*.

141. Tachibana Takashirō, 88; Yoshida, *Mō*, 151.

142. Matsuda, *Natsukashi*.

143. Tachibana Takahiro; Takeda Akira, 237 passim.

144. Takeda Akira, 239; Yume.

145. Yoshida, "Katsuben," 10:41; Yume. The reel is now on the other projector—so to speak—because we in America now read the often inadequate, inelegant English-language subtitles of Japanese films.

146. Yoshida, "Katsuben," 7:50.

147. Reed, 74–75.

148. Ishimaki, *Katsudō*, 182; Yoshida, "Katsuben," 4:48.

149. Furuta, 163–165; Ike; Matsuki, 245–250 passim; Tachibana Takashirō; Tani.

150. Gunji.

151. Lynn F. Reynolds, writer and director; Bluebird Photoplays-Universal, 1917. Copyright description CLL 10691, May 2, 1917. Released in Japan in 1918. No prints are known to survive.

152. Anderson, "Some," 448–450.

153. Translated from text in Yoshida, *Mō*, 109. A variant text appears in Kata, "Taishū," 341. For over seventy years, one of the continuing controversies in Japanese film history is about who first used the phrase "*Haru ya haru*" ("Spring, ah, Spring; Youth, ah youth"). There are claims that Ikoma Raiyū originated it for his ending of the

same film. Ikoma performed *Southern Justice* at the same Tokyo theater as Hayashi Tempū. (For contrasting opinions and conclusions, see Kishi, 13; Misono, "Mukashi," 5; Yoshida, "Katsuben," 6:41–45; Yoshida, *Mō*, 109.)

154. Ike, 63, 75, 94, 100.

155. Takeda Akira, 243.

156. Komatsu and Musser, 74–75; Matsuki et al., 243; Takeda Akira, 237; Yume.

157. Yoshida, "Katsuben," 7:50. Yoshida is not the carping critic. He only reports on this kind of criticism in his history.

158. Matsuki et al., 66–67.

159. Inagaki, 42.

160. Sakai; Yume.

161. Konishi, 354.

162. Katsumura, 189; Koch, 296; Matsuki et al., 66–67.

163. Yoshida, *Mō*, 159–160.

164. From descriptions in Matsuki et al., 245–247; Yume.

165. A representative indication of the social status of *katsuben* is found in Nagai Kafū's short story "Ame shōshō" (translated as "Quiet Rain"). A rich company director who has been keeping a geisha as a mistress decides to abandon her when she starts to dally with a *katsuben*. The businessman confesses that he is a tolerant man of the world who would have expected and ignored the matter if she had had an affair with a Kabuki actor. He would even have put up with her playing around with *shimpa* or modern comedy actors but regards it as aesthetically unacceptable to have a mistress who stoops so low as to run around with the likes of a *katsuben* or chauffeur. (Kafū Nagai, *A Strange Tale from East of the River and Other Stories*, translated by Edward Seidensticker [Tokyo: Tuttle, 1972], 100–101.)

166. Ishimaki, *Katsudō*, 181; Tachibana Takashirō (page reference lost); Takada, 87, 175; Yume. In addition to being a film critic and the writer of a *katsuben* instruction book, Tachibana Takashirō (who also used the pen name of Tachibana Takahiro) was a police official in charge of film censorship in Tokyo.

167. Matsuki et al., 66–67; Takeda Akira, 239.

168. Yoshida, "Katsuben," 7:51.

169. Takeda Akira, 237.

170. Rimer, *Pilgrimages*, 132–133.

171. Matsuki et al. (page reference lost); Takeda Akira, 243.

172. Ike, 247; Misono, "Mukashi," 5.

173. Mifune, 194.

174. The principal organization dedicated to the preservation of the art of the *katsuben* and their films was the Musei Eiga Kanshōkai (Silent Film Appreciation Society) of Tokyo. It was founded by a second-generation *katsuben*, Matsuda Shunsui, who was billed as "the last of the *katsuben*." Matsuda died in 1987. His company, Matsuda Eigasha, continues to sponsor what are unfortunately a decreasing number of *katsuben* performances by Matsuda's pupils. Matsuda was a dedicated saver of old films long before there was any official or major public interest in preservation in Japan. He also sponsored an organization dedicated to the preservation of *kamishibai* (paper play), which is a commingled form discussed later. Audio recordings of *katsuben* continue to be available, as well as video cassettes of films with *katsuben* tracks. In the Works Cited and Consulted section of this article, see Kunii Shika; Musei Eiga Kanshōkai, *Ō katsudō*; Tani Tenrō; and all titles listed under Matsuda Shunsui. I am indebted to Mr. Matsuda for providing the inspiration for this study.

175. Narusawa (page citation lost).

176. Eiga Ongaku.

177. Musei Eiga Kanshōkai, *Jidai eiga*; Tokugawa Ichirō.

178. Satō Yasuhira,4.

179. Furuya, 15; Matsui, 14, 69–71, 127; Satō Yasuhira, 6; Shōji, 274–275; Tachibana Takashirō, 67–79.

180. Furuta, 30, 46, 141–151; Itō, 64; Komota and Shimada, 81–83; Misono, *Ā katsudō*, 76–78; Musei Eiga Kanshōkai, *Jidai eiga; Natsukashi no Nihon eiga*; Sudzuky, 22; Tachibana Takashirō, 60 passim; Yoshida, *Mō*, 12.

181. Tanaka, *Nihon*, 2:71–74, 85–86; Yoshida, *Mō*, 238–241.

182. Furuya, 55.

183. Matsuda, *Natsukashi*.

184. Furuya, 54; Nihon Eiga, 198; Tanaka, *Nihon*, 2:95–96.

185. Reported in Yoshida, *Mō*, 239.

186. Tanaka, *Nihon*, 2:95–98; "Yoki eiga"; Yoshida, *Mō*, 235–236.

187. Satō Tadao, 34.

188. Yoshida, *Mō*, 218.

189. Yoshida, *Mō*, 156–160, 241–242.

190. Kurosawa, 85.

191. Tokugawa Musei, *Wajutsu*, 178–180; Yoshida, *Mō*, 246–248.

192. Nishimura, 424; Tanaka, *Nihon*, 2:270, 279–281.

193. Yoshida, "Katsuben," 7:52–53.

194. Source citation lost but was among materials located in the Waseda Engeki Hakubutsukan Toshoshitsu in Tokyo.

195. Tanaka, *Nihon*, 2:241; other citations lost but were among materials located in the Waseda Engeki Hakubutsukan Toshoshitsu.

196. Yoshida, *Mō*, 245.

197. While it is well established that Japan took a full decade to shift all production to talkies, American conversion to the new technology was slower than conventional film histories indicate. In 1933, 22 percent of all operating American movie theaters were "unwired for sound." A year later this number had fallen only to 15 percent. (Alicoate, 106.) What movies did these unwired theaters play?

198. Quoted by Yoshida, *Mō*, 4.

199. Adachi, 103–104.

200. Kata, *Kamishibai*, 22–30, 269–276: Katō, 143.

201. The pictures are lined up, title card first, inside a wooden frame that suggests the borders of a motion picture screen. The frame that holds the pictures is called a *kamishibai butai* (paper play stage). This frame hangs from a large wooden box that contains drawers for the candy supply as well as the pictures for the rest of the performer's repertoire. The box is attached to the rear fender of his bicycle. The *hyōshiki* behind the *kamishibai* stage are clapped to attract children to the show and are also used for sound effects during the performance.

202. Kata, *Kamishibai*, 22–23, 198–199, 264; Kata, "Taishū," 389.

203. By 1971, there were fewer than 300 professional *kamishibaiya* in Japan. (Kata, *Kamishibai*, 273.) "Educational" and "home" *kamishibai* continue to be produced and sold in a limited market for amateur performance.

204. At the time the picture was taken, he was performing every Sunday afternoon in Nippori Minami Park, Tokyo.

205. Hence the nickname of the program, *tokei dorama* (clock drama).

WORKS CITED AND CONSULTED

Adachi Ken'ichi. *Taishū geijutsu no fukuryū (Undercurrents in the Popular Arts)*. Tokyo: Rironsha, 1967.

Alicoate, Jack, ed. *The Film Daily Year Book, 1959*. New York: Film Daily, 1959.

Altick, Richard D. *The Shows of London*. Cambridge: Harvard UP, 1978.

Amari Fukuyoshi. "Shōnen benshi tanjōki" ("An Account of the Birth of a Boy Benshi"). In *Natsukashi no fukkokuban: puroguramu eiga shi; Taishō kara senchū made (Nostalgic Reprints: A Film History According to Film Programs; From the Taishō Era [1912–25] through World War II)*, edited by the staff of Nihon Eiga Terebi Purodyūsā Kyōkai (Japan Film and Television Producers Association), pp. 421–422. Tokyo: Nihon Hōsō Shuppan Kyōkai, 1978.

Amino Yoshihiko et al., eds. *Daidōgei to misemono (Vagabond Entertainments and Curiosity Shows)*. Taikei Nihon rekishi to geinō daijūsankan (An Outline of Japanese History and Performing Arts, vol. 13). Tokyo: Heibonsha; Nihon Bikutā, 1991. Book and video cassette. VTMV-930.

An Ch'ung Hwa. *Han'guk yŏnghwa ch'ŭngmyŏn pisa (Byways of the Secret History of the Korean Cinema)*. Seoul: Ch'unchu'kak, 1962.

Anderson, Joseph L. Research notes, *Katsuben* performances and conversations. Tokyo, 1949, 1955–57, 1971, 1974–75, 1989.

————. "Some Second and Third Thoughts about the Japanese Film." In *The Japanese Film: Art and Industry (Expanded Version)*, by Joseph L. Anderson and Donald Richie, pp. 439–456. Princeton: Princeton UP, 1982.

Arai Katsuji. "Kamata yori Ōfuna made" ("From Kamata to Ōfuna"). In *Natsukashi no fukkokuban: puroguramu eiga shi; Taishō kara senchū made (Nostalgic Reprints: A Film History According to Film Programs; From the Taishō Era [1912–25] through World War II)*, edited by the staff of Nihon Eiga Terebi Purodyūsā Kyōkai (Japan Film and Television Producers Association), pp. 414–415. Tokyo: Nihon Hōsō Shuppan Kyōkai, 1978.

Aritake Shūji. *Kōdan: dentō no wagei (Kōdan: Traditional Storytelling Art)*. Tokyo: Asahi Shimbunsha, 1973.

Berg, Charles M. "The Human Voice and the Silent Cinema." *Journal of Popular Film* 4 (February 1975): 165–177.

Ei Rokusuke. "Taishū geinō no naka no hankotsuji: iromono" ("The Rebel in Popular Entertainment: Iromono [nonstoryteller *yose* acts]"). In *Dentō to gendai, daihakkan: taishū geinō (Traditional and Contemporary, Vol. 8: Popular Entertainment)*, edited by Nagai Hiroo, pp. 82–95. Tokyo: Gakugei Shorin, 1969.

Eichler, Ulrike. *Bänkelsang und Moritat*. Stuttgart: Staatsgalerie, 1975.

"Eiga jiji zatsudan no yūbe" ("A Night of Small Talk about Current Happenings in Film"). In *Eiga kagaku kenkyū kōza (Lectures on the Science of Motion Pictures)*, edited by Murata Minoru and Ushihara Kiyohiko, 2:158–176. Tokyo: n.p., [ca. 1928].

Eiga Ongaku Kenkyūkai (Society for the Study of Film Music), ed. *Eiga bansō kyokushū: jidai-geki zenshū (Musical Selections for Film Accompaniment: Period Films, First Collection)*. Tokyo: Shinfuonī Gakufu Shuppansha, 1927.

Eiga setsumei kōshū roku (A Course in Film Explanation). Tokyo: Tōyō Eiga Setsumei Kōshūkai, 1929.

Enomoto Shigetami. "Taishū bungaku e no michi: wagei to bungei no kōsaku" ("The Road to Popular Literature: The Blending of Storytelling and Literary Arts"). In *Nihon no koten geinō, daikyūkan: yose (Japanese Traditional Entertainment, Vol. 9: Yose)*, edited by Geinō Kenkyūkai (Entertainment Studies Society), pp. 251–264. Tokyo: Heibonsha, 1971.

"The Filmdom of Japan." *Japan Magazine* 19 (October 1928): 22–24.

Fukuda Noboyuki. "Yūki Magosaburō: makka na karakuri kagebōshi" ("Yūki Magosaburō: Thoroughly Mechanical Shadow Figures"). *Bijutsu Techō (Fine Arts Handbook)* 27 (July 1975): 201–217.

Furukawa Miki. *Zusetsu: shomin geinō: Edo no misemono (Illustrated History: Entertainments of the Common People: The Curiosity Shows of Edo)*. Tokyo: Yūsankaku, 1982.

Furuta Tamotsu. *Waga katsudō daishashin (My Moving Pictures)*. Tokyo: Seiwadō Shobō, 1972.

Furuya Tsunamasa. *Watakushi dake no eiga shi (My Personal Film History)*. Tokyo: Kurashi no Techōsha, 1978.

Geinō Kenkyūkai (Entertainment Studies Society), ed. *Nihon no koten geinō, daikyūkan: yose (Japanese Traditional Entertainment, Vol. 9: Yose)*. Tokyo: Heibonsha, 1971.

Gunji Masakatsu. "Nihon engeki shi seiritsu no tame no josetsu" ("Introduction to the Genesis of Japanese Theatrical History"). *Bungaku* 32 (December 1964): 1–9.

Hall, Mordaunt. "The Screen: A Japanese Production." *New York Times*, 12 March 1929, p. 26.

Hazumi Tsuneo, *Eiga gojū-nen shi (A Fifty-Year History of Motion Pictures)*. Tokyo: Masu Shobō, 1942.

Hibbett, Howard S. "The Role of the Ukiyo-zōshi Illustrator." *Monumenta Nipponica* 13 (1957): 67–82.

Ichinohe Kiyoshi. "Eisha gishi ichidai" ("The Life of a Projectionist"). In *Natsukashi no fukkokuban: puroguramu eiga shi; Taishō kara senchū made (Nostalgic Reprints: A Film History According to Film Programs; From the Taishō Era [1912–25] through World War II)*, edited by the staff of Nihon Eiga Terebi Purodyūsā Kyōkai (Japan Film and Television Producers Association), pp. 411–412. Tokyo: Nihon Hōsō Shuppan Kyōkai, 1978.

Iijima Tadashi. "Nihon eiga no reimei: jun-eiga geki no shūhen" ("The Dawn of the Japanese Film: Round about the Dramatic Films of the Pure Film [Movement]"). In *Nihon eiga no tanjō (The Birth of Japanese Films)*, edited by Imamura Shōhei, Satō Tadao, et al. *Kōza Nihon eiga*, ichi (Lectures on the Japanese Cinema, [vol.] 1), pp. 104–126. Tokyo: Iwanami Shoten, 1985.

––––––. *Waga seishun no eiga to bungaku (The Films and Literature of My Youth)*. Tokyo: Kindai Eigasha, 1969.

Ike Toshiyuki, ed. *Katsudō shashin meiserifu shū (Collection of Famous Dialogue Excerpts from Silent Moving Pictures)*. Tokyo: Mie Shobō, 1978.

Imamura Shōhei, Satō Tadao, et al., eds. *Musei eiga no kansei (Perfection of the Silent Film)*. *Kōza Nihon eiga*, ni (Lectures on the Japanese Cinema, [vol.] 2). Tokyo: Iwanami Shoten, 1986.

––––––. *Nihon eiga no tanjō (The Birth of Japanese Film)*. *Kōza Nihon eiga*, ichi (Lectures on the Japanese Cinema, [vol.] 1). Tokyo: Iwanami Shoten, 1985.

Inagaki Hiroshi. *Hige to chommage: ikite iru eiga shi (Beards and Topknots: A Living Film History)*. Tokyo: Mainichi Shimbunsha, 1976.

Ishimaki Yoshio. "Eiga keizai seisaku" ("Film Economic Policies"). In *Eiga kagaku kenkyū kōza (Lectures on the Science of Motion Pictures)*, edited by Murata Minoru and Ushihara Kiyohiko, 2:24–54. Tokyo: n.p., [ca. 1928].

––––––. *Katsudō shashin keizai ron (On the Economics of Moving Pictures)*. Tokyo: Bungadō, 1923.

Itami Mansaku. "Watakushi no katsudō shashin bōkan shi" ("A History of My Moving Picture Viewing"). In *Itami Mansaku essei shū (Collection of Essays by Itami Mansaku)*, edited by Ōe Kenzaburō, pp. 241–263. Tokyo: Chikuma Shobō, 1971.

Itō Daisuke. *Jidai-geki eiga no shi to shinjitsu* (*The Poetry and Truth of Period Films*). Edited by Katō Tai. Tokyo: Kinema Jumpōsha, 1976.

Kaeriyama Norimasa, ed. *Katsudō shashin eishahō* (*Principles of Moving Picture Projection*). Tokyo: Nihon Kyōzai Eiga, 1932.

———. *Katsudō shashin geki no sōsaku to satsueihō* (*Principles of Moving Picture Scriptwriting and Photography*). Tokyo: Hikōsha, 1917.

Kajita Shō. "Kanda Nikkatsukan" ("The Nikkatsu Theater in Kanda"). In *Musei eiga no kansei* (*Perfection of the Silent Film*), edited by Imamura Shōhei, Satō Tadao, et al. *Kōza Nihon eiga*, ni (Lectures on the Japanese Cinema, [vol.] 2), p. 319. Tokyo: Iwanami Shoten, 1986.

Kasu Sampei. "Minshū to eiga" ("The Masses and Motion Pictures"). In *Renzu kara miru Nihon gendai shi* (*Modern Japanese History as Seen through the Lens*), edited by Satō Tadao et al., pp. 45–69. Tokyo: Gendai Shichōsha, 1959.

Kata Kōji. *Kamishibai Shōwa shi* (*A History of Kamishibai in the Shōwa* [*post-1925*] *Era*). Tokyo: Tachikaze Shobō, 1971.

———. *Rakugo: taishū geijutsu e no shōtai* (*Rakugo: Introduction to the Popular Art*). Tokyo: Shisōsha, 1973.

———. "Taishū geijutsu no nagare: Meiji, Taishō, Shōwa no hyaku-nen no rekishi" ("Currents in the Popular Arts: A Hundred-Year History of the Meiji, Taishō, and Shōwa Eras"). In *Nihon no taishū geijutsu* (*Japanese Popular Arts*), edited by Tsurumi Shunsuke et al., pp. 304–444. Tokyo: Shakai Shisōsha, 1962.

Katō Hidetoshi. *Misemono kara terebi e* (*From Curiosity Shows and Roadside Entertainments to Television*). Tokyo: Iwanami Shoten, 1965.

Katsukichi (*Movie Crazy*), nos. 16–38 (April 1961–January 1977). Tokyo: Musei Eiga Kanshōkai.

Katsumura, T. "Japan's Talking Films." *Japan Magazine* 10 (January 1930): 189–190.

Kawatake Shigetoshi, ed. *Engeki hyakka daijiten* (*Theater Encyclopedia*). 6 vols. Tokyo: Heibonsha, 1961.

Kenchiku Shashin Ruishū Kankōkai (Architecture Photographic Documentation Publication Society), ed. *Katsudō shashinkan* (*Moving Picture Theaters*). Tokyo: Kōyōsha, 1924.

———. *Katsudō shashinkan. Kan ni* (*Moving Picture Theaters. Vol. 2*). Tokyo: Kenchiku Shashin Ruishū Kankōkai, 1926.

Kinugasa Teinosuke. *Waga eiga no seishun* (*My Youth in Films*). Tokyo: Chūō Kōronsha, 1977.

Kirihara, Donald. "A Reconsideration of the Institution of the Benshi." *Film Reader* 6 (1985): 41–53.

Kishi Matsuo. "Katsuben hanayaka narishi goro" ("When *Katsuben* Flourished"). In *Nihon eiga shinario koten, dai-ikkan* (*Comprehensive Collection of Japanese Film Scripts, Vol. 1*), pp. 12–13. Tokyo: Kinema Jumpōsha, 1965.

Kobayashi Ayako. *Utsushie shi* (*A History of Projected Pictures*). Tokyo: Kobayashi Ayako, 1951.

Kobayashi Gentarō. *Utsushie* (*Projected Pictures*). Musashi-shi: Kobayashi Gentarō, 1967.

Kobayashi, Victor N. "Benshi in Hawaii." In *When Strangers Meet—Cross-Cultural Perspectives from the Humanities: Viewers Guide*, pp. 82–83. Honolulu: Hawaii International Film Festival, 1984.

Koch, Carl. "Japanese Cinema." *Close up* 8 (December 1933): 296–299.

Kokusho Kankōkai, ed. *Shashin shū eiga ōgonki: koya to meisaku no fūkei, jōkan* (*A Collection of Photographs from the Golden Age of Motion Pictures: Views of Small Movie Theaters and Masterpieces, Vol. 1*). Tokyo: Kokusho Kankōkai, 1989.

Komatsu, Hiroshi, and Musser, Charles. "Benshi Search." *Wide Angle* 9 (1987): 71–90.

Komota Nobuo and Shimada Yoshibumi. *Nihon hayari uta shi* (*History of Japanese Popular Song*). Tokyo: Shakai Shisōsha, 1970.

Konishi, Jin'ichi. *A History of Japanese Literature. Vol. 2: The Early Middle Ages.* Translated by Aileen Gatten. Princeton: Princeton UP, 1986.

Koszarski, Richard. *An Evening's Entertainment: The Age of the Silent Feature Picture, 1915–28.* History of Cinema, vol. 3. Edited by Charles Harpole. New York: Charles Scribner's, 1990.

Kunii Shika, *katsuben. Eiga setsumei: "Tempō suigyokuden"—"Marubashi Chūya"* (*Film Explanations: "The Water Margin of the Tempō Era" and "Marubashi Chūya"*). Tokyo: Koromubia Rekōdo, 1962. Phonograph record. DL-65.

Kurashikku eiga nyūsu (*Classic Film News*), nos. 110–221 (January 1967–December 1976). Tokyo: Musei Eiga Kanshōkai.

Kurosawa Akira. *Something like an Autobiography.* Translated by Audie E. Bock. New York: Knopf, 1982.

McKechnie, Samuel. *Popular Entertainments through the Ages.* London: Sampson Low, Marston [ca. 1933].

Mair, Victor H. *Painting and Performance: Chinese Picture Recitation and Its Indian Genesis.* Honolulu: University of Hawaii Press, 1988.

Makino Masahiro. *Katsudōya ichidai* (*Life of a Movie Maker*). Tokyo: Eikō Shuppansha, 1968.

Mason, Penelope. "The House-Bound Heart: The Prose-Poetry Genre of Japanese Narrative Illustration." *Monumenta Nipponica* 35 (Spring 1960): 21–43.

Masumoto Kinen. *Jimbutsu: Shōchiku eiga shi: Kamata no jidai* (*Personalities: A History of Shōchiku Films: The Kamata Era*). Tokyo: Heibonsha, 1978.

Matsuda Shunsui. "Benshi to katsudō daishashin" ("Benshi and Moving Pictures"). Jacket notes with *Natsukashi no eiga setsumei shū* (*Collection of Nostalgic Film Explanations*), compiled by Matsuda Shunsui. Yokohama: Nihon Bikutā, n.d. Phonograph record. SJL-542-M.

———, *katsuben. Chikemuri Takadanobaba* (*Bloody Takadanobaba*). Excerpts of a film directed by Itō Daisuke, 1927. Katsudō daishashin shirīzu (Moving Picture Series). Tokyo: Sangurafu [ca. 1970]. Super 8mm film and ¹/₄″ audio tape.

———, *katsuben. Hōrō sammai* (*Wandering Meditation*). Film directed by Inagaki Hiroshi, 1928. Katsuben tōki han—Apollon katsudō daishashin. Tokyo: Matsuda Eiga; Apollon [ca. 1986]. VHS video cassette. APVA-4016.

———, *katsuben. Jiroku Chūshingura* (*The True History of "Chūshingura"* [The Forty-Seven Loyal Rōnin]). Excerpts of a film by Makino Productions, 1928. Katsudō daishashin shirīzu (Moving Picture Series). Tokyo: Sangurafu [ca. 1970]. Super 8mm film and ¹/₄″ audio tape.

———, *katsuben. Kunisada Chūji.* Excerpts of a film directed by Makino Shōzō, 1924. Katsudō daishashin shirīzu (Moving Picture Series). Tokyo: Sangurafu [ca. 1970]. Super 8mm film and ¹/₄″ audio tape.

———, comp. *Natsukashi no eiga setsumei shū* (*Collection of Nostalgic Film Explanations*). Yokohama: Nihon Bikutā, n.d. Phonograph record. SJL-542-M.

———, *katsuben. Orochi* (*Serpent*). Film directed by Futagawa Buntarō, 1925. Katsuben tōki han—Apollon katsudō daishashin. Tokyo: Matsuda Eiga; Apollon [ca. 1986]. VHS video cassette. APVA-4007.

———, *katsuben. Shunsui shinobigusa* (*Recollections of Shunsui*). Tokyo: Matsuda Eigasha; Apollon Ongaku, 1988. Audio cassette with text. X620CT01.

———, *katsuben. Taki no shiraito* (*Taki of the White Streams*). Film directed by Mizoguchi Kenji, 1933. Katsuben tōki han—Apollon katsudō daishashin. Tokyo: Matsuda Eiga; Apollon [ca. 1986]. VHS video cassette. APVA-4010.

———, *katsuben. Tsukigata Hampeita.* Excerpts of a film directed by Kinugasa Teinosuke, 1925. Katsudō daishashin shirīzu (Moving Picture Series). Tokyo: Sangu-rafu [ca. 1970]. Super 8mm film and ¹/₄″ audio tape.

Matsui Suisei. *Eiga ongaku zempan (All about Film Music)*. Tokyo: Shunyōdō, 1931.

Matsuki Yoshishirō et al. *Setsumeisha ni naru chikamichi (Shortcuts to Becoming a Katsuben)*. Osaka: Setsumeisha Dōjinkai, 1926.

Mifune Kiyoshi. "Musei eiga jidai no eigakan" ("Movie Theaters during the Silent Film Period"). In *Musei eiga no kansei (Perfection of the Silent Film)*, edited by Imamura Shōhei, Satō Tadao, et al. *Kōza Nihon eiga*, ni (Lectures on the Japanese Cinema [vol.] 2), pp. 193–195. Tokyo: Iwanami Shoten, 1986.

Mikuni Ichirō. "Katsuben no wagei" ("The Vocal Art of the *Katsuben*"). In *Nihon eiga no tanjō (The Birth of Japanese Films)*, edited by Imamura Shōhei, Satō Tadao, et al. *Kōza Nihon eiga*, ichi (Lectures on the Japanese Cinema, [vol.] 1), pp. 298–308. Tokyo: Iwanami Shoten, 1985.

Minami Hiroshi, Nagai Hiroo, and Ozawa Shōichi, eds. *Etoku: kamishibai, nozoki karakuri utsushie no sekai (Etoku [picture explanation]: The Worlds of Kamishibai [paper plays], Mechanical Peep Shows, and Utsushie [projected pictures])*. Geisōsho hachi (Art Library, [vol.] 8). Tokyo: Hakusuisha, 1982.

Miner, Earl. "The Collective and the Individual: Literary Practice and Its Social Implications." In *Principles of Classical Japanese Literature*, edited by Earl Miner, pp. 17–62. Princeton: Princeton UP, 1985.

Misono Kyōhei. *Ā katsudō daishashin (Ah, Moving Pictures)*. N.p.: Katsudō Shiryō Kenkyūkai, 1966.

———. "Mukashi, katsuben ga atta" ("Long Ago, There Were *Katsuben*"). In *Kōsa Nihon eiga, ni, geppō (Monthly News about Lectures on the Japanese Cinema, 2)*, pp. 3–8. Tokyo: Iwanami Shoten, 1986.

Morioka, Heinz, and Sasaki, Miyoko. *Rakugo: The Popular Narrative Art of Japan*. Cambridge: Harvard UP, 1990.

Morris, Ivan. Introduction to *The Life of an Amorous Woman and Other Writings* by Iharu Saikaku, edited and translated by Ivan Morris, pp. 3–51. New York: New Directions, 1963.

Muramachi Kyōnosuke. *Mukashi natsukashi urigoe (Old-Time Nostalgic Street Sellers' Cries)*. Tokyo: Denon; Nihon Koromubia, 1965. Photograph record. DLS-4165.

Muramatsu Shunkichi. *Tabishibai no seikatsu (The Life of Strolling Players)*. Tokyo: Yūsankaku, 1972.

Murata Minoru and Ushihara Kiyohiko, eds. *Eiga kagaku kenkyū kōza (Lectures on the Science of Motion Pictures)*. 2 vols. Tokyo: n.p. [ca. 1928].

Musei Eiga Kanshōkai (Silent Film Appreciation Society). *Jidai eiga bansō ongaku (Musical Accompaniment for Period Films)*. Tokyo: Matsuda Eiga, 1974. 2 audio cassettes, 801, 802.

———. *Ō katsudō daishashin (Oh, Moving Pictures)*. Tokyo: Kingu Rekōdo, 1973. 2 phonograph records. SKK 799–800.

Nagata Tetsurō, *Tate (Swordfighting Choreography)*. Tokyo: San'ichi Shobō, 1974.

Narusawa Kimpei. *Nihon eiga nenkan: Taishō jūsan' yon-nen (Japan Film Yearbook: 12th and 13th Years of Taishō [1924–25])*. Tokyo: Asahi Shimbunsha, 1925.

Natsukashi no Nihon eiga shūdai kyokushū; senzen senchū hen (Collection of Nostalgic Japanese Film Theme Songs; Prewar and Wartime Section). Tokyo: Den'on; Nihon Koromubia, 1973. 2 phonograph records. ALW-146-7.

Negishi Kōichi. "Hompō eiga jigyō no shōrai" ("The Future of the Japanese Film Business"). In *Eiga kagaku kenkyū kōza (Lectures on the Science of Motion Pictures)*, edited by Murata Minoru and Ushihara Kiyohiko, 2:57–66. Tokyo: n.p., [ca. 1928].

———. "Tōshi jigyō toshite mitaru katsudō shashin" ("Moving Pictures Viewed as an

Investment Enterprise"). In *Eiga kagaku kenkyū kōza* (*Lectures on the Science of Motion Pictures*), edited by Murata Minoru and Ushihara Kiyohiko, 1:55–64. Tokyo: n.p. [ca. 1928].

Nihon Eiga Terebi Purodyūsā Kyōkai (Japan Film and Television Producers Association) ed. staff. *Natsukashi no fukkokuban: puroguramu eiga shi: Taishō kara senchū made* (*Nostalgic Reprints: A Film History According to Film Programs; From the Taishō Era [1912–25] through World War II*). Tokyo: Nihon Hōsō Shuppan Kyōkai, 1978.

Nihon Hōsō Kyōkai Hōsō Shi Henshūshitsu (NHK Broadcast History Compilation Office). *Nihon hōsō shi* (*History of Japanese Broadcasting*). 3 vols. with 4 phonograph records. Tokyo: Nihon Hōsō Shuppan Kyōkai, 1965.

Nishimura Korakuten. "Katsuben ōrai" ("*Katsuben* Comings and Goings"). In *Natsukashi no fukkokuban: puroguramu eiga shi: Taishō kara senchū made* (*Nostalgic Reprints: A Film History According to Film Programs; From the Taishō Era [1912–25] through World War II*), edited by Nihon Eiga Terebi Purodyūsā Kyōkai (Japan Film and Television Producers Association) staff, pp. 422–424. Tokyo: Nihon Hōsō Shuppan Kyōkai, 1978.

Novograd, Paul. "Rakugo: The Storyteller's Art." *Japan Quarterly* 21 (April–June 1974): 188–196.

Ohnuki-Tierney, Emiko. *The Monkey as Mirror: Symbolic Transformations in Japanese History and Ritual*. Princeton: Princeton UP, 1987.

Ōi Hirosuke. *Chambara geijutsu shi* (*A History of Swordfighting [in Film and Theater]*). Tokyo: Jitsugyō no Nihonsha, 1959.

Okamura Shisen. *Katsudō haiyū meimeiden, ichi no maki* (*Biographies of Moving Picture Actors, Vol. 1*). Tokyo: Katsudō Shashin Zasshisha, 1916.

Okudaira, Hideo. *Narrative Picture Scrolls*. Translated by Elizabeth ten Grotenhuis. New York: Weatherhill, 1973.

Ōnishi Nobuyuki. "Rakugo no en: rakugo no makura to sage" ("*Rakugo* in Performance: *Rakugo* Openings and Finishes"). In *Rakugo no subete* (*All about Rakugo*), Kokubungaku Henshūbu (Japanese Literature Editorial Office), pp. 106–114. Tokyo: Gakutōsha, 1973.

Ōta Toshio. *Musei eiga jidai no seishun* (*A Youth in the Age of Silent Movies*). Tokyo: Daiwa Shobō, 1978.

Ozaki Hotsuki. "Iromono no sekai" ("The World of *Iromono* [nonstorytelling *yose* acts]"). In *Nihon no koten geinō, daikyūkan: yose* (*Japanese Traditional Entertainment, Vol. 9: Yose*), edited by Geinō Kenkyūkai (Entertainment Studies Society), pp. 217–231. Tokyo: Heibonsha, 1971.

Pratt, George. "Early Stage and Screen: A Two-Way Street." *Cinema Journal* 14 (Winter 1974–75): 16–19.

Reed, Barbara Mito. "Chikamatsu Shuko: An Inquiry into Narrative Modes in Modern Japanese Fiction." *Journal of Japanese Studies* 14 (Winter 1988): 59–76.

Rimer, J. Thomas. *Modern Japanese Fiction and Its Traditions: An Introduction*. Princeton: Princeton UP, 1978.

———. *Pilgrimages: Aspects of Japanese Literature and Culture*. Honolulu: U of Hawaii P, 1988.

Ruch, Barbara. "Medieval Jongleurs and the Making of a National Literature." In *Japan in the Muromachi Age*, edited by John Whitney Hall, pp. 279–309. Berkeley: U of California P, 1977.

Sakai Makoto. *Eishamakujō no dokusaisha* (*Autocrats of the Movie Screen*). Tokyo: Chūō Kōronsha, 1930.

Satō Tadao. "Nihon eiga no reiritsu shita dodai" ("Foundations for the Creation of the Japanese Cinema"). In *Nihon eiga no tanjō* (*The Birth of Japanese Film*), edited by

Imamura Shōhei, Satō Tadao, et al. *Kōza Nihon eiga,* ichi (Lectures on the Japanese Cinema, [vol.] 1), pp. 2–52. Tokyo: Iwanami Shoten, 1985.

Satō Yasuhira. "Musei eiga no gakushitachi: 'Serohiki no Gōshu' to kakawatte" ("Silent Film Musicians: Their Connection with 'Goush the Cello Player' "). *Kōza Nihon eiga, san, geppō (Monthly News about Lectures on the Japanese Cinema, 3),* pp. 3–8. Tokyo: Iwanami Shoten, 1986.

Schaffner, Neil, and Johnson, Vance. *The Fabulous Toby and Me.* Englewood Heights, N.J.: Prentice-Hall, 1968.

Sekiyama Kazuo. "Etoku no keifu" ("The Lineage of *Etoku* [picture explanation]"). In *Etoku: kamishibai, nozoki karakuri, utsushie no sekai (Etoku [picture explanation]: The Worlds of Kamishibai [paper plays], Mechanical Peep Shows, and Utsushie [projected pictures]),* edited by Minami Hiroshi, Nagi Hiroo, and Ozawa Shōichi. Geisōsho hachi (Art Library, [vol.] 8), pp. 135–157. Tokyo: Hakusuisha, 1982.

Shibata Katsu. *Jitsuen to eiga: rensageki no kiroku (Live Performance and Film: A Record of Chained Drama).* Tokyo: Shibata Katsu, 1982.

―――. *Ōsaka: Dōtombori, Sennichimae; Kōbe: Shinkaichi, Sannomiya shūhen eiga jōsetsukan no kiroku (A Record of Permanent Motion Picture Theaters in the Osaka Areas of Dōtombori and Sennichimae and the Kobe Areas of Shinkaichi and Sannomiya).* Tokyo: Shibata Katsu, 1975.

Shimaji Takamaro, ed. *Nihon eiga shi (History of Japanese Motion Pictures). Sekai no eiga sakka,* sanjūichi (Filmmakers of the World, [vol.] 31). Tokyo: Kinema Jumpōsha, 1976.

Shōji Tamaichi. *Katsudō shashin no chishiki (Learning about Moving Pictures).* Tokyo: Seibundō Shoten, 1927.

Sudzuky, J. Shige. "Cinema in Japan." *Close-up* 4 (February 1929): 16–23.

Tachibana Takahiro. *Kage-e no kuni: kinema zuihitsushū (The Land of Shadow Pictures: A Collection of Miscellaneous Essays on Cinema).* Tokyo: Shuhōkaku, 1925.

Tachibana Takashirō [Tachibana Takahiro]. *Katsudōkyō no techō (Handbook for the Movie-Crazy).* Tokyo: Kōbunsha, 1924.

Takada Kokugan. *Katsudō shashin setsumeisha kōshūkai kōshūroku (Katsuben Training School Lectures).* Tokyo: Dainippon Setsumeisha Kyōkai, 1921.

Takahashi Hiroshi. *Taishū geinō: sono ayumi to geinintachi (Popular Entertainments: Looking Around with the Entertainers).* Tokyo: Kyōiku Shiryō Shuppankai, 1980.

Takeda Akira. *Eiga jūnikō (Twelve Lectures on Motion Pictures).* Tokyo: Shirōtosha, 1925.

Takeda Izumo, Miyoshi Shōraku, and Namiki Senryū. *Chūshingura: The Treasury of Loyal Retainers.* Translated by Donald Keene. New York: Columbia UP, 1971.

Tanaka Jun'ichirō. "Eiga seisaku: kōgyō sōshishatachi" ("Motion Picture Production: The Pioneer Showmen"). In *Nihon eiga no tanjō (The Birth of Japanese Films),* edited by Imamura Shōhei, Satō Tadao, et al. Kōza Nihon eiga, ichi (Lectures on the Japanese Cinema, [vol.] 1), pp. 88–103. Tokyo: Iwanami Shoten, 1985.

―――. *Nihon eiga hattatsu shi (History of the Development of Japanese Film).* 5 vols. Tokyo: Chūō Kōronsha, 1957–76.

―――. *"Uta shigure* gomaku hachiba: Kojima Koshū" ("*Ode to Late Autumn Rain* in Five Acts and Eight Scenes by Kojima Koshū"). In *Nihon eiga shinario koten zenshū: bekkan (Comprehensive Collection of Japanese Film Scripts; Supplementary Volume),* pp. 29–30. Tokyo: Kinema Jumpōsha, 1966.

Tani Tenrō. *Ā katsuben (Ah, Katsuben).* Tokyo: Daiei Rekōdo; Nihon Koromubia, 1971. Phonograph record. G-5007.

Tokugawa Ichirō. *Orijinaru chindon poppsu (The Original Chindonya Pops).* Tokyo: Poridō Rekōdo; Nihon Guramofuon, 1970. Phonograph record. SMP-14339.

Tokugawa Musei. *Musei jiden (Musei's Autobiography).* 3 vols. Tokyo: Hayakawa Shobō, 1962.

———— . *Wajutsu (Storytelling Arts)*. 1949. Reprint. Tokyo: Hakuyōsha, 1987.

Tsubouchi Hakushi Kinen Engeki Hakubutsukan (Doctor Tsubouchi Memorial Theater Museum [at Waseda]) ed. staff. *Kokugeki yōran (A Survey of National [Japanese] Drama)*. Tokyo: Azusa Shobō, 1932.

Tsubouchi Shōyō. "Katsudō shashin to waga geki no kako" ("Moving Pictures and Our Dramatic Past"). In *Shōyō senshū: daishichikan (Selected Works of Shōyō; Vol. 7)*, pp. 229–307. Tokyo: Shun'yōdō, 1927.

Ueda, Makoto. *Literary and Art Theories in Japan*. Cleveland: P of Western Reserve U, 1967.

———— . "The Taxonomy of Sequence: Basic Patterns of Structure in Premodern Japanese Literature." In *Principles of Classical Japanese Literature*, edited by Earl Miner, pp. 63–105. Princeton: Princeton UP, 1985.

Urashima Saburō. *Katsudō shashin taneakashi (The Tricks of Moving Pictures Exposed)*. Tokyo: Tōyō Shuppansha, 1922.

Wade, James. "The Cinema in Korea: A Robust Invalid." In *Korean Dance, Theater, and Cinema*, edited by the Korean National Commission for UNESCO, pp. 175–194. Seoul: Si-sa-yong-o-sa [sic], 1983.

Yamaji Yukio. "Katsuben monogatari sanjū hachi: Sawato Midori-jō no shutsugen" ("*Katsuben* Story 38: The Emergence of Miss Sawato Midori"). *Kurashikku eiga nyūsu*, no. 186 (January 1974): 14.

Yamamoto Kajirō. *Katsudōya jitaden (Stories about Me and Other Movie Makers)*. Tokyo: Shōbunsha, 1972.

Yamane Mikito. *Katsudō shashin no kenkyū (A Study of Moving Pictures)*. Tokyo: Kōbunkan, 1927.

Yanagi Morimasa. *Hakata kōdan: daiyonkan (Hakata Town Talk: Vol. 4)*. Fukuoka-shi: Hakubunsha, 1978.

"Yoki eiga o miru kai" ("Society for the Viewing of Good Films"). Program. Okazaki: Tokiwaza. 27–29 November 1931.

Yoshida Chieo. "Katsuben no rekishi" ("The History of *Katsuben*"). *Eiga shi kenkyū (Studies in Film History)*, nos. 1–10; 12–14 (1973–78).

———— . *Mō hitotsu no eiga shi: katsuben no jidai (One More Film History: The Age of the Katsuben)*. Tokyo: Jiji Tsūshinsha, 1978.

Yūda Yoshio. "The Formation of Early Modern *Jōruri*." *Acta Asiatica* 28 (1975): 20–41.

Yume Sōhei, *Eiga setsumei no kenkyū (A Study of Film Explanation)*. Tokyo: Chōyōsha, 1923.

Zenkoku ni okeru katsudō shashin jōkyū chōsa (A Nationwide Survey of the State of Motion Pictures). Tokyo: Mombushō Futsū Gakumukyoku, 1921.

Sound in the Early Japanese Talkies

Iwamoto Kenji

Translated by Lisa Spalding

During the Japanese silent period, the *katsuben* (or *benshi*) were sometimes more popular than the films they narrated. Consequently, when "talkies" from abroad were introduced into Japan, the film industry was confronted with a host of problems. There was the understandable resistance of the *katsuben*, who simply took unkindly to the idea of becoming obsolete. But in addition, there were two other major problems that needed to be solved: the technological difficulties of the new medium, and the creation of a new means of expression. (Included in this last point was the necessity to formulate a style of speaking that closely approximated everyday conversation.) Iwamoto Kenji, in an essay that is here translated into English for the first time, details these last two problems by concentrating on three films: Mizoguchi's *Furusato* (*Hometown*, 1930), which was made as a part-talkie and which has certain similarities to *The Jazz Singer* (1927); Gosho's *Madamu to nyobo* (*The Neighbor's Wife and Mine*, 1931), the first popular success as an all-talkie film; and Kimura's *Horoyoi jinsei* (*A Tipsy Life*, 1933), the first Japanese musical comedy. Rather than explore in detail the historical development of Japanese sound films—work that very much needs to be done in English—Iwamoto makes a comparative study of the above three films. He not only enables us to see the different approaches that the filmmakers took in their use and expression of sound, but he also gives us an important sense of how these early talkies borrowed from, and built on, their Western counterparts. (Iwamoto's essay, "Talkie shoki no hyogen" ["Sound in the Early Japanese Talkies"], was originally published in *Koza Nihon eiga* [Lectures on Japanese Cinema], Vol. 3 [Tokyo: Iwanami Shoten, 1986], pp. 82–95.)

For further reading, see Joseph L. Anderson and Donald Richie, *The Japanese Film: Art and Industry,* Expanded ed. (Princeton: Princeton UP, 1982), pp. 72–89 (for a brief historical overview of early Japanese talkies); Hattori Tadashi, "Music in the Early Talkies," *Kinema no seishun (Japanese Cinema in Its Youth: The 1920s and 1930s. Interviews)*, ed. Iwamoto Kenji and Saiki Tomonori (Tokyo: Libroport, 1988), pp. 373–393; Kakehi Masanori, "Gosho Heinosuke no sekai: Gosho Heinosuke no entotsu no mieru basho o megutte" ("The World of Gosho Heinosuke: About His Work *Where Chimneys Are Seen*"), in *Nihon eiga o yomu: paionia tachi no isan [Reading Japanese Film: Heritage of the Pioneers]* (Tokyo: Dagereo Shuppan, 1984), pp. 115–138; Keiko McDonald, *Mizoguchi* (Boston: Twayne, 1984), pp. 23–24; and Murakami Tadahisa, "Mizoguchi Kenji," in *Nihon eiga sakka ron [On Japanese Filmmakers]* (Tokyo: Kinema Jumpo, 1936), pp. 201–216.

From Silents to Talkies

The chaos of the period when movies were making the transition from silents to talkies during the late 1920s is delightfully depicted in the Hollywood musical *Singin' in the Rain* (1952). Because sound was recorded directly, there was much agonizing over where to conceal the microphone. The sound was either too loud or not loud enough, and dismay over the leading lady's terrible voice resulted in the use of a double. The film was finally finished, but when the premiere was held, the sound began to slip from the image, and the man spoke in a woman's voice and the woman in a man's. Meanwhile, the actors commuted to elocution classes and practiced tongue twisters.

There does not seem to be a Japanese film comparable to *Singin' in the Rain,* but *Katsuben monogatari (The Katsuben Story,* 1957), a comedy starring Ban Junzaburo, portrays the period when talkies rose to prominence, causing the *benshi* to lose their jobs. The director, Fukuda Seiichi, who made most of the films in the *Nitohei monogatari (The Common Soldier's Story)* series, accords relatively more importance to the silent period, when the hero, an aspiring *benshi,* trains to become a professional, than to the period of the transition to sound.

The popularity of Japanese cinema was due more to its aural aspect (the *benshi*) than to its visual aspect. When the wave of talkies came surging in from abroad like the Black Ships of Admiral Perry, apart from the economic problems of unemployed *benshi* and musicians and costly theater conversions, the Japanese film industry was confronted with the problem of establishing a cinema based on both aural and visual aspects. This involved two major problems: overcoming technological difficulties and devising a means of expression.

Countless episodes like the failures depicted in *Singin' in the Rain* undoubtedly occurred in Japan, but time solved the technological problems. When the period film star Okochi Denjiro appeared in his first talkie, Murata Minoru's contemporary drama *Shanghai* (1932), Wadayama Shigeru voiced this complaint: "Okochi Denjiro assumes a formal posture and speaks. We would like to think that the voice is coming from Okochi Denjiro's moving lips. Regretfully, though, we are inclined to think that it comes from somewhere around his backside, or perhaps around his navel."[1] In the same article Wadayama expresses optimism that such problems will be rectified in due time by technological advances, and within a short time reservations about the new medium were, in fact, dispelled by technological progress. But before discussing technology, I would like to relate an amusing anecdote from around the time when *jidai-geki,* or period films, were confronted by the transition to sound.

In an article entitled "Dialogue in Period Film Talkies," Kiyose Eijiro introduced an episode about a rehearsal for a production of the play *Nezumi kozo tabi makura (Nezumi Kozo's Travels).*[2] The rehearsal was halted as soon as it began because of a lack of uniformity in the way the cast delivered their lines. This was a result of the fact that the actors had completely different theatrical backgrounds. They came from Kabuki troupes, *kengeki* troupes, the *naniwabushi* tradition of rhythmically chanted ballads, female Kabuki troupes performing swordfighting plays, and the amateur ranks. They each delivered their lines as they pleased, be it in the style of the Kabuki actor Ichikawa Sadanji II, or the founder of the Shinkokugeki Theater, Sawada Shojiro, or in the unmodulated tones of the amateur. The performance was totally lacking in coherence.

Although it is difficult to say for certain, because period films such as Kinugasa Teinosuke's *Chūshingura* (1932) are no longer extant, these strange but easily forgotten circumstances may be the reason why contemporary dramas are the only films considered good examples of the early Japanese talkie. In regard to the type of dialogue that would be appropriate for period films in the age of sound, Kiyose proposed standardization: "There is a need for a new style of period film that will provide a standard for those to come; hence there is a need for standard dialogue."[3] But his acknowledgment that "the unique intonations and mannered styles" of theatrical elocution might also become one of the attractions of talkies proved farsighted, since numerous actors with regional accents or mannered styles of speaking became stars after the advent of sound.

Two years after Kiyose expressed these views, Ito Daisuke encountered the same problems when he directed *Tange Sazen* (1933), a period film talkie starring Okochi Denjiro. In a round-table discussion, Ito spoke about his difficulties with the lack of uniformity in the actors' delivery of dialogue. He cited the chaotic delivery of lines resulting from the actors' divergent theatrical backgrounds, and unintelligible pronunciation due to regional accents, then stated, "I would really like to see the creation of a new manner of delivering period film dialogue (elocution). I intend to work on it, too, but I think that it is our most pressing need."[4] It was exactly what Kiyose had pointed out.

There were a number of Japanese films that experimented with sound, including Osanai Kaoru's *Reimei* (*Dawn*, 1927), which employed a sound-on-film system, and Makino Masahiro's *Modori hashi* (1929) and Ushihara Kiyohiko's *Daitokai: rodehen* (*The Great Metropolis: Chapter on Labor*, 1930), which employed sound-on-disc recordings. But these three films were all products of the transitional period that preceded all-sound films and were technically inferior. For this reason it is best to concur with the prevailing view that Gosho Heinosuke's *Madamu to nyobo* (*The Neighbor's Wife and Mine*, 1931), which used the Tsuchihashi sound-on-film system, was the first successful Japanese sound film both technologically and in terms of expression. Nevertheless, it took the Japanese film industry as a whole far longer than the European and American industries to convert to sound, and it wasn't until 1936, when Ozu Yasujiro belatedly made his first talkie, *Hitori musuko* (*The Only Son*), that sound films predominated.

Now, rather than explore in detail the historical development of Japanese sound films, I will try to deal concretely with the problems of expression in talkies by concentrating on two or three films.

The Part-Talkie: *Hometown*

First we shall look at Mizoguchi Kenji's *Furusato* (*Hometown*, 1930), which is the oldest extant Japanese sound film, all the preceding experimental works having regretfully been lost. "Phonofilm," the sound system used for *Hometown*, was brought to Japan from the De Forest research laboratories in the United States by Minagawa Yoshizo. Like its American predecessor, *The Jazz Singer*, *Hometown* is a part-talkie.

With the exception of *Dawn*, which was previewed but never released, Ochiai Namio's *Tai-i no musume* (*The Captain's Daughter*, 1929) and Tsutaya

Hometown. Mizoguchi Kenji at work (*center*).

Takeo's *Kanaya Koume* (*Koume of Kanaya*, 1930) both preceded *Hometown* in using the Phonofilm system (also known as Minatokii). But neither film was anything more than an attempt to render *shimpa* tragedy as part-talkie, and particularly in the case of the latter film, the plays were so out of date that it seems they were incapable of capturing an audience or even being understood by one. Apparently, *shimpa*-style material was already far removed from the mentality of film audiences by 1929 or 1930.

There is a detailed record of a joint critique of *Koume of Kanaya* by twenty-three people who were either engineers, critics, or members of the production team.[5] According to the critique, *Koume of Kanaya* was closer to a play than a film, and despite the fact that it was made specifically as a talkie, sound was used only for dialogue. It was noted that the background music was even created with traditional musical instruments, and that the images appeared flat because the photography lacked any representation of perspective. The story was criticized as too out of date for contemporary audiences to comprehend, and in spite of the pains taken by the staff, the film was deemed a failure.

The Captain's Daugher and *Koume of Kanaya* were both produced by the Hassei Film Company, which used the Minatokii equipment, but *Hometown* was a coproduction with Nikkatsu. Mori Iwao, one of the people in charge of the production of *Hometown*, felt that the Minatokii equipment and the Hassei studio facilities were so inferior that they did not even rate a comparison with what was in use in the United States. They were faced with the question of "what kind of passive structure, or in other words, what method of hiding the defects" to adopt.[6] The "world-class tenor" Fujiwara Yoshie had already been cast, and Mori explained the situation as follows:

> As a sound film, the best approach was the part-talkie. I believed the wisest method of working under those circumstances was to shoot the songs and important dialogue sequences in Minatokii, then construct a grand set at the Nikkatsu studios, and make free use of location shooting for the rest of the film. Afterwards, these sections would be joined harmoniously with the sound sequences by recording music and sound effects.[7]

This is the same method used to make *The Jazz Singer* (released in Japan in 1930), which provided the initial impetus for the development of the age of sound in the United States. Al Jolson, a popular singer of the day, was cast in the leading role of the young Jewish man who leaves home after quarreling with his father and goes on to become a success as a jazz singer. Although *The Jazz Singer* is called a talkie, intertitles are used for most of the dialogue, and a stream of sentimental music flows constantly in the background. It is a success story, but also a story of love within a Jewish family (discord between father and child and reconciliation as the father is at the point of death). The sequences in which Al Jolson sings employ sound, but the overall progression of the story is in the style of a silent film.

Hometown contains many similar elements, and it seems that an instant link was made in the minds of the producers between Fujiwara Yoshie and Al Jolson's success in *The Jazz Singer*. Mizoguchi's film tells the story of Fujimura Yoshio (Fujiwara Yoshie) from the time he returns from abroad until he becomes a successful singer. Although *Hometown* employs more sound dialogue than *The Jazz Singer*, there are still many intertitles, and sentimental music flows constantly in the background. The temporary discord and consequent reconciliation between Fujimura and his devoted young wife (Natsukawa Shizue) are imbued with the sentimentality characteristic of the *shimpa* domestic drama, and scenes without dialogue are performed in silent film–style pantomime.

Contrary to the implications of its title, *The Jazz Singer* is encumbered with Old World Jewish religious and family morals and a rather old-fashioned story. *Hometown*, precisely as its title indicates, is equally encumbered with Japanese sentiments and selfless female devotion, leading one to assume that the use of this type of story for a sound film, which was attempting to break ground for the new age of cinema, may have been a compromise intended to attract audiences.

The producers' decision to make Fujiwara Yoshie's songs the film's selling point meant that little effort was made to exploit the possibilities of even the part-talkie, beyond the addition of sound effects such as the ship's steam whistle in the opening, the sound of cars in the city at night, someone knocking on a door, and the noise of a dance hall. But the use of sound effects for psychological description, even if somewhat trite, can be found in the scene where the ticking of the wall clock echoes forlornly as the wife sits alone impatiently awaiting her husband's return. Given the fact that during the transition to talkies any use of sound was considered a novelty, it was inevitable that works from this period would use songs as a selling point and append sound in a manner that simply duplicated the film track.

As for the cast's reaction to dialogue, Fujiwara Yoshie, who had experience as a stage actor before becoming a singer, said, "Dialogue was the easiest part, but the scenes where I had no lines were difficult."[8] In contrast, Natsukawa Shizue, a silent film actress, commented, "I am useless in talkies. When I speak, my face becomes contorted." Tamura Kunio, who played the boy, Sankichi, admitted, "I had no stage experience so I was very nervous," and he then went on to explain that talkies necessitated the use of correct Japanese, something he had not yet mastered. Mizoguchi, obviously groping in the dark himself, said, "The language of talkies should not be simply an extension of stage dialogue. I think there must be a new form of language that is neither stage dialogue nor everyday conversation."

If you listen to the dialogue in Hometown, the relatively high-pitched and flat voices, the rapid articulation, and the shimpa-style delivery all stand out as unnatural when compared with Shochiku's The Neighbor's Wife and Mine. Technological limitations inevitably made voices sound unnatural as a result of such factors as poor microphone reception and the necessity for the actors to continuously modulate the loudness of their voices in accordance with their distance from the microphone. But there was also a need for such things as correct Japanese, research on the Edo accent, and a standard style of delivering lines in period films, or in Mizoguchi's words, "a new form of language that is neither stage dialogue nor everyday conversation."

Radio broadcasting began in 1925, and listeners were first introduced to the radio drama, which centers around dialogue and sound effects, by a production of Tanko no naka (Danger), translated and directed by Osanai Kaoru.[9] Six years after he made Hometown, Mizoguchi himself used the Osaka dialect rather than the Tokyo accent or standard Japanese in Naniwa erejii (Osaka Elegy, 1936). By leaning toward "everyday conversation" with a strong sense of local color, he was able to produce a splendid fusion of his own personal scrutiny of reality (his eye for realism) with the visual realism brought about by the transition to sound. The distinctive characteristics of the radio drama, with its roots in aural imagery, also provided an impetus for the production of unique works which depicted the everyday world of rural, villages, such as Tasaka Tomotaka's *Bakuon* (*Airplane Drone*, 1939).

The All-Sound Film: *The Neighbor's Wife and Mine*

In contrast to the gloomy works of Mizoguchi and the Nikkatsu school, Shochiku's Kamata studios used realism to produce popular comedies with familiar sounds as motifs. The first, Gosho Heinosuke's *The Neighbor's Wife and Mine*, appeared about fifteen months after *Hometown*. In a review for *Kinema Jumpo*, Tamura Yukihiko praised the film:

> It is not only the first talkie produced by the Kamata studios; it is the first full-fledged talkie to be produced by the Japanese film industry. With this film we can finally announce to the world that we have talkies in Japan, too! I am so impressed by the quality of this film that I would like to express my respect first to those associated with the production.[10]

The talkie system used for *The Neighbor's Wife and Mine* was a sound-on-film process carefully developed by Tsuchihashi Takeo, a man whose name commands a prominent position in the history of Japanese film. He was a violinist by profession and performed in Osaka as a member of the Shochikuza orchestra accompanying silent films and the Shochiku musical troupe.

Apart from the technological advances made in response to the all-sound feature film, the success of *The Neighbor's Wife and Mine* can be attributed to the skillful use of sound devices for the purpose of expression and the manner in which sound was carefully incorporated into the drama. This marks a great contrast with *Hometown*, which used songs simply as a selling point. There are places in *The Neighbor's Wife and Mine* where it is difficult to make out the dialogue, and in one section the synchronization slipped a bit, but the strained and monotonous delivery of lines that marked *Hometown* has been replaced by natural voice tones and a style of speaking that closely approximates everyday conversation. In the same review quoted above, Tamura Yukihiko praises this aspect of the film: "With the exception of Watanabe Atsushi, none of the cast had experience on the stage, but this actually worked in their favor, as lines are spoken in an extremely natural manner. Ensuring that dialogue is delivered in

The Neighbor's Wife and Mine. Watanabe Atsushi (*center*) scowls at noisy neighbor Date Satoko, while Kobayashi Tokuji looks on.

the same tone as everyday conversation should be a matter of the utmost concern to the producers of Japanese talkies."[11]

The Neighbor's Wife and Mine also employs off-screen dialogue, which is not found in *Hometown*, but its use of off-screen sound is not limited to dialogue. For example, in the first scene we see a suburban spring landscape and hear the distant sound of a *chindonya*, a comically costumed band used for advertising. As the camera makes a long pan to the left to reveal a third-rate artist (Yokoo Dekao) painting the scenery, the sound of the *chindonya* grows fainter and disappears. In other words, despite the fact that the *chindonya* is represented solely through the use of sound and never appears on the screen, an attempt is still made to employ the rules of perspective through sound.

Next we hear whistling. The camera closes in from behind the artist and peeks at his canvas. The whistling grows closer. The whistler, a writer (Watanabe Atsushi), appears on the screen and takes a peek at the canvas. The melody he whistles is the theme song from René Clair's first sound film, *Sous les toits de Paris* (*Under the Roofs of Paris*, 1930), which took the world by storm. The film had been released in Japan just three months before *The Neighbor's Wife and Mine*, and it is thought that it influenced the spatial use of sound exemplified by the *chindonya* and the flute.

During the interval of about fifteen months between the release of *Hometown* and *The Neighbor's Wife and Mine,* European and American talkies met with great success in Japan. Films such as Ernst Lubitsch's *The Love Parade* (1930), Lewis Milestone's *All Quiet on the Western Front* (1930), Josef Von Sternberg's *Morocco* (1931), *Der Blaue Engel* (*The Blue Angel,* 1930), and *Dishonored* (1931), and René Clair's *Sous les toits de Paris* proved that the Japanese industry could no longer simply mark time by producing silents. Japanese subtitles, first used for *Morocco,* proved a successful way of dealing with foreign languages and became a decisive factor in the dissemination of Western talkies. Tamura Yukihiko, who greeted *The Neighbor's Wife and Mine* with such great praise, was involved in the production of the subtitled version of *Morocco.*

The technique of introducing an off-screen sound before revealing its source on the film track is also used in *The Neighbor's Wife and Mine* in the scene where the painter and the writer are surprised by the sudden sound of a car honking while they argue in the road. And the purely aural depiction used for the *chindonya,* in which the source of the sound is never revealed on the screen, is utilized again in the scene where the writer, Shinsaku, and his friends play mah-jong late into the night. We hear laughing voices and the sound of mah-jong tiles being scrambled, while on the screen we see only his irritated wife (Tanaka Kinuyo) waiting impatiently for the guests to go home. But in a film in which sound plays the leading role, the most effective scene is the one in which Shinsaku sits down and attempts to work on his manuscript only to be frustrated by the intrusion of various "noises."

The first sound to harass Shinsaku as he tries to write in the middle of the night is made by mice scampering around above the ceiling. His attempts to scare them off by imitating a cat trigger the yowling of a real cat outside, which wakes up the baby, who begins to cry. His elder daughter bursts into tears, yelling "peepee," and his wife calls out, "Honey, please take care of her!" Later we hear the voice of his wife singing a lullaby to the baby, whom she has taken into bed with her. Shinsaku skulks off to bed and falls asleep, only to be awakened by the morning alarm clock. After a spooky peddler (Himori Shinichi) cajoles him into buying medicine he does not want, he sits down again at his desk, but as soon as he is ready to begin writing, jazz music reverberates from outside. A vocalist can also be heard, and the house next door is in a state of noisy chaos. Shinsaku tries everything to escape the "noise," but nothing works, so he heads for the neighbor's house, earplugs in place, to complain.

When he arrives next door, Shinsaku is welcomed by the neighbor's wife (Date Satoko) and the members of her band. Unable to voice his complaint, he ends up staying to listen to their rehearsal. The neighbor's wife sings "Speed Up," the film's theme song, which is a jazz number (composed by Takashina

Tetsuo and Shimada Haruyo) skillfully employed to elicit the air of modernism for which Shochiku's Kamata studios were known. Of course, this modernism can also be seen in the American-style editing, which uses a large number of quick shots. Tsuchihashi Takeo said that the use of as many as three cameras made such a high ratio of shots possible. In one scene, for example, the camera pulls back from a close-up of a cup to reveal Shinsaku tapping out the rhythm on it.

Inspired by the song "Speed Up," Shinsaku is finally able to finish his manuscript (a play). In the last scene, he and his family are walking along a suburban road on their way home from shopping. Hearing an airplane, the whole family looks up at the sky. His wife mutters, "What a beautiful blue sky," and the jazz song "My Blue Heaven" can be heard faintly.

Although I would be reluctant to call the cast's appearance and physical movements stylish, I think that for its time, *The Neighbor's Wife and Mine* was the most stylish of all Japanese films because the filmmaking itself is stylish, especially the modern visual structure (editing, camera angles, and camera movement) and the skillful use of sound (dialogue, sound effects, and music). In other words, this was the Japanese film which most closely approximated its Western counterparts in both its detailed montage and its use of "invisible" sounds to represent perspective.

After Shochiku's success with this film, the popular comedy rooted in the sounds of everyday life became one of their specialties and represented one facet of the so-called petit bourgeois film. Through films such as Gosho Heinosuke's *Hanayome no negoto* (*The Bride Talks in Her Sleep*, 1933) and *Hanamuko no negoto* (*The Groom Talks in His Sleep*, 1935) and Shimazu Yasujiro's *Tonari no Yae-chan* (*Our Neighbor Miss Yae*, 1934), expression in talkies became quite natural. Looking back to when he made his first talkie, Gosho Heinosuke commented: "When we cast Tanaka Kinuyo, who speaks with a Kansai accent, we broke the rule stipulating that all dialogue had to be delivered in standard Japanese, the way radio announcers speak. Contrary to expectations, her delivery imparted lifelike nuances to the dialogue and offered a valuable suggestion for solving the problems faced by the talkies that followed."[12]

The Japanese Musical: *A Tipsy Life*

Even in Japan, where Western music was not yet firmly established, the medium of the talkie brought about a move from films featuring popular singers, such as *The Jazz Singer* and *Hometown*, to the "music" film and the musical film, which integrated drama and music. *Horoyoi jinsei* (*A Tipsy Life*, 1933), directed by

Kimura Sotoji, is considered the first Toho musical, although it was actually produced by the P.C.L. studios before they merged with Toho. Mori Iwao, who wrote the story, specialized in light musical comedies and went on to become a producer and an executive at Toho.

A *Tipsy Life* opens with a scene in the style of a vaudeville turn. The set consists of a station platform where trains bearing the English words *Romance Car* are arriving and departing. The cast includes Fujiwara Kamatari as an ice cream vendor, Chiba Sachiko as a beer vendor, Okawa Heihachiro as the aspiring composer, Yokoo Dekao and Yoshitani Hisao as a pair of bumbling thieves, and Maruyama Sadao as an unemployed worker. At the center of the characters' various entanglements is a love story involving Okawa and Chiba. When Okawa's song "Love Is a Magician" becomes a smash hit, he and Chiba are united, much to the chagrin of the ice cream vendor, who opens a beer hall. The films ends with a large chorus of customers at the beer hall and includes an unusual sequence in which Maruyama Sadao, now a waiter, sings.

The theme song, "Love Is a Magician" (composed by Kanetsune Kiyosuke), is both romantic and sentimental, but still admirable in its suggestion of the French chanson film. At times the acting and the use of motifs call to mind a school performance, and there are some forced laughs, but the large chorus at

A *Tipsy Life*. Fold-out advertisement in the film magazine *Detail*.

the end evokes the atmosphere of German and Austrian operetta films. As its title and the climax in the beer hall attest, it successfully achieves the aims of its sponsor, Dai-Nippon Beer.

A contemporary review was not favorable: "Apart from its novelty value, one would have to say that nothing about the film surpasses the level of an attempt. . . . The soundtrack, produced by Kanetsune Kiyosuke [composer], Kami Kyosuke [composer and arranger], and Okuda Ryozo [sound engineer], is extremely easygoing and unimpressive."[13] Viewed now as Japan's first musical, it proves quite interesting and more enjoyable than one might expect, possibly because the intervening years put one in a more generous mood.

Kami Kyosuke, who was responsible for the score, gives a concrete explanation of the music used for *A Tipsy Life* in an article entitled "Music in Talkies":

> The opening music plays through the top title, then "The Drinkers' Song" [composed by Kami Kyosuke] runs through the rest of the credits and leads directly into the boisterous music heralding the arrival and departure of the trains in the station scene. As the scene begins, I unobtrusively inserted a light jazz number ("Yes, Yes") into the hustle and bustle of the station. Each time a train pulled in or out I added the boisterous train music to the grinding sound effects. . . . I used the thieves' theme for their scene, adding a glissando played on strings to evoke the sensation of falling at the point where the valuables tumble down, and inserted an accordion to mimic the sound they make when they splash into the water. Then I used a trumpet with a mute attachment to express the thieves' disappointment. . . . When you are watching the scene [the large chorus in the beer hall] the music flows without interruption, but there are actually cuts in several places. I was able to do this because the director, Kimura Sotoji, has a very good understanding of music.[14]

As Kami's explanation shows, for the most part he used musical accompaniment either as sound effects or for psychological delineation (including the evocation of mood), and because it was simply appended to the film track, it can be described as flat and monotonous. But it should be noted that his original aim was to make a musical film, and that he carefully thought out the musical structure in order to integrate it with the drama. Even though the integration of music and drama is a basic characteristic of the musical film, the types of sound effects and music it employs were not an integral part of daily life in Japan. From this point of view, *The Neighbor's Wife and Mine*, made two years earlier, was more realistic.

Apart from the problems of expression surrounding dialogue and sound, another issue for debate when the talkies arrived was what to do about Western music. As talkies brought about a more detailed and faithful depiction of reality, directors and composers became perplexed by the question of how to handle Western music. One approach, employed by Japanese musicals such as *A Tipsy*

Life, was to make a bold escape into an unreal and pleasing world. Five years after the release of *A Tipsy Life,* when the journal *Eiga Hyoron* devoted a special issue to Western music, no progress had been made in resolving this problem.[15]

In this special issue, entitled "The Road to Music in the Talkies," Fukai Shiro, musical director for films such as Kumagai Hisatora's *Abe Ichizoku (The Abe Clan,* 1938), expressed concern that realism "leaves no room for Western music, which is still not truly a part of our lives."[16] According to Hattori Tadashi, who worked on the music for films such as Yamamoto Satsuo's *Den'en kokyogaku (Pastoral Symphony,* 1938), directors, audiences, and composers "do not know much about Western music. . . . We do not know what to write, or even what we should write."[17] Although life in Japan is now permeated with Western music, it must be remembered that these were the anxieties of composers living in an age very different from our own.

Ito Noboru also contributed an article to the special issue of *Eiga Hyoron* in which he analyzes the music he composed for films such as Naruse Mikio's *Tsuma yo bara no yo ni (Wife Be like a Rose,* 1935). The pioneering work in prewar film music by these three men, as well as Kami Kyosuke, Horiuchi Keizo, Yamada Kosaku, and Sugawara Meiro, is dealt with in detail in Akiyama Kuniharu's *Nihon eiga ongaku shi (The History of Japanese Film Music).*

Sound Perspective

Let us return once more to the early period of sound films. In American films, the dialogue and music adhere to the image track, permeating it with an impression of flatness, but in French films an impression of spatial depth is developed through techniques such as the sound perspective of *Sous les toits de Paris* and the musical counterpoint of Jean Gremillion's *La petite Lise* (1930). Although we will not consider *La petite Lise,* because it was released later in Japan, there is a contemporary attempt at a detailed analysis of *Sous les toits de Paris* by Nakane Hiroshi, who praised the film's use of music and sound effects as "a splendid expression of sound perspective."[18]

Nakane observes that in the opening scene, as the camera pans slowly down from the sooty chimneys on the roofs of rows of houses, the faint sound of accordion music grows louder, and as the figures of the crowd surrounding the accordion player become closer, the song of the chorus grows louder in a "crescendo from delicate pianissimo to forte."[19] I should add that this scene is indeed as wonderful as he describes it. He goes on to point out that sound perspective is employed throughout the film in scenes such as the one where the hero, Albert, and his friend Louis fight. The moment they are thrown out of the dance hall, the lively music of the hall becomes faint. When the door is opened and another two men are ejected, the music leaks out, then grows faint once again as soon as the door is closed.

Distant sounds are heard faintly, and close sounds are heard loudly. Or an obstructed sound is no longer heard, but when the obstruction is removed it is heard once again. On the one hand, this way of using sound can be thought of as both logical and realistic, but then René Clair is definitely not a director of realistic films. *Sous les toits de Paris* and *Quatorze juillet* (1932) are films with a musical "mood," and both contain "selected sounds" audible only to those who strain their ears. These "selected sounds" are the background, middle ground, and foreground of sound, and the sound close-up. The sound close-up does not consist of a sound which has become physically louder, but the act of straining one's ears to hear a sound which is faint.

In conclusion, the close-up and montage of the silent period correspond, to a certain extent, to aural perspective. Come to think of it, didn't Jean Epstein, who praises the American film's use of close-ups in his book *Bonjour Cinema,* also refer later to the "sound close-up"?[20] I do not intend to escape into easy generalizations about "Western" film, and if I bring up American films, it will raise a whole other set of issues. Nevertheless, it should be said that it was the discriminating ears of the Europeans which produced the "opening up and closing off" of sound.

Although I have dealt with only three films in my discussion of expression in early Japanese talkies, if *Hometown* and *A Tipsy Life* are in the style of the American music film, then *The Neighbor's Wife and Mine* is in the style of "everyday realism," which is closer to the French film but unlike the musically structured films of René Clair. In Japan, this style of "everyday realism" evolved into the mainstream realistic sound film during the 1930s.

This trend in Japanese cinema raises the question of whether the use of sound perspective was really firmly entrenched only in realistic films. Actually, sound perspective was raised as a theoretical issue very early on. About two years before the Japanese release of *Sous les toits de Paris,* Yamamoto Reisho published an article entitled "Methods for Shooting Sound Films Freely," in which he gave concrete examples of slow-motion and fast-motion sound, the sound close-up, sound fade-ins and dissolves, and sound movement while referring to the problems of expressive technique and sound theory.[21] But in Yamamoto's article, the sound close-up is a "sound enlargement" which stops short at the level of a physical expression of largeness. He may have arrived at this view by basing his theories on radio broadcasting, which had already progressed one step ahead of film.

When the arrival of the age of talkies seemed inevitable, the pages of Japan's film journals were enlivened by disputes over whether sound was necessary, debates over proper expression, and the introduction of the theory of the contrapuntal use of sound initiated by Eisenstein and his colleagues in their sound manifesto of 1928. Since the essential points raised by these issues are well summarized in Tanaka Jun'ichiro's *Nihon eiga hattatsu shi* (*History of the Development of Japanese Film*),[22] I would like to discuss the work I have done on these matters at another time.

NOTES

1. In *Kinema Jumpo,* June 1, 1932, p. 42. Wadayama Shigeru was a name used by Kishi Matsuo.

2. Kiyose Eijiro, "Tokii jidai-geki no daiyarogu" ("Dialogue in Period Film Talkies"), *Eiga Kagaku Kenkyu* 9 (September 1931): 100–101.

3. Ibid.

4. "Ito Daisuke o kakonde: jidai-geki tokii zadankai" ("Conversation with Ito Daisuke: Discussion of Period Film Talkies"), *Kinema Jumpo,* January 1, 1934, p. 207.

5. "Gijutsuka ni yoru nihon saisho no tokii hyoban" ("The First Japanese Talkie Critique"), *Eiga Kagaku Kenkyu* 5 (April 1930): 255–282.

6. Mori Iwao, "*Furusato* to jibun no shigoto" ("*Hometown* and My Own Work"), *Eiga Orai,* April 1930, p. 19.

7. Ibid., p. 20.

8. "*Furusato: kankeisha wa kataru*" ("*Hometown*: Talks with the Filmmakers"), *Eiga Orai* (1930), pp. 24–26. All quotations from the cast and director are from this article.

9. *Danger,* written by Richard Hughes, was first broadcast by the BBC in 1924. [Translator's note.]

10. In *Kinema Jumpo,* August 21, 1931, p. 77.

11. Ibid.

12. In *Nihon eiga shinario koten zenshu* (*Screenplays of Japanese Film Classics*), Vol. 2 (Tokyo: Kinema Jumposha, 1966), p. 48.

13. Murakami Hisao, *Kinema Jumpo,* September 1, 1933, p. 157.

14. Kami Kyosuke, "Tokii no ongaku" ("Music in Talkies"), *Kinema Jumpo,* August 11, 1933, pp. 42–43.

15. "Tokii ongaku no jissai" ("Facts on Music in Talkies"), *Kinema Jumpo,* Special Issue on Western Music (June 1938).

16. Ibid., p. 35.

17. Ibid., p. 38.

18. Nakane Hiroshi, "*Pari no yane no shita no insho*" ("*Under the Roofs of Paris*"), *Kinema Jumpo,* July 1, 1931, pp. 56–57.

19. Ibid., p. 56.

20. Jean Epstein, *Bonjour Cinema* (Paris: Editions de la Sirene, 1921).

21. Yamamura Reisho, "Hassei eiga no jiyu satsueiho" ("Methods for Shooting Sound Films Freely"), *Eiga Kagaku Kenkyu* 3 (September 1929): 173–182.

22. Tanaka Jun'ichiro, *Nihon eiga hattatsu shi* (*History of the Development of Japanese Film*), Vol. 2 (Tokyo: Chuko Bunko, 1975), pp. 141–144.

A Cinema of Flourishes: Japanese Decorative Classicism of the Prewar Era

David Bordwell

As a critic, theorist, and historian, Bordwell has combined his interest in articulating an objective definition of film form, of style, with a conviction that the realm of cognitive psychology offers us a better way to make sense of film than do other areas of current film theory. He continues these two interests in this article, an attempt to account for an almost purely decorative presence in Japanese film style of the 1930s. Building on an idea of E. H. Gombrich that human beings possess both a sense of meaning and a sense of order, Bordwell postulates that the purely decorative function that emerges in mainstream Japanese cinema of the prewar era may be attributed to a search for order that outruns the meanings that may be attributed to stylistic or technical devices.

While the article itself is self-contained, it does indeed build on earlier work of Bordwell's. In particular, the concern with "norms" of mainstream film styles of a specific period may be found in two of the author's most influential books: *The Classical Hollywood Cinema*, co-written with Janet Staiger and Kristin Thompson (New York: Columbia UP, 1985), and *Ozu and the Poetics of Cinema* (Princeton: Princeton UP, 1988). Thus we find here the idea that there are conventions, or norms, which may be isolated and defined within the Japanese cinema of the 1930s, and that the mainstream cinema of Japan during this period was as highly conventionalized as the Hollywood cinema of the same period. The difference between these two highly active and varied cinemas is that the Japanese cinema possessed a greater tolerance for a range of stylistic devices, and that Japanese filmmakers and audiences were willing to accept a purely decorative function of film style. That is, film style in many instances is not reducible to a narrative or characterological function. Further, while many stylistic or technical flourishes are associated with particular genres, what we might call "excesses" can be found across generic boundaries.

Bordwell concludes this article with some important observations about Japanese aesthetics and their relation to film, and distinguishes between instances of stylistic flourishes and entirely alternate systems of filmic style and construction.

In one scene of Uchida Tomu's *Police* (*Keisatsukan*, 1933), the plainclothes protagonist leaves his suspect sitting at a café table. Uchida shows the protagonist coming toward us through a curtained doorway (Fig. 1). He walks out frame right. The camera now holds on the narrow slit of the curtain (Fig. 2). Abruptly the policeman's hand shoots into the frame and lifts the curtain away a bit, revealing his prey still sitting at the table (Fig. 3).

1. *Police*

2. *Police*

3. *Police*

This shot occurs in a context that is wholly comprehensible within the norms of ordinary Western filmmaking. The film's narrative line, about a cop who discovers that his boyhood friend is the crook whom he must track down, poses no difficulties to viewers accustomed to 1930s Warner Brothers films. Stylistically, *Police* is also "Western" in its overall reliance upon Hollywood conventions of staging, framing, and editing. In these respects, the film can stand as an emblem of mainstream Japanese cinema of the 1920s and 1930s. Most of the time, Japanese films of this era tend to behave like the majority of American and European films of the same period. This is, on the whole, a "classical" narrative cinema.

Yet this shot seems to deviate from the canon. For one thing, it is oddly gratuitous. Why use the curtain to block and then reveal the villain? Why not simply show the hero peering through the curtain's slit? Why let him act as a sort of impresario of our vision? Moreover, the shot flaunts its virtuosity: the rack-focus from the curtain to the distant villain is exactly timed to the hero's gesture of brushing open the curtain. This is, to put it plainly, a "flashy" shot. And here too the shot is emblematic. For in this classical cinema, some moments stand out by virtue of their ostentatious stylistic features.

At first it might seem that the directors have simply taken over a wider range of stylistic *devices* than Western cinema of the period has accustomed us to. Japanese cinema is eclectic in its free inclusion of unusual technical devices, such as fast-motion, hand-held shots, and whip pans. But of course such devices are not unthinkable in Hollywood; they are simply motivated in other ways. Fast-motion can be justified for comedy, or to speed up a dangerous stunt. A hand-held shot can be justified as the view of a newsreel cameraman. Whip pans can link scenes, as in *The Trial of Vivienne Ware* (1932). A play with vision somewhat like that in *Police* might be found in a scene of murder or seduction. True, such *outré* devices are numerically more common in Japanese films; but they are more common because the functions which they fulfill are more prominent here than in most Hollywood and European cinema. One reason to study the Japanese cinema of the 1930s is that it pushes us toward reflections on the ways in which we may describe and analyze the functions of film style.

1.

Critics and theorists tend to assign three principal roles to film style. First, style is assumed to channel the flow of story information, as when the choice of a framing allows us to grasp pertinent story action. This *denotative* function is usually considered to be so obvious as to require no discussion, but in narrative films it is the principal, most systematic, and most pervasive function of style, and we still have not sufficiently explored it.

A second role often ascribed to style is that of *thematic meaning*. A critic may claim that a shot which shows a man looking into a mirror implies that he is narcissistic, or that a shot which shows him not looking into a mirror implies that he lacks self-knowledge. The thematic function of style has been one which critics have proven very keen to explore; it has become a central object of critical interpretation.[1]

Another function of style, which film critics have fairly often noticed, is the *expressive* one. Here some perceptual qualities of the stylistic device signal a feelingful quality, related either to the action depicted or to a character's inner state. Japanese films of this period, for example, often use style to convey kinesthetic qualities of energetic actions. In another scene from *Police*, a football scrimmage is filmed in a bumpy, hand-held tracking shot. *An Actor's Revenge* (*Yukinojo henge*, 1935) employs very fast cutting in a scene in which the hero hurls a knife into the villain's wrist. Extreme examples of the expressive function are to be found in the *chambara*, or swordfight film. Here a remarkable range of devices become generically conventional in order to increase the sense of frenetic combat: fast-motion, rapid editing, jump cuts, hand-held shots, whip pans, and overlapping shot-changes. In less jolting fashion, films in other genres use style expressively, as when a tearful wife's calling after her husband is presented in a dialogue title that goes out of focus (*Respect for the Emperor* [*Sonno joi*], 1928). Expressive effects quickly become clichés, but the point is that the devices were repeatable because the reigning style reserved a canonized function for them.

Clearly, the "flashy" qualities of Japanese films of the late 1920s are partly traceable to their frequent reliance on expressive functions of film style. There is, however, one more stylistic function which deserves attention—not least because it is most frequently overlooked. I shall call this the *ornamental* or *decorative* function of style. Here style takes narrative denotation or an expressive quality as an occasion for exhibiting perceptual qualities or patterns.

Decorative conceptions of style have gotten a bad reputation in recent centuries. Many theorists have argued that all artworks, or at least all good ones, should be organic wholes in which style functions to convey meaning and to work harmoniously with other components. The organicist would grant that style may function denotatively, thematically, and expressively, but would reject the possibility, or at least the desirability, of its functioning as decoration.

Yet this position overlooks one of art's most historically important functions: the arresting and engagement of our perceptual activity. Poetry is at least as much sound as sense; painting aims to arouse and alter visual habits; music sharpens our discrimination of acoustic texture and structure. Art characteristically invites us to "go all the way down" to the most minute features of the medium, and the decorative function of style fulfills this function by highlighting those features in a particularly vivid way. Initially, we might say, the decorative function of style gives a perceptual *salience* to a particular trait or process of the medium. When a stylistic device seems not to function denotatively, thematically, or expressively, it stands out in itself, as a device utilizing concrete materials and processes.

Beyond this atomistic saliency, there lies the possibility that devices may be patterned. The vividly marked device can be prolonged, developed, or varied. How can this be sustained without relying on denotation, expressivity, or thematic meaning? E. H. Gombrich has proposed the general hypothesis that humans possess both a sense of meaning and a sense of order. Although he does not explain the distinction in detail, I take it that our sense of order is what enables us to scan our environment, to perceive stable patterns and regularly recurring events. Abstract art embodies this search for order in a pure state. On the other hand, the search for meaning includes, for Gombrich, all attempts to interpret our environment, ranging from object recognition to complex attributions of symbolic significance.[2] At moments, Gombrich treats the search for order and the search for meaning as working in tandem, particularly for evolutionary ends. At other times, when discussing decoration, Gombrich treats them as conflicting impulses.

Gombrich's hypothesis is strengthened by research and theorizing in cognitive science. There is little doubt that our perceptual systems are adapted to providing us with a highly reliable representation of a world of three-dimensional objects, events, and states of affairs. In doing this, our perceptual systems necessarily hide from us all the operations which yield that output. Yet such operations start from initial assumptions of unity, regularity, symmetry, constancy—in short, "order." Such assumptions may, of course, be overridden by the nature and structure of the stimulus input; if so, they must then be revised. But the assumptions remain necessary points of departure for any perceptual activity.

My claim that film style can swerve from fulfilling purely narrative functions and can solicit attention in its own right echoes the difference between the sense of meaning and the sense of order. For my purposes here, decorative functions of style emerge when Gombrich's "search for order" outruns the meanings that can plausibly be attributed to the particular devices and patterns we encounter. At a larger level, Gombrich's wealth of examples shows that we need not accept limited *definitions* of style if our purpose is to *analyze the functions* of style. In my terms here: If we think of a film's style as a system of technical choices instantiated in the total form of the work, itself grasped in its relation to pertinent and proximate stylistic norms, then we need not adopt either an organic or an ornamental definition of style a priori. We need say only that in some cases, style may work "organically," to convey meaning or expressive qualities, and that in other cases, it may seem "applied," laid over other components or structures.

The metaphors of superposition in the last sentence should remind us that "decoration" usually implies two kinds of processes. There is, first, the idea of attaching something to a free-standing support—a wall, a page, the human body. In cinema, we might draw the analogy by making the film's narrative and its other stylistic functions serve as the "support" for decorative uses of style.

There is, however, a less metaphorical way of posing the problem. Decoration can also be seen as a process of embellishment, the elaboration of a simpler or "plainer" version. In music, ornamentation can be conceived as the decoration of a simpler structure that is present in the score or that is absent but implicit. Some musical passages seem to be heard as elaborations of more skeletal forms that are implied by the overall organization of the piece.[3] Similarly, in the visual and verbal arts, ornamentation tacitly takes an implicit, more or less recognizable representation as its basis. What the ornament may adorn is not only some physical support but the "output" of a representational construal. In taking an image as distorted or stylized, we must, however tentatively, assign some referential meaning to it. The intertwined curlicues on a wallpaper design are, after a suitable amount of initial processing, revealed as flowers' tendrils; only by positing an earlier, more "realistic" schema for them can we perceive them as "unrealistically" elongated.[4] Constructivist research in perceptual and cognitive psychology has established the priority of object-recognition and story-comprehension schemata in our experience of artworks, and it seems likely that these manifestations of the "sense of meaning" are points of departure for revision in the light of the stimuli afforded by embellishment.[5]

This would seem to be a fruitful way of conceiving of decorative style in cinema, since it brings into play tacit norms and conventions. It seems likely that decorative impulses build upon the more stable responses supplied by familiarity with comparatively simple elements and functions. At least in some cases, the viewer could see style as imposing purely ornamental patterns of technique upon quickly recognized narrative and expressive qualities.[6] The "surplus" in stylistic treatment is construed as decorative elaboration of more conventional forms. Thus in our opening shot from *Police*, the tacit norm for staging and shooting the scene would run something like this: The policeman comes toward the camera, closes the curtain, and turns his back to us in order to peer into the café. Cut to a subjective point-of-view shot that shows the suspect sitting at the table, perhaps framed by masking which simulates the edges of the curtains. The refusal of this more straightforward alternative prompts the spectator to notice the device as such; as critics we can attribute this to the shot's status as an elaboration of the simpler, more conventional representation.

In sum, I argue that a decorative function of style can be identified when a stylistic device or pattern is seen to exceed its denotative, thematic, or expressive function. This obtains when the stylistic device or pattern can plausibly be treated as an elaboration of a simpler, more norm-bound device or pattern that would suffice to achieve these other functions.

It seems likely that such conditions obtain in popular cinema around the world. Hollywood filmmaking often presents intricate montage sequences, self-conscious compositions or camera movements, technical flamboyance (as in Welles or Ophuls), and certain fillips encouraged by genres such as the comedy, the musical, or the thriller. In what follows, I want to show that the Japanese films of the 1920s and 1930s seem striking to us chiefly because they make style more often and more vividly ornamental. Without permanently displacing narrative structure from its central place—without, that is, ceasing to remain "classical"—the films give greater prominence to the decorative functions of style.

2.

One way to point out the greater degree of decorative tendencies in Japanese film style is to consider how often particular tactics become conventional. "Flashy" transitions provide the clearest examples. Like its Hollywood counterpart, Japanese classicism requires linking material between scenes; but the Japanese filmmaker is more likely to take the transition as a pretext for stylistic embroidery. Many filmmakers commonly utilize what I shall call the "dissolve-in-place." Here a durational ellipsis is conveyed by keeping the framing and locale constant while dissolving to action at a later time. The dissolve-in-place can function decoratively because it exceeds simple narrative denotation; the dissolve itself would suffice to convey the passage of time. Moreover, the device usually does not cue thematic meanings or expressive qualities. Instead, it calls the spectator's attention to the image as a graphic configuration by letting the dissolve hold the composition constant across two shots. Like a rhyme in a narrative poem, the dissolve-in-place imposes an abstract pattern upon the telling of the story.

This device recurs in so many films of the period that we may treat it as a decorative cliché. Other conventional transitions include cutaway shots to landscapes or to seasonally significant details. Sometimes transitions are charged with an expressive or commentary role, but frequently they function simply as *poncifs*, set-pieces to prolong the change of scene and to engage our interest in isolated compositions or a suite of connected shots. Naruse's *Apart from You* (*Kimi to wakarete*, 1933) and *Nightly Dreams* (*Yogoto no yume*, 1933) link scenes by having a character walk into the camera, so as to block the lens, and then beginning the next scene with a character walking away from the camera.

Like the transition between scenes, the intertitle is a narrational requirement that can be the point of departure for decorative treatment. In films of the 1920s and early 1930s, intertitles may zoom out at the spectator or pull rapidly into focus. The early 1930s often set titles, either dialogue or expository, against live-action backgrounds. Thus in *Apart from You*, a young woman speaks to a young man at the seashore, and her words are superimposed on the crashing waves. The final title, being a conventional spot for overt narration, is a prime candidate for such embellishment. *Iwami Jutaro* closes with a shot of the colossal swordsman looking down at a beach and laughing; the camera swivels down to reveal "The End" written in the sand.

Almost any clichéd or normalized element—generic, stylistic, or narrational—can function as the basis of ornamental novelty. A montage sequence

4. *The Twenty-Six Japanese Martyrs*

5. *Dr. Kinuyo*

6. *Dr. Kinuyo*

can utilize extreme low angles and wide-angle lenses, as in *The Twenty-Six Japanese Martyrs* (1930) (Fig. 4). (The stylized distortion here in fact predates Slavko Vorkapich's flamboyant montages of the 1930s.) When a subjective sequence is needed, the director can imbue the expressive moment with ornamental force, as Naruse does in *Little Man, Do Your Best* (*Koshiben gambare*, 1931): the father who learns of his son's accident is treated in an orgy of optical-printing effects, including diagonal wipes that slice up the man's face. Even the old standby, the shot/reverse shot conversation scene, can come in for decorative treatment. Take the banter between Saburi Shin and Tanaka Kinuyo in *Dr. Kinuyo* (*Joi Kinuyo sensei*, 1937). Here a shot/reverse shot passage cants each composition sharply (Figs. 5–6). No need to posit expressivity or thematic commentary. ("Their world is out of kilter.") The canted shots decoratively dynamize a static scene, and incidentally camouflage the fact that we have moved from location shooting to the studio. To the objection that such a flagrant device cannot be gratuitous, that it must *mean,* I reply that stylistic decoration may function to awaken our perception, sharpen our attention, and make the scene more vivid. Japanese cinema of the period teems with exactly such arbitrary choices, but they are gratuitous only by standards of the organic theory of style.

The decorative tendency becomes even more explicit when Japanese filmmakers press us to the very limits of visibility. In Shimazu's *First Steps Ashore* (*Joriku dai-ippo,* 1932), for instance, a bar scene is filmed through a grillwork that imposes a grid over the figures (Fig. 7); we must strain to see the action, and we simultaneously appreciate the "modular" differences which shifts in character position can create. Similar compositions make use of the doorways and sliding panels of the Japanese house to create squarish frames within frames that hide and reveal figures on various planes. Perhaps Josef von Sternberg's films became very popular in Japan in this period because they used composition, lighting, movement, and optical transitions such as dissolves to block easy rec-

7. *First Steps Ashore*

ognition of the action and to insist upon the shot as a total design. Here, it would seem, is one premise underlying our shot from *Police*: the embellishment of a scene through a game of vision that arouses, sharpens, and rewards the spectator's attention.

The game appears in another decorative convention of Japanese classicism: the use of selective focus. As a general rule, Japanese filmmakers use a great deal of depth in staging, often with considerable depth of focus. However, 1930s directors also had a great tolerance for putting significant objects and characters out of focus. Sometimes the entire shot will be diffuse to various degrees on all planes, as in the opening of *The Scarlet Bat* (*Beni komori*, 1931). Or one plane will be in focus while a distant one—often an important one—is not. The effect is also evident in another cliché of the period, the rack-focus shot (as, for instance, in Gosho's *L'Amour* [1933]). Such processes create bold geometric shapes and pulverize objects and figures into granular patches of light.

So far, all of my examples have been fairly isolated ones, in which a single shot or pair of shots makes one technical device palpable. But the decorative function of style calls attention to the *patterning* of devices as well. Editing is

8. *Fallen Blossoms*

9. *Fallen Blossoms*

10. *Fallen Blossoms*

the principal means of creating such patterns. Indeed, the Japanese film of any period may use editing to impose an abstract structure on a scene.

This is evident when a conventional scene gets elaborated at the level of style. For example, Japanese cinema of the 1930s frequently shows a character in a static pose, and the style will enliven the scene by what we can call "intensification" cuts: brief shots from disparate angles or distances, usually progressively closer to the figure. In *Fallen Blossoms* (*Hana chirinu,* 1938), as Akira sits thinking about her lover, we get three quick shots of her from three angles (Figs. 8–10). As a swordsman in *Faithful Servant Naosuke* (*Chuboku Naosuke,* 1936) stands poised with his blade raised, four shots rapidly bring us closer to him.

The decorative arrangement of shots is analogous to what Viktor Shklovsky referred to as the "geometricization" of linguistic devices in verse.[7] Through short-range repetition, any device may become "geometricized." Japanese directors are fond of cutting together short, sharp camera movements in simple patterns. In Kinugasa's *An Actor's Revenge,* as a tough actress mocks the protagonist, we get three brief shots, each one a quick pan from her to him. A similar tripartite pattern of camera movements occurs in *Police* and *Lily of the Valley* (*Tsuruganeso,* 1935). Gosho uses an ABA patterning in *Burden of Life* (*Jinsei no onimotsu,* 1935): a scene of a mother and father's conversation is repeatedly interrupted by cutaway track-ins to the son in bed. An action may be framed by symmetrical camera movements, as is the Bat's interrogation of an old man in *The Scarlet Bat.*

Once such tactics have become conventional, however, the filmmaker in the grip of the decorative impulse must go beyond them. A device that has become straightforward and predictable loses its ornamental force. There is thus a tendency for directors to search out less codified devices that can achieve saliency. In the comic *chambara Iwami Jutaro* (1937), a scene begins with a close-up of a small hanging sign that reads, "Put out fires" (Fig. 11), which is then yanked up out of the frame to reveal a woman in her steaming bath (Fig. 12). Titles can also be manipulated in fresh ways. *Three Beauties* (*San ren ka,* ca. 1934) uses a dialogue title which flips over to reveal another title underneath. In *Mito Komon Part II* (1932), a shot of the hero eavesdropping is invaded by a superimposed title reporting what the villains are saying (Fig. 13); later in the same film, the camera pans rapidly from a speaking swordsman to a dialogue title.

If the stylistic norms of a period encourage ornamentation, directors will not only search for idiosyncratic devices; they will prolong and emphasize commonplaces in the hope of restoring their force. Naruse Mikio's work of the period offers several striking examples of this process. Naruse will stress the interplay between sharp and unfocused planes, as in the climactic scene of *Nightly Dreams.* The spectator is urged not only to notice the switch of foreground and

11. *Iwami Jutaro*

12. *Iwami Jutaro*

13. *Mito Komon* Part II

background elements from shot to shot but also to appreciate the way a figure jumps from clear outline to indistinctness (Figs. 14–15). Naruse will also employ marked accentual cutting, as in a deathbed scene in *Street without End* (*Kagiri-naki hodo,* 1934). Here three shots repeat the same pattern: there is a blank frame, into which Sugiko steps; she stops; cut to a new blank frame, into which she steps, moving in a different direction; she stops; cut to a new blank frame; and she steps in from yet a different direction. And Naruse will make insistent use of symmetrical camera movements. In *Nightly Dreams, Apart from You,* and *Wife, Be like a Rose!* (*Tsuma yo bara no yo ni,* 1935), a rapid track-in to a character in close-up will be followed by several more such track-ins or will alternate with equally paced track-backs, so that what starts as an expressive heightening of the action becomes, via immediate repetition, a purely rhythmic pattern—like the zoom-ins and -outs during fight scenes in 1970s martial-arts movies.

Further evidence of this wide-ranging search to refresh decorative common-places may be the tendency toward stylistic flourishes that we find in these films. In decorative art, the term *flourish* retains two of its original senses: ostentatious embellishment and showy movement. The florid stroke of penmanship is the trace of the gesture which produced it. Gombrich treats the flourish as "the expression of the joyful exuberance of the craftsman who displayed both his skill and his inventiveness."[8] The flourish is thus the epitome of the perceptual and ludic possibilities of ornament: "The flourish is easily understood as a playful product, a paradigm of the relation between sign and design. Even where it enters into a symbiosis with the sign, serving as a means of emphasis or enhancement, it never quite surrenders its freedom from the constraints of signification."[9]

Japanese films of this period, I suggest, are full of flourishes. When, in *An Actor's Revenge*, guards who are searching for a thief move aside to reveal the thief far above their heads leaping from roof to roof (Figs. 16–17); when, in any number of *chambara* swordfights, a victim is hurled out at the camera, blocking our view, before falling aside to reveal the hero in another spot, fighting a new adversary; when, in *Mito Komon Part II*, a fight inside a room reaches a climax and a swordsman spins around and slashes his way through a wall, straight out at us (Figs. 18–19); when, in *Marching On* (*Shingun*, 1930), the son's departure for the front is treated in a series of symmetrical, reversed compositions that dissolve into one another; when, in *Little Man, Do Your Best*, a montage sequence mixes negative images, blank frames, and fireworks into a swirl of very short shots—when, in sum, the decorative context of this filmmaking tradition encourages the filmmaker to display his assured mastery over the medium, we are in the presence of that "pleasure in control" which Gombrich attributes to the flourish and which he considers central to decorative art.

In all the cases just cited, the flourish prolongs the game with vision that we have already observed in the abstract patterning of shot composition. A swordfight in *Komatsu Riyuzo Part II* (1930) is handled in a lengthy single shot that keeps a wagon bed in the foreground, seesawing up and down, alternately blocking and freeing our vision. Naruse's mid-1930s films exploit this intermittent masking of sight by means of moving foreground objects that shear across

14. *Nightly Dreams*   15. *Nightly Dreams*

16. *An Actor's Revenge*   17. *An Actor's Revenge*

the frame, erasing or revealing the main action. The stylistic flourish thus becomes one mark of self-conscious narration.[10] A blatant example is the "Put out fires" sign in *Iwami Jutaro* (Fig. 11).

We can, then, best consider the flourish as an unlikely decorative choice that displays a degree of technical virtuosity and that pushes toward a narrational self-consciousness. Our opening shot from *Police* succeeds on all these counts: the more straightforward technical option is avoided in favor of an unusual one; the shot requires a split-second control over timing and focus; and the hand that peels back the curtain acknowledges that this narration addresses itself to the viewer. The shot is made for us, and it declares as much. We have perhaps come full circle: now style, in the furthest reaches of decorative elaboration, affects narrative denotation, governing rather directly how we construct and construe the simplest story action.

The narrational self-consciousness of the flourish makes it ideal for comic scenes, but it is significant that most of my examples in this essay come from dramas. In any genre, the decorative impulse yields a gamelike approach to art, an acceptance of norms as occasions for engaging display. Treating art ludically also asks the spectator to be a sort of connoisseur—knowing the conventions,

18. *Mito Komon* Part II   19. *Mito Komon* Part II

demanding to be dazzled, applauding the artist's virtuosity. In this sense, even the most serious scene can furnish the pretext for a playful handling of style.

Even at its most flamboyant, however, the flourish needs stable stylistic norms to set it off. The discontinuously cut swordfight relies on spatial continuity in the scenes around it. The opaque long-shot alternates with nearer, more legible framings. Out-of-focus planes will be crisp in adjacent shots. The grid laid across the action (Fig. 7) will keep the figures within the central T-composition of classical practice,[11] while the curtained slit of *Police* squeezes the salient information into the vertical axis of the frame (Figs. 2–3). Not only does the ornament revise an implied, simpler device, but it requires a subdued context to set it off. Again, decoration presupposes denotation.

3.

Considering film style's ornamental function will affect the ways in which we do film theory, criticism, and history. It is these domains I want to consider briefly in closing.

By making distinctions among various functions of film style, we can understand how a poetics of cinema can help us identify crucial features of the medium and its culturally varying conventions. In particular, the decorative function of style points to certain aspects of part/whole relations that theorists have neglected. For instance, the *Police* passage I cited at the outset stands out partly because there is nothing else like it in the film. Neither the curtain device, nor the strategy of intermittently blocked vision, nor the quality of self-conscious narration achieved through diegetically implausible character gesture recurs or develops across the film. We have only a momentary flourish. The same holds true, at least as far as I can tell, for the other sequences I have mentioned in this essay. Yet if we pursue the "sense of order" across an entire film's stylistic organization, we may find large-scale systems that are not easily subsumed within the "sense of meaning." Some narrative films can best be analyzed as exhibiting what I have elsewhere called parametric narration: a systematic tendency to detach stylistic patterning from the film's ongoing representation of a fabula (the inferred causal-chronological chain of story events and states of affairs, along with attendant parallel events or states of affairs).[12] Like decorative flourishes, parametric systems are aesthetically motivated; they call attention to the materials and forms of the medium. But, unlike flourishes, parametric narration is organized across the whole film according to distinct and developing principles.[13] Thus when the ranking of perceptual order over meaning is pursued consistently, according to an additive logic of variation and using either a "sparse" or a "replete" range of instantiating devices, we have parametric narration. When the ranking is more occasional or eclectic, we have a narration that is occasionally embellished by isolated moments of aesthetic motivation.

The concept of a decorative use of style can also assist us in doing criticism. When we analyze an individual film, we no longer need to make every salient stylistic event thematically or expressively significant. The foregoing pages should illustrate how the critic might discuss decorative passages. But we want also to talk about filmmakers whose works bear a more complicated relation to the norms of their peers and period. Let me sketch how this might go by taking as an instance the work of one of the most significant filmmakers of the era.

Ozu Yasujiro's 1930s films can be characterized by three simultaneous tendencies. First there is an adherence to classicism, that of Hollywood as well as that of Japan. His films rely upon basic units of narrative composition (scene, summary, transition); they draw upon broad norms of stylistic construction (e.g., eyeline matching, matches on action, centered framing, etc.); they presume that the spectator will understand narrative cinema with the aid of certain pragmatic assumptions about real-world events (e.g., people talking to each other normally face one another). Besides this classical tendency, Ozu also displays a recognition of decorative elaboration as conceived by his colleagues. For instance, Ozu's contemporaries called attention to the narrationally self-conscious transition and the cutaway to items of decor or landscape; he was obviously sensitive to such possibilities. But here enters the third tendency. Ozu goes beyond his peers in organizing the decorative possibilities of film style into a unique parametric system. He restricts his devices to a smaller set than do other directors; he treats that set as possessing a range of minute, sometimes barely noticeable differences; and he spreads that range of differences across the film as a whole, developing them permutationally in complex interaction with the syuzhet. One can study at some length how Ozu's parametric narration obeys its own principles of staging, composition, and cutting, creating a playful but rigorous perceptual-cognitive process.[14] It would be hard to call the dynamically developing nuances of Ozu's style "flourishes" in my sense here. He has, as it were, planed his style down to a level where it is constantly, systematically, very subtly decorative.

If we are justified in speaking of Japanese "classicism," we must also search for the specific historical factors which have allowed decorative aspects of style to gain more prominence than in Western, and particularly Hollywood, filmmaking. Further historical inquiry would, I think, reveal that these decorative emphases are encouraged by many Japanese aesthetic traditions.

Japanese poetics and painting have tended to treat art as a matter of technical skill. In many pre-Meiji arts, the cliché holds an honored place: it is a fixed counter in a formal game, to be deployed in new patterns. Konishi Jin'ichi calls this the tradition of "inorganic" unity, as exemplified by the patterning of images in *renga* (linked) verse or by the *kata,* the decomposed movements of the Noh play.[15] It would be misleading, therefore, to say that Japanese artistic traditions invariably scorn novelty or originality. Art becomes a game of pattern-making within fixed rules which stipulate how the medium is to be handled, and that artist is praiseworthy who can submit the rules to fresh and virtuosic treatment. For the same reason, the decorative impulse in Japanese music and visual arts would be a plausible forerunner of this attitude toward cinema.

Up to this point, the account would be compatible with that offered by Noel Burch in his *To the Distant Observer,* the most thoroughgoing attempt to trace the Japanese cinema of the 1930s back to cultural antecedents. But Burch's frame of reference seems to me to neglect the importance of cultural factors that emerge during the Meiji era and thereafter. For Burch, a unified Japanese aesthetic tradition continues relatively unchanged from the Heian era (794–1155) to the present. This leads him to conclude that Japanese cinema of the present constitutes a film practice essentially different from that of Western countries. Yet such a position ignores the fact that in most respects most films from Japan are comprehensible according to Western protocols of viewing. Because of this, I would argue that there are several distinct Japanese aesthetic traditions, undergirded by significantly varying assumptions about the nature and roles of art. (Indeed, the Heian tradition is at least partly a construct of later centuries.) Moreover, I would argue that representational conventions of form and address are mediated through post-Meiji modernizations (not least the popular urban culture of this century's first decades). There is evidence that by the time such features show up in films, they are not unreflectingly assimilated but are knowingly cited to achieve particular formal ends.

To explain the ornamental function of style in the Japanese filmmaking tradition, I submit, it is not enough to cite distant traditions. The analyst should also recognize that the introduction of cinema participates in broader twentieth-century trends toward the absorption of Western cultural practices. Indicative instances are the adaptation of a compromise Westernized scale for the nation's music, and the mixing of European graphic conventions with more traditional ones. Most important, perhaps, is the Meiji encounter with the long and comparatively unified narrative forms of the West. Historians of Japanese literature agree that lyric poetry, not drama or epic, lies at the center of pre-Meiji poetics. One consequence was an emphasis on short forms and on episodic construction in longer ones.[16] *Renga* verse was composed by creating local connections between relatively independent stanzas. Again, because of the centrality of the lyric, prose narrative tended to grow out of glosses on poems or to become a foil for verse outbursts. It is hardly surprising, then, that the flood of foreign translations in the nineteenth and early twentieth centuries offered Japanese writers new compositional options, as well as difficulties. One of the most frequent results was the synthesis of quasi-European plot structure with "poetic" interludes, as in the *shi-shosetsu* ("I-novel") or in the works of Shimazaki Toson and Tanizaki Jun'ichiro.[17]

The possibilities of synthesis were posed even more acutely for filmmakers. It is clear that by 1925, the norms of Western filmmaking had shaped the narrative construction of Japanese films.[18] Tanizaki's script for *Amateur Club* (*Amachua Kurabu*, 1920) and the Lubitsch-inspired *Woman Who Touched the Leg* (*Ashi ni sowatta onna*, 1926) of Abe Yutaka are only the most illustrious instances of how "modernizing" the cinema meant adapting Hollywood conventions. In accepting Hollywood norms, Japanese filmmakers relegated decorative treatments largely to inserted or hyperstylized moments—themselves marked as "Japanese" touches. Filmmakers could consciously draw on the conventions of *haiku* or *kodan* to punctuate a straightforward plot with the sort of lyrical interludes already common in artistic fiction.[19]

Once in place, the ornamental impulse in cinema remained fairly strong after the 1930s. Although a certain stylistic severity can be seen in films of the Pacific War period, the wartime work of Kurosawa in *Sanshiro Sugata* (1943) or *The Most Beautiful* (*Ichiban utsukushiku*, 1944) perfectly exemplifies the decorative tendency. And certainly films such as *Morning for the Osone Family* (*Osone-ke no asa*, 1946) and *Between War and Peace* (*Senso to heiwa*, 1947) continue to embellish canonical elements of Japanese classicism.

This explanatory frame is far from being sufficiently filled in here, but we have good reason to work under the assumption that most Japanese cinema of the 1920s and 1930s is neither a radical signifying practice nor a direct product of distant Japanese traditions. It is a classical cinema, though perhaps the most variegated, vivid, and vivacious classicism we have yet discovered.

NOTES

1. I discuss how academic film interpretation treats film style in *Making Meaning: Inference and Rhetoric in the Interpretation of Cinema* (Cambridge: Harvard UP, 1989), Chapters 7 and 8.

2. E. H. Gombrich, *The Sense of Order* (Ithaca: Cornell UP, 1979), pp. 134–152.

3. Heinrich Schenker systematized this concept most fully in his ideas of *Stufen* (underlying harmonic regions) and *Ursatz* (fundamental tonal structure). An informal

discussion may be found in Joseph Kernan, *Contemplating Music: Challenges to Musicology* (Cambridge: Harvard UP, 1985), pp. 79–90; a more technical survey is in Nicholas Cook, *A Guide to Musical Analysis* (New York: Braziller, 1987), pp. 27–66. A cognitive reworking of Schenkerism is offered by Fred Lerdahl and Ray Jackendoff in *A Generative Theory of Tonal Music* (Cambridge: MIT Press, 1983), pp. 105–117ff.

4. This is not to downplay the abstraction that is probably inherent in early stages of visual processing. See David Marr, *Vision* (San Francisco: Freeman, 1982), pp. 91–98, 296–328. It is just that judgments of decorative patterning are relatively high-level and top-down, applicable only after what Marr calls the "3-d sketch" has been constructed.

5. David Bordwell, *Narration in the Fiction Film* (Madison: U of Wisconsin, 1985), pp. 30–33.

6. This might be the source of the form/content distinction that is so hard to shake. One can, it seems, always imagine the same "plain version"—the same action or state of affairs—but embellished in different, more or less straightforward ways.

7. Viktor Shklovsky, "Poetry and Prose in Cinematography," *Russian Poetics in Translation* no. 9 (1982): 88.

8. Gombrich, *Sense of Order,* p. 239.

9. Ibid., p. 240.

10. Bordwell, *Narration,* pp. 280–281.

11. See David Bordwell, Janet Staiger, and Kristin Thompson, *The Classical Hollywood Cinema: Film Style and Mode of Production to 1960* (New York: Columbia UP, 1985), p. 51.

12. Bordwell, *Narration,* pp. 49–62.

13. Ibid., p. 281.

14. See David Bordwell, *Ozu and the Poetics of Cinema* (Princeton: Princeton UP, 1988), pp. 73–142.

15. Konishi Jin'ichi, "The Art of Renga," *Journal of Japanese Studies* 2, 1 (Autumn 1975): 47.

16. See, for a brief but penetrating discussion, Donald Keene, *Japanese Literature: An Introduction for Western Readers* (New York: Grove, 1955), pp. 10–13.

17. A brief but suggestive discussion is in Earl Jackson, Jr., "Elaboration of the Moment: The Lyric Tradition in Modern Japanese Narrative," in Wimal Dissanayake and Steven Bradbury, eds., *Literary History, Narrative, and Culture: Selected Conference Papers* (Honolulu: University of Hawaii and the East-West Center, 1989), pp. 5–13.

18. See Joseph Anderson and Donald Richie, *The Japanese Film: Art and Industry* (Princeton: Princeton UP, 1982), pp. 48–62; David Bordwell, "Our Dream-Cinema: Western Historiography and the Japanese Film," *Film Reader* no. 4 (1979): 46–48; and Bordwell, *Ozu and the Poetics of Cinema,* pp. 19–21, 151–159.

19. See Masumura Yasuzo, *Profilo storico del cinema giapponese,* trans. Guido Cincotti (Rome: Bianco e nero, 1955), pp. 19–20; Anderson and Richie, *Japanese Film,* pp. 323–324.

SELECTED BIBLIOGRAPHY

Books in English on Japanese Cinema

Allyn, John. *Kon Ichikawa: A Guide to References and Resources*. Boston: G. K. Hall, 1985.

Anderson, Joseph L., and Donald Richie. *The Japanese Film: Art and Industry*. Expanded ed. Princeton: Princeton UP, 1982.

Andrew, Dudley, and Paul Andrew. *Kenji Mizoguchi: A Guide to References and Resources*. Boston: G. K. Hall, 1981.

Barrett, Gregory. *Archetypes in Japanese Film: The Sociopolitical and Religious Significance of the Principal Heroes and Heroines*. Selinsgrove: Susquehanna UP, 1989.

Bock, Audie. *Japanese Film Directors*. Tokyo: Kodansha, 1978.

Bordwell, David. *Ozu and the Poetics of Cinema*. Princeton: Princeton UP, 1988.

Buehrer, Beverley Bare. *Japanese Films: A Bibliography and Commentary, 1921–1989*. Jefferson, N.C.: McFarland, 1990.

Burch, Noel. *To the Distant Observer: Form and Meaning in the Japanese Cinema*. Berkeley: U of California P, 1979.

Buruma, Ian. *Behind the Mask: On Sexual Demons, Sacred Mothers, Transvestites, Gangsters, Drifters and Other Japanese Cultural Heroes*. New York: Pantheon, 1984.

Desser, David. *Eros plus Massacre: An Introduction to the Japanese New Wave Cinema*. Bloomington and Indianapolis: Indiana UP, 1988.

———. *The Samurai Films of Akira Kurosawa*. Ann Arbor: UMI Research Press, 1983.

Erens, Patricia. *Akira Kurosawa: A Guide to References and Resources*. Boston: G.K. Hall, 1979.

Gillett, John, and David Wilson, eds. *Yasujiro Ozu: A Critical Anthology*. London: British Film Institute, 1976.

Hirano, Kyoko. *The Japanese Cinema under the Occupation*. Washington, D.C.: Smithsonian Institution Press, 1992.

Kirihara, Donald. *Patterns of Time: Kenji Mizoguchi in the 1930s*. Madison: U of Wisconsin P, 1992.

Kurosawa, Akira. *Something like an Autobiography*. Trans. Audie Bock. New York: Knopf, 1982.

McDonald, Keiko. *Cinema East: A Critical Study of Major Japanese Films*. East Brunswick, N.J.: Associated U Presses, 1983.

———. *Mizoguchi*. Boston: Twayne, 1984.

Mellen, Joan. *Voices from the Japanese Cinema*. New York: Liveright, 1975.

———. *The Waves at Genji's Door: Japan through Its Cinema*. New York: Pantheon, 1974.

Prince, Stephen. *The Warrior's Camera: The Cinema of Akira Kurosawa*. Princeton: Princeton UP, 1991.
Richie, Donald. *The Films of Akira Kurosawa*. Rev. ed. Berkeley: U of California P, 1984.
———. *Japanese Cinema: An Introduction*. New York: Oxford UP, 1990.
———. *Japanese Cinema: Film Style and National Character*. Garden City, N.Y.: Anchor, 1971.
———. *The Japanese Movie*. Rev. ed. Tokyo: Kodansha, 1982.
———. *Ozu*. Berkeley: U of California P, 1974.
Sato, Tadao. *Currents in Japanese Cinema*. Trans. Gregory Barrett. Tokyo: Kodansha, 1982.
Silver, Alain. *The Samurai Film*. New York: A. S. Barnes, 1977.
Svensson, Arne. *Japan: Screen Series*. New York: A. S. Barnes, 1971.
Tucker, Richard. *Japan: Film Image*. London: Studio Vista, 1973.

Books in Japanese
(City of publication is Tokyo, unless otherwise noted.)

General

Hatano Tetsuro et al., eds. *Sengo eiga no shuppatsu: gendai Nihon eigaron taikei* (*Departures in Postwar Japanese Film: A Collection of Essays on Contemporary Japanese Cinema*). Vol. 1. Tokisha, 1971.
Imamura Shohei et al. *Koza Nihon eiga* (*Lectures on Japanese Film*). Vols. 2–4. Iwanami Shoten, 1987.
Iwamoto Kenji and Saiki Tomonori. *Kinema no seishun* (*Japanese Cinema in Its Youth: The 1920s and 1930s. Interviews*). Libroport, 1988.
Nihon eiga o yomu: paionia tachi no isan (*Reading Japanese Film: Heritage of the Pioneers*). Dagereo Shuppan, 1984.
Sato Tadao. *Nihon no eiga: kirarekata no bigatu* (*Japanese Movies: The Beauty of Being Murdered*). Chikuma Shobo, 1962.
Sato Tadao and Yoshida Chieo. *Chambara eiga shi* (*The History of Chambara Movies*). Haga Shoten, 1972.
Tanaka Jun'ichiro. *Nihon eiga hattatsu shi* (*History of the Development of Japanese Film*). 5 vols. Chuo Koronsha, 1957–76:
    I. *Katsudo shashin jidai* (*The Age of Moving Pictures*)
    II. *Musei kara tokei e* (*From Silent Movies to Talkies*)
    III. *Sengo eiga no kaiho* (*The Liberation of Movies after World War II*)
    IV. *Shijo saiko no eiga jidai* (*The Peak Period of Movies*)
    V. *Eizo jidai no torai* (*The Arrival of the Movie Generation*)

Directors

Gosho

Gosho Heinosuke. *Waga seishun* (*My Youth*). Nagata Shobo, 1978.
Mizutani Kenji. *Eiga kantoku: Gosho Heinosuke* (*The Movie Director: Gosho Heinosuke*). Nagata Shobo, 1977.
Sato Tadao. *Obake entotsu no sekai. Eiga kantoku Gosho Heinosuke no hito to shigoto*

(*The World of Phantom Chimneys: The Movie Director Gosho Heinosuke, the Man and His Work*). Noberu Shobo, 1977.

Kurosawa

Aoki Makoto et al. "*Ran*—Sono tanjo kara kansei made" ("*Ran*—From Its Birth to Completion"). Special Issue of *Kinema Jumpo* 909 (1985): 19–42.

Imamura Akira et al. "*Ran*." Special Issue of *Kinema Jumpo* 913 (1985): 17–40.

Kurosawa Akira. *Akuma no yo ni saishin ni: tenshi no yo ni daitan ni* (*Careful like the Devil, Bold like an Angel*). Toho, 1975.

Kurosawa Akira eiga taikei (*A Collection of Kurosawa Akira's Films*). Kinema Jumposha, 1971.
1. *Dodesukaden*
2. *Sugata Sanshiro/Waga seishun ni kuinashi* (*No Regrets for My Youth*)
4. *Shizukanaru ketto* (*The Quiet Duel*)/*Nora inu* (*Stray Dog*)
5. *Kakushi toride no san akunin* (*The Hidden Fortress*)
6. *Warui yatsu hodo yoku nemuru* (*The Bad Sleep Well*)

Kusakabe Kyushiro. *Kurosawa Akira no zenbo* (*The Entire Picture of Kurosawa Akira*). Gendai Engeki Kyokai: Sanbyakuhin, 1985.

Nishimura Yujiro. "Miyaguchi Seiji ga kataru Kurosawa Akira no hito to sakuhin" ("The Personality and Works of Kurosawa Akira, Spoken by Miyaguchi Seiji"). *Kinema Jumpo* 911 (1985): 95–99.

Sato Tadao. *Kurosawa Akira no sekai* (*The World of Kurosawa Akira*). Sanichi Shobo, 1969.

Tsuzuki Masaki. *Kurosawa Akira: I. Sono ningen kenkyu; II. Sono sakuhin kenkyu.* (*Kurosawa Akira. I: The Study of the Man; II: The Study of His Works*). 2 vols. Intanaru Shuppanbu, 1976.

Wada Emi. "Kurosawa Akira kantoku to no deai" ("A Meeting with Director Kurosawa Akira"). *Ushio* 326 (1986): 212–215.

Mizoguchi

Shindo Kaneto. *Aru eiga kantoku: Mizoguchi Kenji to Nihon eiga* (*A Movie Director: Japanese Film and Mizoguchi Kenji*). Iwanami Shoten, 1976.

Tsumura Hideo. *Mizoguchi to iu otoko* (*The Man Called Mizoguchi*). Hakama Shoten, 1977.

Yoda Yoshitaka. *Mizoguchi Kenji no geijutsu* (*The Art of Mizoguchi Kenji*). Tabata Shoten, 1970.

Oshima

Matsuda Masao. "Dojidai toshite no Oshima Nagisa" ("Oshima Nagisa as My Contemporary"). *Sekai no eiga sakka 6: Oshima Nagisa* (*Film Directors of the World 6: Oshima Nagisa*). Kinema Jumposha, 1970.

Oshima Nagisa. *Ma to zankoku no hasso* (*My Idea of Evil and Cruelty*). 1968. Haga Shoten, 1972.

Sato Tadao. *Oshima Nagisa no sekai* (*The World of Oshima Nagisa*). Chikuma Shobo, 1973.

Ozu

Hasumi Shigehiko. *Kantoku Ozu Yasujiro* (*Director Ozu Yasujiro*). Tsukuma Shobo, 1984.

Sato Tadao. *Ozu Yasujiro no geijutsu* (*The Art of Ozu Yasujiro*). 2 vols. Asahi Shimbunsha, 1971.

CONTRIBUTORS

J. L. Anderson is Vice President, WGBH Education Foundation, Boston, and Principal Associate, Tokyo Broadcasting System Chair in Japanese Broadcasting, Media, and Culture, NYU Department of Cinema Studies. He is co-author with Donald Richie of *The Japanese Film: Art and Industry* (expanded edition), and has also published in Kodansha's *Encyclopedia of Japan.*

Gregory Barrett was born in Chicago and received his M.A. in Asian studies from the University of California at Berkeley. He has translated *Currents in Japanese Cinema* by Sato Tadao, and has published his own work, *Archetypes in Japanese Film.* Since 1977 he has lived in Tokyo, where he researches Japanese film and teaches English at the School of Intercultural Communication in Yotsuya.

David Bordwell is Jacques Ledoux Professor of Film Studies at the University of Wisconsin-Madison. He is the author of several books, including *Narration in the Fiction Film* and *Ozu and the Poetics of Cinema.*

Robert N. Cohen, a former lecturer in film studies at UCLA and UC Santa Barbara, has published on Japanese cinema in *Film Quarterly, Sight and Sound,* and *Quarterly Review of Film Studies.* He has been a contributor to *Magill's Survey of Cinema: Foreign Language Films* as well as a commentator on Japanese films for PBS. He currently lives in Los Angeles and works as a screenwriter.

David Desser teaches Film in the Unit for Cinema Studies and the Department of Speech Communication at the University of Illinois at Urbana-Champaign. He has published extensively on Japanese cinema, including *The Samurai Films of Akira Kurosawa* and *Eros plus Massacre: An Introduction to the Japanese New Wave Cinema.* He has also published on American films of the Vietnam War and science fiction in the cinema, and is publishing a book on American Jewish film directors.

Linda C. Ehrlich, Assistant Professor of Japanese at the University of Tennessee, Knoxville, has published articles on Asian cinema in *East-West Film Journal, Cinemaya, Journal of Film and Video,* and *Literature/Film Quarterly.*

Kathe Geist is a lecturer in art at Koryo International College in Nagoya,

Japan. She is the author of *The Cinema of Wim Wenders: From Paris, France to Paris, Texas.* Her articles on Ozu have appeared in *Film Quarterly, Art Journal,* and *East-West Film Journal.*

William B. Hauser is Professor of History at the University of Rochester. His publications include *Economic Institutional Change in Tokugawa Japan* and *The Bakufu in Japanese History,* edited with Jeffrey P. Mass. His research interests are the history of Osaka, women's history, and the cultural images of war in Japanese films.

Iwamoto Kenji is a member of the Faculty of Literature at Waseda University, where he teaches film history and theory. He has edited *Kinema no seishun, Nihon eiga to modanisumu,* and *The Eisenstein Reader,* among other books, and he is the author of many essays, including "Film Criticism and the Study of Cinema in Japan: A Historical Survey" (*Iconics,* 1987).

Komatsu Hiroshi is Lecturer in film at Meiji Gakuin University, Tokyo. He has also been working for the National Film Center as a Guest Researcher since 1988. He is author of *Kigen no eiga—sono keishiki to imi* (*Cinema of Origin: Its Form and Meaning*).

Keiko I. McDonald is Associate Professor of Japanese literature and cinema at the University of Pittsburgh. Her books include *Cinema East: A Critical Study of Major Japanese Films* and *Mizoguchi.* She is completing a book entitled *Japanese Classical Theater in Films.* She is also the editor of the volume on *Ugetsu* for the Rutgers World Film series.

Arthur Nolletti, Jr., Professor of English at Framingham State College (Mass.), teaches literature and film studies. He has edited a special issue on Japanese cinema for *Film Criticism,* and has published in such journals and reference works as *Jump Cut, Magill's Survey of Cinema: Foreign Language Films,* and *The International Dictionary of Films and Filmmakers.* He is currently working on a book-length study of director Gosho Heinosuke.

Yuko Okutsu completed an M.A. at John Carroll University in educational psychology and is completing a second M.A. in Japanese linguistics at the Ohio State University.

Donald Richie wrote, with Joseph Anderson, the pioneer study of his subject, *The Japanese Film: Art and Industry.* He later wrote *The Films of Akira Kurosawa* and *Ozu.* His latest work is *Japanese Cinema: An Introduction.*

Lisa Spalding received an M.A. in Japanese Literature from UC-Berkeley and studied film in Tokyo. She is currently working on a film degree in London.

Max Tessier is a noted critic and writer on Japanese film in France. He has published numerous essays and interviews on a wide array of Japanese directors, including Ozu, Mizoguchi, Kurosawa, Oshima, and Yoshida. He is the author of

Images du cinéma japonais and the editor of *Cinéma d'aujourd-hui: Le Cinéma japonais au présent.*

Marice C. Thompson is Professor Emerita of Modern Languages at Framingham State College (Mass.). She received a Bachelor of Arts and a Master's degree from Toulouse University (France), and the *Agrégation d'Anglais* from Paris University. The author of *French 3, French 4, French for Communication One, French for Communication Two,* and *Apropos,* she is currently doing work as a translator and consultant.

INDEX